W9-AUI-621

A
COLLECTION
OF THE
CULTURES
AND
TRADITIONS
OF DANCE

MADE POSSIBLE
BY THE
GLORYA KAUFMAN FUND
AND THE ASSITANCE OF
MANY KIND FRIENDS

ALSO BY VICENTE GARCÍA-MÁRQUEZ

The Ballets Russes: Colonel de Basil's Ballets Russes de Monte Carlo, 1932–1952

Massine

Massine rehearsing the role of Saint Francis in Nobilissima Visione, *1938*

APR 2 4 1996

Massine

A BIOGRAPHY

Vicente García-Márquez

ALFRED A. KNOPF   NEW YORK 1995

THIS IS A BORZOI BOOK
PUBLISHED BY ALFRED A. KNOPF, INC.

Copyright © 1995 by The Estate of Vicente García-Márquez
All rights reserved under International and Pan-American Copyright
Conventions. Published in the United States by Alfred A. Knopf, Inc.,
New York, and simultaneously in Canada by Random House of Canada
Limited, Toronto. Distributed by Random House, Inc., New York.

Owing to limitations of space, acknowledgments for permission to
reprint previously published material may be found on page 445.

Library of Congress Cataloging-in-Publication Data
García-Márquez, Vicente, 1953–1993
Massine : a biography / by Vicente García-Márquez.
p. cm.
Includes bibliographical references (p.) and index.
ISBN 0-394-51003-8
1. Massine, Léonide, 1896–1979. 2. Choreographers—Soviet Union—
Biography. 3. Dancers—Soviet Union—Biography. I. Title.
GV1785.M35G37 1995
792.8'2'092—dc20
[B]   93-35666   CIP

Manufactured in the United States of America
First Edition

Contents

CONTENTS

PART THREE

The 1920s

PART FOUR

Years of Transition: The Symphonic Ballets

CONTENTS

ACKNOWLEDGMENTS

I OFFER SPECIAL THANKS to the following persons who have assisted me since the inception of this book: Youly Algeroff, Alicia Alonso, Antonio, the late Sir Frederick Ashton, Vladimir Augenblick, Jean Babilée, Nancy van Norman Baer, Irina Baronova, André Beaurepaire, Anne Bertrand, Dinko Bogdanie, Richard Buckle, Jan Garden Castro, the late Lucia Chase, Ariane Csonka, Alexandra Danilova, Olga de Basil, Lila de Nobili, Guillermo de Osma, Dame Ninette de Valois, Mary Ann de Vlieg, Robert Descharnes, Eugenia Delarova Doll, the late Sir Anton Dolin, François Duplat, the late Parmenia Migel Ekstrom, the late Luis Escobar (Marqués de las Marismas del Guadalquivir), Ricardo España, Tamara Finch, Frederic Franklin, Lynn Garafola, Daniel Garbade Lachenal, Robert Gaston-Cottin, the late Ettore Giannini, Julio González, Alexander Grant, Tamara Grigorieva, Louisa Horton Hill, the late Jean Hugo, the late Roman Jasinski, the late Robert Joffrey, Valentina Kachuba, the late Boris Kochno, Josseline Le Bourhis, Tatiana Leskova, Irène Lidova, the late Eugene Loring, Felix Lorenzo, Mariemma, Fred and Elena Maroth, Tatiana Massine, Alejandro Medina, Madeleine Milhaud, Curtis Millner, Bruce Nalezny, Ricardo Naymanovich, José Manuel Pacheco, Jean-Pierre Pastori, Duarte Pinto-Coelho, the late Michael Powell, Thelma Schoonmaker Powell, Tatiana Riabouchinska, Marie-Thérèse Rose, Roger Salas, Henri Sauguet, Moira Shearer, Irene Skoric, Vassili Sulich, Ludmilla Tcherina, Tamara Toumanova, Alexandre Vassiliev, Nina Verchinina, Baron Tilo von Watzdorff, Igor Youskevitch, and George Zoritch.

And to the following individuals and institutions: María Isabel de Falla and Elena García de Paredes and the Fundación Archivo Manuel de Falla; Madeleine Nichols and the Dance Collection of the Library of the Performing Arts, New York Public Library; Martine Kahane and the Bibliothèque de l'Opéra de Paris; Brigitte Léal and the Musée Picasso; Ornella Volta and the Fondation Erik Satie; Patrick Bensard and the Cinémathèque Française de la Danse.

I am indebted to Lorca Massine, Peter Massine, and Theodor Massine, with particular gratitude to Tatiana Massine Weinbaum.

I would also like to thank Lynn von Kersting for providing me with a paradisiac retreat while proofreading the text; Kevin Boynton, who typed the first copy of the manuscript and whose editorial work was most valuable; Elizabeth Souritz, who conducted research in Moscow on Massine's early years; Jean Bromage, who devoted many long hours to the final research for this book in the Dance and Theater Collections of the New York Public Library; and Ivan Webster, who typed the final manuscript and whose editorial work on the text was essential. Lastly, my gratitude to Robert Gottlieb and to my editor, Susan Ralston, for her wholehearted support.

INTRODUCTION

MY FIRST ENCOUNTER with Léonide Massine took place in 1978 at Los Angeles International Airport. He had been invited by Tatiana Riabouchinska and me to attend the opening performance of the Southern California Ballet at UCLA. As I waited for him to emerge from the plane, I was filled with anticipation and expectation, for in minutes I was to meet one of the indisputable titans of twentieth-century dance.

Until that day, Massine had been for me a bit of an abstraction, a mythic figure. For years he had been regarded in the dance community as a legendary personality from times gone by. In recent years his activities in the United States had been minimal: he had conducted some master classes and, most importantly, had painstakingly staged revivals of his work for the Joffrey Ballet and, later, the Oakland Ballet.

The wait at the airport seemed endless. After a considerable passage of time—everyone seemed to have deplaned—I grew concerned, fearing that Massine might have missed his flight. Anxiously approaching an attendant to ask if any passengers were still on board the aircraft, I saw emerging through the empty aisle a small, gaunt figure of a man. His presence was authoritative; his eyes, even at a distance, were piercing; he looked like an ascetic monk or a wise, aged philosopher. He was accompanied by an attractive young woman—his assistant, Mary Ann de Vlieg. They made an imposing couple, both studiedly unapproachable. I introduced myself and we exchanged civilities. Massine hardly spoke—only later, in the car, was he the least bit expansive, and then it was to pay a compliment to Ms. de Vlieg. His gaze was disturbing and impenetrable, suggesting the insight of the sage unprepared to divulge any secrets.

The three days Massine spent in Los Angeles were filled with activity. He attended two performances of the company, and after the premiere spoke publicly in praise of the dancers. His master class at Riabouchinska's studio was packed with students and balletomanes eager for a closer glimpse of the legend. The class ended poignantly, and unexpectedly, with Riabouchinska and Massine dancing the opening section of their famous mazurka from *Le Beau Danube*.

My memory of their reunion is still unusually emotional. Their encounter was warm yet somehow distanced, bordering on awkwardness, with an almost total lack of verbal communication; words between them seemed unnecessary, and talk of the past was irrelevant for two people whose lives were linked by the sharing of a common history in the making of dance, perhaps the most ephemeral of the arts. During the first bars of the mazurka their complicity was palpable, when, oblivious to the world around them, they immersed themselves in each other's eyes, perhaps recapturing long-past memories and reasserting the profound bond that, in spite of years of silence, united them.

At the time Massine visited Los Angeles I was already conducting research for my Ballets Russes book. I took advantage of his stay there to discuss with him, whenever possible, his early symphonic ballets. In spite of his apparent aloofness and inaccessibility, which sometimes intimidated me, he was ingratiating, and conscientiously answered my questions. To my surprise he invited me to join him in France, where, later in the summer, he was to teach a choreography workshop in Rennes. I accepted on the spot, without thinking of dates or my own availability.

In Rennes I attended some of his lecture-demonstrations, and we spent time together at lunch and, after class, in the afternoons. Our conversations took in his work from the past and, above all, the new ideas he had for future work. He was particularly keen on creating a ballet where dancers never entered or exited the stage, but metamorphosed themselves continuously, in a different kind of evolution of movement. Despite his laconic manner and elusiveness, I felt a special bond being established between us. Again to my surprise, he invited me to visit him later in the summer on his private islands in the Gulf of Salerno.

If Isole dei Galli are full of timeless legends dating back to the mythical sirens' islands of Ulysses, they are no less legendary as Massine's hermitic retreat for more than fifty years; a refuge for work and rest which had been visited only by some of his closest friends and collaborators: Stravinsky, Hindemith, Reinhardt, Powell, Markevitch, and once, even, the king of Italy. On the island, life was monastic, dominated by Massine's methodical, almost obsessive, regime: swimming at 7:00 a.m., breakfast afterwards, then a walk around the steeply rocky surrounding hills, followed by work in the library until lunchtime, when we assessed his ballets and pored over the many note-books in which, for decades, he had annotated his choreography. Any question of mine that hinted at a personal dimension, or might call for a personal opinion about anyone at all, was simply disregarded, as he continued analyzing his work. After lunch he would disappear into his private rooms, from which he would not emerge until sunset, when he sat with his entourage and visitors—no words were exchanged—on a terrace outside the tower, contemplating the resplendent sun's slow fall into the southern Mediterranean. It was a time of introspection and meditation. When I left the island several weeks later, Massine insisted on accompanying me to the mainland. In a motorboat so tiny I feared for our safety, he lay on the deck impassively, his hat covering his face, as we lurched through the choppy waves and the coastline gradually grew closer. We made plans to meet in New York in the winter. I was never to see him again.

The case for a biography of Massine is at once burning and close to impossible; the artistic giant is so often outfoxed by the man cloaked in mystery. My approach has been essentially historical rather than internal, since time after time the inner man simply could not be coaxed to the surface. If his creative work is well documented by prominent writers, critics, and witnesses of his time, Massine, the man of flesh and bone, remains forever an enigma. As a biographical subject he is in many ways ideal, for in studying his work within the context of the era that produced it, he serves as a unifying thread through decades of the development of art in the West. He was, above all, a man who not only remained for years at the vanguard of dance but was an integral part of the cultural history of our century. Through an amalgam of poetic, aesthetic, and philosophical tendencies he revitalized ballet and validated himself as an artist.

Documenting his body of work was an arduous but fascinating task. Trying to capture the persona, the man's inner life, turned into a quite misbegotten, though endlessly fascinating, crusade. His introspective stance throughout his life became a device and medium for abstracting himself, for withdrawing from the world around him, perhaps, as Jung would put it, "to prevent the object from gaining power over him." For Massine, the creative process, in tandem with theoretical observation, dominated his contribution to the world; and thus, particularly in his case, the creative act constitutes the involuntary biography of his soul. To look for any other clues to his inner self—even from those closest to him—is an insurmountable task. There are glimpses here and there of the essence, but he eludes us constantly, becoming ever more baffling.

PART ONE

Moscow

*What the soul cannot reflect makes no
impact on it; but since the willpower can
control whether the soul reflects something
or not, the soul meets only what it wants
to meet. . . . But one of the soul's strongest
impulses is greed for the new, an
inclination towards the unfamiliar. . . .*

—NIETZSCHE

Miassine with his sister, brothers, and parents, circa 1900

CHAPTER 1

Moscow, July 1895–November 1913

LEONID FEDOROVICH MIASSINE* was born in Moscow on July 27, 1895 (August 8 in the Western calendar), and christened at the St. Pimen Church.¹ His father, Fedor Aphanasievich, was a native of Simbirsk on the Volga River; his mother, Eugenia Nikolaevna Gladkova, came from Kharkov in the Ukraine.

Some years earlier his parents had settled in Moscow, where at the time of Leonid's birth both were employed at the Imperial Theater. Mrs. Miassine (under the name of Miassina) had sung soprano in the Bolshoi Theater Chorus since September 1884. Since September 1891 Mr. Mias-

---

* The spelling was changed to "Léonide Massine" early in his professional career. See page 60.

3

sine had played the French horn in the Bolshoi Orchestra.[2] The household included the couple's five children, Mikhail, Gregori, Konstantin, Raissa, and Leonid, as well as a housekeeper the children came to call Aunt Feodosia, and her three children, Maria, Irina, and Philip.

With his calm and implacable manner, Mr. Miassine was the family bulwark, the ultimate parental authority. Mrs. Miassine's warmth, vivaciousness, and optimism—"without the stubbornness"[3] Massine would later describe as typical of the Ukrainian temperament—held the family together. She controlled the family purse strings, saw to the children's education, and ran the Miassine household.

Firstborn Mikhail was twelve years older than Leonid. As a young man, after completing his engineering studies at Moscow's School of Engineering, he enlisted in the army. In 1904 he was wounded opposing the Japanese incursion into Manchuria. He recovered from his injuries and was awarded the St. Vladimir Medal for military bravery. Afterwards his family took unabashed pride in this honor; and Mikhail's courage under fire deeply awed little Leonid, who idolized his eldest brother. When Mikhail returned home after long tours of duty, what most indelibly impressed Leonid was his brother's remoteness as he stood in his uniform, gleamingly handsome and altogether unapproachable.

Gregori, second-born and ten years older than Leonid, was, Massine wrote, "impulsive and emotional,"[4] the family romantic, which might account for his tendency to run afoul of his father's strict notions of proper conduct. Once, while Gregori was an engineering student (at the same school Konstantin attended), his father learned that he was cutting classes to be with his girlfriend. Mr. Miassine would not abide such breaches of discipline. Gregori was no longer allowed in the house. During this period of estrangement he found temporary employment with the railroad, and dared visit his mother only when his father was not at home. Not long afterward, however, he completed his engineering studies and joined the military, and he soon was stationed in Chelyabinsk, Siberia, as a military construction engineer. Leonid was bewildered by Gregori's retracing of Mikhail's footsteps into the army. The impassioned, gentle Gregori seemed to Leonid a poor choice for the military. And here was another brother gone far away.

Konstantin, the third child, eight years Leonid's senior, was the brother closest to him in age and a tender mentor. Konstantin lavished attention on the baby of the family. He patiently drilled Leonid in the principles of geometry and taught him a healthy respect for skilled marksmanship. Konstantin was a lighthearted taskmaster, and Leonid delighted in his company, even when the two of them were detailed to shovel snow in the deep Russian winter. While Mikhail and Gregori pursued their military careers far from home, Konstantin served as Leonid's loyal male comrade during his formative years.

Leonid's sister, Raissa, was nearest in age to him, and in their combustible rivalry for attention they apparently quarreled often. Raissa poked fun at her brother's solitary dancing, nicknaming him "the circus dancer," while Leonid taunted her as "Baba Yaga," the old witch of Russian folklore.[5]

The Miassines lived on the ground floor of a narrow stone building on Schemilovsky Street, a row of low-roofed dwellings adjacent to a mews in the Sushchevsky Quarter of Moscow, near the imperial stables. On the floor above, the jeweler Sergei Sergeivitch Gagolin kept his workshop, a source of wonder for the young Leonid.

The days in Schemilovsky Street were tranquil. From within the secluded, walled-in courtyard that faced the Miassine house one could hear neighborhood children at play. Often Mrs. Miassine spent most of her day rehearsing at the Bolshoi Theater. While she was away the household ran smoothly, and by late afternoon the "large, high-ceilinged flat was always bursting with activity. The kitchen would be full of women— Aunt Tekla [Mrs. Miassine's closest friend], Aunt Feodosia, her daughters Maria and Irina, my sister Raissa—all helping to prepare our big main meal. In the dining room my elder brothers, Gregori and Konstantin . . . sat working at their higher mathematics, while I wandered from room to room, chatting with the women in the kitchen, listening to my father practicing in the living room, and peering at my brother's geometrical drawings, which looked to me like some strange hieroglyphic language."[6] And Leonid's "great moment" of the day was when he heard "the horse-drawn coach"[7] that brought his mother home from the theater. In the early evening, listening to his father practice his French horn, Leonid would sit transfixed with joy, especially when he was permitted to request his favorite selection, Beethoven's Overture to *Fidelio*.

The year Leonid turned seven, he and the family spent the first of what would become annual summer respites in Zvenigorod-Moskovsky, about forty miles from Moscow. Here the Miassine family built (with financial help from Mr. Miassine's brother Vasili) a wooden dacha on a hill overlooking the Moscow River. The senior Miassines did much of the building and carpentry in and around the house, including bookshelves, cupboards, and an outside fence. The children joined in, and little Leonid helped paint the walls burgundy red and the roof dark forest-green.

These summers in Zvenigorod-Moskovsky were idyllic, with the family blissfully adrift in what Chekhov, in *The Sea Gull*, called Russia's "charming country dullness." They would arrive at the dacha in July, after the elder Miassines had finished their freelance summer engagements during the Bolshoi Theater's off-season. With Mikhail and Gregori away, the summer household consisted of the parents, Konstantin, Raissa, Leonid, and Aunt Feodosia and her children. Mr. Miassine looked after the vegetable garden with his wife, who was also in charge of the flower garden in front of the house. She shared household duties with Aunt Feodosia. Raissa spent most of her free time reading French and Russian novels.

Leonid and Konstantin would escape into the nearby pine forest to hunt partridge and guinea fowl. Leonid relished the athletic Konstantin's company, but even at this early age he began to prefer solitude. He particularly enjoyed rising at dawn to wander alone through the woods to pick wild strawberries and mushrooms for his mother. The singing of the birds or a long swim in the cool river transported him to his own world. He would spend entire days alone fishing and eating handfuls of strawberries before returning home at sunset. Thus, though there were moments at the house when he joined his sister and village children in games, singing old rhymes and learning village dances, such as the *Khorovod,* in his autobiography he reveals that these summer interludes at the dacha endowed him with a critical, secretly longed-for opportunity to commune with nature and learn to stand alone.

Teatime at the dacha was warmly sociable, an occasion for affable village neighbors to come calling. They often included the family's closest friend, a basso named Unitzky who sang in the Bolshoi Theater chorus. The traditional samovar was set out on a wooden table beneath the lilac tree, and on it Aunt Feodosia would arrange freshly baked bread and homemade jam. Mr. Unitzky and Mrs. Miassine delighted everyone with Ukrainian songs. At such moments, Massine recalled, "I would lean back in my chair meditatively sipping my tea and caressing Miltoshka [the family dog], and let myself be lulled by their voices into a waking dream."[8]

During one of the first summers at the dacha, Mr. Miassine took his youngest son to the nearby monastery of St. Saavo. As Leonid gazed upon the onion-domed cupola, the measured peals of its eleventh-century iron and silver bells moved outward in layers of sound, gently caressing the surrounding countryside. Leonid's Russian Orthodox religious upbringing had never been strict, but now, holding his father's hand as he entered the monastery and began wandering its cloisters, he felt a consuming spiritual identification with the chapel's air of sacred mystery and ancient mysticism. The dimly lit space and the candles flickering before the icons worked deeply on the introspective and meditative boy. He had studied the life of Saint Saavo, whose retreat to a hermitage atop a nearby hill had symbolized his rejection of all worldly vanity. Viewing the saint's mortal remains displayed under glass in the chapel, Leonid felt "his presence pervading the building, and in my boyish way I understood his renunciation of the material world, and his search for a contemplative, spiritual life. Sitting in the chapel, gazing at the frescoes and icons there, I felt for the first time a sense of peace and exaltation. . . ." Sixty years later, he would write in his autobiography that "some pattern or pervasive theme in my future creative life began to take shape on that morning. . . ."[9]

Leonid's education began at home, when he was five. His mother and, especially, his Aunt Tekla taught him to read and write and laid out the basic principles of religion, zoology, and mineralogy. With help from his father and Konstantin he tackled geography, geometry, and history. At age eight his home tutoring ceased. At the suggestion of Mme Chernova, a friend of Mrs. Miassine's from the Bolshoi chorus, he was registered to take the entrance exams at the Moscow Imperial Theater School. During her many visits to the Miassine home, Mme Chernova had noticed how charmingly little Leonid played his mouth organ and danced. She wanted these rudimentary artistic inclinations to flourish. Though his parents stressed the importance of an academic education (curiously, music had not been included in their home curriculum), Mme Chernova's persistence and their son's boundless enthusiasm won them over.

Their hesitation seems odd. Music and theater were an integral part of the family environment, and discussion of their work at the Bolshoi no doubt occurred daily. When he was six years old, Leonid had accompanied his mother to a theater in central Moscow where she sang during the summer operetta season. Fascinated, he left her dressing room and roamed backstage, where "all was in semi-darkness, and the curtains and backcloths hung over me like black clouds. As I made my way through the jumble of gilded stairways and papier-mâché hedges, I felt as though I were entering a dream world."[10] Perhaps one can say that at this moment Miassine, gazing from the dimly lit stage at his first empty auditorium, took his initial step toward making ballet history.

Each year after the Bolshoi season ended, Mr. Miassine would obtain part-time jobs playing in open-air concerts at genteel summer resorts. (Although he was in good health, these travels also gave him the chance to take a cure in some of Russia's fashionable spas.) Leonid would sometimes accompany him, once to Pyatigorsk at the foot of Mount Beshtaou, and another summer to Zheleznovodsk (the City of Iron Water), with its promenades, gardens, and grand hotels, where the surrounding mountains included Elbrus and mighty Kazbek, the highest peak in the Caucasus.

Leonid loved attending the orchestra rehearsals. He found himself captivated by the conductor, who, like a magician, appeared to dominate a stage full of musicians by a simple wave of the baton. He delighted in seeing his father play at a nod from the maestro. In rehearsal his father seemed "stronger and more serious" than the other players. While Leonid's tiny feet tapped along to the music of Rimsky-Korsakov, he beamed at his father from where he sat. "But father never smiled back,"[11] so the child's plea for recognition went unanswered. Apparently the pattern persisted. Toward the end of his life he said: "I was the last one in the family, and almost forgotten. I was the freak. They did not know what to do with the little chap."[12]

On examination day at the Imperial Theater School Leonid was filled with anticipation and fear:

> I could hardly eat my breakfast when the morning came for Father to take me to the school. Once there, I sat in the bare waiting-room, holding his hand, until my name was called out and I was shown into a cramped cubicle, where an aggressive little doctor named Kazansky peered at me through rimless spectacles which made his eyes look as large and round as an owl's. He told me to take off my clothes, and there I stood, completely naked, surrounded by white-coated attendants, while he examined my arms, legs, neck and spine, to see if I had the physique necessary for a dancer. As he hammered my knees for reflexes and carefully tested my joints and muscles, I became more and more convinced that I would never pass the test. I felt that I had no talent at all, and that my puny body could never meet the requirements of the Theater School.[13]

Leonid took the entrance examinations for the ballet department of the Theater School, which included religion, Russian language, and arithmetic, and proved competent, earning grades of 4+, 4, and 4, respectively (4 being equivalent to a B in the American system).[14] To his enormous gratification, he was accepted for the regular trial period of one year.

The most important Russian theatrical institution of the nineteenth century was the Imperial Theaters, which included St. Petersburg's Maryinsky Theater (opera and ballet) and Alexandrinsky Theater (drama) as well as Moscow's Bolshoi Theater (opera and ballet) and Maly Theater (drama). These theaters were wholly subsidized by the state. Their recruits came mainly from the Imperial Theater Schools in St. Petersburg and Moscow, which were then the most prestigious institutions of ballet, drama, and opera education and training in Russia. The Moscow school dates from 1773, when a Moscow orphanage, the Vospitatel'nyi Dom, hired instructors to train the inmates as professional singers, actors, and dancers. Part of the school's curriculum required students to participate in theater performances. Systematic instruction began in 1773, at the same time that the orphanage was handed over to the Petrovsky Theater, where the Bolshoi itself has stood since 1825. Throughout the nineteenth century some of Europe's most renowned ballet masters came to work in Moscow. Although during the century's closing decades the Bolshoi Ballet was at something of a creative standstill, its artistic renewal was in fact under way when Leonid entered the Imperial Theater School in 1904.[15]

In St. Petersburg, the ballet classicism of Marius Petipa and Lev Ivanov had reached its peak. In Moscow, the Bolshoi was more restive. Since 1900 Alexander Gorsky had been leading it in new directions, emphasizing a dance-drama approach opposed to the conventions of academic ballet. Before arriving at the Bolshoi, Gorsky had been a pupil of Petipa's, a dancer with the Maryinsky Theater, and a teacher of Vladimir Stepanov's choreographic notation theory (which he later revised) at the Imperial Theater School in St. Petersburg. In 1898 he was invited to stage *The Sleeping Beauty* for the Bolshoi, and in 1900 he was officially transferred there. The artistic renewal Gorsky set in motion at the Bolshoi was in reality part of the modernist movement that was advancing on fin-de-siècle Moscow, a pivotal shift toward bold Russian innovation and experimentation in the arts.[16]

Consequently, though the organizational structure of the Imperial Theaters did not easily accommodate change, it could not remain untouched by the artistic upheaval taking place in Moscow. At the Bolshoi, Gorsky's attraction to the novel theatrical ideas of Konstantin Stanislavsky[17] generated renewed interest in the mise-en-scène as an element that gave added cohesiveness to a ballet production. Breaking from the traditional classical symmetry, Gorsky made the corps de ballet integral to a work's dramatic development. He also introduced character dance steps to the ballet vocabulary, to make it less technical and more expressive. Dance historian Elizabeth Souritz writes: "Gorsky considered that ballet could survive only if it became an art of its time. He felt keenly the need to renew its themes and its language."[18] During his tenure as teacher and choreographer at the Bolshoi, Gorsky made dancers study the expressiveness of the body (torso and arms) and emphasized the fundamental principle that if movement is to have any emotional content, it can come only from the specific context in which the steps are performed. One important result was that the dancers began to rely on acting to enliven their characterizations. Among the generation who exemplified the new Gorsky style were Mikhail Mordkin, Sofia Fedorova, and Yekaterina Geltzer, all of whom personified the dynamism and brio that became the hallmark of the twentieth-century Bolshoi Ballet.

Soon after his acceptance Leonid found himself in the high-ceilinged rehearsal rooms of the Imperial Theater School, where basic ballet class (for six male and six female students) was taught by Nikolai Petrovitch Domachov. This class consumed the morning.[19] The afternoon included lessons in arithmetic, geography, Russian history, literature, and French. Leonid, already the deeply private person he was to remain for the rest of his life, must have found it a blessing to be a day student rather than a boarder. As it was, his daily classes must have made him yearn for the security of home. But he quickly fell in with the school's highly disciplined schedule. Uniforms were mandatory. Boys wore blue jackets with Russian-style, stand-up velvet collars to which were pinned two miniature lyres. Girls wore dark red uniforms and white aprons. On Sunday all students attended mass in the upstairs chapel over the classrooms.

During his year-long trial, Leonid got his first taste of the theatrical world at work. Once, he and a group of students were taken across from the school to the Maly Theater, where they watched a rehearsal of a scene from Gogol's *The Government Inspector*. This first exposure left Leonid "enthralled by the wonderful voices and the expressive gestures." He was so taken by the experience that he felt he "would never be happy until I too could appear on the stage."[20] The experience would focus him in the next few years on acting more than dancing, though when he played with Raissa and their neighbors the Panshin children, he still enjoyed showing off dance steps he had learned in school and dreaming up brief, simple routines with them on the spot.

Once the first-year trial period was completed, a second student examination was required for final acceptance into the school, "this time in

Miassine in the uniform of the Imperial Theater School

an enormous mirrored hall where I was surrounded by flinty-faced examiners staring at me from their benches. Standing alone in the center of the room, I was asked to demonstrate the first five basic positions of the dance. For one moment I felt completely paralysed, and was sure I would not be able to move a muscle. Somehow, as if in a dream, I took a deep breath and found myself moving across the room demonstrating the positions and several dance steps."[21]

How well he did turned out to be irrelevant for a while. Soon after the first-year trial period ended, the school was closed due to the political turmoil that led to the 1905 revolution.

Nineteen hundred five was a momentous year in Russian history; its aborted January revolution in the "Bloody Sunday" massacre at the Winter Palace shocked the world. As the rebellion roiled through Moscow's streets, anxiety permeated the Miassine household. The family remained barricaded in their flat; the only sounds that reached them were screams, gunshots, and, from the nearby imperial stables, the loud galloping of the Cossacks' horses. The commotion terrified Leonid, who suffered recurring nightmares of Cossacks galloping into the courtyard. To allay his little brother's fears, Konstantin read to him and played games with him, but he found that Leonid was most soothed by a minia-ture theater he had built for him:

> I [Leonid] helped him to cut out the characters from cardboard. Then, by
> tying strings to them, we made them glide smoothly across the little stage
> in front of the footlights. The music for our productions was provided by a
> friend, Yuri Ziman, who lived in our block of flats. He had a guitar on
> which he could play two tunes: Strauss's "Vienna, always Vienna" and
> one of Liszt's Hungarian Rhapsodies. We choreographed the Viennese
> waltz by pulling two strings in different directions, and so making our
> characters dance together with jerky, rhythmic movements. Our most am-
> bitious effort was a midnight scene in a wood, lit by one small candle and
> accompanied by the Hungarian Rhapsody played very slowly. For this we
> cut out several witches from sheets of paper, and attached them to threads
> which I manipulated with both hands. But whenever I tried to make them
> fly, the threads got entangled, and the witches hung in a motionless cluster.
>   I got a curious sense of satisfaction out of manoeuvring my little card-
> board characters, making patterns of movement which corresponded to
> Yuri's music. And the sight of them on the stage, lit only by wavering can-
> dlelight, made an impression on me which has remained one of my most
> vivid childhood memories.[22]

Escape from an oppressive reality into theatrical fantasy: the rest of Mas-sine's life would be punctuated by precisely this need to grab for security amidst bewildering uncertainty.

When the worst of the street fighting subsided, Mr. Miassine, Kon-stantin, and Leonid emerged from the house. They were stunned. Leonid, walking between his father and brother and clutching their hands, saw streets with dead bodies sprawled among the remains of bar-ricades, surely a devastating sight for a ten-year-old. The effect on Leonid was to be lasting. For the first time death on a massive scale brought home to his child's world the unpredictable fragility of life. As he later described the scene's impact:

> Twisted and contorted, their limbs had stiffened into every conceivable po-
> sition of suffering. Rows of outstretched arms, torsos, and staring faces
> passed before my eyes as we searched among the dead for people we had
> known. I felt a gnawing ache in the pit of my stomach, and by the time we
> left the scene I was weak and feverish. On my way home I saw a group of
> children playing among the debris of one of the barricades. Listening to

their gay, carefree voices, I felt a sudden sense of detachment from their childhood world of innocence. Suddenly I let go of my father's hand, and walked home on my own.[23]

Somehow, life in Moscow soon returned to normal. Although threats to close down the Imperial Theater School permanently never materialized, no new students were accepted between 1906 and 1910.[24] Leonid was thrilled to be back in school. Now, for the first time he thoroughly enjoyed his dance lessons, and he especially relished his literature classes. Here he was exposed to the works of Lermontov, Pushkin, Fet, and Nikolai Nekrasov. He took particular delight in the Nekrasov poems that dealt with country life, memorizing them and reciting them often.

Leonid proved such a diligent and hard-working pupil that on May 10, 1906, along with his classmate Margarita Kandaurova, he was allowed to advance to the second year of the seniors' department of class I, although he was younger than the required age. On November 13, 1907, he became a "half-pensionary" (a half-scholarship student), at public cost. His school records make no mention of any disciplinary infractions.[25]

In time the curriculum expanded to include elementary physics, drama (dropped from the curriculum in 1910), and dance notation, in which Leonid excelled. (In her unpublished memoirs, Maria Gorshkova, his dance notation teacher from 1910 to 1912, calls him her best student.)[26]

All students were required to participate in Bolshoi and Maly productions. Some ballets were a special treat for them, especially Gorsky's *The Little Humpbacked Horse,* where the apprentices joined the corps de ballet in all three acts plus the finale. Students also got to see famous performers at work. Leonid noticed how meticulously Gorsky coached his dancers during Bolshoi rehearsals. Among the dancers he admired were Maximilian Froman, Vladimir Riabtzev, and Geltzer. (Leonid was deeply amused when, offstage, Mikhail Mordkin sported the ten-gallon hat and raccoon coat he had bought during an American tour.)

The ballerina Margarita Vassilieva's description of Gorsky at work shows how he mapped out his ballets before beginning rehearsals, methods that Massine would later draw on. "[Gorsky] always arrived at rehearsals with the score under his arm, with every scene quite ready and worked out, with sketches for separate dances and a complete plan of the whole production. And when work actually started, one only had to see his burning eyes, the state of creative fervor that seemed to possess him completely, to the oblivion of everything else."[27] There was a flurry

Ballet class at the Theater School; Miassine is third from right.

Miassine partnering Margarita Kandaurova, who became one of the Bolshoi's leading dancers in the 1920s

of excitement when it was announced that the Bolshoi's régisseur would be visiting the school to select a small, dark student to play the role of the dwarf Chernomor in a new production of Glinka's *Ruslan and Ludmilla*. To Leonid's surprise, he was chosen. Not only was this, at an early age, his first solo character role; but, as it turned out, it was also an opportunity that helped set his future artistic course. "I . . . was amazed to discover," he wrote later, "that I had to march on to the stage wearing a heavy turban, a long brocade robe and an even longer white beard, which had to be carried on two cushions by several attendants. Weighed

Ten-year-old Miassine in Ostrovsky's play Poverty Is Not a Crime, *at the Maly Theater*

down by all this, I had practically nothing to do but scowl, look forbidding, wave my arms and cast a spell over the lovely heroine. I was overwhelmed by the splendour of my exotic costume, and became so involved in my part that I was oblivious of the audience and of the rest of the company." The role of Chernomor reignited in the young Leonid his youthful fancy of becoming an actor, and he believed that now "the theater offered me a greater opportunity to express myself and to project my own personality than dancing."²⁸

Leonid's portrayal of Chernomor must have been a considerable accomplishment, for he would go on to be cast in a series of character parts at the Bolshoi and Maly theaters. His next assignment at the Maly came in 1908, as Egorka in Alexander Ostrovsky's *Poverty Is Not a Crime*. In 1909 there were two more roles at the Maly: Dobrotvorsky's Boy in Ostrovsky's *Poor Bride* and Mishka in Gogol's *Government Inspector*. In all of these plays Leonid shared the stage with the Maly's leading performers. His commitments as a juvenile actor meant that he began to spend precious hours in the theater, rehearsing and performing. During the run of *The Government Inspector* he stood

> *enthralled at the side of the stage, watching Konstantin Nikolaevich Rybakov, with his grand sweeping gestures and resonant voice, portray the corrupt old mayor who was trying to present an acceptable image of himself as a benign elderly official. I was equally impressed by the acting of Padarin, a tall distinguished-looking actor playing the part of the Government Inspector's old servant who humbles himself for his master's sake. It was exciting, too, to watch Ostujev's strong, decisive performance as Khlestakov, the adventurer who passes himself off as the Government Inspector, a forthright hero who represents a younger generation seeking to rid Russia of political corruption.*[29]

Leonid's introspective, meditative bent and his penchant for daydreaming had found an appropriate outlet in the make-believe world of the theater. His acting permitted him to venture out into the world; yet once the applause ended he could quickly retreat to his inner reality. He was an avid observer of the actor's craft, of the "manners, voices and gestures" that are the medium of the actor. No doubt his fascination with acting was part of his adolescent search for a more secure identity. But acting had cast a profound spell over him. He found that on his way home from the theater each day he was "still going over the scenes from the play. At home I would repeat Ostujev's lines in exactly his tone of voice." Or he would deliver Rybakov's lines to Aunt Feodosia and her family, mimicking the older actor's movements and gestures. Caught up in his newfound power to move and impress, he also probably affected some of the arrogant offstage posturing of the actors, for he had to be reminded (probably by his mother and Aunt Feodosia) that his dramatic education was not complete and he "was not yet a famous actor."[30] In his autobiography he remembers a visit to his brother Mikhail, who by then was married and living in Helsinki, commanding a military radio station. Upon his departure he waved at the couple from the boat, decked out in his gifts from Mikhail, a new coat and hat, "the latter with its brim turned down at a rakish angle, which I thought very suitable for a promising young actor."[31]

In 1909 Leonid would undergo his first experience of grief at the loss of a loved one. When the family returned to Moscow from Zvenigorod-Moskovsky in September, his brother Konstantin remained behind at the dacha to go hunting with a friend during their expedition and accidentally was shot and killed. He was twenty-one years old and had just graduated with high honors from engineering school; the family was "confident he had a brilliant future before him."[32] Word of his death arrived in a telegram from the family's neighbor and friend Unitzky. Mme Miassine at first refused to believe the horrible news. And in spite of its weeping, the whole family was clearly in a state of shock. Miassine remembered that he

> suddenly felt that I must go and tell some of Konstantin's friends what had happened. I ran out of the house, down the street, past the livery stables, and on to the main boulevard. With only a vague idea of where they lived, I searched for his friends in the back streets and courtyards, but found no one. Driven by an overwhelming feeling of horror, I continued to run through the city, along the boulevards, through parks and squares, until I finally collapsed from exhaustion in an unfamiliar road on the outskirts of Moscow. I lay there for what seemed like hours, until the initial shock of the news had worn off. In the evening I arrived back home, weak and shaken.[33]

Massine fills three pages of his autobiography with his account of the tragic death of his brother and the funeral in Zvenigorod-Moskovsky, which he attended with Raissa and their parents. Konstantin's death left "an ineffaceable scar."[34] And while time seemed to heal the tragedy for the rest of the family, Mr. Miassine would never quite recover from his son's death.

Leonid returned to his young artist's life. With help from a Bolshoi Orchestra colleague of his father's, he began to study the violin. For five years he worked with "great concentration" at mastering the instrument, in order to "enlarge my understanding of serious music."[35] He also enjoyed playing the balalaika, especially during the weekends he spent with his godmother, Alexandra Alexandrovna Puskova, a dramatic soprano with the Bolshoi and one of his mother's most beloved friends.[36]

He seemed to prefer acting more than ever. He writes in his memoirs:

> By the time I was fifteen I had definitely decided that I would be an actor. The theater, to me, was far more stimulating and challenging than the bal-

let, and apart from the fact that the plays I had appeared in held greater interest for me than any of the Bolshoi productions, I found actors more intelligent and articulate than most of the dancers I knew. In comparison with the Maly productions, the ballet was a mediocre form of light entertainment. Except for the ballets of Tchaikovsky, the music was mostly on the level of Pugni and Minkus. Yet I realized too how much of my ballet training had helped me in my acting. Physical control and an understanding of movement were invaluable assets when it came to character interpretation and projection on the legitimate stage. In fact both halves of my education complemented each other. My acting improved through my knowledge of movement, and my experience in the theater helped me to create vivid characterizations in my dancing.[37]

Already by 1912 Leonid appears in the registry of the Moscow Imperial Theaters as the recipient of a six-hundred-ruble scholarship. Beginning in 1911 his acting responsibilities at the Maly had expanded; in a Maly Theater report on the 1911–12 season he is named as performing six roles, three of which were new assignments.

One of these, Mitya in Persianinova's *The Big Ones and the Small Ones*, marked a turning point in Leonid's acting career. The play was premiered in December 1911 as a benefit performance for the acclaimed actress Nadezhda Nikulina (one of Ostrovsky's favorites), who was celebrating fifty years on the Maly stage. The production included some of the Maly's most prestigious actors. That Leonid shared the stage with these luminaries on such an auspicious occasion testifies to his status as the Maly's up-and-coming young actor. The press notices also must have pleased him. According to *Theatre,* "the most interesting among the male performers was Mitya, [played by] the student Miassine . . . ,"[38] and a later review called his performance "excellent."[39] *Season News* glowed: "The boy Miassine who is graduating this year from the Ballet School attracted attention. His performance of the role of the young hero was captivating, youthful and interesting. There was no false note, and such humor and pathos—all was very good. One can predict a great future for this sixteen-year-old actor."[40]

Leonid continued to perform in ballet productions at the Bolshoi: as the Monkey in *Pharaoh's Daughter,* in the Khan's suite in *The Little Humpbacked Horse,* and as Prince Avenan in *The Sleeping Beauty,* all choreographed by Gorsky. As the Monkey he had to "swing down from the branch of an exotic tree, perform a short solo on all fours, and return to my tree without once standing erect. It was a great strain to do this on

Miassine in The Big Ones and the Small Ones, *with actress Nadezhda Nikulina, Maly Theater, 1911*

The Big Ones and the Small Ones, *Maly Theater, 1911; Miassine is on the extreme left.*

the steeply raked stage of the Bolshoi, and afterwards I would be physically exhausted."[41]

Leonid was encouraged by some of the Maly's most prestigious performers to pursue an acting career. Once, during a rehearsal, Mikhail Provich Sadovsky, son of the famous Prov Sadovsky, ostentatiously pointed at Miassine and proclaimed: "There is a boy who has God's spark!"

Leonid's friend Nicholas Zverev, seven years older and a member of the Zimin Theater corps de ballet, also encouraged him, but in another direction. Zverev took Leonid to the studio of the forty-two-year-old Anatoli Petrovich Bolchakov, whose private art school at 4 Miasnitsky Lane attracted a number of male dancers.[42] During 1912 and 1913 Leonid studied drawing and painting under the tutelage of Bolchakov, whom he described as "a friendly, disheveled young man wearing a long white linen smock." According to Bolchakov's widow, Leonid was very keen on drawing and painting and, like the other students, loved the teacher for the genuine interest he took in their lives and careers. It was in this warmly supportive environment that he began to familiarize himself with the works of such artists as van Gogh, Degas, and Toulouse-Lautrec: "Although the reproductions [Bolchakov] showed us were drab and muddy, he had a way of generating enthusiasm as he talked. Until then I had never thought seriously about art, but now I was puzzled and intrigued by such things as the curious angles and positions of the dancers in Degas's pictures, and by the grotesque characterizations in Toulouse-Lautrec's posters. When I stayed on after classes to talk to Bolchakov I found him more like a friend than a teacher."[43]

Leonid's relationship with Anatoli Petrovich became crucial to his growth as man and artist. Their enduring friendship, which began on mentor-pupil terms, without question became Leonid's deepest emotional liaison outside of his family. This was especially true when, after Mr. Miassine's retirement from the Bolshoi in 1911, the family settled permanently at the dacha, making it necessary for Leonid to rent a room near the Theater School. In a 1914 letter to Bolchakov Leonid would acknowledge that it was Anatoli Petrovich who had taught him to love and to live.[44] The relationship was driven by Leonid's thirst for knowledge. The dialectical flow of ideas between them engendered within the young man a firmer sense of mission. He had received only a limited education in the arts and humanities from the Imperial Theater school system. "It was he," Leonid would later write, "who had first aroused my interest in art."[45] As their emotionally charged friendship deepened, Miassine came to discover and appreciate art of a higher order. His exposure to new aesthetic developments enriched his artistic consciousness. The principles underlying the Italian Renaissance and impressionism became freshly available to him, like newfound wisdom. Bolchakov instilled in Miassine an early love for Italy, especially Rome. He showed Leonid "books containing illustrations of Italian cathedrals and of the frescoes and other works of art contained in them. . . . Bolchakov had never been outside Russia, but he could describe the treasures of Tuscany and the paintings in the Louvre as vividly as the most experienced traveller."[46]

In Leonid's letters to Anatoli Petrovich after the dancer's departure from Moscow, their discussions ranged from the early Christian churches and Byzantine mosaics to the contemporary work of Michel Larionov. Anatoli Petrovich prompted Leonid to visit the Tretiakov National Gallery, even though he would later confess that "at the time my taste was not sufficiently developed, and the academic portraits and landscapes I saw there made practically no impression on me."[47]

Anatoli Petrovich's study, with its hodgepodge of easels and plants, provided Miassine with an unfettered and genial setting in which he could meet young artists and students outside the more restrictive environment of the Imperial Theaters. Under their teacher's watchful eye, the young students engaged in intense discussions about art and current affairs. In addition to Zverev and fellow dancer Dmitri Kostrovsky, Leonid also befriended three female classmates, Elena Domiavnova, Elizabeta Stepanovna, and Elena Egorovna.[48]

Leonid graduated in August 1912 and was promptly accepted into the Bolshoi ballet company with a yearly salary of six hundred rubles, plus the customary hundred extra for "équipement."[49] The next year was filled with hard work and achievement.

He danced in ten ballets, including new roles in *Swan Lake* (the Tarantella), *Don Quixote* (the Knight of the Silver Moon and Carasco), and *Le Corsaire* (in the Oriental dream scene). He also appeared in thirteen opera ballets, including those in *The Snow Maiden*, *The Queen of Spades*, *Faust*, *Sadko*, *Eugene Onegin*, and *Les Pêcheurs de perles*, all choreographed by Gorsky. Leonid also danced a menuet and an écossaise in the comedy-divertissement *Assemblée*.

With his new solo parts at the Bolshoi multiplying, his position in the company was solidifying. When Alexander Yuzhin, manager of the Maly drama company, solicited special permission for Leonid's participation as Kolya in C. S. Palynov's play *Ring of Fire*,[50] the Bolshoi's régisseur, A. Bulgakov, replied: "Mr. Miassine distinguished himself during this sea-

Miassine (standing, left) with friends in Moscow, circa 1912

son; I even entrusted him with solo performances; therefore, his absence would be very noticeable. However, I do not have the right to keep him from participating in drama performances, because it is undoubtedly beneficial for his artistic development."[51] Among the other new acting roles Leonid undertook at the Maly were Sergei in Leonid Andreyev's *Professor Storytsyn* and Tsarevich Mikhail Feodorovitch in *1613*. For his role as the tsarevich, Leonid

> *had to learn to employ noble gestures and a grand manner, particularly in the dramatic scene before the young Tsar's coronation when, clad in my sumptuous robes, I confronted my mother, the Tsaritza, played by that*

great actress Alexandra Alexandrovna Yablochkina. This was an impor-
tant part for me, and one in which I gained invaluable experience. After
playing it I felt much more confident on stage, and ready to accept any new
part which was offered me.[52]

His professional schedule during the 1912–13 season was so hectic
that he performed 176 times in ballets, dramas, and operas.

Gorsky's realistic approach to ballet undoubtedly had a substantial
influence on Leonid during his formative years at the Bolshoi, where
he absorbed both the classical academic tradition and Gorsky's determination to revitalize it. As a reformer, Gorsky "pierced the performance
with a clear line of action, dramatized the dance, saturated the ensemble
scenes with playful moments, and introduced details from everyday
life. . . ." This markedly dramatic approach was evident in both his new
ballets and his reworking of the classics. About his version of *Don
Quixote* Souritz writes: "Gorsky added new integrity and meaning to
Petipa's Don Quixote, which had previously been rather eclectic
and amorphous, and in so doing made it more viable."[53] In this work
Gorsky tried "for the first time to break with the clichés of 'balletic-
pseudo Spain.' His major success . . . was the fact that the dancing
was born 'from emotional states that kindled a consuming need for
dance.' "[54] In his 1912 production of *Swan Lake* (in which Leonid
danced) Gorsky "did away with the sedate formation of straight frontal
lines and added character dancing, ending [Act I] with a vigorous, somewhat medieval-looking farandole with torches in the dancers' hands."[55]
According to critic André Levinson, "the finale of the first act of
Swan Lake, listless and sloppy in the St. Petersburg production, in
Gorsky's version has become an artistic, vigorous torch procession of
medieval *fantoccini.*"[56] Interestingly, Leonid was more impressed by
Gorsky's

personality than by his artistic creations. It was enchanting to watch him
glide 'round the stage, demonstrating phrases of movement with an ethe-
real grace which few of his dancers could equal. In Don Quixote he
began to break away from the old academic tradition of rigid rows of
dancers stepping forward at specified moments to perform their set pieces,
attempting to replace this formality by integrated ensembles forming flow-
ing patterns of movement. But it struck me that he was an inventive artist
who could never quite transmit his ideas to his dancers. He lacked the abil-

ity to manipulate large groups on stage, and so his inventions remained only half-realized.[57]

Leonid's favorite work by Gorsky was *Schubertiana*, which he considered "charming, graceful and well composed."[58]

It would be a mistake, however, to undervalue in Massine's future choreographic essays the influence of Gorsky's dramatic expressiveness, his integration of character dance into academic ballet, and his stress on plasticity of movement.

WHAT DIRECTION HAD Leonid's acting training taken after 1910, when drama courses were dropped from the curriculum at the Theater School? How aware was he of Stanislavsky's reforms? Massine does not discuss Stanislavsky in his autobiography, but it seems inconceivable that any serious aspiring actor in Moscow would not have come into contact with the ideas of a man who by 1910 had become a theatrical institution. Stanislavsky's efforts to revolutionize the theater already were being debated during his days with his amateur troupes, the Alexeyev Circle (his family name was Alexeyev) and the Society of Art and Literature, in the 1880s and early 1890s, well before he founded the Art Theater in 1898. And from the early years of the Art Theater, his reforms had had an impact on the Maly. Not only did he enjoy a frank rapport with the Maly actors, who he believed were the strongest spiritual influence on his development; but two of the Maly's most revered teachers, Alexander Lensky (1847–1908) and Alexander Yuzhin (1857–1927), had championed his ideas. Yuzhin (Prince Sumbatov), one of Moscow's most important dramatic coaches, was greatly admired by Stanislavsky, and vice versa: Yuzhin once declared that the Maly should have been taken over by Stanislavsky. Undoubtedly Leonid's acting training from 1908 on had been primarily in Yuzhin's hands, and it was probably Yuzhin who directed him in most of his roles at the Maly. Yuzhin was a thorough director, according to the actress N. L. Tiraspolskaya: "He was able to give very wise and useful advice about principles. He analyzed a play profoundly and cleverly ridiculed the false pathos and the overworked posing of the student. His illustrations glowed with a magnificent skill."[59]

In January 1913, Stanislavsky established the First Art Theater Studio for the purpose of training actors according to his own method. In various interviews, Massine has mentioned meeting Stanislavsky for the first time in the flat of the famous Maly actress Olga Gosvskaya, who joined the Art Theater in 1910.[60] (At the time of the meeting, she and Leonid were working together on Shakespeare's *Antony and Cleopatra*.) And though he himself was never involved with the Art Theater, in conversations with the author, Massine stated that he had been familiar with Stanislavsky's theories and that before leaving Moscow at the beginning of 1914 he had discussed with Stanislavsky himself the possibility of working with him.

PART TWO

Diaghilev

A drive towards unity, reaching beyond
personality, the quotidian, society,
across the chasm of transitoriness: an
impassioned and painful overflowing into
darker, fuller, more buoyant states; an
ecstatic affirmation of the totality of life
[or art] is what remains constant . . . the
eternal will for regeneration, fruitfulness,
recurrence; the awareness that creation
and destruction are inseparable.

—NIETZSCHE

Miassine at the time he joined the Diaghilev company, Moscow, 1914

CHAPTER 2

Moscow, December 1913–Paris, August 1914

THE WINTER SEASON at the Bolshoi Theater proved to be a turning point for Miassine. At the beginning of December he danced again in *Don Quixote* and *Swan Lake,* and at one of these performances Serge Diaghilev was in the audience.

Serge Pavlovich Diaghilev, born in 1872, held a prominent place in the Russian renaissance at the turn of the century. In 1898 he founded the influential St. Petersburg art and literary journal *The World of Art (Mir iskusstva),* which appeared in twelve numbers from 1898 to 1904. Among his associates were the painters Alexandre Benois (who co-edited the magazine with him), Leon Bakst, and Konstantin Somov and Diaghilev's journalist cousin and lover, Dmitri Filosofov.[1] *The World of Art* was a major force in the rise of Russian modernism. Its objectives, fostered also by the important art exhibits it mounted, were to disseminate the tenets of emerging artistic trends in Europe and Russia and to revitalize an interest in the heritage of Russian art. In its first two years the journal paid particular attention to the growth of art nouveau in Europe; later issues focused interest on postimpressionist painters, especially Gauguin and van Gogh. The symbolist poets found a platform in *The World of Art* from which to express their aesthetic principles. In a recent re-evaluation of the journal the Soviet historian Alla Gusarova has observed, "For us *The World of Art* is not only drawings, paintings, books, the embodiment of mental grace, the mind, the high culture of its creators, the reverential love of nature and art. It is a noble enthusiasm for the study of Russian antiquity, a discovery of entire sections of Russian art, almost unknown before. It is examples of artistic criticism, intelligent, sensitive and tolerant of the searchings of their young contemporaries, even those alien in spirit."[2]

Nearly a year after the first issue appeared, Prince Serge Volkonsky, director of the St. Petersburg Imperial Theaters, retained Diaghilev as a coordinator of special projects, a position he held from 1899 to 1901. During this period, Diaghilev edited the Imperial Theaters' yearbook and, later, was entrusted with the production of the ballet *Sylvia,* which led to intrigue and a series of complications that unfortunately resulted in his dismissal.[3]

But neither reversals nor commotion ever stopped Diaghilev; with time, all was made to bend to his indefatigable will. In the midst of the turmoil caused by the abortive 1905 revolution, for example, Diaghilev organized the Russian Historical Portrait Exhibition in St. Petersburg. In 1906, also in St. Petersburg, he mounted a retrospective exhibition of Russian painting, which went on to Paris, where it was presented at the Salon d'Automne.[4] The show was magnificent, surveying everything from fifteenth-century icons to the works of the young artists of the School of Moscow. With the 1906 Paris exhibition of Russian art, Diaghilev began what Alexandre Benois called his "export campaign of Russian art."[5] Setting his sights on Western Europe, Diaghilev in 1907 brought to Paris a series of concerts featuring Russian music, and the following year he presented Mussorgsky's *Boris Godunov* with Chaliapin in the title role.[6]

By 1909 Diaghilev was committing his organizational talents to ballet, introducing to the West the finest fruits of Russian training as exemplified by the dancing of Anna Pavlova, Tamara Karsavina, and Vaslav Nijinsky. Through his efforts Western Europe would witness the revolutionary choreography of Michel Fokine, whose work reflected a shift away from acrobatic virtuosity and Petipa-inspired classicism toward a more naturalistic style. At the same time, stage design and costuming by such artists as Benois and Bakst took on a new fluidity and richness of color. Diaghilev's productions of *Les Sylphides, Firebird, Petrouchka, L'Après-midi d'un faune,* and *Le Sacre du printemps* gave a new beginning to ballet, while in *Firebird, Petrouchka,* and *Le Sacre du printemps* the music of Igor Stravinsky took the theater world by storm.[7]

In the winter of 1913 Diaghilev was in Moscow to recruit a leading dancer for his forthcoming production of Richard Strauss's biblical ballet *The Legend of Joseph,* a work with a libretto by Hugo von Hofmannsthal and Count Harry Kessler, costumes by Bakst, and a sumptuous decor in the Renaissance style of Veronese by José María Sert.[8] When the ballet first was planned in 1912, it was intended that Nijinsky would choreograph and dance the title role, but later events changed everything: Nijinsky's unexpected marriage to Romola de Pulszky in September 1913 led Diaghilev to terminate his association with the dancer, both as his lover and as the company's leading dancer-choreographer.

Diaghilev went to Russia. First he stopped in St. Petersburg to see Fokine, who had left the Ballets Russes once Nijinsky was launched as a choreographer, and persuaded him to take charge of the Strauss ballet. He then traveled to Moscow to meet with the artist Natalia Gontcharova, whom he hoped to engage as the designer for his upcoming production of Rimsky-Korsakov's opera *Le Coq d'or.*[9] Gontcharova and her companion, the artist Michel Larionov, were leaders in the Russian avant-garde art movement, and Diaghilev had much admired their work ever since he had exhibited some of their paintings in his 1906 exhibition. When he arrived in Moscow, she was enjoying great success with a retrospective of nearly eight hundred paintings.[10]

Diaghilev attended ballet performances at the Bolshoi Theater and was captivated by the young Miassine's charismatic presence, his piercing eyes and Byzantine looks, as he danced the Knight of the Silver Moon in *Don Quixote* and the tarantella in *Swan Lake.* Not only had the impresario found his ideal Joseph; he also must have sensed the youth's potential, his pliant sensibility, and his remarkable individuality, for he immediately enlisted Mikhail Savitsky, a Bolshoi dancer who had just joined the Ballets Russes, to arrange a meeting.

The prospect of being sought after by a man of Diaghilev's artistic prominence, international achievements, and personal notoriety must have filled Leonid with high anticipation. He soon found himself visiting the impresario at the Metropole Hotel, located on Theater Square across from the Bolshoi, Maly, and Nezlobin theaters. Massine writes:

> When I walked into the orange, gilded lobby I felt as though I were entering a larger-than-life world of fantasy. Timidly I made my way through rows of potted palms and porters in gold braid. When I asked for Diaghilev at the reception desk, I was shown into the lift and a few moments later was knocking at his door. It was opened by a young Italian with curly black hair and beady eyes. He smiled when I gave him my name, and showed me into a formal little sitting room. "Monsieur Diaghilev will be with you in a moment," he told me.
>
> I sat down stiffly on a plush sofa. The Italian disappeared into another room, and I heard him say, "Signor Baron, Signor Miassine is here to see you." A moment later Diaghilev appeared in a dressing gown. At first glance he appeared tall and imposing, but when I stood up I realized that he was only of medium height, but that he had an unusually large head and broad shoulders. The next thing I noticed was the streak of silver-white hair, like a feather, over his forehead. Peering at me through his monocle, he looked at me like a creature from another planet.[11]

Once the interview was completed, a "dazed and bewildered" Miassine visited the Theater School to tell his friends about Diaghilev's proposal to join his ballet company and to undertake the role of Joseph. His friends counseled against it, contending that it was unwise for him to leave Moscow when in the upcoming *Romeo and Juliet* at the Maly he was being considered for Romeo, a role that could launch him on a serious career as a leading actor.[12]

Days of "restless indecision" followed. Diaghilev clearly represented the potential for artistic recognition on an international scale. For the dreamer that Miassine was, for the child so adept at losing himself in daydreams, for the ambitious young artist he was fast becoming, the choice was between the predictable—the Maly Theater—and the fantastic. Diaghilev appeared like the fairy-tale godfather who could, with the touch of his magic wand, change dreams into reality. But how ready was Leonid for Diaghilev? Was their meeting the act of providence he had been waiting for? Could the impresario catapult him out of his daily routine?

There is no doubt that after his visit to the Metropole Hotel the young man was torn between the security that Moscow provided and his fear of the unknown, a fear magnified by the prospect of replacing Nijinsky in *The Legend of Joseph.* But the actress Masoritznova's oft-repeated tales of Diaghilev's triumphant Parisian premieres[13] continued to grip his imagination; and coupled with Diaghilev's spellbinding personality, they would eventually dispel any doubts. Certainly it was a meeting of two extraordinary men—both narcissistic, gifted, and driven—the younger one discovering his first faith in his talent, the older one always conscious of the indelible stamp he had already left on an art form.

Miassine returned to the Metropole Hotel determined to refuse Diaghilev's offer, reiterating to himself his reasons. But: "I walked in, he peered at me through his monocle, smiled and waited for me to speak. I was just about to tell him that I could not accept his offer when, almost without realizing it, I heard myself say, 'Yes, I shall be delighted to join your company.'"[14]

Miassine and Diaghilev left Moscow on the night train to St. Petersburg.[15] Their first trip together marked the beginning of Diaghilev's tutorship of Miassine. He made clear to his young charge what must be understood above all: the twentieth century was witnessing a radical artistic transition. While Diaghilev talked, Miassine surely only listened. He later wrote that their discussions centered around "an entirely new concept of ballet" that would supersede an "old academic tradition" whose usefulness had been outlived. Diaghilev believed that in the fusion of music, dance, painting, poetry, and drama, in accordance with the examples of Greek and Wagnerian theater, a more complete and cohesive artistic expression might be achieved.

Once they arrived in St. Petersburg, preparations to launch the young dancer began. Miassine's final acceptance into the company was subject to Fokine's approval, so Diaghilev set up an audition with the choreographer. At Fokine's apartment Miassine was asked to reproduce the positions of the figures in a Roman mural and to perform a quick leap over a chair in the center of the room.[16] Once Fokine had accepted the new recruit, Miassine was sent to a photography session at Boissonan and Eggler, which actually provided him with an introductory study of the character of Joseph. Donning the shepherd's costume designed by Bakst, and following Fokine's instructions for the poses, Miassine tried to immerse himself in the character by assuming the expressions he thought appropriate to the role. His anxiety in a new and unfamiliar world, as well as his apprehension about the future, were channeled into an almost Stanislavskian "inner technique." He later wrote: "For a moment, as I shifted my position awkwardly under the glare of the photographer's lights, I had a glimpse of Joseph's character, and felt I could understand his fear and uncertainty when brought before Potiphar." [17] Once more Miassine evinced a tendency and ability to copy and repro- duce the feelings and attitudes of others; a technical strength as well as a survival scheme, it apparently allowed him to work through some of his own internal struggles.

While Diaghilev stayed on in St. Petersburg, Miassine returned to Moscow alone, to make arrangements for his departure. At some point early in December he petitioned the Office of the Imperial Theaters for a leave of absence without salary for one year, beginning on January 14, 1914, due to family circumstances. The petition was denied. [18] By Decem- ber 15, Diaghilev had sent Hofmannsthal a set of photographs of Mias- sine, and the librettist, in a letter to Richard Strauss, expressed his enthusiasm for the new Joseph, promising that Miassine's portrayal "will be the real thing—it has just that quality of purity which is the antithesis of the female character." [19] Diaghilev also wrote Miassine in Moscow set- ting forth the terms of their contract. On December 19 the dancer asked the Imperial Theaters to discharge him as of January 1, 1914, again citing family circumstances. [20] He was issued a passport on January 4, after which he traveled to St. Petersburg to join Diaghilev, who took him to the Hermitage before they left for Cologne to join the company. En route, the two men discussed *The Legend of Joseph* in greater detail. The impresario must have been quite pleased with his discovery, for despite their brief association, already by January 22 Diaghilev was extending the initial length of Miassine's engagement. [21]

As their intimacy deepened, Diaghilev revealed himself to be a fas- cinating human being. Miassine found in him "an underlying humanity and integrity which, I felt, derived from his total commitment to his art." In the presence of his companion Miassine began to feel that "all my past experience had been negligible, and that I was now embarking on an en- tirely new career." His first impression of the older man as "fantastic" and "unreal" began to dissipate, and "by the end of the journey I had begun to feel more at ease with Diaghilev." [22] The impresario had opened to the young man an unknown world, one of unlimited possibilities, where every moment was imbued with brilliant conversation about bold projects to come and the stimulation and excitement of new places. Diaghilev the magician began to cast his spell, and as Miassine's hunger for knowledge and for the new became consuming, he found himself en- chanted by his ever-persuasive companion and steadily drawn into Diaghilev's dreamlike reality. Indeed, Miassine began to erect a near- heroic image of the impresario—doubtless to offset his virtually total dependence. Sexual dominance of the younger man completed Diaghilev's conquest.

In Cologne they stayed at the Domhof Hotel. Miassine was overwhelmed by the luxury of his surroundings; he regarded the hotel as "fairly decadent, completely out of my world," and "felt guilty about being" there. At bottom, he admitted, was the fact that "the hotel merely intensified all the fears and uncertainties which I felt about my new venture."[23]

Being integrated into the company must have been difficult for Miassine. Private and reclusive by nature, he was now thrust into prominence day after day both as Diaghilev's lover and as the center of the impresario's nomadic community. According to the Diaghilev ballerina Lydia Sokolova, Miassine's "impenetrability" was apparent from the beginning; she remembers him as "remarkably like a medical student. . . . He must have been scared. His eyes were so enormous that they seemed to swamp his little pale face, yet when he looked at you they remained completely blank, as if there was a shutter at the back of them. Miassine would stare straight at you, but his eyes never smiled. . . . There was no way of telling what thoughts were in his head."[24]

Nevertheless, Miassine found the company's collective spirit exhilarating, and also came to see how radically different its aesthetic approach was from the academicism of the Bolshoi. He was soon assigned the role of the Night Watchman in *Petrouchka* so that he might observe and understand Fokine's style. This 1911 ballet had a powerful impact on him; he found in it evidence of the "synthesis of elements" of which Diaghilev had spoken so enthusiastically. He marveled at *Petrouchka*'s integration of drama, music, painting, and dance, and saw that a whole new grammar of art had opened up to him. Moreover, he now saw that this choreographic style was "universal in its depth and intensity." In Fokine's choreography Miassine came to admire the intricate ensembles that dispensed with the "convenient academic groupings"; he found in them a "sharply observed, realistically interpreted interplay" between the characters even while "all the movements were held together by a sustaining and unifying rhythm."[25] Thus, gradually, his understanding of Fokine's conception deepened. He began to see in *Petrouchka* not only "a statement of the dramatic human contrast to the world of puppets," but also the ballet's inner truth in the "profoundly human character" of Petrouchka, a "tragic figure, symbolizing innocence caught up in a world of corruption."[26] (Fokine himself danced Petrouchka in these performances, with Karsavina as the Ballerina.)

Massine

Miassine received his first taste of the Ballets Russes' creative process during rehearsals for *The Legend of Joseph*, which already had begun. Working with Fokine was stimulating but strenuous:

> I was fascinated by the flowing, rounded movements which Fokine had devised for me, but when I tried to execute them I found that I was restricted by the stiff academic positions in which I had for so long been drilled. During the first week of rehearsals I struggled to readjust my body so as to achieve the effortless rhythm which Fokine demanded. He remained noncommittal about my progress, and although Diaghilev did all he could to bolster up my confidence, I remained convinced that I had undertaken a task which was beyond me.
>
> In my first dance Fokine's typically free and flowing movements, in which big elevation steps were followed by poses on one knee, evolution of the arms during fast running steps and occasional broad arm and body movements in a small spatial area, created a perfect visual equilibrium between movement and immobility. I found it very taxing, while under such a great physical strain, to maintain for so long the illusion that my movements were spontaneous and effortless, and I was exhausted long before the end of the dance.[27]

Miassine with Michel Georges-Michel and Diaghilev near Nice, 1914

By the time they came to rehearse the second scene, Miassine felt more comfortable. For the mime, he drew on his acting experience. Moreover, Fokine was a thorough and meticulous choreographer, offering descriptive images to help the dancer form his image of the shepherd. Now, in true Stanislavskian fashion, Miassine identified the qualities that linked him to the character, devising a convincingly acted interpretation. For instance, in visualizing the conflict with Potiphar's Wife as the embodiment of his inner anxiety, he found that "each time I struggled with her, I seemed to project into my acting all my own anguish and heartbreak at having left Russia to take on the incredibly taxing part." And "when Froman, who was playing the part of the Archangel, finally rescued me from Potiphar's cruelties and led me away with a firm and kindly handclasp, I almost felt that I was in truth being delivered from my own fears and uncertainties."[28]

Rehearsals for *The Legend of Joseph* were conducted throughout the German tour, but the schedule was intensified while the company was in Berlin. Leon Bakst arrived from Paris and sent back an enthusiastic telegram to Misia Edwards, Diaghilev's close friend and staunchest supporter: "Miassine marvelous and astonishing with sincerity, fluency of movement, fantastic figure, great art."[29]

After engagements in Hamburg, Leipzig, Hanover, Breslau, Berlin, and Zurich, the Ballets Russes arrived in Monte Carlo for a spring season from April 6 to May 6. Miassine was dazzled by Monte Carlo's "pink-painted hotels, outdoor cafés and whimsical houses," and "curved balconies"; it was like a "make-believe city, a set for a pretty operetta."[30] He and Diaghilev embarked upon a public social life. There were dinners with Misia and her lover José María Sert, the Spanish painter who was designing the sets for *Joseph*. They approved of Diaghilev's new companion, and helped Miassine to feel more at ease and less inadequate in his new environment. At a party at the Hôtel de Paris, the young dancer met and waltzed with the legendary Isadora Duncan. She reminded him of a figure on a Greek vase; he was struck by her harmonious gestures and by her "extraordinary freedom and expressiveness of movement."[31]

But mostly Miassine concentrated on *Joseph*. The celebrated teacher Enrico Cecchetti, who had worked with the greatest dancers of his time, gave him intensive private classes to strengthen his technique, and he continued to do so in Paris when the Ballets Russes moved there for a season at the Opéra.

Paris, the city that since the turn of the century had been fertile ground for a host of movements in modern art, exceeded all Miassine's expectations. He took in the broad, beautifully designed parks, strolled about the area around the Champs-Elysées, and leisurely ambled across the place Vendôme and the Faubourg-Saint-Honoré. All too aware of the differences between France and Russia, he puzzled over the social pastime of café conversation; though he admired Paris, he felt "very out of place, very much the oafish stranger in this elegant city."[32]

Miassine's schedule soon became hectic. Although he had time for a few visits to the Louvre, life centered around the forthcoming premiere. Cecchetti continued to coach him both privately and in his public class at the Opéra, a class also attended by Nijinsky, whom Diaghilev wanted Miassine to observe at work.

Excitement pervaded the Opéra stage. Diaghilev was surrounded by his collaborators, such artistic luminaries as Strauss, Hofmannsthal, Kessler, Fokine, Bakst, and Sert. Miassine began to comprehend the sources of the admiration, respect, and authority Diaghilev commanded when, during rehearsal, the impresario remarked that one musical passage was too long, and unnecessary besides. Strauss took his pencil and, following Diaghilev's suggestion, deleted about ten pages from the score.[33] Stravinsky also attended the rehearsals, and Miassine met the composer for the first time. At another session he was introduced to the poet Jean Cocteau and to the exquisite young artist Valentine Gross, a friend of Marcel Proust and a well-known personality in Parisian intellectual and artistic circles. (At one of these rehearsals Kessler introduced Cocteau to Gross—a meeting that would have major repercussions in the poet's life and, indirectly, for Miassine and the Ballets Russes.)[34] The keen interest aroused by the new discovery prompted Gross to seek, through the publisher Jacques de Brunhoff, Diaghilev's permission to draw Miassine. Probably still smarting from the outcome of his relationship with Nijinsky, Diaghilev denied the request. (The impresario's characteristic possessiveness was always apparent in his relationships with lovers and friends, and even in his dealings with his collaborators.)

Miassine's only concern, however, was the new ballet; he was particularly worried about the Opéra's stage, which was so steeply raked that he had difficulty keeping his balance. On May 14 the ballet had its *répétition générale,* with the striking Russian soprano Maria Kuznetsova as Potiphar's Wife, a mime role. For Miassine, life and art were once again intertwined, as he utilized his existential experience in the service of the theatrical one. He describes his mental state during that first performance:

By the time the curtain went up I was in a pitiable state of nervous tension. As I was carried on stage in my hammock I kept my eyes tightly shut, and when I finally opened them the glare of the footlights nearly blinded me. Struggling to retain my balance on the huge sloping stage during my solo dance, I felt my ordeal was far worse than anything that Joseph had been called upon to endure. During a long stretch of almost uninterrupted movement I became increasingly dizzy, but fortunately Joseph's brothers stepped forward to support me, and after a momentary respite I was able to finish the rest of the dance. After the agony of the opening scene the rest of the performance passed off easily enough, though my own buried fears nearly got the upper hand of me again during my struggles with Potiphar's wife, and by the time the final curtain came down I was almost fainting with exhaustion. As I lay sweating on the sofa in my dressing room, Diaghilev, Strauss and Benois came 'round to congratulate me. To my dazed mind they seemed as unreal as the imposing figures of Potiphar and his wife.[35]

Relying more on Miassine's physical appearance and his acting ability than on his ballet technique, Fokine had tailored the role of Joseph to exploit the best qualities of the young dancer. Miassine's lambskin costume, designed by Benois (his only contribution to this ballet) to personify youthful innocence and vulnerability, was so scanty (for its day) that the press dubbed the ballet *Les Jambes de Joseph*, or *Joseph's Legs*. Despite insinuations in the press that his dancing posed no threat to Nijinsky (who attended the premiere), Miassine was praised for his sensitive portrayal.

After Paris, the company began a London season at the Drury Lane Theatre on June 8. Anticipation ran high for *The Legend of Joseph*, and the press covered the preparations for the local premiere as thoroughly as they had in Paris. Strauss was undoubtedly one of the major attractions. One reporter wrote: "Seldom has a musical event provoked such interest in London beforehand as that which Dr. Strauss's ballet was able to command. When the great night arrived Drury Lane was packed, and literally humming with anticipation."[36] Strauss received a thunderous ovation when he appeared on the podium.

After a dress rehearsal attended by London society, Miassine made his British debut on June 23. Reviewers complimented him on his appearance and stage presence even as they acknowledged his lack of technical command. The *Sunday Times* wrote: "M. Miassine is not a very experienced dancer, but his youthful, ingenuous appearance was a great

*Four studio portraits of Miassine in
The Legend of Joseph,
wearing the lambskin tunic
designed by Benois*

asset."[37] This time Karsavina took the part of Potiphar's Wife. She thought Miassine was "quite remarkable" as Joseph; his "lack of virtuosity in those days lent pathos to the image he created."[38]

Life in London was more settled than in Paris. Diaghilev arranged for a tutor to provide Miassine with English lessons; and there were leisurely visits to the National Gallery, the Tate, and the Wallace Collection, where Diaghilev pointed out the works of Fra Angelico, Giotto, Uccello, and Mantegna, probably in preparation for Miassine's forthcoming Italian sojourn.

Since leaving Russia Miassine had maintained a close correspondence with his family and with his former art teacher, Anatoli Petrovich Bolchakov. His frequent letters to Anatoli Petrovich, which seem to have stopped at the outbreak of the revolution,[39] are permeated with Miassine's sincere love and affection and his emotional commitment to friendship. In June he wrote from London:

> I miss [art] school, Anatoli Petrovich. At times I feel such an urge to start working again, with new strength and love. How could one find a model class here? It was possible in Paris, but I did not have time. Here I am not so busy, I work only in Joseph.
>
> Now I take walks in London, and I was in the museum. How many interesting things there are in the British Museum and also in the National Gallery.
>
> In the company, of course, there are many hostile people. Our group [the contingent of Moscow dancers who knew Bolchakov] is well disposed. Tarasov was helping me for some time. I have a close relationship with Matveich [Nicholas Zverev]. He is the kind of person I imagine him to be.
>
> What can I say about the Fokines? They have their own world and their own life. He is indifferent to me, same as she. The fact is that he does not recognize anyone else but himself. When he wanted to get by without Nijinsky—whose name he does not want to hear—he started to work with me and in three months, even less, he made something out of me. In his creative work he has become labored and somehow sugared. Vera is ruining him.
>
> Now I am working diligently at Cecchetti's almost every day. It seems that I am making progress. . . . Dancing is my weak side and now I am trying to work seriously.
>
> Kolya [Nikolai Kremev] is studying every day. Sometimes during performances I can see him jumping somewhere offstage. A very hardworking fellow. I see him seldom, but we feel close. And his English lady [Lydia

Sokolova, née Hilda Munnings] is a very fine person; they are such a good match, it really surprises me.

I have met Nijinsky, but did not see his works yet. He will be here for four performances. When Fokine is here, I suppose Nijinsky is not going to be here. Fokine will not allow that. . . .

Is it really true that after all your work you cannot allow yourself to have a vacation in Italy?[40]

By July 28, Diaghilev and Miassine were back in Paris. That night, at Misia's apartment, they listened to Erik Satie and the Spanish pianist Ricardo Viñes play Satie's *Trois Morceaux en forme de poire.* To everyone's consternation, a friend arrived to announce that Austria-Hungary had declared war on Serbia. On August 1, Germany declared war on Russia. On the third, the two men left for Italy. When they crossed the border the following day, Germany had declared war on France and invaded Belgium.

Italy, summer 1914

CHAPTER 3

Italy, August 1914–United States, April 1916

ON AUGUST 4 Diaghilev and Miassine arrived in Milan to begin their holiday.¹ They planned to reassemble the company in Berlin by October 1; but once in Milan they realized that events in Europe were taking a much more serious turn than they had imagined. Miassine's impulse was to return to Russia to share in her destiny; but, as he explains in his autobiography, he was reluctant to walk away from what promised to be a brilliant future. Overcome with guilt and very much yearning for his family's approval, he wrote to them and to Anatoli Petrovich explaining his predicament. They supported him, urging him to pursue the artistic possibilities and to take advantage of the rare chance he had been given.

After a round of sightseeing in an oppressively hot Milan, Diaghilev and Miassine left for the much cooler seaside resort of Viareggio. The

Cecchettis joined them there, and the maestro resumed his daily regimen with the dancer. Miassine also enjoyed the city's open-air Marionette Theater, where he intently watched commedia dell'arte characters for hours at a time.[2] Pulcinella, Pimpinella, Capitano Spavento, and the other characters soon held him spellbound; he was "intrigued by their grotesque masks and their jerky, loose-limbed movements."[3] Their influence would soon be felt in his own work.

From Viareggio Miassine and Diaghilev drove to Pisa to visit its ancient cemetery, the Campo Santo, and then to San Gimignano and Monte Oliveto Maggiore. They went on to Siena,[4] and reached Florence at the end of September. There they took lodgings in a spacious flat at 4 Viale Toricelli. Despite the beauty that surrounded him, a lonely Miassine pined for his loved ones, and the theater, back home. He wrote to Anatoli Petrovich: "I recollect the time of work and love, for that you taught me, how to love, and I feel again as if I was burdening you, my dear Anatoli Petrovich. . . . What is going on at your place; who is working and where is Kolya Zverev? I will be here until times get better. Now it is rather difficult and sad. If you have a moment write about the theater in Moscow."[5]

As matters turned out, the Tuscan city was their base for the next month and a half. From there they made trips to Pistoia, Pescia, Lucca, and Ravenna. Miassine's artistic education continued in earnest now as Diaghilev patiently showed him the glories of Florence.[6] Under Diaghilev's tutelage, Miassine studied mosaics, frescoes, paintings, sculpture, and architecture and learned to appreciate the Byzantine, Gothic, Renaissance, and baroque styles. Among the painters he came to admire were Cimabue, Duccio, Donatello, Fra Angelico, Pietro Lorenzelli, Fra Filippo Lippi, Tintoretto, and Michelangelo.[7] For Miassine, "it was not merely the stylistic achievements of these early painters which affected me: it was their spiritual beauty and mysticism."[8]

Miassine was most deeply impressed by paintings whose theme was sacrifice, especially as portrayed in the figure of the grieving Christ. Such works as Cimabue's *Crucifixion*, Duccio's *Rucellai Madonna*, Berlinghieri's *Stigmata of St. Francis* and his triptych titled *Virgin and Child, Saints and Crucifixion*, along with the anonymous *Crucifixion* in the cathedral of Pistoia, he came to regard as lucid symbols of "innocence and humility."[9]

In Ravenna he found much to admire in the sixteenth-century Byzantine mosaics in the church of Sant' Apollinare Nuovo. He was particularly taken by the "beautiful depiction of the miracle of the loaves and fishes, with its gleaming golden background, and the stylized groupings of Christ, and the four disciples tightly placed together with the stylized arm and torso movements."[10] Once more, however, it was the figure of Christ that most moved Miassine: "What gives the mosaic its hypnotic power is the figure of Christ himself, presented as a young man in a purple robe, His arms extended to receive the loaves and fishes. . . . His compassionate, penetrating expression haunted my imagination."[11]

Miassine's Florentine experience reconfirmed the religious longings to which he had been prone since childhood. Now, as he walked through "the churches and museums of Florence I felt again the sense of peace and exaltation which I had experienced as a child of eight, and I could remember vividly my feelings when I had first seen, preserved under glass, the mortal remains of the monastery's patron saint, who had renounced the world in favor of a contemplative life. Perhaps it had been an unconscious identification of myself with St. Saavo which had stirred my youthful emotions."[12] The more absorbed in the sacred subject matter of these works he became, the more he felt "my response to these primitive paintings derived from the same longing for a contemplative, spiritual life."[13] This was an early sign of the growing spirituality that would lead Miassine toward the sanctification of art and his later asceticism.

These affirmations of religious fervor were a natural outgrowth of Miassine's personality, characterized since childhood by longings that would eventually lead him to seek a personal, transcendent meaning to existence. He had avidly read Dostoevsky and Lermontov before leaving Moscow,[14] and one can see a clear relationship between Dostoevsky's profound dismay at man's alienation from his spiritual world and the mature Miassine's sense of the tragedy of human existence. Miassine's fascination with the figure of Christ, bordering on quasi-identification, suggests either a messianic streak in his makeup ("I am the way, the truth, and the life") or an intuitive conviction that self-sacrifice would lead to redemption, a harmonious fusion of spirit and flesh.

Florence unquestionably nourished Miassine's spiritual side, while at the same time Diaghilev concentrated on giving his young charge a practical education in the arts. The impresario believed that meticulous analysis of paintings could teach a choreographer invaluable lessons in perspective, an understanding that he must have in order to place and configure dancers expressively on stage: "In the classical ballet," Miassine elaborated further,

dancers mostly dance in a 180-degree contact with the audience. This eye-to-eye contact destroyed the scenic illusion. The study of paintings pro-

vided a concept of construction, bringing to the attention the focus of the scene. By studying the different painters it is possible to have a better understanding of how they used angles, perspective, and how they manipulated the stage to develop the subject. In painting all space is utilized. Paintings were also an example of how one could realistically and harmoniously conceive the arrangement of a scene. They also served as a guide to human behavior in order to convincingly create a character in his or her idiosyncratic gestures and in interaction with other characters.[15]

Diaghilev rounded out his teaching with improvisational exercises, calling on Miassine to reproduce poses from the paintings he had studied. And then, Miassine remembered:

One afternoon in the Uffizi, while I was looking up at Fra Filippo Lippi's Madonna and Child, *Diaghilev said to me, "Do you think you could compose a ballet?" "No," I answered without thinking, "I'm sure I never could." Then, as we passed on into another room I was suddenly aware of the luminous colors of Simone Martini's* Annunciation. *As I looked at the delicate postures of Gabriel and the Virgin Mary, I felt as if everything I had seen in Florence had finally culminated in this painting. It seemed to be offering me the key to an unknown world, beckoning me along a path which I knew I must follow to the end. "Yes," I said to Diaghilev, "I think I can create a ballet. Not only one, but a hundred, I promise you."*[16]

In this mystical way, Miassine's creative path was revealed to him. The opportunity for artistic fulfillment had arrived, and he knew it. Now his life had direction: he would try to synthesize the contrasting realities of the material world and the mysterious world of the spirit. And his idealism was total. He believed that his efforts, if solemnly undertaken, should lead to moments of divine exaltation and religious ecstasy. From now on his life would be a ceaseless striving after greater spiritual and artistic development.

The two men left Florence for Rome, where on November 10 they took up residence at the Grand Hotel.[17] Dazzled by the ancient city's beauty and vitality, Miassine wrote Anatoli Petrovich to sing the praises of Roman life and the Italian countryside. This letter clearly shows Diaghilev's overmastering influence. His perceptions are appropriated by Miassine; the younger man's insights and grasp of the world are mediated by the older man's:

It is impossible to visit Rome without thinking of you. I know you would be happy here, and I wish you could be with me. What sun, sky, air! The spirit of God is everywhere in this city.

I have just had the most beautiful trip. Starting from Viareggio, I drove with friends through Tuscany and the Campania. I have never seen such incredibly rich yet simple landscapes—everywhere deep green cypresses set against a rolling backcloth of golden fields. At sunset the Tuscan hills were a burning amber, their gentle silhouettes etched against a rosy sky. It was the landscape of all the Renaissance artists who have glorified Madonnas and sunsets! For me the beauty of their painting took on a new reality. After this trip I can understand the truth of their Tuscan coloring. . . . Traveling by car is much more exciting than going by train, for one can see the landscape unfolding all 'round you as you speed along the winding roads. There is a certain moment, just before twilight, when the country-side takes on its purest coloring and everything becomes more intense and more clearly defined. In the slowly fading light you can feel the landscape enveloping and penetrating into your soul.

For me those Tuscan sunsets transcended all earthly beauty and achieved a mystical tranquility of their own. I know that I have been very fortunate, for it is rare that one comes so close to this blessed land. I am writing this to you, Anatoli Petrovich, because I know that Italy means as much to you as it does to me. Truly this country is, as Dostoevski described it, a "cemetery of miracles."[18]

In the eternal city they visited archaeological sites as well as museums, monuments, and churches. (They were particularly astonished by the underground churches dating from the first century.) Miassine also managed to keep working at his drawing. He wrote to Anatoli Petrovich: "You know, I am working on drawing rather seriously. I work two hours daily and I am extremely happy."[19] Two days later he again told his old art teacher: "I continue to draw; my sight has become keener and [the result is] most interesting. I remember the precepts of the school and I keep them in order not to go astray."[20]

Florence had been devoted to the study of history. In Rome Miassine and Diaghilev were caught up in the intense fermentation and multiform experimentation of futurism, a movement conceived by the Italian poet Filippo Tommaso Marinetti and announced by him in a manifesto published on the front page of *Le Figaro* on February 20, 1909. He proclaimed the end of the art of the past and the birth of an art for the future. Futurism hailed modernity, revolution, electricity, speed, and

scientific advance, and aimed to alter man's mentality not only by revital-
izing the arts but by creating a new language that would incorporate the
experiences of modern man. Marinetti gathered around himself a group
of prominent Italian artists, including Umberto Boccioni, Carlo Carrà,
Luigi Russolo, Giacomo Balla, and Gino Severini. Soon the futurists were
producing other manifestos, using the 1909 document as a model, treating in turn painting, architecture, language, theater, and film.

Diaghilev and Miassine witnessed the experimental efforts of the
futurists at close hand. They attended many *serate futuriste,* or futurist
evenings, which took place mostly in theaters. These manifesto readings
combined with theater, concert, and political assembly inevitably ended
in riot or scandal.[21] By 1914 the *serate* had become primarily a forum for
theatrical experiments governed by Marinetti's "Dynamic and Synoptic
Declamations"—poetry readings that integrated onomatopoeia with the
principles of one art form or another. The new theatrical language of the
futurists also demanded audience participation. One of the most talked-
about *serate* took place in Rome in March 1914, at Giuseppe Sproviere's
gallery. A reading of Francesco Cangiullo's poem "Piedigrotta," complete with costumes, scenery, and lighting designed by Balla, was accompanied by onomatopoeic instruments.[22] Diaghilev and Miassine attended
one of the subsequent performances the following autumn, and
Diaghilev became interested enough to discuss with Cangiullo the possibility of adapting the poem into a ballet with music by the futurist composer Francesco Balilla Pratella.[23]

But even more absorbing than their involvement with this artistic
movement was Miassine's first choreographic essay and the preparations
for it. In view of Miassine's Florentine experience, Diaghilev encouraged
him to create a ballet on a religious theme. He asked Ivan Meštrović, the
Serbian sculptor, then living in Rome, to design it. Diaghilev wrote to
Stravinsky: "I cannot tell you about the subject in any detail, but let me
say that what I have in mind is a performance of the mass in six or seven
short scenes. The epoch will be Byzantine, which Meštrović will arrange
in his own way. The music, a series of a cappella sacred choruses, should
perhaps be inspired by Gregorian chant, but of that more later."[24] He
would later decide that the work was to have no music and that Orthodox chants would be heard during the intervals.

As always, Diaghilev and Miassine found time to enter into the hectic social whirl, even in the midst of work. Among the people they saw
frequently were Gerald Tyrwhitt (later Lord Berners) of the British embassy and Vasily Khvoshchinsky, from the Russian embassy, with his wife.

The highly cultured Khvoshchinskys were prominent figures in Roman diplomatic and artistic circles. He wrote extensively about Tuscan painters, and together they founded a string quartet in Rome. The young and attractive Mme Khvoshchinsky befriended Stravinsky; their correspondence is unusually affectionate. It was at the Khvoshchinskys' flat that Miassine met Rodin, who was in Rome working on a commission for a statue of the Pope.

As the new year arrived, Rome was jolted by an earthquake, which Miassine found unnerving. "The new year came in a strange and frightful manner," he writes to Anatoli Petrovich:

> I am still feverish. It was an unforgettable day and morning. In those seconds that brought death to so many people, I felt my worthlessness and pitiful helplessness. The shocks were so strong that it seemed that two or three seconds longer and everything would be finished. Afterwards it was pleasant and joyful, the sunshine and a perfect sky. It all ended like a fairy tale; where the ground broke a huge lake was formed. If it were not for the newspapers and processions with stretchers it would be like the fifth act of a nightmarish fairy-play.[25]

At this time Diaghilev decided that since the war would seriously restrict activities in Paris, he would send for Stravinsky, who was in Switzerland, and present the composer to Italian artistic circles. He channeled a great deal of energy into organizing this visit, and finally, on February 8, the composer arrived. In his honor Diaghilev put together a musical soirée at the Grand Hotel. The program featured the four-handed piano version of *The Rite of Spring*, performed by Stravinsky and the Italian composer Alfredo Casella, and excerpts from *The Firebird* played by Stravinsky, who also accompanied the singer Mayra Freund in a selection of his songs. On the following evening Casella conducted *Petrouchka* at the Augusteo Theater in the presence of the Roman intelligentsia.[26]

On March 3 Diaghilev's Russian compatriot Sergei Prokofiev arrived in Rome to discuss the possibility of collaboration. On the seventh he gave a recital, conducted by Bernardino Molinari in the Santa Cecilia Conservatory, in which he was the soloist in his Second Piano Concerto. Miassine found Prokofiev's company delightful.

Miassine and Diaghilev next spent a week and a half in Naples and Palermo, then returned to Rome, where they accepted Marinetti's invitation to visit him in Milan at the beginning of April. The visit was being arranged so that Diaghilev, Miassine, and Stravinsky, who was to join them, could attend a performance of Luigi Russolo's *intuonarumori*, or noise intoners. These were boxes of different sizes that projected a variety of sounds from individual speakers attached to each box; the aim was to explore noise as a new dimension of music. These "sounds" might well find their way into Miassine's new ballet. Diaghilev wrote to Stravinsky:

> *After 32 rehearsals* for* Liturgie, *we have concluded that absolute silence is Death, and that there is and can be no absolute silence in any air space. Thus the action must have some accompaniment, not musical accompaniment but, rather, sounds. The source of the sounds must not be revealed, and the passage from one to another must not be noticeable to the ear, i.e., they must flow into each other. No rhythm should exist at all, because the beginning and the end of sound should be imperceptible. The proposed instruments are guzli (psalters), bells with tongues wrapped in felt, aeolian harps, sirens, tops, and so on. Of course, this all has to be worked over. Marinetti urges us to plan a meeting in Milan, if just for a day, in order to discuss matters with the orchestra's representatives and to examine all of their instruments. In addition, he is going to send Pratella to Milan to acquaint us with his latest works, which are, as he puts it, stunning.*[27]

The demonstration in Milan took place in Marinetti's home and was attended by Diaghilev, Miassine, Stravinsky, and the futurists Pratella, Boccioni, Carrà, Cangiullo, and the Viscount of Madrone, among others. Cangiullo later wrote:

> *A Cracker crackled and sent up a thousand sparks like a gloom torrent. Stravinsky leapt from the divan like an exploding bedspring, with a whistle of overjoyed excitement. At this time a Rustler rustled like silk skirts, or like new leaves in April. The frenetic composer hurled himself on the piano in an attempt to find the prodigious onomatopoeic sound, but in vain did his avid fingers explore all the semitones. Meanwhile, the male dancer [Miassine] swung his professional legs, Diaghilev went ah, ah, like a startled quail, and that for him was the highest sign of approval. By moving his legs the dancer was trying to say that this strange symphony*

---

* Diaghilev must mean thirty-two working sessions with Massine, since the company was not in Rome.

was danceable, while Marinetti, happier than ever, ordered tea, cakes and liqueurs. Boccioni whispered to Carrà that the guests were won over.[28]

Much talk about possible joint ventures between the futurists and the Ballets Russes followed, though no actual collaboration took place until 1916. At the time of the demonstration in Milan, Diaghilev was negotiating a tour of North America with Otto Kahn, chairman of the board of the Metropolitan Opera. He decided to have his collaborators and the company meet together in Switzerland, where they would begin making preparations for the tour, which eventually got under way in January 1916.

Diaghilev and Miassine returned to Rome and met up with Misia and Sert, and at the end of April the foursome left for Switzerland. They drove north via Milan and Montreux (where they stayed at the Palace Hotel) to the outskirts of Lausanne, where Diaghilev had rented a villa called Bellerive, in Ouchy, on Lake Geneva. Here began one of the most peaceful intervals in the history of the Ballets Russes, a period when the company lived and worked with a hopeful sense of artistic community.

Diaghilev, who had grown dissatisfied with the work Meštrović had done on *Liturgie,* considered asking Gontcharova to design the ballet. Her expertise in adapting the style of Byzantine religious art and her deep knowledge of Russian icons made her an ideal choice. Diaghilev invited her to Ouchy, but his cables went unanswered until he extended an invitation to her companion, the painter Michel Larionov.[29] When the couple arrived on July 16, he set them up in a studio in the garden of Bellerive. He enjoyed their company. The brunet Gontcharova, a born aristocrat, was brilliant, subdued, and tranquil, while Larionov, tall and blond with slanted blue eyes, possessed a witty, volatile disposition. Diaghilev would develop a close association with them in his deliberate move toward modern Russian painting and away from the decorative theatrical designs of his early period, dominated by Benois and Bakst. The conservative Benois (along with another *World of Art* painter, Somov) had been inclined to identify himself with the West and had written articles in his native country denouncing the Russian avant-garde.[30]

Soon dancers began arriving in Lausanne. Some were original members of the Ballets Russes who had scattered once the war broke out; others had been recruited in Russia and Poland by régisseur Serge Grigoriev. They settled in pensions around Ouchy. Cecchetti taught three classes: nine a.m. for the corps de ballet, ten for the soloists, eleven for

Natalia Gontcharova at Bellerive,
Lausanne, 1915

Miassine's private instruction. After lunch came rehearsals. Some were conducted in a market (used only in the early morning) at the top of a hill. Others took place at Bellerive. Many of them lasted for up to six hours.[31]

When the company reconvened in Switzerland in 1915, Miassine's prominent position had clearly been solidified. His alliance with Diaghilev and their obvious sexual intimacy were discreetly acknowledged by everyone. The Ballets Russes' structure was strictly hierarchical, and Diaghilev, the supreme seigneur, presided along with his attendant prince, Miassine. Next in line came the council of collaborators, and below them were the various court strata who made up the balance of the company. But Diaghilev and Miassine's public behavior was always restrained, particularly during any interaction with others in the company. Valentina Kachuba, who had come from Moscow to join the troupe, remembers that whenever the two men were in public with other company members, Miassine circumspectly stood behind Diaghilev, remaining at a distance from him and not stepping forward unless he was needed.[32]

Despite the anguish of the war in Europe, the creative ambiance at Bellerive was confident, congenial, and conducive to work. As one visitor, the young composer Maurice Sandoz, described it: "The big Louis XIV house, spread out on its terraces, is dominated by the grassy slopes. Huge clumps of trees, judiciously planted by the English gardeners a hundred years or so ago, did not hide the house or deprive it of its famous view."[33] And: "It was an ideal spot of several acres, abounding in dates and oleanders, pines and maples, lilacs and roses. Following a little path through the miniature woodland, we emerged on a little garden surrounding the smaller villa. 'Here,' [Diaghilev] said, 'is where most members of my colony live,' and then leading me within, we visited half a dozen rooms, in each of which I found a young woman or man busy with pen, pencil, or brush."[34]

Predictably, much of the group's activity centered around Miassine's apprenticeship. Diaghilev had charged Gontcharova and Larionov with furthering Miassine's education in art and choreography. As mentors to pupil, they began working with him on *Liturgie*. As Gontcharova watched over the choreographic sessions, she worked on her designs. Her surviving sketches for this ballet, which show her keen aesthetic grasp of the power of icons, are of finely crafted apostles, gold and silver seraphim, and vermilion-winged angels, all in the Byzantine geometrical style. Gontcharova also worked on the concept of the staging and on the backdrop, in which she depicted Christ, the Madonna, and the apostles in the style of Italian primitives. As the ballet moved toward its final form, Larionov offered further advice on the choreography.

Liturgie was a series of scenes from the life of Christ, centering on the Passion. For the first scene, the Annunciation, Miassine "devised a succession of angular gestures and still, open-hand movements inspired by Cimabue's *Virgin*. For the Ascension I arranged two groups of angels with their arms raised and hands crossed to create the illusion of wings ascending to heaven."[35] These poses were linked to Gontcharova's designs; Miassine later recalled her sketches stressing "such vital details as the Byzantine hand positions and the angular, in-turned arm movements of Christ for the scene of the Resurrection, evoking the effect I was striving for. . . ."[36] He described his rapport with Gontcharova in a letter to Anatoli Petrovich:

I am very enthusiastic about Gontcharova's work, and, perhaps, she is the only one that interests me now. Larionov is a very well-educated artist and much was revealed to me in the course of conversations with him, and I

A rehearsal of the Garden of Gethsemane scene in Liturgie, *Bellerive, 1915*

would like to do much, of course, everything in my sphere, what I feel to be more and more as most congenial to me and at this time I believe the most interesting.

I work on a huge ballet, it seems to me I had written to you already but in few words. The movements will be without music. . . . Music choruses begin only when the curtain comes down and end when the curtain is again risen. It is difficult to say how this came about, one thing followed the other. . . . Costumes and sets are by Gontcharova and she made many interesting things.

Even if it is going to be done in America you have to come to the premiere.[37]

Stimulating friends visited Bellerive. Bakst came from Paris. Stravinsky, who lived at Clarens, frequently made two-hour bicycle trips to Ouchy. There the composer played, for the first time, passages from *Les Noces,* already planned as one of Miassine's future choreographic projects. Of it Leonid wrote to Anatoli Petrovich: "It is extremely interesting and congenial to me and I will be in heaven if I succeed in doing it well. The music is really wonderful and if you like Stravinsky it will be a great joy."[38] Shortly after Diaghilev set up quarters at Bellerive, Mme Khvoshchinsky arrived from Rome to manage the house—whether at the impresario's request isn't entirely clear. But Diaghilev, never altogether comfortable with visits from women, must have been a bit unsettled by the figure cut by this attractive, intelligent young woman, especially since Miassine obviously had taken a fancy to her. (She remained for two months.)[39] Stravinsky introduced another important newcomer, the Swiss musician Ernest Ansermet, into the inner circle. With Pierre Monteux away in the French army, Ansermet eventually became Diaghilev's conductor. Thus, with Diaghilev's collaborators contributing their varied talents, Miassine's apprenticeship was well and truly begun.

Although by now Miassine had choreographed most of *Liturgie,* the work still had to overcome a series of hurdles, not the least of which was

Stravinsky, Mme Khvoshchinsky, Diaghilev, and Bakst at Bellerive, 1915

finding suitable music. Diaghilev had tried to persuade Stravinsky to collaborate, but he refused.[40] Miassine's autobiography tells us that Diaghilev then decided that the ballet would be performed without music, that instead, during the intervals Orthodox chants like those the impresario had heard in Kiev would be heard; but when Diaghilev was unable to obtain the music for them from Russia, the entire project was dropped. In fact, there were production as well as musical problems: In an interview with the Paris-based Russian newspaper *Les Nouvelles Russes* in 1953, Gontcharova discussed the complex, multitiered decor, which was very difficult to execute. She also mentioned that the producers had intended to allow the public to hear the steps of the dancers as a sort of background accompaniment to the choreography;[41] still, Miassine must have been right when he said that the unresolved doubts about the music were one of the reasons that the ballet was abandoned. In any case, *Liturgie* never went beyond the experimental stage.

In the fall preparations got under way for the American tour, which Otto Kahn was to sponsor under the auspices of the Metropolitan Opera. Before leaving Europe, however, Diaghilev arranged two Red Cross benefit performances, one in Geneva, the other in Paris.

Diaghilev needed a new work to introduce before leaving for America and suggested to Miassine that he begin another ballet, one that would not require such a long preparation. *Liturgie* had been an exceedingly personal choice of subject, but this time Miassine opted for one that was straightforwardly, unabashedly Russian: the dances from Rimsky-Korsakov's opera *The Snow Maiden*. When Diaghilev played him the score, Miassine was delighted, for the dances recalled to him the "singing games" of his childhood.[42]

But Diaghilev, as always, was making another, deeper point at the same time. He chose Russian music in order to tap Miassine's cultural roots. And this was in keeping with his own instincts as well, for the impresario shared in the widespread Slavophile stirrings that sought to revive and preserve the venerated Russian virtues and traditions that had been disrupted by the westernizing reforms of Peter the Great.

Diaghilev asked Larionov, who was very knowledgeable about Russian folklore, to design the ballet and assist Miassine in its creation. Gontcharova acted as unofficial collaborator. According to Miassine, Larionov "was intrigued by the idea of a ballet based on Russian folklore, and suggested that it should revolve 'round the person of the sun god Yarila, to whom the peasants pay tribute in ritual ceremonies and dances, fusing with it the legend of the Snow Maiden, the daughter of King

Frost, who is destined to melt in the heat of the sun when she falls in love with a mortal." Miassine also decided to "incorporate into the action the character of Bobyl, the 'innocent' or village half-wit, and to end the ballet with the traditional dance of the Buffoons, for which I devised a succession of interwoven leaps, twists, and turns."[43]

The result of this collective effort was *Le Soleil de nuit*. Larionov and Miassine discussed the structure of the work, and in exploring the anthropological meaning of the old ritual peasant dances Larionov gave the younger man a clearer understanding of their essence. For the choreography Miassine "drew on my childhood memories of the *chorovod* and *'Gori, gori jasno,'* which [Larionov] helped me to embellish with suitably primitive, earthy gestures."[44]

Le Soleil de nuit had no literal story line and, like Fokine's innovative *Les Sylphides,* was conceived strictly in terms of dance; pantomime was unnecessary. Grigoriev saw early on that Miassine possessed originality and skill in the configuration of groups, and had "succeeded in inventing a great many interesting and varied steps and patterns."[45]

During rehearsals Miassine was a bit remote but entirely gracious, treating everyone with the utmost politeness, both in his tactful instructions and in his taking care to use "Mademoiselle" or "Monsieur" when addressing the dancers.[46] Sokolova remembered the dancers' delight not only in performing *Le Soleil de nuit* but in putting the inventions of the young choreographer to the test. His style was eccentric and intensely personal, and they warmly approved.[47] Kachuba admired Miassine's authority and daring in getting his dancers to sit, lie, and roll on the floor.[48]

In addition, in *Le Soleil de nuit* Miassine created a role for himself that set off his charismatic stage presence to greater advantage than ever before:

In my own role as the Midnight Sun I had to match the power of Rimsky-Korsakov's music with a driving energy which permeated my whole body. In my dance, which was based on classical movements, I made use of broad arm movements, and strengthened my performance with rapidly repeated elevations. Larionov had designed for me a sumptuous glittering costume with a fantastic headdress of burning red suns which glowed against the inky-blue of the midnight sky. Attached to my hands by elastic were two more gold suns, the size of dinner plates, decorated with jazzed red borders. As I danced, I flashed them in rapidly alternating rhythms, to the left, to the right, over my head, down below my knees. In order to sus-

tain the illusion of a revolving sun, I was forced to keep every muscle in my body in constant motion until the end of the dance. But I could feel power pulsating within me, and by the end I had reached a fever pitch of excitement.[49]

Miassine's dance was his projection of himself as the star he was to become. As his description suggests, this ballet carried a strong visual impact. Larionov's decor included stage wings painted as huge trees in yellow and green that at first could not be recognized as such; the backdrop depicted a primitive idol against a starred sky.[50] The costumes were variations on traditional Russian costumes with enormous headpieces known as *kitchki* or *kokochniki;* in fact, the headpieces were so large that Miassine asked that his be modified to allow him to jump.[51]

Misia and Sert came from Paris to see the new work. The assurance of Miassine's choreography came as a surprise, since they had blamed him for the failure of *The Legend of Joseph.* Now, in a letter to Cocteau, Misia described "last night, a dress rehearsal for us of what has been done these past months. Something completely new, very beautiful, in which Miassine proves that he really is someone. And how prejudiced we were against him, Sert and I!!!"[52]

The ballet was introduced on December 20 in a single performance at the Grand Théâtre in Geneva, in a program that included *Carnaval, The Firebird,* and *Prince Igor.* On December 22 the *Journal de Genève* reported: "*Le Soleil de nuit* was a delight. It was like a box of Russian toys brought to life and laughter, shining with gold papers and splashed with color. Comic costumes for peasants and clowns, with, among them, Bobyl, a simpleton in a white blouse, and Miassine, the much applauded choreographer, as a puppet with cymbals and a vermillion face."[53]

The enthusiastic reception of *Le Soleil de nuit* gave Miassine a shot of youthful self-confidence. At the age of nineteen he was enjoying his first taste of success and public acclaim. But he soon was brought down to earth by Diaghilev, who after the performance remarked dryly, "I did not hear them cheering."[54] This barb cut deeply enough for Miassine to quote it in his autobiography fifty years later, a sign of how hungry for approval he must have been at the time. The Ouchy period, for all its personal and artistic rewards, was without doubt a time of stress and conflicting demands for Miassine. One can imagine how eager he must have been to prove his artistic worth, not only to himself but, more importantly, to Diaghilev. And he needed the recognition not just to validate his artistic achievement but as compensation for how much he feared he was sacrificing in the process.

Needless to say, Miassine's growing self-confidence was not easy for Diaghilev to accept. He was, after all, a man whose work was a means of self-fulfillment and an extension of himself: Miassine's role was to be an instrument of Diaghilev's own realization, a well-behaved acquisition. Full acknowledgment of his protégé's achievement amounted to granting him an identity and thus an independence that, at least in the early stages of their relationship, he could not bring himself to give. By withholding praise from Miassine's creative efforts at crucial moments—a pattern that would often be repeated—Diaghilev would help to poison some of Miassine's subsequent attitudes toward others.

During his formative years Miassine appropriated much of his identity from Diaghilev's, enough so that assessing the adult Miassine becomes difficult without understanding Diaghilev's aggressive fusion of lightning brilliance with sinister deviousness. For the naive Miassine Diaghilev was a role model, an ideal to which he aspired. Admiring Diaghilev, Miassine also wanted to please him. But at this stage of his life humility and gratitude were the only coinage in which he could do so, and Diaghilev signaled to Miassine the surest way to continue to please him: with *more* humility and gratitude. The unavoidable, if unconscious, anger that this process built up in Miassine in the ensuing years had its seed in these early manipulations of Diaghilev's. The end of their relationship truly was right there in its beginning.

Diaghilev and Miassine spent the holidays in Paris. On Christmas Day a group of friends gathered at Misia's house, where, with Miassine turning the pages of the score, Stravinsky played the first scene of *Les Noces.* The Ballets Russes performed a charity matinée to benefit the British Red Cross on December 29 at the Paris Opéra. The program consisted of *Schéhérazade, The Firebird* (conducted by Stravinsky), *Le Soleil de nuit,* the Bluebird Pas de Deux, and *Prince Igor.* Then, on January 1, 1916, the company sailed from Bordeaux to New York to begin its American tour.

The voyage across the choppy Atlantic was rough, and the smallness of the vessel did nothing to allay the impresario's terror of ocean travel; so Diaghilev distracted himself by poring over the schedules and programs for the tour. Indeed, he became so immersed in the planning that he rarely left his cabin. Miassine, on the other hand, spent a great deal of time on deck, "gazing at the wintry seascape on which the rolling Atlantic breakers formed vast hillocks of foam."[55] Diaghilev never appeared on the open deck without donning a life jacket, and by journey's end his deep dread of the sea had pushed his nerves nearly to the point of collapse. The sudden scream of the onboard sirens sent the skittish traveler scurrying, with Miassine in tow, to the safety of a lifeboat that had been designated for his use in an emergency. To his great relief, he was informed that the siren meant simply that the vessel was passing the Statue of Liberty in New York harbor. As they drew closer and the island lifted its foggy veil, the city and its great skyline stimulated Miassine's imagination; the imposing arrangement suggested to him the geometrical simplicity of "elongated Babylonian temples."[56] Much later he wrote: "What particularly interested me was the fact that each unit of those monumental constructions represented a different aspect of life in New York. I thought it would be amusing to make a choreographic composition based on six individual rooms, superimposed one on another, seen simultaneously, a sort of spiritual and visual counterpoint of various characters and their moods, typical of the daily happenings in this great city."[57]

Since the Metropolitan Opera was still conducting its season, the American debut of the Ballets Russes took place at the Century Theatre. Opening night, January 17, saw the inevitable retirement of "Miassine" and the debut of "Massine." The new spelling was hit upon by Diaghilev, who thought it easier for non-Russians to pronounce. (The Gallicized "Léonide" had been with the dancer from the start of his Ballets Russes career.) The first program consisted of *Firebird*, *La Princesse enchantée* (as the Bluebird pas de deux was sometimes billed), *Le Soleil de nuit*, and *Schéhérazade*; the repertory for the rest of the engagement included the Polovtsian Dances from *Prince Igor*, *L'Après-midi d'un faune*, *Carnaval*, *Petrouchka*, *Les Sylphides*, and *Le Pavillon d'Armide*. In addition to his role in *Le Soleil de nuit*, Massine also danced the Faun, Petrouchka, the Golden Slave in *Schéhérazade*, and the Tsarevich in *Firebird*. Later in the tour he danced the role of Amoun in *Cléopâtre*.

Though the Ballets Russes performed well and found favor with American audiences, the press was quick to note the absence of Nijinsky and Karsavina. Generally, the notices were mixed. Of course there were those in the audience for whom classical ballet meant little more than a pretty ballerina floating across the stage in a tutu. Others, like *New Republic* writer Troy Kinney, praised Diaghilev for his synthesis of the old and the new, which engendered what Kinney called "the freedom of richer convention."[58] Diaghilev himself concluded that the barrier was the repertory; New York audiences seemed frankly puzzled by artistic innovations for which perhaps they simply weren't ready.[59] He also confided to Massine that "Americans still seemed to think of ballet as light entertainment, to be enjoyed after a hard day at the office."[60]

Two of the ballets, *Schéhérazade* and *L'Après-midi d'un faune*, were met with shocked protests from the public and the press over their supposed immorality and bad taste. In *Schéhérazade*, the depiction of an interracial orgy in which a white woman takes a black slave as her lover was simply too much for the American public of 1916; the ballet set off an explosive political furor. Grenville Vernon, a writer for the *New York Tribune*, believed that "the remarkable impersonation of the Negro favorite of Zobeide, Princess of Samarcande, by M. [Adolph] Bolm, will render the ballet impossible for production south of Mason and Dixon's line. Even to Northern minds it was repulsive."[61] And of course the simulated act of masturbation in the final moments of *L'Après-midi d'un faune* fared no better, earning from the Catholic Theatre Movement a broadside denouncing certain "objectionable features of the Russian Ballets." The controversy culminated in a hearing in the chambers of Judge McAdoo on January 25. According to the *New York Sun*:

> *M. Serge de Diaghilev and the Russians listened with the grave patience and the puzzled amusement with which intelligent folk from Continental Europe have often watched the workings of the censorship of municipal authorities over the American theater. They were particularly impressed by the abnormal perceptions of some of the protectors of public morals, who discovered "meanings" that had never occurred to those that had many times set the two pieces on the stage. "I believe," said M. de Diaghilev, half amused and half perturbed, "that my mind and the minds of those who planned and executed the ballets are less vicious than the minds of those that made the protest."*
>
> *The spokesmen of sundry "vice" societies were arrogant and vociferous until M. de Diaghilev and the representatives of the Metropolitan Opera House, being quiet men of the world, naturally wearied of noisy bickering and agreed to alter certain items, so that even the agents of the societies in question could not possibly imagine anything into anything.*[62]

In keeping with the agreement, *L'Après-midi d'un faune* was performed that night with the offending finale sanitized; it ended as the Faun (Massine) "placed the drapery gently on the rock and sat gazing at its silken folds."[63] With the performance safely over, huge floral tributes were presented to Massine on stage. A disgusted Diaghilev rose stiffly to take his leave of general manager Giulio Gatti-Casazza, business director John Brown, and the other Metropolitan officials who sat nearby; turning to them all he taunted in French: "America is saved!" [64]

In this charged atmosphere the New York season ended on January 29. Two days later the company opened in Boston, the first leg of a tour that would include sixteen more American cities. Massine soon discovered that the lengthy train rides gave him "the nightmare illusion of being locked in a prison cell while speeding off to an unknown fathomless abyss." [65] Fits of insomnia accompanied his bouts of claustrophobia, causing him to spend many sleepless nights in the cold corridor, staring out windows as the inky landscape sped by. The larger cities allowed the company the luxury of longer presentations and the brief illusion of continuity in their personal lives. In the smaller towns and communities they endured one-night stands. But though Massine found these short, abrupt stopovers exhausting, he enjoyed discovering the various styles of American architecture. He wrote to Anatoli Petrovich: "I take off my hat to these magnificent skyscrapers. They are more beautiful than anything I have ever seen. . . . their simplicity is so much better than all the decorative sculpture which ruins so much European architecture." [66]

The difficult schedule had one advantage: it gave Massine an opportunity to delve into the company's repertory, to take on roles that demanded well-defined and rigorous characterization. In analyzing *Cléopâtre* and *L'Après-midi d'un faune,* ballets in which Fokine and Nijinsky, respectively, had attempted to create a two-dimensional effect reminiscent of bas-relief, Massine concluded that Nijinsky had surpassed Fokine. For him, Nijinsky's choreography achieved the desired effect: by "suppressing the sense of depth, and dispensing with the usual graceful positions, and by twisting sharply in opposite directions the upper part of the body against the lower, Nijinsky evolved a sculptural line which gave an effect of organic beauty such as I had never seen in any ballet." [67] Without ever having seen Nijinsky perform the role, Massine brought to his portrayal of the Faun a similar conception, derived from his own study of Greek statuary and Greek and Roman bas-reliefs. We can assume that Massine discussed the ballet with Diaghilev, and we can be reasonably sure that the impresario was instrumental in Massine's understanding of the work's innovations. But as Massine pointed out in his autobiography, he would receive no praise from Diaghilev for his portrayal of the Faun. The older man's approval of his assuming the role seemed to be enough.

Of the many new roles that Massine undertook, he found Petrouchka the "most rewarding," because in it "my sense of identification with the half-human puppet helped me to project much of my own personality."[68] The most demanding aspect of the role was making explicit "Petrouchka's divided nature, his hopeless love for the ballerina, and his humiliation; all had to be conveyed by constant variations of tiny, grotesque steps woven together to create a pathetic whole."[69] Commentators have often mentioned the parallels between *Petrouchka*'s "triangle" and Nijinsky's emotional and existential conflicts. Some of the triangle's psychological dynamics apply to Massine as well.

Massine's extraordinary good looks and piercing eyes were fit for a Georgian prince, and it is certain that more than one woman in the company fell in love with him. Massine himself was attracted to some of the female dancers, especially those from Moscow. "All the Moscow ladies are kind," he wrote to Anatoli Petrovich, "their manner of speech excites me and causes joy to my ears, as if I hear birds chirping: there is the whole of Moscow in them."[70] Even though flirting with him was "against all the rules," Sokolova recalls that "many of [the women] had a crush on him although no one seemed to be able to penetrate his 'frozen stare.' "[71] As the tour progressed, however, Massine himself—to the amazement of nearly everyone in the company—began to flirt with the company's seductress, the beautiful Lubov Tchernicheva, who was also Grigoriev's wife. This ended abruptly when the company reached Washington, D.C. There, Massine danced Amoun opposite Tchernicheva's impressive Cléopâtre; but later, at an embassy benefit for the Russian Red Cross, the cat came home and sent all the mice scurrying. According to Sokolova:

We performed several dances in the middle of the ballroom, including that of the nursemaids from Petrouchka, and afterwards we joined in the ballroom dancing. There was a terrific crush, and my partner saw a little room which was empty, so he guided me through the door. Almost immediately we were followed by Massine and his would-be girlfriend. We were all laughing and flirting and having a wonderful time, when to our horror we saw Diaghilev standing in the doorway, a champagne bottle under his arm and glasses in his hand. We froze. He had seen enough; he turned and walked away. The following morning a message came 'round via the bush telegraph—that is, by Vassili, Diaghilev's servant and spy—that anybody who interfered with the peace of the company by disturbing Massine in his work would be expelled immediately. Léonide and the lady did not speak to each other for many a day after that. As for the rest of us, any girl who valued her position in the company was careful to steer clear of Massine.[72]

In Washington Massine watched a group of Sioux Indians perform a series of war dances at the National Theater. From this event he conceived his idea for a ballet based on an American subject. With Ernest Ansermet he visited the Smithsonian Institution, where the conductor studied Native American musical instruments while Massine read up on material dealing with tribal moon dances, nuptial ceremonies, and funeral rites. He had been drawn to the story of the Indian maiden Pocahontas and had decided that she would be the source for his new ballet. Ansermet forwarded to Bakst in Paris colored prints of American Indians and engravings depicting the life of Pocahontas in order to aid the artist in designing a decor. Massine intended to create a *suite de danses* modeled on *Le Soleil de nuit*. In the meantime, the company left Washington for engagements in Philadelphia and Atlantic City before returning to New York to open at the Metropolitan Opera House on April 3.

Ever since negotiations had begun for the United States tour, Diaghilev had hoped to re-engage Nijinsky as the company's premier danseur. However, during the war the Nijinskys were interned twice, first in Budapest and later in Vienna. Finally, through the extraordinary efforts of Diaghilev and Otto Kahn, who called upon the influence and connections of Queen Alexandra of England and her sister the dowager empress Maria Feodorovna, Emperor Franz Joseph of Austria, King Alfonso XIII of Spain, and the Pope (whose intercession was at the request of the Spanish monarch), the dancer and his family were released. They traveled via Switzerland and Paris to Bordeaux and sailed from there for the United States on March 26. They landed in New York on April 4, the day after the Ballets Russes had opened at the Metropolitan.

But no sooner had they arrived than an embarrassing squabble arose between Diaghilev and Nijinsky. In London Nijinsky had won a back-salary judgment against the impresario amounting to half a million gold francs. Now, as he enjoyed his freedom in New York, Nijinsky conveniently overlooked Diaghilev's crucial role in securing his safe passage out of Europe and threatened to boycott the Ballets Russes until he was paid. The press, of course, quickly sniffed out the quarrel and bared the episode in sensational headlines. Nijinsky eventually set aside his argument with his former lover and made his American debut on April 12, but only after Otto Kahn had negotiated a settlement of the dispute.

Nijinsky was once again part of Diaghilev's Ballets Russes, and Massine now alternated with the legendary dancer in some of Nijinsky's own roles. Massine knew that comparisons were inevitable, so he must have been quietly pleased by a favorable review of Nijinsky's Petrouchka that took appreciative measure of both men's abilities: Nijinsky "had to stand a very severe comparison because of the superb work of Massine in the same role. Mr. Nijinsky paid more attention to the puppet's soul and less to his mechanism than Mr. Massine. Those who like this conception will prefer Nijinsky; those who prefer to have the fact that Petrouchka is a puppet emphasized, Massine. Both are as fine as can be in their respective characterizations."[73]

Lydia Lopokova, who had rejoined the company when it arrived in the States and danced the Ballerina opposite both dancers, wrote: "Massine mimed the part with his hands, stiff and hanging—in Massine's mime the hands are very important. Nijinsky moved more with his whole body. Massine's was an intellectual creation, Nijinsky's of inward bodily genius, only half conscious. But both were great creations."[74]

Offstage, Massine found Nijinsky aloof and reserved. But to see him dance! To watch Nijinsky transform himself on stage, to marvel at his effortless control, to be captivated by the fluidity and harmony of his movements, and to witness his profound emotional expressiveness— all this put Massine in ecstasy. He especially respected Nijinsky's Petrouchka, a "poignant representation of a puppet-like but recognizable human figure."[75] He felt that the role came more easily to Nijinsky than to him. He also admired Nijinsky's Bluebird and his Spectre; but what he found even more fascinating was his meticulous coaching of the nymphs in L'Après-midi d'un faune.

In New York, social life for Diaghilev and Massine centered on late-night suppers at the Plaza Hotel, where they enjoyed the company of Grigoriev, Lopokova, Kahn, and Prince Paul Troubetzkoy. They also found time for "delightful parties" coordinated by the well-known society orchestrator Elsa Maxwell. And because the war had driven many Europeans to New York, Diaghilev was able to renew old friendships with, among others, the eccentric photographer Baron Alfred de Meyer and his wife, Olga. For his part, the solitary Massine found time to enjoy the treasures at the Metropolitan Museum and to study and photograph the Morgan Collection of Mayan sculpture.

To follow the Metropolitan engagement, which ended on April 29, Otto Kahn had organized another American tour. He hoped to avoid friction between Diaghilev and Nijinsky by making Diaghilev's presence unnecessary. To that end he proposed renting the company from the impresario. Diaghilev could see that his returning to Europe alone while the war continued would surely disrupt the company, but he also knew that the American tour would secure for the Ballets Russes the continuity it needed. So he accepted Kahn's proposal, but on one condition: the company would first travel to Spain for a string of brief engagements in Madrid, San Sebastián, and Bilbao; Nijinsky would remain in America, awaiting the troupe's return.

*Massine outside the Teatro Real,
Madrid, 1916*

CHAPTER 4

Spain, May–September 1916

ON MAY 6 the Ballets Russes sailed aboard the *Dante Alighieri* for Spain, where at King Alfonso XIII's invitation the troupe was to perform its first engagement ever at Madrid's Teatro Real. The threat of torpedoes, coupled with Diaghilev's water phobia, made for a nerve-racking Atlantic crossing.[1]

When the *Dante Alighieri* reached Cádiz, the Spanish composer Manuel de Falla was probably at the dock to greet it. He had seen the Ballets Russes perform in Paris and had met Diaghilev there, but it seems to have been Stravinsky who suggested that he travel to Cádiz to welcome the company to Spain. Falla, whose French was impeccable, was a native of Cádiz. He kindly offered his services as cicerone and took everyone sightseeing, exposing the company to its first taste of flamenco.

Despite his rather subdued personality, Falla's intelligence and refinement quickly won over Diaghilev and Massine, both of whom soon befriended him.

Massine was completely charmed by the port town. Its "whitewashed houses [were] smothered in bougainvillea, and the tiny plazas, with their baroque fountains,"[2] were dusted with the scent of lemon blossoms. After the pressures of the American tour and an anxious ocean voyage, Cádiz must have seemed a haven. The young choreographer was very much taken with Andalusia. This first contact with Spain marked the beginning of his lifelong love affair with the country, a passionate attachment that would inspire one of his greatest ballets, *Le Tricorne*. (Cervantes's *Don Quixote*, in Spanish, eventually became one of his favorite books.)

From Cádiz the company set out for Madrid, where the Teatro Real opening was scheduled for May 26.

With Europe at war, Spain had become a refuge for an elegant congregation of citizens without a country, as well as a center of espionage and counterespionage. Despite the deterioration of the local economy, due especially to the catastrophe of the Spanish-American War, for those whom the wartime upheaval had made rich, Madrid was the preferred city for regaining their bearings and recovering their composure. Largely untouched by the hardships of war, the city vibrated with excitement and a sense of anticipation. The grand hotels, notably the Ritz and the recently opened Palace, were crowded with glamorous "survivors." Aristocrats, millionaires, artists, and swindlers all compounded the intrigue. Every newly arrived bejeweled woman sighted at the Ritz or the opera was taken for an American millionairess, a Russian princess traveling incognito, or a cunning spy. Any sleek new male face was thought to be that of an exiled king or a filthy-rich gangster.

Diaghilev and Massine checked into the Ritz, one of the most exclusive quarters in town. Across the street sit the Palacio de Villahermosa and the Palace Hotel; further west stands Parliament. Along the Paseo del Prado is the Canovas del Castillo Square with its fountain of Neptune emerging from the waters. Next to it is the Prado. The entire scene is dominated by the sixteenth-century San Jerónimo Basilica. The Paseo del Prado had long been a fashionable stretch for early-evening promenades. As pedestrians strolled through its park and fountain areas, members of the upper classes, sitting in prominent view in their open carriages, moved alongside them at a stately pace. Massine was enchanted by "how beautiful people are, and the costumes, the shawls."[3] Passing through the famous domed lobby of the Palace, Diaghilev and Massine encountered many of the hotel's celebrated guests; two of the more notorious were the renowned spies Mata Hari and Marthe Richer (who was also one of the first female pilots).

The Teatro Real, opposite the Royal Palace, was the city's most prominent cultural showcase. Opera was enjoying a renaissance. There was fierce competition in the public fancy between long-cherished Italian favorites and the torrential works of Wagner. At the Real it was possible to see the *Ring* cycle performed by some of the best singers and conductors from Bayreuth and Munich. Performances of *Parsifal* extended from the afternoon into the evening, and the audience dined during the intermission, as was the custom in Germany. Two striking divas dominated the scene at the Real. From France there was the red-haired, blue-eyed Geneviève Vix, who had created a sensation there in Richard Strauss's *Salome,* more for her provocative costume than for her vocal abilities. From Russia there was Maria Kuznetsova, who had created the role of Potiphar's Wife opposite Massine's Joseph. She had been romantically linked to Bakst, and Massenet had written his *Roma* for her. In Madrid she created a stir on stage and off. She directed and supervised the premiere of *Parsifal* and sang the role of Kundry as well. Beautiful and enigmatic, she appeared offstage with her arms and head covered with precious stones, the embodiment of Oriental opulence and mystery. She promptly took the Ballets Russes under her wing. An invitation to one of her Russian teas was highly coveted, and Diaghilev, Massine, and other members of the company were often in attendance.

Eager, as usual, to explore new trends in all the arts, Diaghilev and Massine soon were immersed in musical life outside the Teatro Real, attending concerts and recitals at the Ateneo, the Círculo de Bellas Artes, and the Ritz Hotel. These performances featured the most recent compositions of European and Spanish composers performed by prominent musicians and singers, among them Falla, Ricardo Viñes, and Arthur Rubinstein.

The ballet engagement at the Real opened on May 26, with a program consisting of *Les Sylphides, Carnaval, Schéhérazade,* and *Le Soleil de nuit.* It was a glittering social event attended by the royal family, in full regalia, and practically all of Madrid. But the performances immediately following were not supported by the general public. *ABC,* a leading newspaper, reported that although the balcony had been sold out, the tiers and the orchestra seats were only two-thirds filled.[4] Word of mouth must have been good, however, for on May 30 *ABC* reported that the Ballets Russes had become a triumph, playing to consistently full houses.[5]

With the Ballets Russes at the Real, Diaghilev and Massine themselves became an attraction on Madrid's brilliant social scene. Among their most distinguished hosts were the Duchess de Montellanos (at whose home Rubinstein was a frequent guest and performer), the Duchess de Durcal, the Count de Romanones, the Marquise de Ganay, and Mme Eugenia Errazuriz. Yet, true to his custom, Diaghilev soon gathered around him his own entourage, over which he presided with Massine at the Ritz or the Palace. Among the city's luminaries to whom Falla introduced them were the Count de Casa Miranda, the great Swedish diva Christine Nilsson (mother-in-law to the count), the musicians Joaquín Turina, José Cubiles, and Conrado del Campo, and the playwrights Gregorio and María Martínez Sierra. In 1914, after Falla had returned from Paris to Spain, he had traveled with the itinerant theater company of the Martínez Sierras, composing incidental music for them. It was for this group that he created his *El amor brujo* as a vehicle for Pastora Imperio, the greatest flamenco *bailaora* (dancer) of the period. Newcomers to Madrid were entranced by Imperio; Ansermet dubbed her "la Divina."

Stravinsky joined the Ballets Russes for its Madrid engagement. His *Firebird* was performed on May 28, and at his curtain call a thunderous ovation filled the hall.[6] At the first performance of *Petrouchka*, on June 5, the pianist Cubiles played the cymbals as a personal tribute to the composer. While in Madrid, Stravinsky attended bullfights with Falla and visited Toledo and the Escorial with his friends.[7] Both sites made a deep impression on the composer, who thought them a "revelation of the profoundly religious temperament of the people and the mystic power of their Catholicism, so closely akin in its essentials to the religious feelings and spirit of Russia."[8] Massine wrote to Anatoli Petrovich: "The Escorial impressed me more than any other art. I did not find it solemn. In some parts there is the simplicity of Byzantium and everywhere there is powerful spirit and mighty form. I cannot compare it to anything. There are no decorations; only architecture."[9]

At the Martínez Sierras', Stravinsky played passages from *Les Noces* and listened to Falla's work in progress, *El corregidor y la molinera*, a pantomime he was composing for the Martínez Sierras.[10] It was also at one of the playwrights' musical soirées that Diaghilev and Massine heard for the first time Falla's *Noches en los jardines de España* (formerly called *Nocturnos*). They were enamored of the piece; Diaghilev felt that the score offered Massine an ideal opportunity to fashion a ballet on a Spanish theme. But Falla was not keen to hear his music, conceived for the concert hall rather than the theater, accompanying a ballet.[11] To overcome Falla's resistance, Diaghilev enlisted the support of Stravinsky, who cited *Petrouchka* as an example of a work written originally for piano and orchestra and later adapted into a ballet.[12] To entice the wary Falla, Diaghilev proposed a setting: a *fête de nuit* under a starlit sky in the gardens of the Alhambra, with magnificently shawled women and men in evening dress (*"tout à fait vingtième siècle,"* Falla commented).[13] But Falla was even less enthusiastic about this idea, which he felt was more suited to the music hall. He offered another option: he would turn *El corregidor y la molinera* into a ballet.[14]

"El corregidor y la molinera" is a traditional Spanish tale based on the anonymous eighteenth-century romance *El molinero de arcos,* and best remembered as the 1874 novel *El sombrero de tres picos* by Pedro Antonio de Alarcón. (Hugo Wolf based his 1896 opera *Der Corregidor* on the same story.) The Martínez Sierras' two-scene pantomime followed Alarcón closely. Since Falla's compositional draft for the completed first scene is dated August 8, 1916, Diaghilev and Massine could have heard only a partial score for the first scene at the Martínez Sierras'. In any case, the tale interested both men, especially Massine, who hoped to produce his first Spanish ballet in December or January in Rome.[15]

By June 18, Diaghilev submitted a written offer to Falla to produce *El corregidor y la molinera* in ballet form and to do the same with his *Noches.*[16] Falla thought the terms of the offer unfair and made Diaghilev a counteroffer, which the impresario met only halfway.[17] He gave Falla permission to produce *El corregidor* in Spain in the Martínez Sierras' pantomime form.[18] As for the *Noches,* Falla was unable to best Diaghilev, who insisted that he alone would produce it.

In Madrid Diaghilev and Massine delighted in seeing for the first time the works of the great Spanish painters, as well as the impressive collection of Titians in the Prado and the magnificent Goya tapestries at the Royal Palace. In a postcard to Anatoli Petrovich, Massine wrote, "We are all crazy about what we see in the Prado. . . . There is nothing in common with Italy; everything seems new and different to me."[19] Spanish painting would have a lasting influence on Massine, and he now spent most of his free time at the Prado studying the works of Ribera, Murillo, Zurbarán, Goya, Velázquez, and El Greco. Though Goya would inspire the actual choreographic designs of Massine's future works, he was most impressed by Velázquez. This artist, in "the simplicity of his brushwork, the deftness with which he conveyed the forms, and the texture of the surfaces," possessed a style that Massine respected for leaving "much to the imagination, suggesting movement rather than laboring over a minute detail."[20]

On June 4 Massine presented a certificate from Dr. Juan Bergara to the Russian embassy in Madrid and was subsequently exempted from military service on the grounds of pulmonary weakness, which necessitated his remaining in a warm climate.[21]

After the season at the Real ended on June 9, Diaghilev invited Falla to join him and Massine in their travels during the remainder of the month to Seville, Granada, and Córdoba. As they toured these cities Diaghilev and Massine discovered that Falla, a native of Andalusia and a student of Spanish folklore, was a key figure in the revitalization of interest in *cante jondo*—the ancestral southern Iberian form of singing as an expression of pain or joy. With Falla's help they slowly came to appreciate its essence and its finest tradition in the south. The cultural treasures of the region were a revelation. In Seville, Massine was taken to see the most windowed cathedral in the world. He was impressed by its organ as well as by "the altar dances with castanets, and the orchestra in front of the altar." He was amazed, too, by the dancing "accompanied by singing, by little boys, who were also dancing. The singing is really shouting; the dance consists of various steps involving swaying from side to side, and many figures."[22] In Seville he also met the greatest flamenco *cantaora* (singer) of that time, *La Niña de los Peines*. Warm, leisurely evenings were spent at the Café Novedades. Here they met Felix Fernández García, a dancer who would play a major role in the creation of Massine's Spanish ballet.

> *One evening, at our favorite café, the Novedades, we noticed a small, dark young dancer whose elegant movements and compelling intensity singled him out from the rest of the group. When he had finished dancing Diaghilev invited him to join us at our table. . . . As we talked to him I sensed that he was a nervous and highly strung creature with a very original talent. He soon made it clear to us that he was not happy in his present life, and although it amused him to dance in the café, he did not find it very rewarding. We made a habit of going every night to see him dance, and were more and more impressed by his exquisite flamenco style, the precision and rhythm of his movements, and by his perfect control.*[23]

Massine and Diaghilev found Granada, framed by mountains and olive groves, spellbinding. To Anatoli Petrovich Massine wrote: "I saw a

*Massine with
Manuel de Falla in
Granada, 1916*

miracle, or was it a wonderful, uncommon dream? Such is my impression of what I saw in the Alhambra. There is not a thing equal to that; only St. Mark, however strange it may seem."[24] Here they attended two nocturnal Gypsy feasts, one of them in a garden beneath the Alhambra that looked out onto the adjoining quarter of Albaicin, the old Arabic town. Their host was the famous matador Juan Belmonte. Under a starlit summer sky they revisited the Alhambra.

The evening before they left Granada, they attended a performance by the Madrid orchestra of Falla's *Noches en los jardines de España* at the Palacio de Carlos V.[25] In Córdoba they visited the mosque and came to a fuller appreciation of Andalusia's rich cultural roots in Islam, Judaism, Christianity, and the folkways and beliefs of the Gypsies. It was during this expedition that the gestation of the ballet based on *El corregidor y la molinera* truly began. In a July 7 letter to Stravinsky, Falla reports that by the time he had returned to Madrid from his trip to the south he began revising parts of the score for *El corregidor* and developing the dances.[26]

After returning to Madrid, Diaghilev and Massine proceeded overland to San Sebastián, on the northwest coast. At this time San Sebastián was a fashionable summer resort, along with Santander, where the royal family and the court spent their holidays. Summer in San Sebastián was filled with festive diversions, including sports, the casino, and the theater season. In early July a racetrack was opened to the public for the first time, with the royal family presiding over the inauguration. Diaghilev and Massine's mission in San Sebastián was to arrange for two gala performances of the Ballets Russes at the end of August. Except for a short trip to Paris, they spent the summer between San Sebastián and a small fishing village some forty kilometers south of Barcelona called Sitges, where Misia and Sert were on holiday.

In the early 1890s Sitges was still a quiet fishing village, but by the end of the decade a number of Catalonian painters, most notably Santiago Rusiñol, had made it their home. Rusiñol was the spiritual leader of a group of bohemian artists that included Ramon Casas and Miguel Utrillo. These painters, who had lived in Paris during the 1880s, had enjoyed the admiration and friendship of such Parisian notables as Debussy, Proust, Léon Daudet, and Mallarmé.

At the time that Rusiñol moved to Sitges, it was a simple Mediterranean cove with modest old houses perched along the stone ramparts overlooking it. It was also the site of a church, a medieval hospital, and the chapel of San Juan Bautista. In this quiet, unadorned setting, Rusiñol acquired a pair of old houses next to the hospital and installed in them his vast collection of objets d'art, including two El Grecos, *San Pedro* and *Santa Magdalena.* By the turn of the century, however, Sitges found itself the center of the *modernismo* movement[27] and soon began attracting international personalities. One of these was the Chicago millionaire Charles Deering, who in 1910, with Utrillo's help, acquired the old hospital and several of the old houses around it. Utrillo designed Deering's Mediterranean residence, known as Maricel, by combining elements of the traditional Mediterranean Romanesque, Gothic, and Renaissance styles of architecture. This dwelling became the home of Deering's extensive collection of El Grecos, Zurbaráns, and Goyas as well as works by such contemporary artists as Rusiñol and Casas. Sitges shortly became a gathering place for European artists, many of whom, like Marie Laurencin, were waiting out the war in Spain. Deering invited Misia and

Sert to Maricel in the summer of 1916. So many like-minded people in such a congenial setting proved irresistible to Diaghilev and Massine, who were immediately taken with this charming little village. The intelligent company, plus surroundings that encompassed nature and art at their most magnificent, made Sitges a pleasurable stopover on many of their future visits to Spain.

For the San Sebastián gala Diaghilev planned to offer a ballet on a Spanish theme as a tribute to the Spanish monarchs and an expression of gratitude for their support, with a ballet on a Russian theme as a companion piece. Gontcharova and Larionov, who at Diaghilev's invitation had joined the group in Sitges, once again were delegated to work with Massine. But choosing a subject proved difficult. Diaghilev suggested that they adapt the score of Fauré's *Pavane*. Massine wanted to take Velázquez's *Las meninas*, a portrait of the royal family, as a point of reference and for inspiration.[28] The painting had moved him deeply, and the ballet would be Massine's homage to the Spanish painter.

Diaghilev approved, and the plans proceeded at a steady pace. Sert was to design the elaborate period costumes. Carlo Socrate, the Italian scene painter, was to create the decor, which eventually featured a garden overlooked by a balcony. The story concerns two ladies-in-waiting who secretly, or so they think, meet with two courtiers. The couples perform a pavane as a dwarf—introduced by a cello played pizzicato—makes her presence known and then rushes off, conveying in mime her intention to spread the scandal of illicit love. Massine set a series of pas de deux designed to evoke the ambience of the court of Philip IV. His idea was to communicate "a personal interpretation of the formality and underlying sadness that I had glimpsed in Velázquez . . . counter-balanced by the flowing movements which blended with melancholy strains of Fauré's evocative music."[29]

The ballet was rehearsed in San Sebastián. The dancers were Sokolova, Olga Khokhlova, Leon Woizikowski, Massine, and, as the dwarf, Elena Antonova. At first it had seemed to Diaghilev that a real dwarf was needed in the role. Sokolova describes how things went when a dwarf was brought to Diaghilev's hotel room for the requisite interview with the impresario: "The little man sat for a while, trying to understand what the talk—partly in Russian, partly in French, partly in Spanish—was all about. Then he got bored, slipped off the chair onto his tiny legs, grabbed a lot of cherries from a dish, filled his mouth with as many as it could hold, and began prancing up and down the room, shooting out the stones at everyone in sight. Diaghilev in hysteria kept asking Larionov to 'get rid of the little brute.' "[30] Much to the relief of Sert, who was to design the ballet—and, one suspects, to the relief of just about everyone else—the notion was dropped.

For the Russian novelty Diaghilev suggested one of the fairy-tale settings of Liadov. Massine happily agreed; while a young boy, he had been fascinated by the traditional folk stories he heard in Zvenigorod-Moskovsky. They decided to adapt Liadov's *Kikimora,* the story of a witch who forces her cat to rock her cradle and then, in a fit of rage, decapitates the poor feline. Larionov's decor was inspired by a peasant interior at Abramtsevo, depicting in cubist terms a bright yellow *isba* (a Russian log hut); Gontcharova's two costumes were neoprimitive in style.

San Sebastián that August belonged to the Ballets Russes. Diaghilev and Massine stayed at the Hotel Continental overlooking the Concha. Here they encountered Arthur Rubinstein, and the three men were soon lunching together daily.[31] Rubinstein became closely linked with the ballet company, attending its morning rehearsals and enjoying long afternoons with Gontcharova, Larionov, and Ansermet at the Café Terrace. At night the dancers escorted the young pianist to the empty hall of the casino, where he played for them, and where he became enamored of the beautiful Valentina Kachuba.

In San Sebastián Diaghilev and Massine encountered many familiar faces, among them that of Mme Khvoshchinsky, who planned to spend part of the summer in the old aristocratic enclave. But since she had arrived without her husband,[32] Diaghilev sensed trouble; he feared that her mere presence could awaken Massine's assiduously buried heterosexual leanings. He was right. The agent provocateur, as Diaghilev called her, precipitated the first major crisis between him and Massine.

Exactly how intimate matters became between Massine and Mme Khvoshchinsky is unclear. It's possible they simply promenaded together in plain view or shared amusing conversation over coffee at the hotel, nothing more. They may have gone so far as to flirt openly, perhaps even in Diaghilev's presence. Both Massine and the lady were certainly capable of feigning innocence as they secretly enjoyed skewering Diaghilev's massive ego. In their own eyes the couple may simply have been having a bit of fun, but they were hurting Diaghilev, a man accustomed to exerting monumental control with surgical precision, where he was most vulnerable.

In fact they were playing with fire. For what is known is that they pounded a raw nerve in the tempestuous impresario; he fumed over their flirtation, if that is what it was, for months afterward. Diaghilev had painful memories of women who had threatened his homosexual relationships. First, back in St. Petersburg, the poet Zinaida Hippius (a.k.a. Gippius), in a draining and devastatingly protracted struggle spanning years, had finally claimed for herself Dmitri Filosofov, Diaghilev's longtime lover.[33] The Nijinsky-Romola affair followed, and in that episode the price was not only Diaghilev's loss of his lover but his company's loss of its leading dancer and new, rising choreographer. Now these old wounds to Diaghilev's psyche ached anew. Mme Khvoshchinsky stirred deepseated fears and doubts. Diaghilev was again confronted with the fact that he had taken as a lover a man who was ambivalent about his true sexual orientation, and history suggested to him that he could lose this latest companion to the opposite sex as well.

The first San Sebastián gala took place on August 21; the program included *Les Sylphides, Sadko, Prince Igor,* and *Schéhérazade.* On August 25 *Las meninas* and *Kikimora* were premiered.[34] *Las meninas* was well received; the press was charmed by its "ceremonious and solemn" evocation of ancient Spain, and King Alfonso XIII, who had formally declared himself Diaghilev's protector, came to San Sebastián expressly to attend the performance.[35] Adolfo Salazar, the prominent music critic, wrote: "When we saw that tiny delicate work performed on stage we understood clearly what exquisite and refined art was contained in that production; what fine and subtle talent had been involved in its creation. . . . We are dealing above all with the sketch of an epoch and of a character as conceived by an artistic mind that creates according to sentiments it has been handed down, but that does not attempt to merely copy in a vulgar fashion."[36] When *Las meninas* was shown in Paris, Debussy wrote to Diaghilev, "It has been your pleasure, my dear Diaghilev, that the typical French charm of Fauré's *Pavane* should clad itself in Spanish seriousness. That was a tour de force for which you should be congratulated —you and your prodigious Massine as well."[37] According to Massine, Diaghilev loved *Las meninas* very much, preserving it in the repertory until his very last season in 1929.[38]

Since King Alfonso had become a benefactor of the Ballets Russes, the authorities of Bilbao scheduled series of galas for the end of August to coincide with the monarch's visit to their city to review the fleet. Following the Bilbao galas Diaghilev, Massine, and Ansermet made a short trip to Paris to engage Monteux and Anselm Goetz as conductors to tour with the company. From there they went to Bordeaux, whence on September 8 part of the company sailed for New York. Grigoriev and a nucleus of dancers would remain in Europe to work with Massine.

Diaghilev and Massine returned from Bordeaux to San Sebastián to attend the music festival at the Gran Casino. Misia joined them, probably owing to a request from Diaghilev, who in periods of emotional need or personal crisis counted on her as a confidante (the Mme Khvoshchinsky affair still rankled). The three became inseparable, and together they attended Rubinstein's performance of Rachmaninov's First Piano Concerto on September 20. Falla also came to San Sebastián to help draft the contract for *El corregidor y la molinera,* or *Le Tricorne,* as the ballet was now called, in French, after the title of Alarcón's novel. According to this September 15 draft,[39] Diaghilev would produce the ballet in 1917 in Rome. Falla was to deliver his piano score by November 15, 1916, and the orchestral score would follow on December 15. The draft of the contract does not mention *Noches,* so Falla apparently, with Ansermet's help, succeeded in extricating himself from his original agreement with Diaghilev concerning this work and its future.[40] On September 22 the music festival ended, and Diaghilev, Massine, Misia, and Sert left San Sebastián for Italy.

The Chinese Conjuror in Parade, *1917*

CHAPTER 5

Rome, September 1916–Paris, May 1917

MISIA, SERT, DIAGHILEV, AND MASSINE drove to Italy, making leisurely stops at Verona, Bologna, Padua, and Venice. At the end of October, in Rome, Diaghilev and Massine rented a furnished apartment, complete with piano, at the Corso Umberto, via del Parlamento 9. And since they were soon joined in Rome by Gontcharova, Larionov, Ansermet, and the Cecchettis, this apartment would turn out to be their headquarters until the following May. While the others reviewed plans for new productions, Maestro Cecchetti gave Massine a daily private class at the little old Teatro Metastasio.

Stravinsky arrived in November to discuss the ballet *Le Chant du rossignol,* a reworking of the opera he had begun in 1909, *Le Rossignol.* In 1913 the Free Theater of Moscow had sought to perform the opera, but before the project materialized the company went bankrupt, in 1914. Diaghilev succeeded in producing the opera that same year. Then in September 1916 at Santander he commissioned Stravinsky to prepare a ballet version by combining the second and third acts of the opera.[1] He visited Stravinsky at Morges later that fall to monitor the work's progress; but now, when Diaghilev once again wanted to discuss *Le Rossignol* in ballet form, Stravinsky had another idea: to turn the second and third acts into a symphonic poem without voices. Diaghilev accepted the new proposition. Feeling confident that he would be able to produce the piece later in Rome, Diaghilev left the composer, who had already begun to revise the music and the scenario for what he now was calling *Le Chant du rossignol.*

Mikhail Semenov, a former music critic from St. Petersburg, joined the Diaghilev circle in Rome, a city he visited frequently from his home in Positano, about twenty miles south of Naples. He, Diaghilev, and Massine would meet at the Caffè Ariana (across the street from the Corso Umberto) for long afternoons of conversation about art and music. Massine in particular drew close to Semenov, a sort of father figure who would eventually provide Massine staunch support during and after his breakup with Diaghilev.

As they had been in other cities, Diaghilev and Massine were soon at the center of Rome's artistic life. Despite the war, the Italian capital provided some of the social and cultural excitement then missing from a beleaguered Paris. They rekindled their association with those futurist painters who were not at the front, particularly Balla and his young follower Fortunato Depero. The futurists stimulated the Russians. In the two years since his first exposure to futurism, Diaghilev had gained a more perceptive understanding of its aesthetic principles, and this visit would mark the first actual collaborations between the Ballets Russes and the futurist artists. (In 1917 Diaghilev would tell Nijinsky: "Futurism [and] Cubism are the last word. . . . I do not wish to lose my place as an artistic guide.")[2]

Massine too felt the pulse of futurism. He later acknowledged that by the time of this stay in Rome futurist painters "had already begun to influence my choreography."[3] Undoubtedly he was beguiled by Marinetti's notion of "total art" (as articulated by Apollinaire), whose aim was to produce a theatrical spectacle with painting, music, and movement equally represented. Marinetti's concept, apart from its emphasis on music hall (variety theater) elements and its affinity for audience participation, coincided in its theory as a theater of synthesis with both the ideal of total theater for which Diaghilev had long prodded Massine to strive and the innovations of the Moscow theater. Futurist theatrical experimentation would infuse *Parade,* the ballet Massine would create in Rome in 1917 with the collaboration of Cocteau, Satie, and Picasso. For the remainder of his life Massine repeatedly singled out *Parade* as an example of a total work of art whose elements were equally represented.[4]

The sojourn in Rome was meant to provide the company with a working period to develop new works, and, above all, to give Massine a chance to sharpen his choreographic skills. During his stay at Bellerive he had worked on *Liturgie* and created *Le Soleil de nuit,* and later, in Spain, he had come up with *Las meninas* and *Kikimora.* With this apprenticeship behind him, at age twenty he was refining the stylistic preferences that would propel his work for the next fifteen years.

Unfortunately, plans for *Le Tricorne* and Stravinsky's *Le Chant du rossignol* had to be postponed because the scores were not ready. Diaghilev began to look for new ideas. Ensconced in Italy, he sensed that an Italian subject would be fitting, as *Las meninas* had been for Spain. Aside from Russia, Italy was the country he loved most, and an homage to her seemed felicitous. He suggested that Massine read Goldoni's comedy *Le donne di buon umore.* Massine quickly seized on Goldoni's musicality and his technique in the manner of commedia dell'arte, a style that blended mime, dance, and acrobatics. This appealed to Massine's own sense of theater and dovetailed with a curiosity about commedia dell'arte that had been apparent on the Russian stage since the turn of the century.

Diaghilev and Massine began to search the libraries of Rome for old Italian music. The composer they lit upon was Domenico Scarlatti (1685–1757), a contemporary of Goldoni. They hired a musician to play some of Scarlatti's more than five hundred harpsichord sonatas on the piano at the Corso Umberto. Of the twenty pieces chosen for the ballet, only two were familiar to concertgoers: a capriccio and a pastorale, both usually performed on the piano in Karl Tausig's arrangements. Vincenzo Tommasini (a young composer whose opera *Uguale fortuna* had won first prize in a 1913 competition organized by the city of Rome) was commissioned to work with Massine on the score and to orchestrate the sonatas. Rehearsals began at the Cantina Taglioni, the dance studio in Piazza Venezia where the company worked throughout its six-and-a-half-month stay in Rome.

Extensive rehearsal time was dedicated to *Les Femmes de bonne humeur,* as the new work came to be known, and the ballet was conceived and created in unhurried fashion. Yet Massine's near-obsessive absorption in his work turned the composition of *Les Femmes* into an intense intellectual and creative exercise. To evoke the style and manner of the period, he began a conscientious study of the seventeenth- and eighteenth-century choreographic treatises Diaghilev recently had acquired for him at auction in Paris. These included first editions of works by Carlo Blasis, Raoul Feuillet and Louis Pecour, Malpied, and Jean-Philippe Rameau.[5] At Diaghilev's suggestion, Massine spent much of his free time studying the paintings of Guardi, Watteau, and Longhi in galleries and art books. He later wrote:

> From Watteau's "Fêtes Galantes" I took the languorous gestures of the women, their delicate hand movements, and the ineffable sadness of their backward glances. Pietro Longhi, with his sharp sense of domestic detail, was an invaluable help when I came to do the choreography for the main scene, the supper-party given by the maid Mariuccia to her admirers, Leonardo, Battista, and the Marchese de Luca, during the absence of her mistress, La Marchesa Silvestra. In this I emphasized the elaborate setting of the table, the placing of knives, forks and plates, the carving of the chicken and the pouring out of the wine.[6]

In transforming the three-act Goldoni play into a one-act ballet, however, Massine was hampered by the stylistic devices and technical trappings of commedia dell'arte, with its masks, disguises, and heightened gestures. To make the complex manageable, he "balanced the action simultaneously on both sides of the stage."[7] In later years he concluded that his solution "worked well in the supper-party scene, but was more difficult in the slower liquid passages."[8]

Massine's steady emergence from apprenticeship to a surer command of his art underlies these passages in his memoirs, which show that he already possessed a keener sense of his identity as an artist than the novice Diaghilev had taken up such a short time before.

Les Femmes was the first Massine ballet notable for both individual and collective characterization, and the first to demonstrate his ability to compose phrases out of idiosyncratic gestures and to intertwine intricate yet cohesive ensembles in which the characters retain their personalities. The contrasts Massine contrived for them served to reinforce their individuality, a result most pronounced in the role of Niccolò, the waiter. Massine confesses that in "pondering over the problem of contrasting him stylistically with the other, more graceful characters, I remembered

Les Femmes de bonne humeur,
Rome, 1917

the puppets I had seen in Viareggio, and decided to give him their floppy, loose-jointed movements."[9]

To intensify this diversity Massine used musical counterpoint to juxtapose the movements of two characters within the same phrase. Moreover, he fixed counterpoint for each dancer by contrasting the torso and the leg movements, devising "broken, angular movements for the upper part of the body while the lower limbs continued to move in the usual harmonic academic style."[10] Sokolova described it as the "jerky, flickering movements of marionettes."[11] Lopokova, who created the role of Mariuccia, believed that "the movements of the dancers' bodies were something quite new in this ballet, different both from classical and from character dancing. . . . The movements were so new that at the rehearsals our bodies began to ache as never before. The knee was always bent and the arms akimbo—the limbs never in a straight line."[12]

This new approach to choreographic movement brought to ballet the aesthetics of angularity as a predominating trend. Lynn Garafola writes:

> Angularity was perhaps the most dramatic sign of the modernist revolution in ballet. Thanks to Massine, wrote French critic Fernand Divoire in the 1930s, "the invention of the later Ballets Russes in the area of dance was the angular angle, the angle more or less deforming, more or less comic and caricaturing." Under the tutelage of Larionov, Gontcharova, and the futurists, Massine hardened ballet's soft and "beautiful" line. He staunched the flow and cramped the openness of classical movement and substituted contorted gestures for the rounded arms of the traditional port de bras. "All that is plastic, graceful, free from angularity is excluded," wrote Valerian Svetlov. . . . "The times of the 'choreographic tenor,' M. Fokine, in the smart phrase of Massine, are gone for ever. All the movements of the dancers are short, angular, mechanical."[13]

Characterization in *Les Femmes* was not psychological; it reflected the conventions of commedia dell'arte, in which each character was representative of a type or a personality trait.

Mime—expressive gesture—and dance movement flowed into one another just as, in eighteenth-century opera, recitatives tell the story and the arias that follow let the emotions soar. In most narrative ballets the mime passages remain strictly pantomime (like the *recitativo secco* in opera), but in *Les Femmes* they resembled a *cantinella*, a recitative set to melody (*recitativo stromentato* or *accompagnato*) that was harmoniously blended into the whole work, enhancing its rhythmic cohesion.

Another source of inspiration for Massine was film, with its speeded-up, broken movement and the rapid montage technique for simultaneous action. Nineteen sixteen was also a productive year for futurist cinema, and surely Massine, through his association with this movement, was aware of its developments. The film *Vita futurista*, produced with the participation of Balla, Marinetti, and other futurists, included a dance sequence with transparent figures, achieved by the use of double exposures. (Balla, a close friend of Diaghilev's and Massine's, was one of the signers of the "Manifesto of Futurist Cinema" published in the November 1916 issue of *Italia Futurista*.) And in the same year we find the photographer Bragaglia, who had done experimental work with photodynamism, launching his own company, La Novissima, which produced three full-length films—*Thais, Il perfido incanto,* and *Il mio cadavere*—as well as the comic short film *Dramma in Olimpo.*[14] The futurists' interest in the speed and simultaneity of cinema also touched the theater. In his *Notes on the Theater,* published in the Italian press in installments during 1915–17, Fortunato Depero proposed that "it is necessary to add to the theater everything that is suggested by cinematography."

Another source of Massine's interest in film may have been Gontcharova and Larionov, who had worked with Vladimir Mayakovsky and the Burliuk brothers on the experimental film *Drama at Cabaret 13* before they left Russia.[15] (Gontcharova and Larionov remained committed to Massine throughout his early artistic and intellectual development, not only as mentors but as close friends; Gontcharova served as his confidante, and both were parental figures to him.) Yet another influence came from Massine's fascination with Charlie Chaplin.[16]

Les Femmes was in rehearsal throughout the month of November 1916, and on December 17 Diaghilev wrote to Mme Stravinsky: "Tell Igor that Massine has finished Scarlatti. As an involved colleague it is hard for me to judge, but I think it is a small masterpiece—all merriment and loveliness from beginning to end."[17]

Les Femmes was made on the dancers who had remained in Europe, except for Lopokova, who took over the rôle of Mariuccia when she returned from the United States tour. The cast Massine chose proved ideal; an indisputable triumph emerged from his meticulous coaching and the dancers' responsiveness to his contrapuntal and angular style.

Diaghilev asked Bakst, who had a great flair for the eighteenth century, to design the production, and in December Bakst left Paris to join his collaborators in Rome. He created a Venetian piazza with buildings that curved inward, as if seen through a concave mirror, giving the work a modernistic semblance. But after the ballet had been performed in Rome and Paris, Diaghilev rejected the concept in favor of the more traditional style of the eighteenth-century Venetian painter Francesco Guardi. Bakst modified his decor,[18] but his costumes were left intact: elaborate gowns richly embroidered in gold and lace for the women, velvet jackets and knee-length breeches for the men, and period wigs for all.

WITH *LES FEMMES DE BONNE HUMEUR* completed, Massine was exhilarated. But as Christmas drew nearer he was stricken with nostalgia for Moscow, which he expressed in letters full of longing to Anatoli Petrovich.

Not everything in Rome had gone as harmoniously as *Les Femmes.* The mere presence in the city of Vasily Khvoshchinsky, in his post at the Russian embassy, revived the fear and jealousy that had racked Diaghilev in San Sebastián, even though Mme Khvoshchinsky was not in Rome. (From San Sebastián she had gone directly to a nearby sanatorium, where she remained throughout most of this period.) Relations between Diaghilev and Khvoshchinsky snapped at a concert on November 19. Arturo Toscanini, conducting Siegfried's Funeral March, was prevented from finishing the piece by shouts from the balcony protesting a performance of Wagner when Italy was at war with Germany. In the theater foyer afterwards, Khvoshchinsky defended the performance and Diaghilev vehemently sided with the protesters, setting off a scandalous row that, according to Diaghilev, ended only "when we called in our seconds, and the affair was settled peacefully, but with great difficulty."[19]

Irrational and out of proportion by itself, the Wagner incident was obviously an excuse for Diaghilev to avenge himself upon Mme Khvoshchinsky, and an outlet for his pent-up anxiety and rage. And, as he would later write to Stravinsky, it afforded him the opportunity he needed to break off his relations, manageably pleasant until then, with the couple.[20] But this was an episode from which Diaghilev would not easily recover, and despite all the exciting work being done in Rome during this period, he confessed to Stravinsky in a letter dated December 3 just how deeply affected by the affair he was. "But my spirit has been depressed. That awful business with Khvoshchinsky is over, but it will be better to talk about it in person." Diaghilev's desperate need for a confidant is made clear in the same letter, in which he declares to Stravinsky, "I will come to Paris when you are there. I am writing all of this to you because of our friendship."[21]

Of course all this turbulence began to erode the bond between Diaghilev and Massine. Diaghilev's uncontrolled fits of temper made life at the Corso Umberto trying. In his fury he was apt to smash the furniture; he once "tore the telephone from the wall and shattered it on the ground."[22] Massine's reaction to such raving was to immerse himself in work. Not only were his spirit and intellect being sorely tested, but his appreciation of Diaghilev as a great man—brilliant, often magnanimous, capable of radical devotion and self-sacrifice in the pursuit of artistic ideals—had to be set against the demanding, sometimes merciless, mistrustful, possessive, and self-centered tyrant he now faced. Nevertheless, since Massine's personal credo dictated the sacrifice of himself to art as to a religion,* any distress his personal situation may have caused him was justified in his mind by the work that grew out of their affiliation. In the creative process he could insist upon an alternative reality, sublimating his private needs to his work and its realization. The dark side of this bargain was that as the years went on art increasingly became for Massine a substitute for and a refuge from real intimacy.

After *Les Femmes*, Massine began a Spanish ballet set to Albéniz's "Triana," from *Iberia*, with decor and costumes by Gontcharova; but this work never advanced beyond the rehearsal stage. Nevertheless, the fascination Spain held for Diaghilev and Massine inspired them to plan more works on Spanish themes. For instance, in notes and sketches surviving from this period, they set out their ideas for *España*, set to Ravel's *Rhapsodie espagnole*, with designs by Gontcharova. (At a certain point this work was probably titled *Rhapsodie espagnole*.) Diaghilev also wanted to produce two additional ballets to accompany the projected *Le Tricorne* on a "Spanish" program, first in Rome, later in Paris. Unfortunately, when Falla was unable to complete his score on time, the other two projects were scrapped.

Diaghilev had hoped that after *Triana* Massine could begin rehearsals for *Le Chant du rossignol*. By November 1916, Fortunato Depero had been contracted to design the new work, for which he envisioned a "fantastic garden scene of huge plastic flowers," and for the costumes,

---

* The sanctity of art was a prevailing belief among the Russian artists of the Silver Age, the Russian cultural renaissance of the turn of the century. As an article of faith it was discussed at length by, for example, Stanislavsky.

"geometrical Chinese masks, cylindrical sleeves, and heads in compartments."[23] Diaghilev found Depero "brilliant," his work on the ballet "marvelous," and his decorations "splendid." Massine, he reported, "was dreaming about presenting the work"[24]—his first collaboration with the composer of *Sacre*. But Stravinsky did not finish the score in time for Diaghilev to produce the ballet in Rome. It was not staged until 1920, with scenery and costumes by Henri Matisse.

With both their ambitious projects, *Le Chant du rossignol* and *Le Tricorne* (the latter's score was not completed until 1919), in limbo, Diaghilev suggested that Massine and Larionov devote some time to the one-act *Kikimora* as the starting point of a full-length ballet incorporating other Russian legends, again to music by Liadov.[25] The ballet eventually consisted of three episodes: the story of Kikimora and the cat; the story of the swan princess under a spell cast by a three-headed dragon, who is finally set free by a knight; and the story of the ogress Baba Yaga, whose plot to capture and devour a young girl lost in the forest is thwarted when the girl saves herself by making the sign of the cross.

Contes russes, as the ballet was titled, grew out of another close creative partnership between Massine and Larionov, just as *Le Soleil de nuit* had done. Massine later said of Larionov's contribution that his "costumes and decor for the whole ballet were among his most delightful creations, the elements of Russian folk art being even more cleverly adapted than in *Le Soleil du nuit*."[26] But the knight's horse in the second episode, entrusted to Depero, elicited one of Diaghilev's hysterical reactions. Massine describes how he and Diaghilev

> *were summoned to [Depero's] studio on the outskirts of Rome. As we walked into the room the artist pointed proudly to his construction—a bulbous outsized elephant! We stood staring at it silently for a few moments until Diaghilev, in a sudden outburst of rage, smashed the papier-mâché animal with his walking stick. I tried to pacify the shocked and bewildered Depero by explaining to him that although his construction no doubt had great charm, it was not quite the horse we had envisaged. But poor Depero was still puzzled, and explained that he had done his best. This was exactly how he had imagined the animal. The problem was not finally solved until Larionov designed a primitive but graceful animal cut out of thin wood and painted white.*[27]

On February 18, 1917, Cocteau and Picasso arrived in Rome to begin their collaboration with the Russians on a new ballet called *Parade*.

Cocteau had first met Diaghilev at Misia Edwards's Quai Voltaire apartment several days after the sensational opening of the Ballets Russes at the Châtelet on May 9, 1909. It had been through the good offices of Misia and Bakst that Cocteau was able to penetrate the inner circle of the Ballets Russes, and it was following Bakst's suggestion that Diaghilev's impresario in France, Gabriel Astruc, commissioned Cocteau to design the publicity posters for the 1911 ballet season, one of which was the famous rose and mauve poster of Nijinsky in *Le Spectre de la rose.* Cocteau had been engaged by Diaghilev for the first time in 1912, when for the ballet *Le Dieu bleu* he provided the libretto, Reynaldo Hahn the score, Bakst the scenery and costumes, and Fokine the choreography.

But even then Diaghilev had been eager to strike out in new artistic directions, such as Nijinsky's angular, innovative choreography for *L'Après-midi d'un faune* (1912). The formulaic *Le Dieu bleu* did not interest him. He disliked Hahn's score which Prince Peter Lieven, a member of Diaghilev's Parisian entourage, once characterized as "India seen through the eyes of Massenet, sweet and insipid."[28] Diaghilev's decision to employ Cocteau, a poet he did not admire, as librettist on *Le Dieu bleu* in fact had been a scheme to snag Hahn, since, according to Stravinsky, "Diaghilev needed Hahn. . . . He was the salon idol of Paris, and salon support was very useful to Diaghilev at that time."[29] Unfortunately, *Le Dieu bleu* had not been a success, and in a moment of exasperation after its premiere Diaghilev hurled at Cocteau the famous challenge: "Astound me! . . . I will wait for you to astound me . . . !"[30]

These words would come to be the driving force behind *Parade.*

In 1913 the Ballets Russes had premiered Nijinsky's *Le Sacre du printemps,* a succès de scandale. The following year Cocteau, in his indefatigable ambition to be associated with all important artistic events, tried to persuade Stravinsky to collaborate with him on a new ballet libretto he had written called *David.* The project went unrealized; but Cocteau, refusing to abandon it wholly, in 1916 asked Erik Satie to collaborate on a work Cocteau now called *Parade,* an adaptation of his original *David* libretto. Satie, who had gained notoriety in the 1880s and 1890s with his *Gymnopédies* and *Gnossiennes* for piano, was living an obscure and rather bohemian life in Arcueil-Cachan. He accepted Cocteau's offer. Cocteau then asked Picasso, to whom he had been introduced in 1915 by Edgar Varèse, to join the project as designer, and to the utter astonishment of Montparnasse, Picasso accepted the offer from the dubious poet of the Right Bank. Of course, once Satie and Picasso agreed to collaborate,

Cocteau easily secured a commitment from Diaghilev, who admired the composer and the painter immensely.

When Picasso joined Cocteau and Satie in August to begin work on *Parade*, his overbearing personality caused trouble. Two letters to Valentine Gross, who had introduced Cocteau to Satie, tell the tale. In one, dated September 4, 1916, Cocteau implores Gross to

> make Satie understand, if you can cut through the aperitif fog, that I really do count for something in Parade, and that he and Picasso are not the only ones involved. I consider Parade a kind of renovation of the theater, and not a simple pretext for music. It hurts me when he dances around Picasso screaming, "It's you I'm following! You are my master!" and seems to be hearing for the first time, from Picasso's mouth, things that I have told him time and time again. Does he hear anything I say? Perhaps it's all an acoustical phenomenon.[31]

The other key letter in the episode, Satie's to Gross, dated September 14, is a confession to her of his dilemma:

> Chère et douce amie—if you knew how sad I am! Parade is changing for the better, behind Cocteau's back! Picasso has ideas that I like better than our Jean's! How awful! And I am all for Picasso! Picasso tells me to go ahead, following Jean's text, and he, Picasso, will work on another text, his own—which is dazzling! Prodigious! I'm half crazy, depressed! What am I to do? Now that I know Picasso's wonderful ideas, I am heartbroken to have to set to music the less wonderful ideas of our good Jean—oh! yes! less wonderful. What am I to do? What am I to do? Write and advise me. I am beside myself. . . .[32]

In Cocteau's original libretto for *Parade* three circus performers—a Chinese Conjuror, a Young American Girl, and an Acrobat—emerge from the circus tent to entice passersby in to see the show. Cocteau wanted each character introduced through a megaphone with a sung announcement, in the style of a Greek chorus. "After each music-hall number," he proposed, "an anonymous voice issuing from an amplifying orifice (a theatrical imitation of a circus megaphone, the mask of antiquity in modern guise) was to sing a type phrase outlining the performer's activity so as to open up the world of make-believe."[33] Satie and Picasso opposed this idea. According to Picasso scholar Douglas Cooper, the painter shared Satie's belief that the voices would interfere not only with the music but with the choreography and decor as well. Instead, Picasso proposed adding three new characters—who became the French, American, and Negro managers—to introduce the performers. He argued that these additions would exploit "the contrast between three characters [the conjuror, the girl, and the acrobat, played by dancers] . . . and the more solemnly transposed inhuman, or superhuman, characters [the three managers, three-dimensional constructions with dancers inside] who would become in fact the false reality on stage, to the point of reducing the real dancers [the conjuror, the girl, and the acrobat] to the stature of puppets."[34] Disagreement on this point, however, quickly led to arguments, hysterical invective, and threats from Cocteau and Satie to quit the project. But on the eve of their trip to Rome Cocteau finally acceded to Picasso's ideas.

Meanwhile, in Rome, Massine was choreographing Satie's *Gymnopédies* for the Marchesa Casati, one of the very few women admired by the futurists. This gave him an opportunity to experiment with Satie's music and to expose himself further to the composer's style before staging *Parade*. Even though Massine's musical taste, formed at the Bolshoi, was quite traditional, he deeply enjoyed Satie's music, finding it amusing and charmingly original.[35]

Once in Rome, Cocteau and Picasso easily blended into the working dynamic that characterized Diaghilev's ballet productions. They stayed at the Hotel de Russie on the Via Babuino, facing the Piazza del Popolo with its large back garden and its winding paths leading to the slopes of the Pincio. From here Picasso could walk the short distance to his rented studio on Via Margutta, where he continued to work on *Parade*. Activity on the ballet centered around Picasso's studio and the Cantina Taglioni, where the company rehearsed. Despite their hectic schedule, Diaghilev and Massine were delighted to show their beloved Rome to the newcomers; the nights in particular proved ideal for relaxing in the balmy Roman weather. Cocteau, as the group strolled about in the city "made of fountains, shadows and moonlight," was inspired to write his poem "Rome, la nuit."

Meeting Picasso was a momentous occasion for the twenty-one-year-old Massine. Their friendly collaboration would produce four ballets over the next seven years and was critical in refining Massine's aesthetic ideas and orienting his taste. "It seemed to me," he wrote, "that whatever [Picasso] looked at—whether it was a flower, a statue or an architectural composition—went through a process of abstraction in his mind, and emerged as a cubist creation. He was at that time trying to transpose and simplify nature in much the same way primitive African sculptors did in carving their powerful wooden figures and masks. By dissolving surface barriers and clearing away sentimental layers of association, he widened his vision to encompass previously unknown perspectives."[36] Picasso's working methods in fact figured in the evolution of Massine's own approach. Massine was enthralled by the way the painter "would design several dozen of sketches, starting from very realistic ones, before attempting to arrive at a final thought. Then, little by little, this realism would subside like something unnecessary."[37] Massine saw at work beneath Picasso's method the painter's guiding creative principle, a process of trial and error that eventually led to a crystalline idea. "This is something that remained in me," Massine later said, recalling Picasso's admonition "not to take for granted your first step as a final result, but as a point of departure to clear up your thoughts in order to eliminate those elements that could be detrimental to the final conception. An artist arrives at a final result, not as something occasional—because he likes it—but following a principle and a process of thought."[38]

In Rome, Picasso and Cocteau associated not only with other Ballets Russes collaborators, such as Gontcharova and Larionov, but also with the futurists, especially Balla and Depero. Despite their differences, these artists developed a rapport that was founded on mutual respect as much as on the experimental climate of the times.

As *Parade* rehearsals proceeded, Cocteau once again tried to persuade Massine to use voices in the ballet, but Diaghilev and Massine continued to side with Picasso and reject the concept. Massine undoubtedly realized the choreographic potential of the managers, and he saw, too, that the voices would constrain choreography that, if expressive enough, should be able to stand alone. Fortunately, when Cocteau saw Picasso's sketches for the managers, he was won over by the painter's brilliant conception.[39]

During rehearsals some changes were made, the most significant of which was Massine's addition of a female acrobat as part of a parody pas de deux. In adding this character Massine showed a new assertiveness that suggests a view of himself as the creative equal of his collaborators. He also suggested that the Negro Manager, who was to appear on a horse, be omitted altogether, because the "human" figure kept falling off its steed. Picasso discarded the structure of the Negro Manager, but the horse (with two dancers inside) remained.

Another important change resulted from a suggestion by Cocteau. According to a letter from the poet to Misia, Massine was originally slated to dance the male Acrobat, but in rehearsals he imparted such power to the Chinese Conjuror that Cocteau asked him to undertake the latter role in performance.[40]

How rewarding it must have been for Massine that his collaborators made him feel from the very beginning that he was their equal! Indeed, Cocteau sent the young choreographer a letter assuring him of their confidence in him and his work (not a bad tactic, either, for winning Diaghilev's favor):

> My dear Massine:
> Collaborations are full of surprises.
> My theme has surprised Satie and Picasso; their treatment of it in turn has surprised me.
> There remains a blank
> On purpose
> It is yours; it is up to you to fill it, to "surprise" us, so that only the public remains to be surprised. Do not take that blank to stand for something vague, but instead accept it as a manifestation of the excellent construction of Parade, and how much we trust you.[41]

In the midst of their exhilarating and rewarding work, Diaghilev, Massine, Cocteau, and Picasso took time out at the beginning of March to visit Naples.[42] In an exploratory mood the friends visited historical sites (but did not cease thrashing out their vision of Parade). From Naples they made trips to Positano, Pompeii, and Herculaneum. Massine remembered how "Picasso was thrilled by the majestic ruins, and climbed endlessly over broken columns to stand staring at the fragments of Roman statuary."[43] Cocteau captured the occasion with his Kodak. The excursion gave the quartet the opportunity to enjoy both classical art and Neapolitan culture, including good food and fine wine. A special joy accompanied their examination of archaeological sites, historical buildings, and works of art. The introverted Massine, always given to solitude, spent time alone, during the stillness of siesta, "walking through the narrow streets behind the Piazza Garibaldi."[44] An intent observer, he was aware of and admired "the zest and ingenuity of the citizens who, whether they were craftsmen at their work or street sellers displaying their fish and fruit, performed their tasks with such high-spirited style, humor and bravura."[45] Massine was discovering the "richness and diversity of life" in a region to which his future life would be intimately linked.

*Picasso, Diaghilev,
Cocteau, and
Massine in Pompeii
and Positano, 1917.
The photos were
taken with
Cocteau's Kodak.*

In Rome again, the group resumed work on *Parade* armed with fresh ideas. Diaghilev again presided at long luncheons, usually at the Grand Hotel, where Cocteau's scalding wit amused his friends and sometimes irritated the impresario. On other occasions they would gather in Diaghilev and Massine's domed Corso Umberto salon, where, undoubtedly, one of the topics of discussion was the political upheaval in Russia —for by March 15, the tsar had abdicated the throne and a revolutionary government had been formed by Oleg Kerensky.

The American Ballets Russes contingent was back in Rome by early April,[46] and before the month was out Diaghilev scheduled a short engagement for the company at the Teatro Costanzi. On one of its nights a charity gala was attended by Marchesa Casati and Colette. A second gala, on April 12, saw the premiere of *Les Femmes de bonne humeur.* Eleonora Duse watched the performance from the wings, then came onstage to congratulate the cast. The work scored a great success with the Romans. With *Les Femmes,* Massine had created the first modern comedy-of-manners ballet.

The second part of the evening was a program of Stravinsky's music, conducted by the composer including the fourth tableau of *Petrouchka,* along with the berceuse and final apotheosis of *The Firebird,* which Stravinsky had recently adapted for concert performance. The musical highlight was the 1908 *Fireworks,* which Diaghilev presented as a "ballet without dancers." For this occasion Balla had designed a complex wooden structure covered by paint and canvas, topped by smaller structures covered with a translucent fabric and lit from inside. Against a black background were projected forty-nine combinations of lights (some were repeated), in which scarlet and green predominated. Shadow projectors were also used. The program notes described this experiment as "a purely musical organism that visually evolves at the same pace as fireworks."[47] Balla took a curtain call dressed in a futurist suit and purple straw hat, carrying a square-cut walking stick.

At the time Massine joined the Ballets Russes, Diaghilev had begun to acquire contemporary art works as gifts for him. Shortly, Massine began to buy for himself. Now an impressive selection from his collection was exhibited in the foyer of the theater, including two Baksts, one Braque, six Carràs, one de Chirico, five Deperos, one Derain, two Gleizeses, three Gontcharovas, three Grises, one Larionov, three Legers, three Lhôtes, six Picassos, four Riveras, one Severini, four Survages, and two Zarregas. Taken together, the exhibition and Balla's *Fireworks* made it an evening reminiscent of a *serata futurista.*

When the Costanzi engagement ended, Cocteau returned to Paris. The finale of *Parade* was still being hammered out, and in letters to Massine the poet proposed an ending (which, with some slight modifications by Massine, was close to the actual ending):

> *Here's a good ending which came to me in my sleep. It fits Serge and places emphasis on* Parade: *As the managers collapse in the finale, the acrobats, the young American girl, and the Chinese man could show up timorously, so that they are present and watch terrifiedly as the managers fall, and then they can begin to point with all their strength to the "ingresso," while understanding that the managers have given up on it. That would be a fair way to bring those characters back upon the stage and to help clarify that they are the parade and not the internal spectacle.*[48]

Following their triumph in Rome, the company moved to the Teatro San Carlo in Naples for five performances. This time Stravinsky journeyed south with his friends. En route on the train the others bet Picasso that he could not draw Massine in less than five minutes; he won by doing a pencil portrait of the choreographer in the swiftest academic manner. In Naples they visited the aquarium, which according to Stravinsky was easily the city's greatest attraction for Picasso and himself, a place where they all spent many happy hours together.

After the final performance at the San Carlo, Massine accepted Semenov's invitation to spend several days with him and his wife at their retreat in Positano. The invitation offered him a rare stretch of time away from Diaghilev, who hardly ever let him out of his sight. In Positano Massine was delighted by the "cluster of whitewashed cottages, which looked as if they had been piled up one above the other in a vast cleft in the mountains."[49] In the Semenovs' lovely home, a converted mill discreetly set at the edge of the village, Massine found deep enjoyment in their company.

It was during this visit that he first glimpsed the Isole dei Galli, a group of islands reputed to be part of the legendary sirens' islands braved by Ulysses. The words that follow, written more than half a century later, underscore Massine's yearning for independence at the time:

> *On my first night there I happened to look out my window, and noticed a desolate rocky island several miles off the coast. When I asked Mikhail Nikolaevich about it next morning, he told me that it was the largest of the three islands of Galli, the two smaller ones being hidden from view.*

*The Semenovs'
house in Positano*

*They belong to a local family called Parlato, who used them only for quail
hunting in the spring. During the day we took a boat to the island I had
seen, and discovered that it was composed of rough grey rock with no veg-
etation except for a few sun-scorched bushes. I was overcome by the beauty
of the view across the sea, with the Gulf of Salerno spreading out in the
distance. With Paestum to the south and the three Faralioni of Capri at
the northern tip of the Gulf, it had all the drama and mystery of a painting by Salvator Rosa. The silence was broken only by the murmur of these
and the occasional cry of a gull. I knew that here I would find the solitude
I had been seeking, a refuge from the exhausting pressure of my chosen career. I decided then and there that I would one day buy the island and
make it my home.*[50]

En route from Rome to Paris, the Ballets Russes gave one performance in Florence.

By the end of April 1917 *Parade* was nearing its definitive form. Following Diaghilev's suggestion, Picasso designed a front curtain that was to appear (after the theater's own velvet curtain had been parted) to the accompaniment of Satie's "Prelude to the Red Curtain." The curtain, which drew its inspiration from circus posters, depicted a theater stage framed by red drapes. Seven circus characters sat at a table: two harlequins (one in blue, the other in red), a black man wearing a turban, a toreador with a guitar, a sailor, and two young girls. To the left was a foal beside a winged white mare, and at the top was a ballerina, with small wings, stretching her arms toward a tiny monkey atop a ladder. A dog slept on the floor next to an acrobat's ball and drum. In the background were a garden, an arch in ruins, and, in the distance, Mount Vesuvius. The predominant colors were the greens and reds Picasso had favored in his *saltimbanques.*

The eight characters turned out to be Picasso's friends and collaborators, disguised by him as a private joke.[51] The blue harlequin was Cocteau; the red one, Massine (in a 1917 drawing of Massine by Picasso the dancer appears in the same outfit); the turbaned black was Stravinsky. The toreador was Picasso; the sailor, Diaghilev. The romantic girl next to Cocteau was Maria Chabelska, the dancer who created the role of the American girl; the girl in the hat was Olga Khokhlova, Picasso's future wife; and the ballerina was Lydia Lopokova (who created the role of the female Acrobat). Of course the background, with its view of Vesuvius reminiscent of Naples, had a special meaning for this group.

After the Satie prelude, the front curtain rose to reveal a painted backdrop: a monochromatic urban scene made up of a street, buildings, and trees without perspective and conceived in cubist terms. In the center a crooked rectangular opening, with a balustrade on both sides and covered with a curtain, served as the gateway to the performance tent, through which the four entertainers entered and exited the stage.

The gigantic constructions for the French and American managers were eleven-foot-tall collages of arms, trees, boulevards, skyscrapers, an Uncle Sam hat, megaphones, and signs. Only the legs of the dancers under these structures were visible. The horse (which had been fashioned to carry the figure of the Negro Manager), with a face reminiscent of an African mask, actually had two dancers inside. The Chinese Conjuror wore an Oriental-style outfit in bright yellow, bright red, and black, with a three-cornered hat and a long braid (Massine made up his face with expressionistic features). The American Girl, a bow in her hair, wore a pleated skirt and middy jacket; the Acrobats wore blue and white unitards gaily decorated with spirals and stars.

Massine's choreography fleshed out Cocteau's indications of the personality of each character with a great economy of expressive movement. The Managers marched, turned about, and stomped pompously; the Chinese Conjuror breathed fire, ate an egg that would later be retrieved from his foot, and ran about the stage performing mechanical jumps; the American Girl danced jazzy, Chaplinesque steps. In a parody of the silent serial *The Perils of Pauline,* she swam across a river, drove a car, took pictures with a Kodak, and so on. The horse ingeniously stomped out, and the Acrobats jumped and pretended to walk a tightrope. As the curtain fell, the Managers, frustrated in their efforts to lure the passersby inside, fainted and fell to the floor, the Girl sobbed, and the Conjuror remained frozen in place.

In this unusual ballet, Massine went a step beyond naturalism. The influence of Picasso could be seen in *Parade's* stylization and deformation of movement, an aesthetic tendency already present in the stylized angular baroquism of *Les Femmes de bonne humeur.* Now, through cubism, Massine undertook a more radical assault on the bodily image, an image that in his hands proved far from a faithful visual sign for actual human gestures.

Sections of the front curtain had been painted in Rome, where Depero helped to construct the large figures of the Managers.[52] When the company arrived in Paris on May 1, Picasso immediately began supervising the reproduction of his designs and also helped to finish painting the curtain. Meanwhile, rehearsals continued. Criticism and comments from the poet Apollinaire helped shape the final form of the ballet.[53] His commentary, published in the *Excelsior* on May 11, was reprinted in the performance program:

> The Cubist painter Picasso and that most daring of choreographers, Léonide Massine, have staged Parade, thus consummating for the first time this union of painting and dance—of plastic and mime—which heralds the advent of a more complete art.
>
> This new union—for up until now stage sets and costumes on the one hand and choreography on the other were only superficially linked—has given rise in Parade to a kind of super-realism [sur-réalisme]. This I see is the starting point of a succession of manifestations of the "esprit nouveau": now that it has had an opportunity to reveal itself, it will not fail

to seduce the elite, and it hopes to change arts and manners from top to bottom. . . .

. . . Massine . . . has produced a complete novelty, one so marvelously seductive, of a truth so lyrical, so human, so joyous, that it might well be capable of illuminating (if this were worthwhile) the frightful black sun of Durer's Melancholia—*this thing that Jean Cocteau calls a "realistic ballet." Picasso's Cubist sets and costumes bear witness to the realism of his art.*

The sets and costumes of Parade *clearly disclose his concern to extract from an object all the aesthetic emotion it is capable of arousing. Frequent attempts have been made to reduce painting to its own rigorously pictorial elements. There is hardly anything but painting in most of the Dutch school, in Chardin and the Impressionists.*

Picasso goes a good deal further than any of them. Those who see him in Parade *will experience a surprise that will turn into admiration. His main purpose is to render reality. However, the motif is no longer reproduced, but merely represented; or, more accurately, it is suggested by a combination of analysis and synthesis bearing upon all its visible elements —and, if possible, something more, namely, an integral schematization that might be intended to reconcile contradictions, and sometimes deliberately renounces the rendering of the obvious outward appearance of the object. Massine has adapted himself with it, and art has been enriched by adorable inventions like the realistic steps of the horse in* Parade *whose forelegs are supplied by one dancer and the hind legs by another.*[54]

Paris awaited the forthcoming premiere with rapt anticipation. The Châtelet was sold out fifteen days in advance. The season opened on May 11 with a *répétition générale* at four in the afternoon. The evening's program included *Firebird*, the French premieres of *Les Femmes* and *Contes russes*, and the Polovtsian Dances from *Prince Igor*. André Levinson, the prestigious Franco-Russian ballet critic noted for his partiality to the classical tradition, congratulated Massine on his achievement in *Les Femmes de bonne humeur*: "The inspiration of this humorous ballet is so adroit, the execution so homogeneous and free from constraint, the whole so well composed that I freely surrendered myself to the sweetness of living that exquisite hour of forgetfulness."[55] He considered the ballet "a living and original work where the past only appears in the form of a distant suggestion, an echo softened by the passing of centuries."[56] (Levinson once had severely criticized Fokine for relying in his ballets on "ethnography and archaeology" when reconstructing the past.) Levinson admired Mas-

The Chinese Conjuror in
Parade, *1917*

sine's choreography for combining "a sense of delicacy with a feeling of fitness in which the laws of the classic dance are rarely abrogated, its normal movements distorted and parodied, heightened and dispersed by the rhythm."[57] He described Massine's style as *"perpetuum mobile,* a movement falling on each note, a gesture on each semiquaver, a continual fidget to which we owe the breathless and spirited animation of *The Good-Humoured Ladies;* now, this restless style, with its insistence on distorted or broken lines, is bound to the imperative of polyrhythmic musical movement or tyrannical syncopation that a Stravinsky imposes on the orchestra.[58]

On the afternoon of May 18, *Parade* received its premiere at a war benefit that had been sold out two weeks in advance. The eclectic audience brought together the Rive Droite and the Rive Gauche: the Ballets Russes circle (the Princess de Polignac, the Count and Countess de Beaumont, the Countess Greffuhle, Misia Sert) and the bohemians of Montmartre and Montparnasse (Juan Gris, Severini, Apollinaire) were joined by Paris' musical elite (Roland Manuel, Ricardo Viñes, Francis Poulenc, Germaine Tailleferre, Louis Durey, and Georges Auric). Picasso's evocative and romantic front curtain was greeted with unanimous applause as it was displayed to the accompaniment of Satie's harmonious prelude— generous welcome from a public that might not have been so warm had it known what was to follow. After the front curtain rose to reveal the cubist decor, the audience was confronted with the huge, sensational constructions of the Managers just as Satie's rhythmic music, composed of integrated noises, began. Of the pandemonium that then seized the auditorium, Poulenc remarked: "For the first time—it has happened often enough since, God knows—the music hall was invading Art with a capital A. A one-step is danced in *Parade!* When that began the audience let loose with boos and applause. All Montparnasse, in the top gallery, shouted, 'Vive Picasso!' Auric, Roland Manuel, Tailleferre, Durey and many other musicians shouted, 'Vive Satie!' It was real bedlam."[59]

By now one segment of the audience was shouting obscenities and loudly demanding that the authors be sent to the front lines. Cocteau described what followed:

> *Women rushed at us armed with hatpins. We were saved by Apollinaire because his head was bandaged, he was in uniform and was therefore respected; he set himself in front of us like a rampart. The piece lasted twenty minutes. After the curtain went down the audience was uproarious for fifteen, and finally fistfights broke out. I was crossing the theater with*

Apollinaire to join Picasso and Satie, who were waiting for us in a box, when a large lady singer recognized me. "There's one of them!" she cried—she meant the authors. And she lunged at me, brandishing a hatpin, trying to put my eyes out.[60]

The press either massacred the ballet or condescended to it. Pierre Lalo, son of the composer, virulently attacked it in *Les Temps*. Jean Poueigh, in *Le Carnet de la semaine*, declared Satie without purpose, humor, technique, or professionalism. In response Satie sent Poueigh a postcard bearing the observation that the critic was an ass, and an unmusical ass at that. Unfortunately, since the postcard was not in an envelope and thus could be read by anyone, Poueigh was able to file a libel suit against Satie that would go before two tribunals. Eventually, a thoroughly chastened Satie was sentenced to a week in jail and ordered to pay Poueigh a fine of one thousand francs. Cocteau was a witness at the second trial. Surrounded by reporters, he not only screamed at them, but raised his walking stick in a threatening gesture toward Poueigh's lawyer. For this act Cocteau, too, was fined by the judge.[61]

One vocal segment of the audience at *Parade* considered it a thoroughly lame joke—a joke they resented. The press was especially outraged at Cocteau's audacity in subtitling it "a realist ballet." (To Cocteau, it was "more true than truth.") The artistic community, on the contrary, expressed its appreciation and recognition of the ballet's achievement. It left Stravinsky, for instance, with "the impression of freshness and real originality."[62] Juan Gris "liked *Parade* because it is unpretentious, gay and distinctly comic. Picasso's decor has lots of style and is simple, and Satie's music is elegant. It is not figurative, has no fairy tale element, no lavish effects, no dramatic subject. It's a sort of musical joke in the best of taste and without high artistic pretensions. That's why it stands right out and is better than the other ballets. I even believe that it is an attempt to do something quite new in the theater."[63] And in a letter to Cocteau, Proust expressed his pleasure: "I cannot tell you how delighted I am by the considerable stir made by your ballet. It would be almost an insult to you and your collaborators to call it a 'success.' And yet, inexplicable though it may seem, the success is real and very great. Even though in this case the success is no more than a mere foretaste, a propitious aura emanating from the future, it is not to be belittled."[64]

Proust's words were prophetic. As the 1913 *Sacre* is thought to have been a portent of Europe's forthcoming tragedy, so *Parade* anticipates the 1920s in its juxtaposition of reality and unreality. With a sort of magical realism, *Parade* prepared the way for dadaism and for surrealism. (Apollinaire's usage of *"sur-réalisme"* in his commentary anticipates the aesthetic value the term would come to have in the following decade.) Satie's ragtime passages announced the arrival of the Jazz Age and the Roaring Twenties. The Chinese Conjuror's movements were founded in the contraction and relaxation of tension (energy), accurately predicting the dance expressionism of the following decade. *Parade*'s mobile decor—Picasso's and Massine's joint achievement was the fusing of the decor with the musical structure—preceded Oskar Schlemmer's *Abstrakter Tanz,* in the Bauhaus style that forged dance from the joining together of painting and sculpture. Already present in *Parade* were seeds of the pictorial visualizations, or frescoes in movement, Massine would create in the 1930s with Joan Miró, André Masson, and Henri Matisse. One can even find in *Parade* premonitions of the pop creations of the 1960s. If the importance of a work of art is measured by its transcending the moment and perpetuating itself in history, then *Parade* is undoubtedly one of the twentieth century's most significant and enduring monuments.

For everyone involved in the creation of *Parade,* the ballet marked a turning point. Satie immediately became a prominent figure in the Parisian musical world. Notwithstanding the influential Apollinaire's dislike for him, Cocteau succeeded in establishing himself as a key personality in the avant-garde; he remained not only a catalyst in the arts but a continuing force for infusing content into the French aesthetic of the twentieth century. His association with Picasso, as Cocteau himself expressed it, meant he gained a better understanding of common reality, the reality that from then on, as he ranged beyond it, became integral to his own creative process. For Picasso, who had not had an individual exhibition in Paris since 1902, the theater clearly offered greater exposure than any gallery could; *Parade* would eventually be seen in Madrid, Barcelona, and London. His work on the ballet reawakened his interest in the human figure, an interest that had waned while he explored the stylistic problems of cubism. He fell in love with and married Olga Khokhlova, and, with Paul Rosenberg as his dealer, left Montparnasse behind and began his rapid rise into high society.

Diaghilev had for some time wanted to attract the artists of the School of Paris; the first of his ultramodern productions, *Parade* was the opening gambit in his campaign to convert his Ballets Russes into an expressive vehicle for the avant-garde. And as for Massine, overnight he ceased to occupy the periphery of Diaghilev's entourage and became a figure of importance in his own right. The young and immature dancer who three years earlier had made his debut in *The Legend of Joseph* now returned to Paris as one of the leading avant-garde artists of the time. Apollinaire wrote to him two days after the premiere of *Parade*:

> You have taken up alongside Diaghilev the most prominent position to date as far as scenic art goes.
>
> But what interests us the most is the way in which you embroider with such strangely powerful grace upon those ballets.
>
> It's that force and, I should say, that simplicity of yours, which makes you stand out. . . .
>
> Choreography and music are surreal art forms par excellence, since reality, as expressed by them, always goes beyond nature.
>
> And therein lies the importance of your art and your own artistic importance.
>
> It seemed to me that you are so intent upon penetrating the secrets of the choreographically unforeseeable, that I do not fear in the least for the future of that modern art form.
>
> As for *Parade*, and even perhaps all ballets in general, I believe that the knees and the elbows have not been paid all the attention they deserve. . . .
>
> There is no doubt that you are the first one to make justifiable the use of the word "art" when speaking of dance.[65]

As a performer and as a groundbreaking choreographer, Massine would dominate ballet for the next thirty years. When the Ballets Russes left Paris in May to return to Spain, the future of modern ballet was his.

Diaghilev and Massine with the company, Seville, 1918

CHAPTER 6

ⅅ⅁⅊⅌⅍

Spain, June 1917–July 1918

AT THE END of May the Ballets Russes was back in Madrid, and so were Picasso, Stravinsky, and Ansermet. Nijinsky, who had remained in Spain with his family since the American Ballets Russes contingent had returned to Europe in April, made his long-awaited official Spanish debut at the company's June 2 opening.[1] That night audiences at the Teatro Real had the rare opportunity of seeing Nijinsky as Harlequin and Massine as Eusebius in *Carnaval*. The first performance was a wild success with public and press alike; and the final curtain came down triumphantly night after night. Once again, the Spanish monarchs attended every performance. In a letter to María Martínez Sierra, who was in Paris at the time, Falla noted that there was not a seat to be had.[2] In addition to the season at the Teatro Real, a number of special performances were given for the royal family and the court at the private Royal Palace Theater.

Diaghilev and Massine quickly joined Madrid's artistic and social life. Arthur Rubinstein was still in town, as were two newcomers to Diaghilev's inner circle, Sonia and Robert Delaunay. These two artists had been much influenced by French chemist Eugène Chevreul's 1839 theory of simultaneous contrasts ("the breaking up of color tone into its component elements").[3] This led them to coin the term *simultanéisme* for the placement of human figures and objects in the same painting. The notion had two main emphases: color, as subject and form, and the rendering of light. The couple were important members of the artistic community of prewar Paris; their studio at rue des Grands-Augustins was a gathering-place for the avant-garde.

The Delaunays had first arrived in Madrid in 1915, then moved on to the Vila do Conde in Portugal, and later to Vigo in northern Spain. By 1917 Sonia's private Russian income had been cut off, so they returned to Madrid looking for financial opportunities. Diaghilev introduced the couple to the capital's elite, and these contacts helped Sonia to open a successful clothing and interior design boutique in the elegant Serrano quarter of the city. In designing clothes for members of the royal court she found herself in competition with the French painter Marie Laurencin, who was also in Madrid. But Sonia's dresses, shawls, purses, umbrellas, and furniture were such hits that she later opened two more shops, in Barcelona and Bilbao.

By day Diaghilev, Massine, Picasso, Stravinsky, Ansermet, the Nijinskys, Falla, and the Delaunays would congregate at the bullfights, and by night they plunged into Madrid's unique after-dark scene, where they relished seeing authentic flamenco and often stayed out until the wee hours of the morning.

Massine and Diaghilev resumed their collaboration with Falla. Soon after they were reunited, Falla played for them his score for the pantomime *El corregidor y la molinera,* which had been successfully premiered in Madrid the previous April. Diaghilev's and Massine's first reactions were relayed to María Martínez Sierra by Falla in a June 8 letter, in which the composer confessed: "As I feared, I will have to make important modifications in the second scene . . . to make it more choreographic. . . . Consequently there will be two versions: the original that will remain as is for the theater companies, and the choreographic one, for the Russians."[4] Although these changes had not yet been discussed in detail, "the only certain thing at the moment is that I have to create a long finale, develop further the scene of the fight and even, perhaps, make it possible for the Miller to return followed by the corregidor's policemen."⁵ Diaghilev and Massine agreed that the composer would surely strengthen the piece by "omitting some of the pastiche writing of the music for the corregidor's dance, and expanding the ending into a fuller, more powerful finale."⁶ Falla readily concurred. For one thing, *Les Femmes de bonne humeur,* which he had just seen at the Real, had given him a sense of Massine's originality and creative power, and Falla was excited and eager to work with him.⁷ Falla continued to revamp his score, and by June 22 María Martínez Sierra had praised some of his changes in the finale.⁸ But more hard work lay ahead. According to Massine, the composer felt that in order to expand the score he would have to spend "more time studying native dances and music before I could successfully translate the *jota* or the *farruca* into a modern idiom."⁹

When did Picasso join the project? Douglas Cooper and others believe that when he returned to Paris after his visit to Spain with the Ballets Russes in the summer and autumn of 1917 he was still unaware of Diaghilev's plans to create a Spanish ballet.¹⁰ But it is highly likely that the Russians had already discussed their plans with Picasso in Rome, since *Le Tricorne* was one of the projected ballets for the Roman season. It seems safe to assume that Picasso, a member of Diaghilev's informal artistic council, would not be left out of any discussion of forthcoming productions, especially plans for a Spanish ballet. Another piece of evidence bolsters this assumption. Carlos Bosch, who also frequented Diaghilev's Madrid circle, claims that around this time he introduced the artist Pedro Muguruza to Diaghilev as a possible designer for *Le Tricorne.* Indeed Muguruza prepared preliminary sketches for Diaghilev, but the matter went no further since, according to Bosch, Picasso was already involved in the project.¹¹

In Madrid relations between Nijinsky and Massine—past and present lovers of Diaghilev—were cordial but distant. Massine deeply admired Nijinsky as dancer and choreographer and seized every opportunity to observe him at work. He watched transfixed as Nijinsky, rehearsing *L'Après-midi d'un faune,* "demonstrated the most minute details of gesture and movement."¹² And Nijinsky in turn genuinely admired Massine's work; after a performance of *Les Femmes de bonne humeur* the great dancer was unrestrained in his praise. "I was surprised," writes Massine, "to receive a visit from Nijinsky, who came to my dressing room, embraced me, and told me what a beautiful ballet I had created. I was taken by surprise, as I did not feel I knew him very well; but when he said that he would love to dance Battista—one of the principal parts—I felt very honored."[13]

The engagement at the Teatro Real ended with two performances, including *Parade,* which was added at the request of the king. The company then spent June 23 to 30 in Barcelona at the Gran Teatre del Liceu. Picasso accompanied them in order to introduce Olga to his family and friends.

The rapport that had developed between Picasso and Massine during the creation of *Parade* went deeper than an understanding between professional collaborators; the two men thoroughly enjoyed one another's company. In Barcelona, as in Madrid, Paris, Rome, and Naples, they spent many hours together. They would meet at the café-restaurant Lion d'Or, their favorite hangout, or go sightseeing. Of course their talk focused mainly on art. In my conversations with Massine he remembered that on this trip to Barcelona he and Picasso began work on *Le Tricorne.* A sort of personal testament to these fertile Barcelona days is the famous Harlequin that Picasso painted here, for which, back in Rome, Massine had been the model.

The Spanish dancer Felix Fernández García was also in Barcelona. Diaghilev and Massine had become reacquainted with him in June in Madrid, where, during the Teatro Real engagement, they ran across him in a working-class café. Right on the spot Diaghilev had invited Felix to a performance at the Real,[14] and after the dancer had seen *Schéhérazade* and *Thamar* he was eager to join the company. Diaghilev had promptly signed him before leaving for Barcelona. Sokolova saw this as a crucial move:

> *The employment of Felix was the first step towards the realization of the great Spanish ballet which Massine intended to create, though at that time neither Diaghilev nor Massine could have known exactly what form it would take. The essential was that Massine and the company should learn to perform Spanish steps in a Spanish way: and Massine in particular had to master the grammar of the Spanish dance before he could work out his choreography. At this stage Diaghilev and Massine probably saw Felix as the eventual star of their Spanish ballet, for if they had only needed a professor, it would surely have been more reasonable to engage an older man with experience of teaching.*[15]

In Barcelona, Felix, whom Massine thought "a naturally gifted dancer," began to teach him flamenco.[16] He also introduced Massine to his old Barcelona teacher Señor de Molina, who would give Massine his first lessons in the intricate technique of *zapateado*.

Unfortunately, Barcelona also became the site of renewed antagonism between Diaghilev and Nijinsky. While both men no doubt avoided dwelling on their stormy history, Nijinsky may nonetheless have resented the attention now being paid to Massine, and very likely felt some rejection at being left out of the company's creative process. He realized, too, that Massine had completely replaced him in Diaghilev's life.[17] Perhaps to salve his injured pride—and ill advised by his wife—Nijinsky suddenly balked at going to South America, where he was under contract to appear with the company immediately after the Barcelona run. He rashly tried to flee Barcelona for Madrid, but Diaghilev countered with stern legal measures; according to Spanish law, the dancer was bound both to perform in Barcelona and to tour with the company. Nijinsky was found in a Barcelona train station, arrested, and returned to the company.[18] Thus, after the Teatre Liceu engagement ended, Nijinsky sailed for South America with the Ballets Russes on July 4. (For this tour Grigoriev was in charge and Ansermet was company conductor.)

The Nijinsky incident was quite unsettling to Massine. He wrote to Anatoli Petrovich:

> I have not written to you for such a long time because everything was not clear in my mind, I could not visualize the future.
>
> Today is a special day: the whole company departed for Brazil and with them went Nijinsky, such a difficult and complicated subject. . . .
>
> Nijinsky is unacceptable and it seems to me that it is impossible to work with him. In spite of this I have great love for him as a great master who is troubled by thoughts that are similar to mine.[19]

With the company abroad, Diaghilev and Massine decided to resettle in Barcelona, partly because in hot weather the Mediterranean city was more agreeable than Madrid. Nearby Sitges had become their favorite summer resort on the Iberian peninsula. José María Sert was there during this time, and when not preoccupied with redecorating Charles Deering's home, he would take frequent jaunts into the city. Falla arrived in Barcelona and took Diaghilev and Massine to a performance of *El corregidor y la molinera* at the Teatro Novedades. For the first time Diaghilev and Massine heard the score played by an orchestra, and the music's "pulsating rhythms, played by eleven brass instruments, seemed to us very exciting, and in its blend of violence and passion was similar to much of the music of the local folk-dances."[20]

Few ballets have been as meticulously planned as *Le Tricorne*. In July, Diaghilev organized an excursion to give Falla the opportunity to do still more research on popular tunes, and to allow Massine to immerse himself in Spanish culture studying the personality types and dances that were to find their way into the new ballet. Felix Fernández García came along. The foursome journeyed from Zaragoza, the home of *jota*; to Burgos, the city of the medieval hero El Cid; to the high Renaissance of Salamanca; to El Greco's Toledo, with its blend of Sephardic and Arabic influences; and on through Córdoba, Seville, and Granada, the three southern cities that Diaghilev, Massine, and Falla had visited the year before. The dry, scorching summer heat did not keep them from visiting cathedrals, monasteries, and museums. At night they abandoned themselves to café life and soaked up regional music. Felix outdid himself trying to impress his traveling companions. He was a great asset, for "wherever we went he was automatically accepted as a friend by the local dancers. He was able to arrange several performances for us, and we spent many late nights listening to selected groups of singers, guitarists, and dancers doing the *jota,* the *farruca,* or the *fandango.*"[21]

Through Falla and Felix, the Russians were exposed to the best of flamenco. In Seville, where the previous year they had met La Niña de los Peines, they now met the famous flamenco dancers Ramírez and Macarrona. Massine was able to film some of their performances on the 16mm camera he had bought in Rome. These dancers impressed him with their "ferocious power and elegance."[22] In Seville they also watched "a *sevillana* performed by a group of dancers on the roof of an old house in the Triana quarter, lit by warm blue moonlight. In Córdoba Felix organized a performance in a cavern on the outskirts of the city, gathering together the group of cobblers, barbers and pastry cooks who were considered the best dancers in that part of town. After a meal of raw ham and Jerez they danced with such pleasure, spontaneity and native fire that the performances went on until the early hours of the morning."[23]

In Granada they revisited the Alhambra and the Generalife gardens, this time on donkeys. (To the amusement of the others, on the first slope the donkey bearing Diaghilev collapsed under his weight.)

As Massine got to know Falla more intimately, the composer's religious fervor, his ascetic views, and his almost monastic lifestyle, so detached from worldly vanities, all made a deep impression on the younger man. "His natural dignity and humility," Massine wrote, "were expressed in his thin, El Greco shaped face which, with it finely chiselled features and sallow skin, was like an instrument tautly strung."[24] Falla was "an extraordinary, inspiring man . . . unassertive, yet his remarks were often sharp and penetrating. He spoke with compelling intensity, and his conversation—particularly on art and music—was curiously exhilarating."[25] They reached a level of intimacy in which they exchanged anecdotes about their childhoods, about their love for the theater, and about their fascination with puppets. This trip marked the beginning of a friendship that would last until the composer's death in 1946.

Throughout the journey Massine was intrigued by Falla's method of compiling musical sources; he was "continually writing down passages of music in the notebook he habitually carried."[26] Once, in Granada, on their way back to the hotel after "wandering through long Moorish patios and courtyards," they "stopped to listen to a blind man playing a guitar. Falla spoke to the man, asking him to repeat the mournful little tune. . . . While he did so, Falla stood with his eyes closed humming it through and then methodically writing it down in his notebook. He later used that melody for the *sevillana* in the second part of the ballet. . . ."[27]

As the trip continued, *Le Tricorne* began to assume its final shape.[28] First the characters were modified. The miller in the pantomime, as in the novel, was ugly and humpbacked; for the ballet he was metamorphosed into an attractive young man. The names of the two central characters, Lucas and Frasquita, were changed to the Miller and the Miller's Wife, to accentuate their symbolic value in Alarcón's social allegory of the common folk's victory over the aristocracy. The intricate scenario of the pantomime was simplified in order to smooth its transition to dance, and Falla replaced the descriptive musical passages with dance numbers. Yet the action and the score of the first section of the pantomime and those of the corresponding part of the ballet were to remain remarkably similar.

But in the second scene *Le Tricorne* began to assume much larger dimensions. The first scene revolved around the actions of the two main characters, but the second required a full corps de ballet. This was a significant departure for Massine, since in *Les Femmes* and *Parade* he had used only a limited number of dancers. In *Le Tricorne* he would prove his skill in the deployment of large ensembles. And to match Massine's conception for the finale, for the first time in the evolution of the work Falla introduced a full orchestra.

Besides swapping ideas about the new ballet, Massine and Falla talked long and deeply about folklore.[29] For Falla, popular thematic sources served only as a point of departure. He wanted to capture the mood, rhythm, melodic forms, and cadences, but eschewed the perpetuation of the literal popular form, opting instead to try for a personal and original interpretation. According to him, "the essential elements of music, the sources of inspiration, are the nations and their people. I am opposed to music that takes as its base the authentic folkloric documents; on the contrary, I believe that it is necessary to have as a point of reference the live, natural sources and to utilize their sonorities and rhythms in its essence, but not for their exterior appearance."[30] In the first of Massine's ballets rooted in folklore—*Le Soleil de nuit* (1916) and *Contes russes* (1917)—he had unwittingly carried out Falla's dictum. His objective had been to take the essence of the popular dance movement and distort it in order to produce his own personal expressive and suggestive movement. And undoubtedly these conversations on folklore with Falla during the gestation of *Le Tricorne* influenced and altered the course of that ballet as well.

When Diaghilev left Spain in 1916, his intention had been to produce a Spanish ballet in Rome with Spanish dancers, as evidenced by the numerous letters in which he asked Falla to hire Spanish dancers to come to Rome.[31] In the Falla Archives one can read a contract signed in Seville on October 1, 1916, by Falla (acting on Diaghilev's behalf) and the dancer Angela Morillo, who was to join the Ballets Russes in Rome the following November 1.[32] It is possible that in 1917 Diaghilev still felt inclined toward Spanish dancers and that he envisioned Felix Fernández García, as Sokolova suggested, as the leading male dancer of *Le Tricorne*. However, as Massine developed his concept of the work as a stylization of Spanish folklore instead of an authentic interpretation, or re-creation, the choreographer must have realized that Felix was not as suitable for the role of the Miller as he himself was, especially since he was now much more confident in his knowledge of the native dance idiom. By the time their excursion ended and Diaghilev, Felix, and Falla returned to Madrid, Massine was fully imbued with the Spanish temperament, proving again his ability to take what he needed from his cultural surroundings.

Once back in Madrid, Falla set to work on the score, but, deliberate worker that he was, it would take him several more months to complete a satisfactory draft. In the meantime, Diaghilev warded off the stagnation of inactivity by suggesting to Massine that he begin preparing a new ballet. They decided to set it on a series of unpublished pieces by Rossini,

Péchés de vieillesse, which had been brought to their attention in Rome by the composer Ottorino Respighi, and devised a libretto based on the German ballet *Die Puppenfee,* which dealt with toys that come to life. (This work had first been produced in Vienna in 1888, and again in St. Petersburg in 1903 with choreography by the Legat brothers.) Massine liked the music's gaiety and variety, and he easily

> *visualized first two Italian peasant dolls who would dance a* tarantella. *Then, for Rossini's rousing mazurka, I pictured a quartet of characters from a pack of cards: The Queen of Diamonds and of Clubs, the King of Spades and of Hearts. Another piece of music, an ingenious parody of Offenbach, naturally suggested two vivacious cancan dancers in the spirit of Toulouse-Lautrec's paintings. We all agreed that the ballet should be taken at top speed, the dancers following each other without a break. I much enjoyed making the first rough sketches for the new ballet, which we called* La Boutique Fantasque. . . .[33]

Rehearsals got under way as soon as the company returned from South America in October.

The next Ballets Russes season took place in Barcelona, November 5–18, 1917. *Parade* was presented on November 10. The cubist ballet was not acclaimed by the press. At the end of November the company returned to the Teatro Real in Madrid. But neither autumn season equaled the success of the spring season, for the country was being swept by influenza. In Barcelona the flu had caused the death of many employees at the British consulate, and in Madrid half the populace had fled to the countryside.

For Massine the presence of the Delaunays in Madrid was comforting. His introspective personality made it difficult for him to open up and establish friendships, but he seems to have been able to communicate with certain women, one of whom was Sonia. Happily married, she was no threat to Diaghilev. Like Gontcharova, the other woman close to Massine, Delaunay—also Russian, a painter, and highly intellectual—would come to play a maternal role for the young choreographer.

After the season at the Teatro Real, prospects for the Ballets Russes were more uncertain than ever before. Aside from a forthcoming engagement in Lisbon in December, Diaghilev had not been able to arrange any other bookings. With the rest of Europe at war and with the impresario cut off from his private income as a result of the revolution in Russia, the survival of the troupe was in serious jeopardy.

Upon the company's arrival in Lisbon, revolution broke out, with the aim of overthrowing the government of Bernardino Machado. The upheaval lasted three days and nights, during which Massine and Diaghilev remained barricaded under the main staircase of the Avenida Palace Hotel. While Diaghilev fretted that they were losing valuable rehearsal time, Massine, with his capacity to retreat into the world of his imagination, felt rather stimulated and creative in the presence of so much turbulence:

> *Instead of succumbing to the general panic, I found myself remembering the gaiety and fantasy of Rossini's music. While the fighting raged outside my thoughts went back to the beach at Viareggio, where I had seen two white fox terriers coquettishly chasing and teasing each other. With a vivid picture in my mind of their frisky, flirtatious movements I mentally composed the poodles' dance for the new ballet. Throughout the revolution I remained in a highly creative mood and as a result, once the fighting had stopped, I was able to compose the major part of* La Boutique fantasque *in a few days.*[34]

When the political turmoil came to an end, the company opened its season a day behind schedule at the Coliseu dos Recreios, then moved for two performances to the San Carlos Opera, whose auditorium, at Diaghilev's request, was reopened especially for the Ballets Russes.

During the Lisbon engagements Massine began to rehearse, with Sokolova and Alexander Gavrilov, a Venetian waltz for his Rossini ballet. He also introduced into *Le Soleil de nuit* a solo for Lopokova set to the music of the shepherd's aria from *The Snow Maiden*. (Lopokova first danced it when the company went to London in 1918.)

The performances at the San Carlos ended, and prospects grew dire. Diaghilev and Massine returned to Madrid, leaving an almost starved company behind. Immediately upon their arrival, Diaghilev sent for Falla, who came at once to the Palace Hotel to find him desperate, with tears in his eyes. He confided to Falla the company's circumstances. "I am lost," he said. "What is going to become of me? My only solution is to go into a monastery."[35] Falla offered to help by approaching his friend and solicitor, Leopoldo Matos. Matos had successfully negotiated the rights to adapt Alarcón's *Sombrero de tres picos* to the stage, despite the fact that the writer's will had stipulated that the novel was to remain in its original form. With Matos's assistance the Spanish impresarios Arturo Serrano and Méndez Vigo came to Diaghilev's rescue, offering to organize a forty-seven-performance tour of the Ballets Russes throughout Spain. From Madrid, Diaghilev and Massine returned to Barcelona to spend the rest of the winter at the Hotel Angleterre.

In Barcelona, Massine began to set the tarantella for *La Boutique fantasque*. When the bullfighting season opened he attended the corridas regularly. He especially enjoyed the "poise, control and elegant movement of Juan Belmonte, Gaona, and Joselito."[36] He studied their styles and movements to acquire a better understanding of folk dances like the *farruca*, and befriended Belmonte, who fascinated him in long conversations about bullfighting. In *Le Tricorne*, Massine's inspiration was to give full expression to what he took Spain to be, including the perilous position of the matador and his flirtation with death in the arena. He collected all the illustrated bullfighting periodicals; and when as the Miller he performed his *farruca*—for him more than a dance, "it was a trance"—he envisioned a bull confronting him. Massine poured into his solo "all the highly emotional feelings I had when spending the afternoons at the *corridas*."[37]

Diaghilev, who had been in touch with Oswald Stoll to arrange an engagement at the London Coliseum, went to Madrid to see about transferring the company to England. By now he felt that he had squeezed Spain of all prospects, and to him the Ballets Russes' future looked grimmer than ever.

By March the tour of Spain had been arranged, to begin at the end of the month in Valladolid. Diaghilev traveled to Lisbon to share the good news with the company. One of his chief hopes was to recruit a superior orchestra. With Falla's assistance, he was able to persuade Joaquín Turina to become the company's musical director and assemble a group of musicians that included members of the orchestras of the Teatro Real, the Madrid Sinfónica, and the Filarmónica.

The tour covered about four thousand kilometers; the company's eighty-six dancers visited Valladolid, Salamanca, San Sebastián, Bilbao, Logroño, Zaragoza, Valencia, Alcoy, Cartagena (where with Serrano's help a threatened musicians' strike was averted), Córdoba, Seville, and Granada. The most successful engagements were the last two. In Seville, Diaghilev invited the company to celebrate at a *venta* (an open-air café) surrounded by orange groves, where Felix danced. In Granada, they performed at the Teatro Isabel la Católica and danced *Schéhérazade* at the Alhambra, for invited guests only, to Diaghilev's immense satisfaction and to high praise from those who later said the company had soared on this special occasion. From Granada they returned to Madrid, where they performed from May 25 through June 2, then moved on to Barcelona.

During this trying period, Massine's privileged position in the company brought on some grumbling among the dancers. During Turina's short association with the Ballets Russes, he clearly perceived its hierarchical structure: "A quite picturesque and rare society of nomadic people. It was classified into three sections: the higher echelon, the bourgeoisie, and the working class, who had the least possible contact among themselves and who kept a most rigorous protocol. The leading dancer, Massine, replaced the famous Nijinsky with very little sympathy from the other dancers who resented his rapid rise to eminence."[38]

The company's ongoing crisis of survival weighed heavily on Diaghilev's shoulders. Three years into the war, he found himself penniless, cut off from most of his friends and supporters, and responsible not only for his company's continuity but for the well-being of a great number of people. This overwhelming burden, added to his other cares, gradually wore him down. The lack of funds, a spreading dread, and repeated sleepless nights drained him, and their effect began to show in the shabbiness of his physical appearance. His dear friend Misia had advised him to drop it all, apparently forgetting that Diaghilev's imperious will would not allow him to surrender.

Diaghilev exhausted every possible connection to help get the company to England. He went to Madrid to make a personal appeal to King Alfonso, and through the intercession of the monarch, the Spanish ambassador in London and the English ambassador in Madrid arranged for the company's entry into England via France. Diaghilev wrote to Massine, who was still in Barcelona with the company:

> I am working here from 9:00 a.m. until nighttime. Upon arrival, I found out that the French will not let us through and are falling back on their last refusal. . . . I became like a storm and challenged everybody to their feet. The French did not give in, and again wanted to ask the English to let us go by sea. Again, I howled—new obstacles arose—I did more than I could. There was no one in Madrid who was not somehow involved in helping us! I begged the King three times to let us through and finally obtained the authorization. As soon as I did my nerves cracked and my whole system collapsed.[39]

All of this agitation placed further strains on Diaghilev's intimate relations with Massine. He turned more anxiously than ever to his young companion for emotional fulfillment and love. Massine was unable to respond fully to Diaghilev's needs, adding even more stress to an already unhappy situation. Diaghilev's demands were desperate, histrionic, and permeated with fear. He adopted the role of victim, and the resulting hysteria was calculated to fill Massine with guilt. This classic victim-victimizer scenario was Diaghilev's characteristic modus operandi; its dynamic defined his relationship with Massine. Perhaps unaware that his behavior would inevitably shatter that relationship, by clinging desperately to the younger man Diaghilev drove him away. In the same letter to Massine, Diaghilev dispatched a lover's reproach:

> At times, it's probably necessary to explain oneself, given that you don't want to understand or to feel. . . . I sent you a cable thinking that I was victorious, and received only a cable from the Lopokovs. From you not one word of tenderness, not one word of joy in return for my warmth. I asked frequently whether there was a note from you. . . .
>
> I was very depressed and cried constantly, having to leave the table when I would not hold back my tears. The Delaunays wanted to cheer me up and took me out to a restaurant. . . .
>
> I was ready to leave when I got your note asking me, for the sake of the dancers, to wait and wait and wait. I wanted so badly to go to the sea . . . didn't I deserve a break? If no one is concerned about my tired head then I need to think about it myself.
>
> It is very hard for me to be without my family, my dear ones, without friends, without a drop of tenderness. . . .
>
> Someday you will understand all this and someday a ray of light will illuminate your heart of glass. . . . Can it be that it is not my destiny to infuse you with the warmth of a Russian spring sun?[40]

Before returning to Barcelona, Diaghilev invited the Delaunays to join him and Massine for a short stay in Sitges. With most of Diaghilev's closest friends unavailable to him, the Delaunays had been supportive, and during his frequent visits to Madrid he had spent most of his free time with the couple. In Sitges the four friends settled down in a lovely villa (probably lent to Diaghilev, in view of the catastrophic state of his finances).

This was not the first time that Sonia and Robert had joined Diaghilev and Massine in Sitges, but this sojourn would mark the initial collaboration of the Delaunays with the Ballets Russes. Diaghilev had asked them to redesign *Cléopâtre* for the projected London engagement.

Robert designed a new decor, and Sonia designed some of the costumes, including Cleopatra's. A more creative collaboration, however, took place when Sonia, Robert, and Massine, all of whom had wanted for some time to work together on a ballet, began preparing *Football*, inspired by Robert's 1913 painting *L'Equipe de Cardiff*. Robert wanted to create something with a joyous and mad life, a work that would have repercussions for ballet.[41] Sonia wanted the space around the players (dancers) to remain mobile; as she explained to Massine, art in the past had been characterized by static laws, but the laws of modern art were dynamic. In her view, *Parade* had been a new beginning for a "universal spectacle," with every movement fresh and true and rooted in simplicity; she saw it as a point of departure.[42]

Working with the Delaunays afforded Massine another in a series of insights into art. Gontcharova and Larionov had provided his first important exposure to Russian and modern art; the futurists had given him a taste for experimentation; Picasso had introduced him to the principles of cubism; now the Delaunays would help him explore other artistic movements, including abstraction. They enjoyed his company, and respected his insatiable artistic curiosity and willingness to cross new frontiers. Robert wrote to him: "I find that you are making unbelievable progress and it is work that makes you superior, and in the way you have abandoned certain little prejudices of our friends from yesterday. . . . We see through it that you have also been taken by the liberating and regenerating movement, because a new era begins for the ballet."[43]

Sonia and Léonide spent long afternoons at the beach discussing art, theater, and films. Massine was fascinated by moving pictures and wondered exactly how they would affect the theater arts. Sonia argued that film would not achieve the stature of the other arts until it was delivered into the hands of artists,[44] but Massine, of course, had already proven in *Les Femmes de bonne humeur* the influence of film on his own work.

On July 29, 1918, the French consulate in Barcelona issued a transit visa enabling Massine and Diaghilev to enter France between August 4 and 7 and traverse it on their way to England. Leaving Barcelona on a midnight train, they entered France at Cerbère on the fourth.

The trip was not uneventful. At the French border, two detectives in dark glasses interrogated Diaghilev about his connections in Spain with Mata Hari, who had been executed in France for espionage on October 15, 1917. Fortunately, the letters she had sent to Diaghilev at the Palace Hotel imploring him to take her into the Ballets Russes had been left behind in Madrid.

The Cancan Dancer in La Boutique
fantasque, *1919*

CHAPTER 7

Paris, August 1918–London, August 1919

IN PARIS, Diaghilev and Massine took a taxi from the St-Lazare station to the Hôtel Meurice. They were shocked at the devastation the City of Light had suffered during the war, in stark contrast to the untroubled Spanish landscape they had just left. The façades of the buildings were covered with grime, the city's "boarded-up shops and kiosks"[1] looked like barracks, and the few people they encountered showed the weariness of war in their thin, pale faces and stricken appearance. Everyone seemed "fearful of the shells from 'Big Bertha' which burst over the town every few minutes."[2]

At the hotel, Diaghilev and Massine were joined by Misia and Sert and during luncheon the foursome recounted the travails of the past several months. But they clung to their hopes for the upcoming London season and for Massine's ballets in progress, *Le Tricorne* and *La Boutique fan-tasque*. Diaghilev was also optimistic about his plans to produce the eighteenth-century Cimarosa opera *Le astuzie femminili*, with, he hoped, a design by Sert.

During their six-day sojourn in Paris, Diaghilev and Massine were overjoyed to embrace old friends. At the Palais Royal apartment of Valentine Gross and her fiancée, the artist Jean Hugo, Stravinsky, just in from Switzerland, played his brand new composition *Ragtime* for, among other guests, Diaghilev, Massine, Picasso, Auric, and Poulenc.[3]

On August 9 Massine and Diaghilev left via Le Havre for England. As they were leaving Paris, a house on rue des Capucines was bombed, and pieces of glass and stone pummeled the roof of their taxi. They soon discovered that London, too, had been dramatically transformed by the war. Victoria Station hummed, and "Oxford Street, Trafalgar Square, the Savoy Hotel, the Coliseum—all were in a perpetual bristle."[4] The two travelers checked into the Savoy and got to work on their Coliseum engagement, which was only four weeks away. Diaghilev soon held auditions to replace those dancers who had defected in Spain when the troupe's survival had seemed most doubtful. Into the Ballets Russes came a group of dancers whose English names were immediately Russianized. The sole exception was petite Vera Clark, who was identified by her real name in company programs for a short while before she changed it to Vera Savina. She would play a decisive role in Massine's future.

The Coliseum engagement was the Ballets Russes' first in a music-hall theater. The company appeared on both afternoon and evening programs; according to Massine, Diaghilev detested seeing his ballets "sandwiched between performing dogs and acrobats, and clowns."[5] Diaghilev also cursed the theater's deficient lighting equipment.

As opening night drew closer, a weighty responsibility fell on Massine. Since Nijinsky and Karsavina were no longer with the company, much of the season's success depended on him. Diaghilev, with good reason, was jittery, particularly about the reception of *Les Femmes de bonne humeur*.[6] London audiences had not seen Massine dance since before the war, and then only in brief appearances as Joseph. Now he returned as both leading dancer and choreographer of the Ballets Russes; the novelties in the repertory would doubly depend on him.

The Ballets Russes opened at the Coliseum on the afternoon of September 5, when Massine was reintroduced to London as Amoun in *Cléopâtre*. The welcome was warm. The dancers were no doubt buoyed to see many of their longstanding society friends and supporters in the audience, including Lady Juliet Duff, Lady Ottoline Morrell, Lady Cunard, the Duchess of Rutland, Catherine d'Erlanger, and the Sitwell brothers. In the evening the company presented its first premiere, *Les Femmes de bonne humeur,* with a new, more realistic decor by Bakst.

To Diaghilev's immense relief and deep satisfaction, *Les Femmes* and its dancers were a sensation. The ballet's cinematic movements and simultaneous action were a revelation to British balletomanes. Wrote *The Observer*: "The merry adventures are unfolded with a rapidity of action that only perfect precision can sustain, and it is this precision with which every gesture is linked to its accompanying musical phrase that is the secret of this remarkable feat of stage production. . . . The result is not only a brilliant work of art, but the most exhilarating entertainment. Wordless wit is not easy of accomplishment, but Massine's choreography has attained to it."[7]

Still, the work's distinctive style and rhythm took the general public by surprise, and even ballet aficionados found it a bit puzzling. The dance historian Cyril Beaumont described his own first impression: "I was not sure whether I liked the ballet or not. The unusual speed of the performance was a little bewildering, and I could not get accustomed to the jerky, puppetlike quality of Massine's choreography, so different from the rounded and flowing movements of Fokine's compositions."[8] Only after repeated viewing did he determine that Massine's "dances did far more than accompany the music and accord with its rhythmical structure; they really translated the spirit of the music in terms of choreography."[9] Beaumont was also much taken by Massine's new, *cantinella*-like mime, which he found "unusual in that it was not separated from the actual dancing but, so to speak, grafted on it. Thus the whole ballet was a continuous flow of expressive movement unbroken until the very end, the sequence being adroitly subjected to variations in mood and speed to afford contrast and variety."[10] If Fokine's dramatic ballets had made their action cohere in terms of pantomime and dance—distinct from one another but of a piece with the narrative—Massine's synthesis of mime and dance, welded to the musical structure, produced a new, quintessentially balletic style of storytelling.

London's artistic and literary lights, unimpressed by Diaghilev's earlier, prewar seasons, now eagerly adopted the company. Osbert Sitwell observed: "Now the leaders of the intellectuals, seven lean years too late, had given the signal OK, and their followers flocked to it, replacing the old kid-glove and tiara audience of Covent Garden and Drury Lane."[11] This new interest was partly motivated by an awareness of Diaghilev's association with Gontcharova and Larionov, and of the controversial creation of *Parade* the year before, tales of which had been circulating ever since. Moreover, the collaboration of Cocteau, Satie, and Picasso had made the Ballets Russes an integrated brigade in the continental avant-garde. England was beginning to feel the sweep of this movement largely thanks to Roger Fry, who was instrumental in bringing foreign art before the tradition-bound British public. (In 1917 Fry had organized an exhibition in Birmingham that included canvases by Constantin Brancusi, Juan Gris, André Marchand, André Derain, and Maurice de Vlaminck, as well as such British painters as Duncan Grant and Vanessa Bell.) Thus Massine—associate of Picasso, Gontcharova, and Larionov, artists whose works marked such a radical stylistic departure from the prewar repertory held in contempt by Bloomsbury—now found himself the focus of that coterie's rapture and respect.

The Sitwell siblings lost no time in capitalizing on their prewar connection with Diaghilev, electing themselves unofficial Ballets Russes hosts for all of Bloomsbury. (It was in their home at Swan Walk that Maynard Keynes met his future wife, Lydia Lopokova.) On a rainy night in November they gave a dinner party for Diaghilev and Massine that coincided with the Armistice, much to Osbert's delight. The official end of the war that had seen the slaughter of more than ten million Europeans left everyone overwhelmed with relief and excitement, so they all left Swan Walk to attend another party at the flat of the collector Montague Shearman. Osbert, Diaghilev, and Massine took a taxi around Trafalgar Square, where it seemed that all of London had gathered to participate in a euphoric celebration. At Shearman's they found the "dark flower of Bloomsbury," as Osbert liked to call the set: Virginia Woolf, Roger Fry, Lytton Strachey, Clive Bell, Maynard Keynes, Duncan Grant, David Garnett, D.H. and Frieda Lawrence, Aldous Huxley, Sacheverell Sitwell, Ottoline Morrell, and Lydia Lopokova. It was an important and jubilant occasion, and with Diaghilev alone abstaining, the revelers danced into the next day.[12]

On November 21, *Le Soleil de nuit,* now titled *Midnight Sun,* was premiered; it now included the solo for Lopokova that Massine had added in Lisbon. Wrote Sydney Carrol in the *Sunday Times:* "Emblematic of Pagan Russia—the savage vitality, the crude color and design, the primitive exuberance of this village dance thrill the senses and arrest the mind."[13] With this neoprimitive Russian ballet, Massine scored another success with both press and public. In a letter to his daughter Pamela, Fry described it as "a sort of peasant festival in honor of the Midnight Sun. Dances of peasant women in wonderful dresses with buffoons and village idiot. Then Lopokova is the Snow Maiden and has a most strange and poetical *pas seul* expressing her longing for the Midnight Sun. Massine, Midnight Sun, dark scarlet red and gold with two great golden discs. He rushes backwards and forwards across the stage, while the peasants keep up a ceaseless dance, very complicated and almost chaotic, but very beautiful. . . ."[14]

On December 23 came the London premiere of *Contes russes*, retitled *Children's Tales*, and Massine enjoyed yet another triumph. Some changes had been made. In order to link the three unrelated episodes Massine had made two additions: a prologue for a street vendor carrying puppets representing the characters in each story; and at the end of the Swan Princess episode, a funeral procession for the dragon slain by the knight Bova Korolevich. The finale, according to Grigoriev, also had been modified and improved.[15] *The Times* declared that Massine had "strung together three old Russian legends in a very ingenious way; the grotesque setting is so quaint and so unlike anything that one usually associates with a children's entertainment, the dancing of the whole team is so exhilarating, that one cannot wonder at the enthusiasm which greeted it."[16] There were also alterations to the decor; because some scenery had been destroyed in a fire in South America, Larionov redesigned the backdrop for the Swan Princess scene. Diaghilev also asked his scene painter, Vladimir Polunin, to change the yellow backdrop of the Baba Yaga episode to green (a decision that displeased Larionov). Even so, Fry was so much taken by Larionov's work in *Le Soleil de nuit* and *Contes russes* that in March 1919 he published, in *Burlington Magazine*, two appreciative articles on these designs.

The successful engagement at the Coliseum closed on March 29 with more than seventeen curtain calls. The six-month season had established Massine as a sublime craftsman and a formidable artistic force, which gave his ego a powerful boost. Massine the "star" began to emerge. In his book *The Diaghilev Ballet in London*, Cyril Beaumont describes an incident that clearly demonstrates how absorbed Massine had become in his newly won status. Entering the theater well before curtain time at a gala performance one evening, he noticed that the name of Lopokova, who also had conquered London and whose popularity was enormous, had been printed in larger type than his own. In a display of temperament, Massine promptly locked himself in his dressing room, fell completely silent, and refused to come out. It was not until much later, after Diaghilev and Grigoriev had pleaded and begged, that the choreographer finally emerged—only moments before curtain time—and went on stage.[17]

Massine's artistic maturation and the recognition it brought accelerated his independence from Diaghilev. He relished running his own life, forming friendships with people like Ottoline Morrell and going off alone to visit Duncan Grant's studio on the top floor of a house in Fitzroy Street, where Grant and his circle of friends held forth. These were Massine's first decisive moves toward becoming his own person.

Their Coliseum engagement over, the Ballets Russes performed in April at the Hippodrome in Manchester, then returned to open a second season in London on April 10 at the Alhambra Theatre, which, like the Coliseum, was under the management of Sir Oswald Stoll. Now in a suitable venue, the company could present its customary three-ballet program. As Massine began rehearsals for *La Boutique fantasque* and *Le Tricorne*, London, like Rome in the spring of 1917, became for Ballets Russes a setting for exhilarating creative collaboration. Ansermet came to conduct the Alhambra season, and in May Picasso and André Derain, the French *fauve* painter, arrived to work on the new ballets. Picasso and Olga took up residence at the Savoy, and Derain stayed at 36 Regent Square in a small flat lent to him by Vanessa Bell.

La Boutique fantasque, the first world premiere scheduled for the Alhambra season, was also the first Diaghilev ballet to be created in England. Planning for it had begun in Italy in 1917. Bakst, who then was working with Massine on *Les Femmes de bonne humeur* and who had designed the Legats' *Puppenfee,* was commissioned to design the new ballet. Throughout 1918, Massine and the painter exchanged letters on various aspects of the production.[18] But when Bakst's preliminary sketches reached Diaghilev in London, he was disappointed: for him, the artist's "pre-war style had lost its appeal."[19]

At the end of the Coliseum engagement, Diaghilev asked Massine to meet with Derain in Paris to discuss his possible collaboration on *Boutique fantasque.* In Derain's rue Bonaparte flat, Massine outlined the plot and explained how he and Diaghilev envisioned the toy shop, "something entirely *fantastique* and imaginary."[20] As he described the characters he hummed the music, and Derain, highly excited by the project, boldly proceeded to sketch the four playing cards, the tarantella dancers, and the cancan dancers.

When the news that he had been replaced reached Bakst, he was, of course, terribly hurt. The breach that opened between him and Diaghilev lasted for two years. But Diaghilev was merely obeying his dictum "In the theater there are no friends."[21] Although Massine believed that "it was certainly a ruthless thing to do," he admitted that "it did not surprise me, for I had long ago realized that Diaghilev was ruthless in anything that affected the work of the company. The artistic perfection of his productions was the most important thing in his life and he would allow nothing, not even a longstanding friendship, to stand in the way of it. When an artist was no longer useful to him, he did not hesitate to drop him. At the time I am afraid I did not consider this a defect in his character, but rather an unavoidable aspect of his professionalism."[22]

When rehearsals began in London, most of the choreography for the characters who had emerged from conversations between Massine and Diaghilev had been laid down. In the first of three scenes, the keeper of the toy shop is displaying his goods to his customers, who include three English ladies, an American family, and a Russian family. The windup toys include an Italian couple, who dance a tarantella, a quartet of playing cards (two kings and two queens), a snob, a melon dealer, a group of Cossacks, a pair of poodles, and two cancan dancers. Unfortunately, each family wants to buy only one cancan dancer, separating the loving couple. As the customers leave the shop, the cancan dancers are placed in separate boxes for future delivery. The second scene takes place at night, when the shop is closed. The toys come out of their boxes and trolleys eager for their lives to continue, but they are saddened by the lovers' tragic separation. An escape is planned for the couple, and the scene ends in a spirited mood as all of the remaining toys dance in celebration of their scheme.

When, in the third scene, the families return the following day to pick up their merchandise, they are dismayed to find the boxes empty. Believing that they have been cheated, they attack the shopkeeper and his assistant. The toys, however, come to the rescue of the owner and his helper and make war on the customers, driving them, terrorized, out of the shop. As the shoppers peer through the window from the street, the toys forgive the shopkeeper; then all unite in a joyous grand finale.

The juxtaposition of human beings and toys that come to life only under the right conditions gave Massine the opportunity to assemble an ironic comedy of manners in which the nonhuman characters win the sympathy of the audience. His people are caricatures—the affected, aristocratic English ladies, the crass, nouveau-riche American family and its merchant-class Russian counterpart—but the toys become ever more human and admirable. The grotesque and satirical elements serve as distancing devices to keep all sentimentality out of the plot.

With *La Boutique fantasque* Massine hoped to give ballet a new kind of realism, what he called "naturalistic realism."[23] The poodles' sexual frolicking and antics (such as the male poodle lifting his leg on the American boy) were examples of this. His burlesque treatment of an old theme was a further departure from the conventions of neoromanticism and was regarded by conservative critics as excessive, cause for extreme uneasiness. According to Clive Bell, "*La Boutique* reminds one oddly of the sculpture of Bernini. It skims the edge of vulgarity: Need I say that there is never the least chance of its falling in? M. Massine has chosen to construct his work of art out of the banalities that have haunted the variety stage these sixty years. There are white frills and pink roses and an apotheosis of *la prima ballerina assoluta*: and Madame Lopokova gives the final touch to an unmitigated can-can with an authentic 'split.' No, Massine is not in the least frightened, but he contrives, like an accomplished funambulist, to give his cultivated audience a twinge of fearful joy."[24]

Massine clearly separated the pantomime from the dance passages. Each expressive mode was reserved for one kind of character: melodic mime for the human beings, dance for the toys. For each toy, dance passages and stylized gestures were so narrowly idiosyncratic that even the toy's nationality was recognizable. It was precisely the absence of any superficially human qualities from the toys' movements and gestures that accentuated the internal human qualities with which Massine endowed them. Each character stood out as an individual, so much so that Sokolova felt that "the interpreters of even the smallest parts could flatter themselves that Massine had taken so much trouble to show them off to advantage as if they had been the stars of the ballet."[25]

For the creation of *Boutique,* Massine owed a debt to two major influences. The general pictorial sources can be traced to the paintings of Seurat and Toulouse-Lautrec, the inspiration for the ballet's period atmosphere and style (the male cancan dancer comes directly from Seurat's *Le Cirque*).[26] The ballet's language, its intricate footwork, derives from Massine's recent immersion in Spanish folk dance, especially flamenco. In *Boutique* he invented a new balletic language of the floor, with constant movement transitions of heel-toe-heel and frequent use of stomping. His choreographic effects tend toward self-containment (for which he was indebted to his classical training under Cecchetti), avoiding open and large movements. In the program notes, Diaghilev noted that Massine's "choreographic mind derives chiefly from the Spanish school

... which is what is termed in pictorial art 'miniature.' "[27] Alexandra Danilova, a ballerina who later was to be closely identified with the role of the cancan dancer, remembered: "What made Massine's choreography interesting was its *fantastique* rhythm. The rhythm was all in the feet, the way it is in Spanish dancing, which fascinated him . . . Massine would use heel work . . . His steps came from character dancing: the *farruca,* the *tarantella* . . . always the talking feet."[28]

Rehearsals were in progress, but Massine had yet to devise a finale. He had departed considerably from *Die Puppenfee,* introducing many new characters and imposing upon the work a satiric edge that required a new dénouement. Derain hit upon the solution—the fracas between the toys and the customers.[29] The clash between human and mechanical characters served as a safety valve for the ironic tension, and the image of the ousted customers peering through the shop window provided an object for the work's spirited ridicule and satire.

La Boutique fantasque was Massine's first contribution to a new genre that he himself created: the modern demi-caractère divertissement ballet, in which the dance and mime passages make up an organic whole, and the divertissement is essential in advancing the plot. One of the defining elements of this genre is the "Massine finale," a dramatic expansion of the coda of the traditional classical divertissement. The inner dynamic of Massine's finale is based on escalating tensions, the contrast in mood and tempo as individuals or groups of dancers join the ensemble, one after the other, in ever-increasing numbers, establishing the momentum leading to the climax. But such was Massine's emphasis on characterization that despite their cohesion as a group, the dancers retained their individuality as well as the specific meaning of their movements.

Derain designed a front curtain depicting two figures, a man with a guitar and a dancing woman. The stage decor consisted of a backdrop of arched windows overlooking an exotic bay with foliage and an old, white-wheeled paddle-steamer, and stage wings painted with charts and tables. London audiences lauded the designs and admired Derain's work for its simplicity. Ansermet commended him as "the first painter that I find very much a musician."[30]

The premiere was one of those rare occasions when an audience is completely carried away by its enthusiasm. Indeed, before the curtain had gone up the theater vibrated with the promise of an extraordinary feat. Beaumont had expected a full house but "was not prepared for the enormous audience that had gathered":[31] even the space in the back of the stalls had been taken, and the packed foyer was impossible to navigate. Throughout the performance there was continual applause, which swelled to roars of approval as Lopokova and Massine came on to dance the cancan, whereupon the full house screamed ecstatically: "Massine! Lopokova!" After the finale "the applause was literally deafening. But when the collaborators came forward to call in their turn, Derain was frightened at the warmth of his welcome and had to be dragged on the stage. Massine made repeated graceful bows while Lopokova, half crying, seemed divided between sadness and delight."[32]

London's reception of *La Boutique fantasque* was one of the greatest outpourings of love and acceptance accorded any theatrical event during the years immediately after the war, if not *the* greatest. The ballet won unanimous plaudits from the critics as well as the public and, said *Vogue,* was immediately elevated to the status of a "popular cult."[33] Britain was in need of an antidote to the ravages of war, something to divert its attention, even temporarily, from the depressing social, political, and economic conditions of postwar life. *La Boutique fantasque* fit the bill perfectly, and the public responded with elation. Although "the world was going awry . . . here before our eyes something was enacted which achieved perfection. We could console ourselves that man's powers were not decaying."[34]

As soon as Picasso arrived in London in early May, he vigorously set to work on *Le Tricorne.* Soon the top-floor studio across from the gallery entrance of the opera house (occupied today by offices and the Covent Garden Archives) was his center of operations, with sketches hung at eye level from the ceiling. Meanwhile, Vladimir Polunin and his wife, Elizabeth, busied themselves painting the scenery with their long-handled broom brushes. From the many surviving preliminary sketches one can sense the amount of work Picasso poured into the project. Studying the drawings proved instructive for Massine. He and Picasso held long discussions on the new ballet, and, as before, their talks inevitably came down to crucial aesthetic decisions. One pivotal issue was the recurring question of symmetry versus asymmetry in art. Picasso believed that symmetry was binding and rigid. He directed Massine's attention to his decor for *Le Tricorne,* pointing out that "if I put a house on the right, I do not put a house on the left."[35] From these discussions Massine drew the courage he needed to transform his own choreography; ever afterward he would consciously seek to avoid symmetry in his configurations (though it was not until the 1930s that his work achieved its broadest freedom in movement and spatial formation, when he began to make asymmetry a dominant feature of his symphonic ballets).

Picasso's designs for *Le Tricorne* began with a painted front curtain depicting a bullfighting arena, from which a dead bull is being dragged out by horses. Seated in an arched spectator's box are four women in traditional garb, complete with mantillas, and a man in a scarlet cape. A little boy selling oranges completes the tableau.[36] The arena scene was framed on each side by gray curtains. The front curtain enhanced the theatrical experience in much the same manner as had the curtain Picasso created for *Parade*. Picasso's decor, with very simple lines, in a style that seemed unrelated to cubism, presented a stage landscape in ocher, rose, and salmon. To the right stood the Miller's house, with a porch, a well, and a birdcage. The silhouette of a town could be seen beyond a bridge in the distance. Picasso took Diaghilev's suggestion and enhanced the Miller's home by adding a vine. The costumes were an elaborate collection of traditional regional attire in the spirit of Goya, combining black and gray with a riot of yellows, greens, blues, scarlets, pinks, and mauves.

As in *Parade*, Picasso wanted the front curtain visible during the playing of a prelude. Since Falla's score had none, Diaghilev hastily wrote to him in Madrid, requesting more music and relaying Picasso's idea that Falla use voices in this overture to enhance the emotional impact of the corrida scene.[37] Falla concurred and immediately began working on it.[38]

From Alarcón to Martínez Sierra to Falla—who also made some final additions to the ballet's libretto—the story of *Le Tricorne* had been radically simplified. In Falla's hands the first scene related the story. The second was an allegory that ended with an apotheosis symbolizing the people triumphant over an ineffectual monarchy.

The eighteenth-century tale, which remained the bedrock for Falla's inventions, recounts the intrigues of a miller and his beautiful wife and the attempts of the corregidor (the local governor) to seduce her. And Falla stays with this essential framework. First the Miller and then his Wife are introduced, followed by the Corregidor, who is borne aloft on a sedan chair and is about to make his way, accompanied by his faithful entourage, through the village. The Miller's Wife flirts shamelessly with him, but before the Corregidor can respond, the Miller returns, to the extreme consternation of the Corregidor, who sullenly leaves the scene. With the Governor gone, the Miller and his Wife join their neighbors in a joyous dance.

In the ballet's second part, the Corregidor, determined to seduce the Miller's Wife, arranges to get the Miller out of the way by having him arrested. He then returns to the Wife, who is now alone. They engage in a perilously seductive dance, during which she cleverly manages to send him off the side of the bridge into the mill stream below. She rushes off to find help. The Governor emerges from the stream, removes his wet coat, hangs it out to dry, and lies down to rest upon the bed inside the house.

The Miller returns home, sees his sleeping rival, and dons the Corregidor's coat. As the Miller turns to leave again, he stops and writes upon the wall: "Your wife is no less beautiful than mine."

When the Corregidor wakes to find his coat gone, he puts on the Miller's clothes. As he leaves the house he encounters police officers, who abuse him in the belief that he is the Miller. Villagers congregate, soon becoming an unruly mob. Undeceived by the Corregidor's disguise, the crowd surrounds him and the people take turns beating and berating him. At the finale the villagers, led by the Miller and his Wife, join in a celebration of the Governor's downfall and gleefully dance a mad *jota* as they roll his effigy into a blanket and toss it about.

At the beginning of rehearsals, the role of the Miller's Wife was assigned to Sokolova, with Woizikowski and Massine as the Corregidor and the Miller. Sokolova recalled: "Massine spent hours with me on the stage of the Alhambra in the afternoons, practicing Spanish dancing and working out scenes and numbers we were to do together. We did amazing things with our heads, hands, and arms, and tried out every combination of heel-beats which Massine had taken down from Felix or which he invented. . . . Diaghilev would sit patiently watching us: I think he enjoyed seeing us master the subtle steps."[39] Felix Fernández García, who also attended these rehearsals, "must have thought as he sat there how sadly he had been cheated: for he had taught Massine and the rest of us all we knew about Spanish dancing, and yet he was neither to dance the chief part in the ballet nor to have any credit for his share in the creation. It must have been too much for him to see Léonide, who was not even a Spaniard, dancing what was to all intents and purposes his own *farruca*."[40]

Earlier, in Spain, Massine had been apprehensive about giving the role of the Miller to Felix; now, in London, he had no doubt that Felix was both unsuited to the part and incapable of taking it over. Like most flamenco dancers, Felix was all spontaneity; his dancing was largely improvisational, and it was nearly impossible for him to perform the same step twice in succession. Massine wanted very much to give Felix an opportunity to dance, so he offered him the tarantella in *La Boutique fan-*

tasque.[41] But the result was a disaster. Sokolova recalls: "Massine gave him a metronome to help him learn the dance on time," but instead of being aided by this, Felix would simply "become nervous and hysterical."[42] The tarantella fell to Woizikowski. In another effort to make use of Felix, Massine tried him in the corps de ballet; but the only role in which he did well was the Peddler in *Petrouchka,* which allowed him to improvise as much as he wished.

Soon after the opening night of the Alhambra season, Karsavina joined the company and took over the role of the Miller's Wife in rehearsals of *Le Tricorne.* Although she had not seen Massine since the 1914 London season, when they had danced together in *The Legend of Joseph,* she soon realized that he now was clearly a different person. "I was strongly impressed," she wrote, "by the amazing development of Massine. . . . I found him now no more a timid youth . . . he now possessed accomplished skill as a dancer, and his precocious ripeness and uncommon mastery of the stage singled him out, in my mind, as an exceptional ballet master. It was his complete command of Spanish dancing that amazed me the most. On the Russian stage we had been used to the balletic stylization of Spanish dancing, sugary at its best, but this was the very essence of Spanish folk dancing."[43] Despite her confidence in Massine, though, Karsavina had serious misgivings about undertaking a part that she knew was inappropriate for her: unlike the others, she had not been immersed in Spanish culture. So, to inspire the ballerina, Diaghilev asked Felix to dance for her at the Savoy Hotel. Karsavina recalled the occasion:

> It was fairly late when, after supper, we went downstairs to the ballroom and Felix began. I followed him with open-mouthed admiration, breathless at his outward reserve when I could feel the impetuous, half-savage instincts within him. He needed no begging, and gave us dance after dance. In between, he sang the guttural songs of his country accompanying himself on the guitar. I was completely carried away, forgetful that I was sitting in an ornate hotel ballroom 'til I noticed a whispering group of waiters. It was late, very late. The performance must cease or they would be compelled to put the lights out. They went over to Felix too, but he took not the slightest notice. He was far away. The performance had given me something of the same feeling as listening to the gypsy singers of my own country—savagery and nostalgia. There, no hotel official would come to bring us brusquely back to earth again. To a Russian such a curfew is incomprehensible. A warning flicker and the lights went out. Felix continued

*like one possessed. The rhythm of his steps—now staccato, now lan-
guorous, now almost a whisper, and then again seeming to fill the large
room with thunder—made this unseen performance all the more dramatic.
We listened to the dancing enthralled.*[44]

The endless frenetic dancing at the Savoy was only the latest sign of
Felix's disturbed mental state. His behavior, erratic enough before this
episode, had marked him among the members of the company as an eccentric. But this evening and the dramatic events that followed made it
clear that whatever gave Felix his tenuous hold on sanity was rapidly de-
serting him altogether. About his final descent into madness, Sokolova
wrote:

*It cannot have been more than two or three days after Felix had danced at
the Savoy—and it may have been the very next morning—that his behavior at rehearsal became stranger than ever. We were working in the club
room in Shaftesbury Avenue, where the men had to dress behind a sort of
bar or cloakroom counter. Felix began to pop his head up from behind the
counter, wearing different hats and making faces. This was quite funny at
first, and we all laughed, but he would not stop. Grigoriev tried to control
him without success, and as Felix kept on and on, appearing and disap-
pearing in a variety of hats, one could feel a wave of concern go around
the room. At lunch time he went off, with his metronome ticking. Leon
Woidzikovsky followed him to the Hotel Dieppe in Old Compton Street,
where he was staying, and found him lunching in his room—he was not
allowed to have meals in the restaurant, as he behaved strangely and upset
people. Felix was eating to the rhythm of the ticking metronome, stopping
now and again to adjust it to a different speed. Leon could get no sense out
of him and went away.*

*That night, when Felix should have been on stage he was discovered in
the men's dressing room, his face spotted with a mixture of grease paints,
grimacing at himself in the mirror. Nothing could be done about this while
the performance was in progress, and by the time the ballet was over he
was nowhere to be found. He did not return to his hotel, and his disappearance was reported. Later that night he was found doing a demented
dance on the altar steps of a South London Church.*[45]

Felix was certified insane and taken to a mental asylum at Epsom,
where he remained until his death in 1941. Massine wondered if "the seed
of his mental illness was not inherent to his genius."[46] Reluctantly, one

wonders too if Felix was something of a sacrificial lamb in the creation of Massine's Spanish masterpiece.

As Massine put the finishing touches on his choreography, Picasso was also readying his second work for the stage. The Polunins found it a pleasure to work with him, for not only did he visit the studio daily to supervise the creation of his maquettes, he also took an active interest in the completion of the entire work. Picasso painted directly onto the decor the silhouette of the town in the distance and the seven stars in the sky, and as the Polunins prepared the colors and assisted him in other ways, he painted most of the corrida scene on the front curtain. To Vladimir Polunin, who had reproduced Bakst's elaborate designs, Picasso's decor was amazing in "its total absence of unnecessary detail; the composition and unity of coloring was astounding. It was just as if one had spent a long time in a hot room and then passed into the fresh air." [47]

Diaghilev's lighting design for the mise-en-scène graduated downward from a bright bleached quality for the first part of the ballet to, near the close, almost pitch darkness (with a hopeful dawn at the very end). According to Falla, the progression of the choreographic action and the orchestration was directly inverse to this lighting scheme; that is, in the first part the number of dancers was kept to a minimum in order to keep the focus on the principal characters, and the orchestra was limited by Falla to the size of "a chamber orchestra. Later, on the contrary, from the beginning of the second part the choreographic and orchestral elements gradually increase to culminate in the final dance." [48] Thus in the ballet's first part, which revolved around the personal conflict of the leading characters, the music was intimate, while in the allegorical second part it was more grandiose. According to Polunin, Diaghilev's gradations of lighting, from day to night and night to dawn, were quite effective: "The scene, owing to the presence of some soft reddish tints, acquired the aspect of a Japanese print which, so far from impairing its beauty, endowed it with a certain unexpected charm." [49] For Beaumont, "the disturbing brilliance of the day, and the cool, tender night pervaded the auditorium." [50]

The first performance of *Le Tricorne* was scheduled for July 22. Falla reached London several days in advance, but hours before he was to conduct the premiere he received a cable saying that his mother was critically ill. The company was very supportive, and Ansermet accompanied his friend to the station and saw him off. Sad to say, Falla never saw his mother alive again, for she died that very day. Ansermet conducted the premiere in his stead.

That night at the Alhambra Theater, as the stage was being readied for *Le Tricorne,* Picasso himself applied greasepaint to the faces of the policemen with a "mass of blue, green and yellow dots which under the stage lighting, gave . . . a pockmarked, ruffianly appearance."[51] He gave Woizikowski, the Governor, a most effective makeup, matched-up "dabs of the same blue which was used in the costumes of his bodyguard of policemen."[52] When the stage curtains parted to reveal Picasso's corrida scene, and Falla's vibrating rhythms were heard, shouts of "Olé!," the tapping of heels, and the click of castanets filled the theater. The evening's tone was set, its charged atmosphere established, and the delighted house roared its approval. When the final curtain came down on the *jota,* the entire audience was caught up in a sense of enchantment. The *Sunday Times* summed up the new work's artistic relevance: "In conception and workmanship it rivals all other stories of Russia, Italy, France, and the Orient, told with such splendor, colors and audacity in poetic movement."[53]

However, Picasso's constructionlike dresses and the grotesque colored makeup he employed to dehumanize the minor characters were most disturbing to some critics. For W. A. Propert, the moment the secondary characters entered, "one began to feel less at ease. The beauty began to fade with the insistence of those noisy dresses, dresses that never seemed to move with the wearers or assume the changing curves of their bodies, that looked as if they were cut in cardboard, harshly striped and rayed, with all their contours heavily outlined in black."[54]

In its final form, Alarcón's story line, with its sociopolitical satire and regional localization, was of secondary importance to the creators of *Le Tricorne.* The tale gave the ballet its narrative structure, but it was essentially an excuse for Falla, Picasso, and Massine to present a personal artistic expression of their feelings for Spain, its folklore, temperament, and way of life. Ethnic popular sources were vital to modernist artists, especially those from Spain and Russia, who found in folklore a strong source of inspiration. However, the goal of modernism was not to reproduce folklore but to take it as a point of departure, to stylize it while purging it of banality, and subject it to a process of purification to get closer to its essence. Falla, one of the greatest folklorists of his time, adhered to this principle completely, utilizing popular thematic sources only as a source of inspiration.

For Picasso, *Le Tricorne* occurred during an important transitional moment in his development, bringing about a fusion of predominant elements from his previous creative phase: cubism and his omnipresent concern for the concepts of space and perspective. If the front curtain and the characters of the acrobats in *Parade* already had hinted at a tendency toward a classically oriented aesthetic, then *Le Tricorne* signaled the neoclassical style that came to the fore soon after. As Marilyn Mc-Cully has stated, *"Le Tricorne* is a prime example of the synthesis of styles Picasso achieved at this time, and it was, perhaps more than any other, the project that helped him attain this synthesis."[55]

The lengthy period of collaboration and friendship between Falla and Picasso strongly influenced the young Massine. (He was twenty-four when *Le Tricorne* was premiered.) The choreographer already had been exposed to "ethnic modernism" through his association with the neo-primitivist/cubo-futurist Gontcharova and Larionov. Throughout the three-year apprenticeship that culminated in *Le Tricorne* he was able to extend ethnic modernism into its fullest choreographic possibilities.

Massine's work on *Le Tricorne* had been long and arduous, but the result was unquestionably gratifying. He saw in Karsavina's "virtuoso performance" all the "zest and sensuality of a Spaniard," and found that the "languorous, seductive movements of her first entrance quickly established the character of the Miller's bored, dissatisfied wife. . . ."[56] The choreographer also declared Woizikowski as the Corregidor a "wonderful grotesque character, all trembling lust and licentious leers."[57] Yet the personal high point of the ballet for Massine was the *farruca* he danced:

> *I began by stamping my feet repeatedly and twirling my hands over my head. As the music quickened I did a series of high jumps, ending with a turn in mid-air and a savage stamp of the foot as I landed. Throughout the dance my movements were slow and contorted, and to the style and rhythm which I had learned from Felix I added many twisted and broken gestures of my own. I felt instinctively that something more than perfect technique was needed here, but it was not until I had worked myself up in a frenzy that I was able to transcend my usual limitations. The mental image of an enraged bull going in to the attack unleashed some inner force which generated power within me. I felt an almost electrical interaction between myself and the spectators. Their mounting excitement had the effect of heightening my physical strength until I was dancing with a sustained force that seemed far beyond my reach at other times. For one moment it seemed as if some other person within me was performing the dance.*[58]

Beaumont was convinced that "few of those who saw the first night will have forgotten the color and bravura with which he invested his

The Miller in Le Tricorne, *in the early 1950s*

farruca, the slow snap of the fingers followed by the pulsating thump of his feet, then the flickering movement of his hands held horizontally before him, palms facing and almost touching his breast. All at once this gave place to a new movement in which his feet chopped the ground faster and faster until suddenly he dropped to the ground on his hands, and quickly leapt to his feet and stopped dead, his efforts greeted with thunderous applause."[59] The *farruca* invariably drove audiences into a delirious frenzy. Massine's charismatic stage presence, his ability to enthrall his audience, triumphed. Even motionless, he could marshal a degree of expressiveness that left the audience spellbound.

Le Tricorne is particularly noteworthy for its synthesis of classical movement with the basic styles of Spanish folk dance. Massine skillfully assimilated into his own personal idiom the *farruca*, the fandango, the *sevillana*, and the *jota*, without sacrificing their individual characteristics. Moreover, he used the internal dynamics of Spanish dancing, specifically that tantalizing quality of increasing-decreasing speed, "pursuit of tension, teasing, advancing and retreating,"[60] to establish a mood. He wrote: "*Le Tricorne* had begun as an attempt to synthesize Spanish folk-dancing with classical techniques, but in the process of evolution it emerged as a choreographic interpretation of the Spanish temperament and way of life."[61] Massine had created yet another genre: the modern folk-character ballet.

In homage to Goya, the three *Tricorne* collaborators devised the climactic *jota*, in which the whole ensemble joined to form a magical fresco in movement. Falla's musical inspiration had come from a 1917 visit with the painter Ignacio Zuloaga to Fuendetodos, Goya's native town; Picasso's costume designs sprang from Goya's art and style; and Massine borrowed the tossing of the effigy from his *El pelele*.

Boutique and *Tricorne* had made it apparent to most observers that Massine commanded an impressive range of talent. In a brief career, he had produced ballets on Russian and Spanish themes and had articulated styles that went from commedia dell'arte to the satiric comedy of manners to modernism. He had done wholly narrative ballets and ballets with no story line. And with each work he had enriched and extended his choreographic language. On the personal level, his exploration of new possibilities and his ever-vigilant struggle against repetition had grown out of his ideal of self-perfection. In a short three years, a new page had been turned in ballet history. Writing in *The New Republic* at the end of the Alhambra engagement, Clive Bell compared the "old" and the "new" ballet and concluded that Massine possessed "a creative genius and therefore an authority, which has carried the ballet to a degree of seriousness and artistic importance of which Nijinsky can scarcely have dreamt. It is extraordinary how thin and essentially unimportant the ballets of six years ago seem."[62] In Bell's estimation, only Fokine's *Petrouchka* held its own, yet even that,

> *under the Massine influence . . . is something distinctly different from and superior to the* Petrouchka *of M. Fokine. M. Massine has emptied the puppets of their superfluous humanity, and the protagonists (when Madame Lopokova dances) are more doll-like than dolls, and the ballet, by becoming less theatrical, has become more of a work of art, and infinitely more dramatic . . . [Massine's] greatest achievement has been to rescue the ballet from "the stage"—I use the word in the commonest and most disobliging sense—putting it on the level of literature, music and the graphic arts. His idea of the ballet is an organized whole, detached from circumstance, and significant in itself. . . . The fact is, with his creative imagination and positive intelligence, M. Massine has realized the dream which Mr. Gordon Craig half dreamt, fumbled, dreamt again differently, and never came near realizing. He has given us "an art of the theater."[63]*

Of Massine's many innovations, perhaps the most daring was a new kind of characterization. He sought to transfer the center of gravity from the audience to the work itself: the life of each character was to be understood from the interaction of all the characters and their theatrical reality rather than in direct presentation to the audience. Bell compared Karsavina, the embodiment of pre-Massine interpretive technique, with Lopokova, who embodied the new kind of dancer. Karsavina "communicates her gracious and attractive personality directly to the audience . . . ; when not preoccupied with purely technical subtleties, she is apt to express herself, not through the work of art she is interpreting, but immediately, as in conversation. There is complicity between her and the audience."[64] But Lopokova was likened to Mozart or Fra Angelico: "The point is that neither Mozart nor Fra Angelico, nor Lopokova, express themselves directly to the public. They transmute personality into something more precious. The public gets no raw material from them. They pour themselves into works of art from which the public might deduce what it can." Bell continued:

> *Since to be a work of art, the ballet must have the detachment of a picture or a symphony, the mimes, it seems, should go through their motions as in*

an imaginary screen between themselves and the rest of the world. They have relations with each other, with the music and the scenery, and with nothing else. They may be personal as they please on their own side of the curtain. It is because she sometimes crosses to ours that Madame Karsavina is not perfectly in key with the new ballet: whereas little Lopokova, bouncing in her box, making vivid contacts with every line and color on the stage, impressing her personality on each gesture of her own, and so helping to build up an organic whole, is the choreographer's first violin. In the difference between Madame Karsavina and Madame Lopokova is epitomized the essential differences between the old and the new ballet.[65]

Massine himself proved to be the quintessential actor-dancer, and London's cognoscenti paused to admire. T. S. Eliot wrote: "Massine . . . seems to me the greatest actor whom we have in London. Massine, the most completely unhuman, impersonal, abstract, belongs to the future stage." The poet felt that next to the "conventional gesture of the ordinary stage which is supposed to *express* emotion . . . the abstract gesture of Massine, which *symbolizes* emotion, is enormous." Massine's interpretations bore out Eliot's contention that emotion in art must be transmitted through physical images analogous to the emotion—what he came to call the objective correlative. Such images should derive not precisely from nature but from life experiences. In a similar vein, "the art of every actor is in relation to his own age, and would perhaps be unintelligible to any other. But as the age is not an instant, but an infinite span of time including part of the future, we can still, with our retrospective selves, appreciate such artistry as that of Bernhardt, though we move toward satisfaction in the direction which moves Léonide Massine."[66]

In Ouchy and San Sebastián, where Massine produced *Le Soleil de nuit*, *Kikimora*, and *Las Meninas*, he served his choreographic apprenticeship. Rome, where he fashioned *Les Femmes de bonne humeur*, *Contes russes*, and *Parade*, was the site of his initiation into the ranks of his profession. Then came the Alhambra season in London, where the creation of *La Boutique fantasque* and *Le Tricorne* led to his consecration as a hero in a new balletic age. He was bombarded with rave reviews and flurries of congratulatory letters and cables; he was inundated with invitations, adulation, recognition, and respect. He was sought after by both high society and the intelligentsia. Massine left London in August 1919 haloed in his own light and the light of no other. He was no longer a planet in the solar system of Serge Pavlovich Diaghilev.

London, 1920

CHAPTER 8

London, August 1919–Rome, February 1921

AFTER THE ALHAMBRA SEASON ended on July 30, Diaghilev and Massine left London for Paris, then proceeded on to their beloved Italy. Most of their vacation would be spent at the Lido in Venice and in Naples. In a familiar pattern, they spent their holiday preparing new works. This time a ballet based on the character of Pulcinella began to germinate.

But Italy also put Massine in a reflective mood. "I began," he recalls, "to think seriously about the work I had been doing since 1917, and although I felt I had made great advances in technique, I was far from satisfied with what I had accomplished. Now that I had thoroughly absorbed the theories of Blasis, Feuillet and Rameau, I realized that mere mastery of their notations would not help me to go beyond the so-called 'technical regime' of the classical tradition. In fact, I began to see that their work, if followed too closely, could limit the scope of my choreographic evolution."[1]

His personal life was not all he wanted it to be, either. After six years of a nomadic existence he yearned for the privacy of his own retreat, a home base. The Isole dei Galli beckoned again, and on this Neapolitan excursion Massine moved his dream of ownership a little closer to reality.

In Naples he and Diaghilev renewed ties with their friend Mikhail Semenov, whom they had last seen in 1917. That year, shortly after the exhibition of his art collection at the Teatro Costanzi in Rome, Massine had left the collection in Semenov's care. He also had authorized him to act in his behalf in securing the purchase of the Isole dei Galli. Unfortunately, the "negotiations had been prolonged because the numerous members of the Parlato family could not decide among themselves how much they wanted for [the property]."[2] Those negotiations were still going forward while Massine, on this present excursion to Italy, stopped to see the Semenovs in Positano and to take "another delightful trip to Galli." He became more committed than ever "to buy them, and hoped one day to go and live there."[3]

In September Massine and Diaghilev left Italy and returned to Paris to begin work on *Pulcinella*. Fragments from his past were coming together to make the subject appealing to him now. On his first visit to Italy in 1914 he had become fascinated by the commedia dell'arte. In 1917 he had been charmed by commedia dell'arte street performers in Naples; and that same year, while researching the genre for *Les Femmes de bonne humeur,* he had come across a manuscript, circa 1700, entitled *Les Quatre Polichinelles semblables.* He was beginning to see how a ballet based on Pulcinella might work.[4]

But *Pulcinella* remained in embryonic form in 1917. Preparations for producing it began only after Diaghilev's return to London from Spain in 1918. That year he obtained from the British Museum a sheaf of pieces then attributed to Pergolesi which he hoped to consider for the score. By September, at Diaghilev's direction, the musicologist E. van der Straeten had worked into a score selected movements from several of the sonatas for violin and bass (which are no longer thought to be by Pergolesi). Still more music came from the Bibliothèque Nationale in Paris, and the richest lode of all was found in Professor Ricci's Casa Musicale, a commercial outlet where copies of musical compositions from the Conservatorio di Musica in Naples were sold.[5] Diaghilev probably offered Picasso the commission to design *Pulcinella* in 1919, while the painter was in London working on *Le Tricorne*. In a June 10 letter to Stravinsky written in London, the conductor Ansermet mentions a projected "Pergolesi-Picasso" ballet.[6]

Ideas for *Pulcinella* kept blossoming. In Naples in 1919 Massine continued his research on the commedia dell'arte at the Royal Palace Library. Meanwhile, at the Conservatorio di S. Pietro a Mailla, Diaghilev found yet another collection of compositions by Pergolesi; on the strength of a preliminary selection from these he would later commission Stravinsky to orchestrate the ballet score. In *Expositions and Developments* Robert Craft quotes Stravinsky recalling that "the suggestion that was to lead to *Pulcinella* came from Diaghilev one spring afternoon while we were walking together in the Place de la Concorde: . . . 'I have an idea that I think will amuse you . . . I want you to look at some delightful eighteenth-century music with the idea of orchestrating it for a ballet.' When he said that the composer was Pergolesi, I thought he must be deranged. . . . I wasn't in the least excited by it. I did promise to look, however, and to give him my opinion. I looked, and I fell in love."[7] (Stravinsky errs in placing this conversation in the spring. It was in September, and before the month was out he was conferring with Diaghilev, Massine, and Picasso about the new ballet.)[8]

In truth, in the spring of 1919 relations between the impresario and the composer had been stormy. Between May and July they had quarreled bitterly through intermediaries over the royalties from *Firebird* and *Petrouchka*. And such bickering was not new. Their relationship in and out of the theater had always been plagued by feuds over money and over Stravinsky's loyalty to the Ballets Russes—and to Diaghilev. The staging of any Stravinsky work outside the Ballets Russes inevitably provoked Diaghilev's jealousy and possessiveness, especially when such efforts were successful, as the recent production of *L'Histoire du soldat* in Switzerland had been. Now, however, the complainant was Stravinsky, who accused Diaghilev of robbing him and threatened a lawsuit. Ansermet and Misia were called in to mediate the dispute, and the matter was settled just before Diaghilev and Massine left for their vacation at the end of July. Diaghilev may have still felt sour over the incident, though, since he deliberately avoided seeing the composer that August as he journeyed from Paris to Italy.[9]

Happily, a correspondence between Diaghilev and Stravinsky was resumed that same month, and by September all of the collaborators had arrived in Paris to begin working on *Pulcinella*. By then Stravinsky saw that "the proposal that I should work with Picasso, who was to do the scenery and costumes and whose art was particularly near and dear to me, recollections of our walks together and the impressions of Naples we had shared [in the spring of 1917], the great pleasure I had experienced from Massine's choreography in *The Good Humoured Ladies*—all this combined to overcome my reluctance."[10] He composed the tarantella between September 7 and 10; on the eighth Picasso gave him an inscribed drawing of two figures for the ballet. Diaghilev, Stravinsky, and Massine worked on the libretto and finished it in October.

Pulcinella was not the only ballet that Diaghilev hoped to mount in 1920 with Stravinsky's help. During their reunion in Paris, Diaghilev once again turned his attention to *Le Chant du rossignol*, which he had hoped to stage in Rome back in 1917. At that time, he had commissioned the futurist artist Fortunato Depero to create the scenery and costumes, but now Diaghilev much preferred to work with Henri Matisse.

Ever since his first collaboration, in 1917, with the painters of the school of Paris, Diaghilev repeatedly had tried to enlist Matisse for a Ballets Russes project. In September of 1919 the painter was at his residence in Issy-les-Moulineaux, on the outskirts of Paris, when Diaghilev and Stravinsky arrived unannounced one morning. Stravinsky played the piano score of *Rossignol* for Matisse, who responded with some ideas about decor and costumes.[11] The visitors tried to persuade Matisse to design the ballet, but he refused. As the days went by, however, his ideas continued to ferment; and when Diaghilev approached him again, he easily gave in.

With the collaboration of Stravinsky, Picasso, and Matisse assured, Diaghilev and Massine returned to London. The third ballet season had begun on September 20 at the Empire Theatre. Since the English premiere of *Parade* was the only novelty scheduled during the twelve-week engagement, Massine was able to devote himself to the new ballets. In October Diaghilev invited Matisse to come to London for a day, as an adviser.[12] Matisse's sojourn at the Savoy Hotel had been beautifully—cunningly—prepared for by Diaghilev, who immediately asked Matisse to remain in London not for twenty-four hours but for fifteen days, to supervise the execution of his designs. This opportunity tantalized Matisse, though he was hesitant about neglecting his other work in Paris. Diaghilev prevailed. Matisse would in fact remain in London for more than a month. Toward the end of his stay he was also persuaded by Diaghilev to design the ballet's front curtain.[13]

Matisse and Massine began to sketch out their conception of the ballet, agreeing that the overall look should be achieved through the precise allocation of color as on a canvas. "Those colors were the costumes," said Matisse years later. "The deployment of colors allows the decor's expression to remain the same. It is imperative that a great expression dominates the colors in order to create an ensemble without demolishing the harmony in the rest of the work."[14] In attaining this shared goal, Matisse admitted that he was aided by Massine, who understood what he was trying to achieve.[15] (Five years later, Matisse was terribly disappointed by Balanchine's revised version of the ballet, feeling that the original work had been turned into "a real candy jar.")[16]

During one of their Sunday outings, Matisse, Diaghilev, and Massine paid a visit to Felix Fernández García, whom Massine would continue to visit at the asylum until the outbreak of war in 1939.[17]

Matisse and Massine became fast friends during their collaboration in London. In subsequent years, during engagements in Monte Carlo, Massine made regular Sunday calls on the painter at his home in Nice. Matisse described these visits as the dancer's "Sunday recreation because the rest of the week was very hard on Massine."[18] In his autobiography Massine writes that in Matisse's flat in Nice "one of the best rooms was occupied by a giant bird cage. He had hundreds of exotic birds from all over the world, and was so proud of them that he carried about an official document testifying to the vocal range of his favorite nightingale."[19]* But after Le Chant, twenty years would pass before the two would collaborate again.

On December 20, 1919, the Ballets Russes completed its season at the Empire, then moved on to the Paris Opéra, where the season was to be divided into two engagements. The first would begin on December 24 and feature, on January 23, 1920, the French premieres of Le Tricorne and La Boutique fantasque, followed on February 2 by the world premiere of Le Chant du rossignol. The second engagement, slated to begin on May 8, would include the world premieres of Pulcinella on May 15 and Le astuzie femminili on May 27. During the early days of the run Massine prepared for the premiere of Le Chant while, at the atelier of the famous couturier Paul Poiret, Matisse supervised the building of the Emperor's sumptuous cape.[20]

Le Chant du rossignol, which was based on a story by Hans Christian

---

* Massine's recollection of seeing the painter's birds in his flat in Nice may actually come from later visits, for according to Matisse he had not yet acquired them at the time of the creation of Le Chant du rossignol.

Andersen, was highly praised by the French press. Louis Laloy wrote in *Comoedia:*

> *The most remarkable aspect of this version is the composition of the ensembles. M. Massine is not only a ballet master who choreographs steps and formations, he is a painter who executed a series of moving tableaux in space. M. Henri Matisse has furnished decors of elegant simplicity and costumes whose brilliant colors lend themselves to the most divine combinations. M. Massine is thus able to exercise his inspiration without directly copying the style of the Orient; instead he can imply the most daring essence of the style.*[21]

Massine's choreography depended on groupings that suggested sculpted images like those seen in Chinese porcelain, paintings, and screens. Sokolova found these groupings "ingenious": "They built themselves up into flat friezes, rather in the way that acrobats do, but their bodies were packed tight and knitted close together, some men on one leg, some upside down resting on a bent arm, some in a kind of hand stand. These groups suggested to me the grotesque combinations of figures on carved ivory boxes, and I wondered if it was from these that Massine had taken them."[22]

Massine's groupings, in static, pyramid-like configurations, enhanced the theatrical space. The close collaboration between choreographer and designer was felt throughout the ballet:

> *One of Matisse's concerns in designing* Le Chant du Rossignol *was the manner in which individual costumes could be made to interact and combine. The sculptural poses and ensemble movement of the uniformly clad corps de ballet allowed the artist to think in terms of volumetrical modeling. Matisse designed geometrically cut costumes for the Mourners and Mandarins that deliberately masked the curves of the body, thereby transforming the dancers into building blocks of Massine's accumulative architectonic structures. When the costumes were isolated and placed in movement by the figures inside, they became part of an overall fluctuating pattern of stylized shape and color. The Mourners' all-encompassing white felt cloaks and hoods, appliquéd with midnight blue velvet chevrons and triangles, converted the dancer's figure into a planar surface—an abstract shape—as did the saffron yellow satin robes of the Mandarins. In scene two, matching his choreography to the spare design, Massine caused these alternately shimmering and absorbent surfaces to move "silently be-*

*fore the pale background . . . like spirits passing at dawn . . . [as] the pale
hand of Death was outstretched over [all]."*[23]

The London critics, who first saw the ballet in July 1920, were not as
enthusiastic about these innovations as the French press had been. *The
Times* commented that although the dance of the Nightingale was "brilliantly designed and carried out," in it there was "something wrong between the dance and the music. It halts and wavers. . . ."[24] Ernest
Newman of the *Sunday Times* declared that since the music was "mostly
without rhythm, it has baffled even the genius of Massine to invent a satisfactory"[25] choreography for it. However, the *Daily Herald* admired the
production for its theatrical ingenuity. "There are no big dancing opportunities but it is full of quaint devices, of curious and unexpected effects,
and consistently remains a fairy tale. It is a fairy tale such as one would
never have dared to see in the flesh. Who could have thought they would
have lived to see the Emperor really walking on the backs of his
courtiers—or, death defeated, see his funeral robes turn magically to an
indescribable magnificence?"[26]

As the Paris Opéra engagement continued, Diaghilev and Picasso
began an intense struggle over *Pulcinella*. Picasso's first thought was to
move the setting to modern times, a notion that Diaghilev immediately
rejected. The painter then produced preliminary sketches of a false
proscenium framed by tiers of theater boxes, with a nocturnal Neapolitan scene at stage center. These, too, were turned down. According to
Douglas Cooper, this particular design was probably inspired by the
Teatro San Carlo in Naples. Cooper speculates that "the baroque
tradition was probably considered too grand for the occasion, but it
shows that from the start Picasso wanted to underline the artificiality
of the action, its puppet show element, for the dancers would have to
perform in the middle of the false theatre and in front of the inner
stage."[27]

Picasso next offered a group of designs transposing the idea of a
theater-within-a-theater to the Paris of the Second Empire. Diaghilev exploded in fury. Stravinsky writes that the "designs were Offenbach-period
costumes with side-whiskered faces instead of masks. When he [saw]
them, Diaghilev was very brusque: 'Oh, this isn't it at all,' and proceeded
to tell Picasso how to do it. The evening concluded with Diaghilev actually throwing the drawings on the floor, stamping on them and slam-
ming the door."[28]

Picasso submitted yet another version of the stage-within-a-stage before he produced his final decor, which consisted simply of three panels depicting a Neapolitan night scene. Between two houses a little street stretches away and disappears into a background where a solitary boat sits in the bay and a radiant moon hangs over Mount Vesuvius. Cyril Beaumont described it as a "cubist study in black, blue-grey and white, admirably conveying with a remarkable economy of means a moonlit street overlooking the Bay of Naples."[29] The stage was covered with a floor cloth whose surface was freshly painted white for each performance. As with *Le Tricorne*, Picasso's palette of soft colors for the decor contrasted with the traditional commedia dell'arte costumes of bright red, green, plum, rose, white, and black.

Since his arrival in Paris, Stravinsky had been drawn into the

> *frequent disputes which ended up in pretty stormy scenes. . . . Sometimes my orchestration proved a disappointment. Massine was composing his choreography to the piano reduction, which I was sending to him section by section as I made it from the orchestral score. It often happened that when I was shown certain steps and movements that had already been decided upon I saw to my horror that in their character and importance they in no way corresponded to the very modest volume of my little chamber orchestra. . . . The choreography had, therefore, to be altered and adapted to the volume of my music, and that caused them no little annoyance, though they realized that there was no other solution.*[30]

The completed *Pulcinella* was remarkable in its modernist juxtaposition of traditional and new elements. Stravinsky reinterpreted eighteenth-century melodies in his own musical idiom; Picasso's cubist decor stood in contrast to his traditional commedia dell'arte costumes; and Massine once more expanded his choreographic language by fusing Neapolitan folk dances and commedia dell'arte gesticulation with the academic balletic vocabulary.

Before the second Paris Opéra engagement in May, the Ballets Russes presented seasons in Rome, Milan, and Monte Carlo. During this period Diaghilev and Massine embarked on *Le astuzie femminili*. Diaghilev's avid pursuit of eighteenth-century Italian music had netted him the scores for *Les Femmes* and *Pulcinella,* and now, hoping for a third such success, he was eager to begin work on Domenico Cimarosa's opera. *Astuzie* was composed after Cimarosa's three-year residency in St. Petersburg, where in 1798 he had replaced Paisiello as director of the Italian Theater. The plot concerns a rich heiress who, refusing to wed her

Lubov Tchernicheva, Massine, and Vera Nemtchinova rehearsing Pulcinella, *1920*

guardian or the man her father chose for her before his death, in the end manages secretly to marry the man she loves. Diaghilev commissioned Ottorino Respighi to arrange the music and José María Sert to design the costumes. Massine would direct the movements of the singers in the opera—the first two scenes—and choreograph the ballet which was the work's third and final scene.

In Rome, rehearsals for *Le astuzie* were marked by the first violent creative disagreement between Diaghilev and Massine. "For the last scene," writes Massine, "which was supposed to be a performance of *'Ballo Russo,'* I devised a series of short divertissements. . . . When Diaghilev came to a rehearsal and saw what I was doing, he objected strongly. He said that the divertissements were entirely unnecessary and wanted to dispense with them. I, on the other hand, insisted that a suite of dances was entirely in keeping with the pervading eighteenth-century style of production. This led to a heated argument, but I finally persuaded Diaghilev to let me have my way. . . ."[31] According to Grigoriev, Diaghilev "wanted a connected suite of dances. Their arguments were interminable, but Massine held out. . . . They had, of course, argued before on points of detail. But hitherto Massine had always yielded to Diaghilev's reasoning. So this was a new departure; and whether or not it signified a rebellion on Massine's part, whether or not he had decided to assert himself, it marked in fact the opening of a rift between them, which was to widen as time went on."[32] In other words, Massine, knowing full well that Diaghilev was rigidly uncompromising toward the aesthetic convictions of others, signaled his determination to press new claims both for his own artistic territory and for personal autonomy. His surprising readiness for confrontation must have shaken the impresario. Unaccustomed to having his will thwarted, the man who brooked no disagreement gave in. Why? Was it because he could, or because he could not, see that Massine was after his freedom?

The tremendous success of the postwar London and Paris seasons secured the company's immediate continuity as well as Massine's reputation. To Diaghilev, his protégé's triumph was undoubtedly a source of deep satisfaction. He had sensed Massine's potential, advanced his education, nurtured him, and surrounded him with some of the most prestigious and innovative artists of the era. Indeed, Massine was Diaghilev's greatest creation—a young man made of uncommonly rich clay, which Diaghilev modeled largely for the realization of his own needs. But the mentor-pupil relationship was nearing a crisis, and their remaining months together would be an emotional and professional tug-of-war.

More than fifty years later, Massine regarded the *Astuzie* confrontation with Diaghilev as the "false daring of a young man who is convinced that he is right. The false authority due to age and immaturity."[33] But by then, of course, Diaghilev already had become for Massine an idealized figure, infallible and larger than life.

When the Rome and Milan engagements concluded, the Ballets Russes appeared in Monte Carlo for the first time since the war. From the principality they proceeded to Paris, where they arrived after an unexpected delay:

> On the day we were due to leave Monte Carlo for Paris a railway strike started. Diaghilev was in despair, for our engagement in Paris was scheduled to begin in four days time. Fortunately, at the last minute we heard that there was one train leaving Monte Carlo with four sleepers, enough for Diaghilev, Karsavina, Matisse and myself. Early next morning, as we were speeding toward Paris, I was suddenly aware of a violent jolting, and a heavy ashtray hit me on the nose. The train had been derailed, and turned over on its side. . . . When I climbed out of the carriage I found Diaghilev

and Karsavina a bit shaken, but not injured. Matisse too had emerged safely, and as we all stood there in dazed bewilderment one of the passengers took a photograph of us. We were at a small place called Bar le Duc, about three hours from Paris, and we heard afterwards that a group of strikers had deliberately cut through the railway line. I can still remember standing there in the cold morning air, staring in amazement at the smashed locomotive with the rails jutting up like a broken iron fence.[34]

The four travelers were driven to Paris.

At the Paris Opéra, the premiere of *Pulcinella* on May 15, 1920, marked another triumph for Massine. André Levinson reported:

Just as Stravinsky in the enchanting score has confined the gushing melodies that might be by Pergolesi within a sarcastic harmonic scheme, where the trombone utters insolent persiflage and the bassoon hiccoughs asthmatically, so Massine has used the technique of classic virtuosity in an ironic sense. He treats the great "temps d'école" (like the double turns in the air, the caper or that brilliant ornament the "fouetté") as so many comic themes, expressing the exuberance and mannerisms of cavaliers costumed by Picasso. The "classic" is no longer the grand style, abstract and synthetic. It is used purposely to create character in the same way that the czardas, the bolero and the jig were used in the classic Coppélia. *Only now the roles are reversed. In* Pulcinella *the traditional steps are used to stylize the pantomime.*[35]

When the ballet was premiered in London on June 10, it was warmly received by the British press. Richard Capell wrote in the *Daily Mail:* "It is a comic view of the human puppet show. It looks through the spectacles of the eighteenth century's dry fun and crackling wit."[36] *The Observer* wrote that "the lapses from Italian melodious purity into unadulterated Stravinsky do not jar, as Massine's wonderful choreography follows the changes with such understanding that the dancers—the perfect ensemble—seem to take the lead, and the orchestra merely to follow their spontaneous movements."[37] For Cyril Beaumont:

The whole production was dominated by Massine as Pulcinella, for which character he had invented all manner of grotesque steps, obviously inspired by a careful study of the many pictorial representations of the Mask in question. Massine's dancing was particularly interesting for the way in which he caused certain steps to be expressive in themselves. Remember,

*too, that his features were almost hidden by his bird-like mask. Yet it was
extraordinary to observe how, by the tilt of his head and the angle of his
body, and by the varying speed and variety of his movements, he was able
to suggest his thoughts and emotions. When I saw his subtle, intensely expressive, and beautifully timed dancing, I was reminded of Garrick's com-
ment on the Italian harlequin Carlin—"Behold how the very back of
Carlin has a physiognomy and an expression."*[38]

The choreography for each character became a stylistic manifestation of that character, so that while the "two gallants and the girls . . .
were cast in a modish vein,"[39] the peasant Pimpinella's dances were
rooted in folk style. Edward Dent, writing in *Athenaeum*, called it a "more
elaborate *Parade*."[40] Stravinsky felt that in *Pulcinella* "all elements—subject, music, dancing, and artistic setting—formed a coherent and homogeneous whole."[41]

While Paris was not much taken by *Le astuzie femminili*, the second
premiere (May 27) of the Opéra season, the ballet was a tremendous success in London. Ernest Newman wrote in the *Sunday Times*:

> *There must be a good deal of eighteenth-century light opera that is worth
> reviving (Mozart by no means exhausted the vein), and apparently it is to
> M. Diaghilev that we must look for the revivals, for only he, with his thor-
> ough methods of preparation, and his equal understanding of all the ele-
> ments of a production, can deprive us of any excuse for condescension
> towards these old works. This rippling, sparkling music should be the
> delight of the town. The new principles of gesture and movement that
> Massine has gone upon for the opera singers deserve more detailed consid-
> eration than I can give them today: briefly, no gesture is made that is not
> necessary and pertinent. The acting thus wins a curious and paradoxical
> repose as well as an animation. Massine's ballet (that follows the opera) is
> one of the most beautiful creations of the extraordinary young genius; it
> has the quiet harmony that one or two of his later inventions, brilliant as
> they have been, have lacked.*[42]

Edward Dent congratulated Massine as an opera director by remarking
that "in the operatic part M. Massine has really succeeded in carrying out
convincingly what only a very few producers have even attempted before. . . . What M. Massine has realized is that formal music requires formal movements and groupings. There is no attempt at realistic acting.

Nor are there any of the usual ridiculous movements which we associate with operatic acting. The singers at every moment form a composed group. . . . It is perfectly simple, harmonious and expressive."[43] The choreography for the ballet scene was a variation of the Petipa divertissement which included a pas de trois, a pas de six, a tarantella, a *pas rustique,* a *contredanse* for eight couples, a classical pas de deux, and the finale.[44] Massine juxtaposed numbers based on character dances, such as the tarantella, with numbers strictly based on the *danse d'école,* such as the pas de deux. Diaghilev incorporated the *Astuzie* ballet into the repertory in 1924, and it was thenceforth called *Cimarosiana.*

When the second season at the Opéra ended, the Ballets Russes moved back to England. In June and July at Covent Garden the company performed *Pulcinella, Astuzie,* and *Chant du rossignol.* Diaghilev and Massine then left London for the Lido. On this holiday, however, Massine set aside valuable time for himself. Diaghilev had entrusted him with launching a revival of *Le Sacre du printemps,* and on his own Massine went to Switzerland to discuss the project with Stravinsky.

In autumn the Ballets Russes toured the provinces in Britain. After performances in Liverpool and Birmingham Massine returned to London—surprisingly, without Diaghilev. With him instead were Sokolova, who had been cast as the Chosen Virgin in *Le Sacre,* and Vera Savina, who came along so that Massine could coach her in *Les Sylphides.* On this sojourn in London the delicate balance between Diaghilev and Massine finally collapsed.

Savina, the English Vera Clark, was born in Hempstead on July 12, 1897. The daughter of Jane Helen Kerasly and Ralph Clark, a post office clerk, she received her early training at Stedman's Academy in London, but truly grew as a dancer under the tutelage of Maestro Cecchetti. She had joined the Ballets Russes in 1918. Two years younger than Massine, she was small and technically strong, "with well formed limbs and exceedingly attractive head, blonde, slightly suggestive of [the ballerina Lydia] Kyasht at times."[45] According to Arnold Haskell, she suffered from "stage modesty probably due to her English temperament."[46] She created the role of the female poodle in *La Boutique*; and according to Beaumont, Massine created the *Astuzie* pas de deux for her, although the premiere was given to Karsavina. Savina later danced it brilliantly. Sokolova said that she had "a lovely, long jump with delicate hand and arm movements"[47] and that her dancing of the Mazurka in *Les Sylphides* was done "beautifully and with a wonderful quality of lightness."[48]

Two forces in Savina's life were about to collide, and nothing would be the same for her once they did. First, Diaghilev recently had chosen her to learn the Mazurka, a sure sign of his high hopes for her as a future ballerina. Second, Massine fell in love with her. Sokolova would later write of Savina that "being English and not speaking two words of Russian, [she] was as innocent as a new-born lamb, and she was the only person in the company who had no idea of Massine's situation. But Massine had fallen in love with her. Without realizing any of the implications, she must have been flattered."[49] It must have been liberating for Massine to feel someone utterly unlike Diaghilev responding to him emotionally, guilelessly, passionately. Savina's return of his affections probably emboldened him, too. Here at last, in the flesh, was a personal, obvious challenge to Diaghilev.

From London the Ballets Russes went to Paris for a season at the Théâtre des Champs-Elysées, where Massine's version of *Le Sacre du printemps* received its world premiere. The first choreographic version had been the powerfully erotic handiwork of Nijinsky, and its premiere at the same theater on May 29, 1913, had marked one of the great theatrical scandals of the century. Stravinsky had lauded Nijinsky's controversial choreography at the time, but by 1920 the composer was openly expressing dissatisfaction with it. The essence of his complaint was that Nijinsky had become "subjected to the tyranny of the bar"[50] in trying to achieve a perfect metrical synchronization between the choreography and the music. When Diaghilev offered to produce a new version of the work, Stravinsky, sensing that a whole new estimation of *Le Sacre* lay in prospect, eagerly collaborated with Massine. Before rehearsals began, as the two men discussed the music at length, Massine's own concept of *Le Sacre* began to take shape. His idea was to attempt "a counterpoint in emphasis between it [the music] and the choreography."[51] The solution lay in creating "a bridge over certain passages of music not counting every bar and every note, and to create a counterpoint over it, then, to create another bridge over other passages of so many bars. . . . I did not account each bar as an individual thing to choreograph. From here to there I do a bridge and I do my own rhythm as I felt I should."[52] Stravinsky readily agreed, and the choreographer began to formulate the work.

Neither man hesitated to discard the original libretto. Massine in particular, in a clear departure from his recent work, looked forward to producing a work void of all literal story, one emerging solely out of a synthesis of music and dance. According to the program notes, *"Le Sacre du printemps* is a spectacle of pagan Russia. The work is divided in two parts and has no subject. It is choreography. It is choreography freely created to the music." As the composer himself commented, "[Massine] and I have suppressed all anecdotal detail, symbolism, etc. [that might] obscure this work of purely musical construction. . . . There is no story at all and no point in looking for one."[53]

In fashioning the choreography, Massine "studied numerous archaic Russian icons and wood carvings and found no justification for the bent wrist and ankle movements which Nijinsky had used. I therefore decided to base my production on the simple movements of the Russian peasants' round dances, strengthened when necessary by the use of angular and broken lines which I had evolved from my study of Byzantine mosaic and perhaps unconsciously also from the captivating spirit of cubism."[54] This *Sacre* would depend on the juxtaposition and counterpoint of groups, and on the contrast between tensed, heavy movements and light ones. To set the work consistently in abstract dance terms, Massine used less exaggerated gestures and a cleaner, classical vocabulary. One example was the choreography for the Chosen Virgin. Though Massine gave this dance a barbaric intensity and emotion, he filled it with recognizable *danse d'école* steps such as *grands jetés en tournant* even as, through stylization, he distorted them.

Sokolova, one of five remaining members of the company who had danced in Nijinsky's *Sacre*, described the differences between the two versions.

> *This was a typical Massine production, clear-cut and methodical, with each group counting like mad against the others, but each holding its own. In Massine's choreography nothing was ever left to chance, and if anybody was in doubt about what he had to do or why he had to do it, he had only to ask and everything was explained. I think it was lucky for Massine that he had never seen the Nijinsky production, which had been staged a year before he joined the company: he might have felt obliged to imitate something which had been conceived in a style quite alien to him. The Nijinsky ballet had a sadness about it, with its groups of ancient men with enormous beards, trembling and shuffling. . . . It was a vague work, far less complicated and accurate than Massine's.*[55]

Massine gave Sokolova her greatest triumph as the Chosen Virgin. She describes the choreography:

There were some enormous sideways jumps, which had to be performed very slowly, and every second one had an extra movement in it. . . . The steps Massine had invented for my sacrificial dance bore so little relation to any kind of dancing that had ever been done before and were so violently contrasted one with the other, and followed each other so swiftly with such sudden changes of rhythm, that I think the impression I gave was of a creature galvanized by an electric current. The dance was tragic: it evoked pity and terror.[56]

Grigoriev wrote:

Massine's choreography was highly expert, but to my mind lacked pathos, in which it differed notably from Nijinsky's. It was as if Massine had paid greater heed to the complicated rhythms of the music than to its meaning; and the result was something almost mechanical, without depth, which failed to be moving. Nijinsky's version, comparatively helpless though it was, had better captured the spirit of the music, and whereas it had brought out the general theme and, in particular, the contrast between the two scenes, these somehow became obscured in Massine's composition.[57]

A grateful Stravinsky commended Massine's efforts, explaining to the press, first in Paris and later in London, how Massine had allowed the music and dance to free and not restrict one another:

What enlightened Massine was to hear [Le Sacre] in concert. . . . Thus from the first he perceived that, far from being descriptive, the music was an "objective construction." Massine does not follow the music note by note, or even measure by measure. . . . Take, for example, this measure of four followed by one of five: Massine's dancers stress a rhythm of three times three. . . .

 The choreographic construction of Nijinsky was one of great plastic beauty but subjected to the tyranny of the bar: that of Massine is based on phrases, each composed of several bars. This last is the sense in which is conceived the free connection of the choreographic construction with the musical construction. . . . [Le Sacre] exists as a piece of music, first and last.[58]

When Massine's *Sacre* was premiered in Paris on December 15, 1920 (performed in its entirety before the stark backcloth that Nicholas Roerich had designed solely for Part Two of Nijinsky's production), the reception was mixed. In *La Revue Musicale* Emile Vuillermoz, piqued by Stravinsky's pronouncements, counterattacked in a four-page vindication of Nijinsky's choreography, accusing the composer of "ingratitude" toward his previous collaborator, especially when Stravinsky declared that it was "Massine who made him understand the real meaning of his work." Vuillermoz found Massine's version "less novel and less personal" than Nijinsky's.[59] Levinson commented:

> [Massine] denies, with—it would seem—the consent of the composer, the magnificently human motivating basis of the work to conform to a purely abstract conception, which has been consciously emptied of all significance. He simplifies the actions by eliminating all historical reminiscence, all archeological association. To be sure the theatre is not a museum, but Massine filled the void with a succession of illogical movements of niggardly design, without plastic reason for being. Mere plastic exercises, denuded of all expression.[60]

For Jean Bernier, Massine's dancers were men and women rather than anthropological, mythic archetypes, though they belonged to a primitive tribe. "It is not a question of ballet; Léonide Massine dictates a sacred ceremony. Only instinct—no longer science or taste—is his master, his demon. . . . Symbolist with Nijinsky, *Sacre* by Massine is brutal, of implacable realism." For Bernier it was "an explosion of life."[61]

Julie Sasonova felt that "it presented a tremendous contrast to the ethereal classical dance. . . . The male dancers underlined their efforts in lifting the inert bodies of the women. The final dance was a frenzy . . . that seemed to be carved out of stone, so strongly was it permeated with the sensation of weight—one of the rare occasions that Diaghilev's ballet was a precursor of modern dance technique. It was as if Massine wished to show the expressiveness and the constructive possibilities of the contrast between weight and lightness."[62]

In June of the following year the ballet's abstraction was roundly decried in London. Said the reviewer for the *Morning Post*: "Mr. Massine has turned his back on any idea so definite as the ceremonial action which Mr. Nijinsky fitted to the music eight years ago."[63] According to *The Times*:

> There is no drama, no story; only a passionless ritual, in which the men lunge and spar at one another, and lift the women on their shoulders. In the second scene the Chosen Virgin stands in the centre of the stage in a

striking pose, the other participants grouped around her. Sometimes they
cluster closely and indulge in a curious spasmodic quiver. At last the chosen
one deigns to move in a high-leaping, ungainly dance which is at least a
triumph of calisthenic skill. The others leave her to herself; her dance be-
comes more extravagant, till at last she falls to the ground exhausted. That
is all that happens, and through it all Stravinsky's orchestra tears its way
in ever-increasing harshness.[64]

Massine's *Sacre* remained in the Ballets Russes repertory off and on
until the company's final season in London in 1929. Although by then
Diaghilev was in poor health and his visits to the theater were rarer, he
did show up at Covent Garden to see *Le Lac de cygnes* and *Le Sacre du*
printemps. According to the critic P. W. Manchester, in its 1929 revival at
Covent Garden *Le Sacre* achieved a triumph greater than its successes of
1913 and 1920. In the gallery the audiences "were stomping and screaming
and yelling and you thought the place would come down that night."[65]
The Times's critic declared Massine's version the true landmark: "The revival of Stravinsky's *Le Sacre du Printemps* was devised, no doubt, to form
the climax to the season of the Diaghilev Ballet. . . . It is the charter of
the modern ballet. . . . After its first presentation, Léonide Massine designed a choreography which not only freed it from the vulgarity of
story-telling, but even eschewed any recognisable symbolism or 'programme.' . . . *Le Sacre* is 'absolute' ballet and we are assured that it will
come to be regarded as having a significance for the 20th Century equal
to that of Beethoven's Choral Symphony in the 19th."[66]

Massine's turn to abstraction in *Sacre* shows him extending his expressive grasp, reaching out to include ballet freed from literal story
in favor of the pure integration of music and dance. This not-quite-
conscious sense of mission, which intensified during the 1920s, set in motion a developing aesthetic that came to fruition during the next decade
with his abstract symphonic ballets. From the 1930s to the end of his life
these abstract ballets would continue to appear alongside his dramatic
works. He felt especially close to *Le Sacre,* reviving it on four more occasions during his lifetime.

As the season at the Théâtre des Champs-Elysées advanced, so did
Massine's pursuit of Savina. Sokolova remembers:

It was about six in the evening, and the place was dark. Vera Savina was
standing in the far corner of the stage, when Mme. Sert suddenly came

through a door nearby. Misia Sert was a clever, attractive woman of the world, besides being Diaghilev's devoted friend, and there were no secrets between them. Crossing the stage, I overheard Vera say, "Mme. Sert, have you seen Mr. Massine?" "No, Verotchka. Did you want him for anything in particular?" "I have an appointment with him." At this, of course, Mme. Sert pricked up her ears—and so did I. "Oh? Where is your appointment?" "At the Arc de Triomphe, but it's such a big place I don't know exactly where to meet him." "Then," said Mme. Sert, "I should stand right in the middle of the arch if I were you." I was staggered by this, but said nothing. I imagined Misia hurrying off to tell Diaghilev about the appointment, and Vera standing in the centre of the Etoile, waiting in vain.[67]

It was highly probable that Diaghilev was already aware of the latest developments, and Misia's discovery would only have confirmed his misgivings. One day Sokolova

heard Massine calling to me. His room was next to mine, and the door was open. As I walked in, Léonide Feodorovitch congratulated me for the first time in my life. He said, "We could not have achieved this work without each other." I was surprised and touched. I told him I was grateful for all he had done for me. He put his hands on my shoulders and kissed me quite naturally on each cheek. This was done with such sincerity, and I was so overwhelmed to hear these words from the handsome Massine, who never praised anybody, that I returned his embrace with emotion. As he moved away he suddenly froze. Looking round, I saw Diaghilev standing in the doorway. Without a word, he walked past me. I mumbled something and slipped out, leaving an icy atmosphere behind.

Diaghilev must have known at this time that Massine was interested in someone, but I think he may have been uncertain whether it was Savina or [me]. As Mme. Sert had undoubtedly passed on the information about the rendezvous under the Arc de Triomphe I suppose that his suspicions now rested on Vera.[68]

At the dinner after the premiere of *Le Sacre du printemps*, Savina

was seated half-way down the table, and as the evening went on the Diaghilev group began to rag her unmercifully. As she spoke no Russian she was an easy butt. She wore a short pink dress with shoulder-straps, which looked very English among all these sophisticated gowns by Lanvin and Chanel. There was a lot of laughter and they kept saying, "Have a little more champagne, Verotchka." . . . *Diaghilev must have been anxious about Massine; and Massine must have been longing for some sort of life of his own with Vera. I should have liked to sit quietly listening to Stravinsky, who could be very amusing, and who had, besides, many complimentary things to say about my performance. However, our conversation was interrupted by Massine who jumped to his feet and climbed onto the piano.*

"Quiet, everybody!" he shouted. "I have an announcement to make." There were a few encouraging cheers, then everybody was silent. We all realized that he was tight, for he was much too quiet and well-behaved in the normal course of events to make any demonstration.

"The time has come," he said. "I have made up my mind that I am going to run away."

Everyone shouted, "Come on! Tell us who with. Who is it to be?"

"There's no secret about it," cried Massine. "I am going to run away with Sokolova."

The guests all cheered and laughed, taking this for a great joke—pretending to think it funnier than they did—since they were all embarrassed. Diaghilev . . . can have found it no more amusing than I did. Massine jumped off the piano, came round the table to where I sat petrified, and kissed my hand. . . . I could not imagine what had possessed Léonide Feodorovitch. Was it just a bit of nonsense on the spur of the moment? Was he trying to annoy Diaghilev, in a spirit of frustration? Or was he trying to put him off the scent?[69]

Throughout the Paris season Diaghilev was ill-tempered and irritable. During a lighting rehearsal he asked Grigoriev:

"What would you think if Massine suddenly left us?" This was so unexpected I merely looked surprised; so Diaghilev went on: "Yes," he said, "we are to part." As soon as I could collect my thoughts, I answered that as a dancer Massine could certainly be replaced. But as a choreographer—to replace him at all quickly would be extremely difficult. "You think so?" asked Diaghilev, as if not so sure. Then looking at his watch, he asked me to continue by myself; after which he stood up and went away, leaving me much perturbed.[70]

According to Grigoriev, the "season in Paris ran its customary course; and the only evidence Diaghilev exhibited of the private conflict that was distressing him was that he showed less than his usual interest in the details of our performances. He looked more and more sombre, however; and it was clear that his relations with Massine were rapidly deteriorating."[71]

By New Year's Eve, when the company moved to Rome to open a season at the Costanzi on January 1, Massine's involvement with Savina had become so serious that Diaghilev had hired detectives to follow the pair about and report on their activities. Massine was not intimidated and pursued Vera openly.[72] Diaghilev's next, clearly desperate, tactic was to offer Savina a contract that would assure her of leading roles in the company—if she would leave Massine.[73] Beneath Diaghilev's outlandish bullying and manipulation was the devastating pain he was experiencing in watching his lover go. But Massine had reached the point of no return.

Stories about the remaining emotionally strenuous days abound. One of the most unpleasant has Diaghilev inviting Savina to his room, getting her drunk, stripping her naked, then throwing her into Massine's room next door.[74] Grigoriev writes that one day in Rome he was summoned by Diaghilev and

> found him in a state of great agitation. "I am definitely parting with Massine," he declared. "I have come to the conclusion that we can no longer work together. His contract has expired; and I should like you, as régisseur, to inform him before today's rehearsal that I have no more need of his services, and that he may accordingly consider himself at liberty." Diaghilev's face was flushed as he told me this, and he could not keep still, but kept walking up and down the room. I knew, as before over Fokine, that it was useless to argue or make any attempt to overpersuade him. So I remained silent; on which, realizing that I did not agree, he continued even more heatedly. Hadn't he, he cried, done everything for Massine? Hadn't he made him? What had Massine's contribution been? "Nothing but a good-looking face and poor legs!" And now, when, owing to Diaghilev, he had become the dancer and choreographer he was; when, working together, they could have created the most wonderful things—everything had collapsed and they must needs part company!—His voice was full of pain and bitterness. He grew more and more agitated, and continued his pacing to and fro. Then he poured himself out a glass of wine, which he

drank off quickly, and, suddenly controlling himself: "So, my dear Serge Leonidovich," he said, "go and deliver my message, please. We'll talk further about this later on."[75]

When Massine arrived at the rehearsal, Grigoriev "immediately took him aside and gave him Diaghilev's message."[76] The choreographer "went deathly pale and turned and walked out of the room."[77] According to Grigoriev, "that night Massine called on me and asked me in detail what Diaghilev had said. I told him as much as I could, adding that I was convinced no power on earth could make Diaghilev revoke his decision. Massine agreed that this was probably so; after which we shook hands and said goodbye."[78] In the theater that evening Sokolova "went to see Vera to find out what was going on, but her dressing-room was empty. I asked the wardrobe mistress where she was and was told she had been put upstairs. I traced her to a room at the top, which she was sharing with three other girls. She had been banished to the corps de ballet . . . I told her she must stand by Massine whatever happened."[79] On February 2 Savina was replaced in a lead role in *Les Sylphides* and Massine's performance as Petrouchka was canceled.

Diaghilev disappeared for several days. Only Walter Nouvel and the impresario's servants were close to him during his collapse. They "feared for his health and even for his reason" and "watched him anxiously day and night."[80] When he finally "emerged, he had such black rings under his eyes that he was barely recognizable."[81]

For Diaghilev, forty-nine years old, the familiar story was repeating itself: a younger man he had skillfully shepherded to international acclaim now fought free of his grasp. Yet he maintained that his attachment to Massine possessed a unique dimension, unlike his liaisons with earlier or future lovers. He eventually called Massine "the most brilliant mind I have ever met in a dancer."[82] Nevertheless, according to Serge Lifar, after their breakup Diaghilev would also blame Massine for all his future misfortunes, including the diabetes that ended his days. No clear resolution of the affair would be possible for him. He once said that of all the friends he had loved, none but Massine had "provided him so many moments of happiness or anguish."[83]

Apparently no civil parting, arrived at in mutual respect, was feasible. In their final months together Massine's need for independence grew stronger, while Diaghilev grew more truculent, turning vicious when faced with his inevitable loss. One can see Massine driving him to the breaking point. First came the artistic disagreement over *Le astuzie,* with the choreographer tenaciously and victoriously holding his ground. Then came a demand by Massine that he be given the title of *maître de ballet* during the final Paris season. Diaghilev at first rejected this out of hand, then complied after the creation of *Le astuzie*—compromising, bitterly, one final time. But Massine, twenty-five years old, forged ahead without regard for the consequences.

PART THREE

The 1920s

*The man who has achieved intellectual
freedom is not so much a traveler towards
a goal as a wanderer on the face of the earth.*

—NIETZSCHE

Massine with Nicolas Efimov in Les Fâcheux, *1927*

CHAPTER 9

ジカスチム

Rome, February 1921–Paris, September 1928

NO LONGER UNDER the protection and guidance of Diaghilev, Massine now had to answer life's most persistent question for himself: which way should he go next? Ever since his departure from Russia in 1914, his "life and work had been entirely bound up with the Ballets Russes."[1] In a letter to Anatoli Petrovich written just after the company's departure for South America in 1917, the lonely youth had disclosed that "I have affection for the company as if it was my family."[2] Now, separated from the company once more, he again "felt abandoned and alone."[3] But he proved more resilient than his dejected tone would suggest and before long had taken control of his situation. He had much in his favor: youth, fame, and connections to a network of well-placed, powerful insiders he was soon to exploit brilliantly.

It is difficult to assess Massine's finances at the time of his breakup with Diaghilev. As a member of the Ballets Russes—a company chronically short of cash—he never had been able to save much; so when he was dismissed he was probably not financially secure enough to support Savina and himself indefinitely. But for the moment the happy couple showed no signs of money worries.

One reason may have been Massine's knowledge that he had his valuable art collection to fall back on. Back in December 1917, to keep the collection safe from Diaghilev's maneuvering, he had wired his friend Semenov in Italy to "protect it against all eventuality."[4] Diaghilev had been corresponding with Semenov during this same period, and it is possible that he had proposed the sale of some of the paintings as a stopgap measure to alleviate his own financial problems.[5]

Massine began to enjoy his new life, proudly squiring his future bride to Rome's museums, libraries, and monuments. He also immersed himself in planning future ballets.

By the second week of February, he had his first offer of work. The Italian impresario Walter Mocchi, of Rome's Teatro Costanzi, asked Massine to organize a small ballet company to tour a chain of theaters Mocchi managed in Brazil, Argentina, and Uruguay. The troupe would present ballet programs and also appear with Mocchi's touring opera company. Massine immediately set to work.

He invited Jan Kawetzky, a dancer from the Ballets Russes, to join the venture as régisseur. Kawetzky, unhappy with Diaghilev, seized the moment and quickly recruited other defectors, including Gala Chabelska, Kostecki, Statkiewicz, Grabowska, Edinska, and Norwicka. (Still another group of dancers would join this contingent once the company reached South America.) But Massine's personal attempts to lure Stanislas Idzikowski into leaving Diaghilev proved unsuccessful.[6] With Kawetzky in charge of assembling the dancers, Massine began to prepare the repertory. First he acquired the rights to the music for two of his own ballets, *Les Femmes de bonne humeur* and *Le Tricorne,* and to several pieces that he could use in the future, including Satie's *Gymnopédies,* Liadov's Eight Russian Folk Songs, and the March and Dance from Glinka's *Ruslan and Ludmilla.* A number of sources came through with material: Falla, the music publishers Ricordi, J. and W. Chester, and Durand et Cie, the archives of the Opéra-Comique. Massine then commissioned composer Gian Francesco Malipiero to orchestrate four dances by Cimarosa and a selection of pieces by Johann Strauss the Younger and engaged Respighi to orchestrate a series of Chopin piano pieces.

Massine and Savina were married in London on April 26, 1921, but for the rest of the three-month preparation period they divided their time between Rome and Paris. During this time Mocchi arranged for Massine to meet with Raoul Gunsbourg of Monte Carlo's Casino Theater. On May 24 Gunsbourg offered the newlyweds a tempting contract: following its South American tour their new company would present ballets at the Casino Theater and join the theater's opera season from February through April 1922. Gunsbourg gave Massine until September to accept his offer.[7]

The contract with Mocchi had been signed during the first week of May. It called for Massine to be lead dancer and choreographer, with Savina as ballerina, for four months, during which they would perform in Rio de Janeiro, São Paulo, Buenos Aires, and Montevideo. Among the operas Massine agreed to stage were *Samson et Dalila, Aïda, La Gioconda, Carmen, Marouf,* and *Tannhäuser.* The roster of the opera company was headed by Beniamino Gigli. The new company sailed from Genoa for South America on May 27 aboard the *Principe di Udine.*

While Massine was happy to be directing his own company, the rigorous schedule did not leave him enough time for thorough creative work. When he worked with Diaghilev, he had been given ample time for meticulous planning of his ballets. He now found himself pressed to produce a full repertory and manage a company at the same time. During the first four weeks in Rio de Janeiro he conducted sixty-five rehearsals, choreographed several ballets, and staged eight operas. Of course, not all of that work was grueling; most of the repertory consisted of excerpts or divertissement ballets, though Massine included the full-length *Femmes de bonne humeur.* He considered the tour "physically and mentally more exhausting than any I had ever undertaken. Besides dancing every night, I had to run the company, and felt far from confident in my role as director. Nor did I have any time in which to do my own work."[8] Nevertheless, throughout the hectic months Massine found time to maintain his correspondence with Picasso. From the dancer in São Paulo to the painter in Fontainebleau:

All the blacks here dress themselves like the blackman in Parade's *front curtain. They have such an air of innocence as if America had just been discovered yesterday. All in all, it is a bit curious. Young people wear neck-collars like those from the time of Boutique and one finds in small cafés people wearing wooden hats in the shape of straw hats.*

Nature surpasses all imagination . . . a hundred times more beautiful than what we see in photographs. One eats extraordinary fruits with a taste as strange as their name. . . .

I have had a success as I have never had before, which frightens me, and Vera also. . . . I continue my [choreographic] research although I have very little time for it; however, I feel very comforted by the discoveries I have made.[9]

In another letter he spoke more openly about his work and state of mind: "I think that I am freeing myself of various faults that cluttered my head and my eyes and which were an obstacle toward the realization of my choreographic goals. Here I lack the technical means and the company has such a limited number of dancers that it has affected what I can achieve choreographically. . . . The lines and their harmony have been broken and muddled up, as have all of my ideas. The only thing that sustains itself is *Le Sacre*, which marked the turning point of my present ideas."[10]

Fortunately, the company, billed as Compañia de Bailes Rusos, was enthusiastically received. South America had already seen such famous ballet artists as Olga Preobrajenska, Virginia Zucchi, and Ana Pavlova, as well as the Ballets Russes in 1913 and 1917. A cultivated public awaited Massine's troupe, especially in Buenos Aires and Montevideo. As matters turned out, after his obligations to Mocchi had been satisfied Massine extended the tour on his own. From late October to mid-December the company performed twice a day at the Empire Theater in Buenos Aires; on December 19 it opened a two-shows-a-day, ten-day engagement at Montevideo's Teatro Artigas. But despite success Massine was homesick for Europe and his friends, and his letters to Picasso became more frequent. On November 18 he cabled: "Let me hear about your news. Loneliness unbearable."[11]

Far from Europe, and thriving, Massine was probably better able to grasp the significance of his dramatic break from Diaghilev. As in 1914, when he wrestled with the decision to *remain* with Diaghilev, he wrote to Moscow for his family's blessing and acceptance. His letter was unusually open and heartfelt. He had "left them as a boy" without knowing "that God would send us so many long and painful experiences"; unquestionably his journey "had been very lonely." His recent decision to leave Diaghilev and to marry had been "a turning point in my private and social life." Living with Diaghilev had become unbearable. "I felt as though I was in a gilded cage which suffocated and oppressed my entire spirit. This ended a seven-year period of my life in which I have endured more than others will endure in a lifetime!" He described Savina as "charming" and "humble" and "a great source of support in my life."[12]

On January 12, 1922, the Massines sailed for Europe on the Italian ship *Duca d'Aosta,* which docked in Monte Carlo on February 1. They proceeded to Paris (the contract with Gunsbourg having collapsed after a financial disagreement),[13] where the Hôtel Normandie once again served as their headquarters. While Semenov continued to negotiate the acquisition of the Isole dei Galli, Massine set his professional sights across the Channel.

London was to become Massine's base of operations for most of the 1920s. His extended Ballets Russes engagements there had given him entrée to the city's cultural elite; social and professional relationships with prominent Londoners had followed. Most important, despite Britain's depressed postwar economy, London enjoyed a dynamic theatrical life, and dance was turning from a craze into an obsession. Soon London would (until World War II) replace Paris as the world's ballet capital.

From the Hôtel Normandie, Massine negotiated with Sir Oswald Stoll and with the Hollywood producer Walter Wanger, who had leased the Royal Opera House at Covent Garden, to book performances in London.[14] Covent Garden was undergoing a severe financial crisis during the postwar period; to remain open, it had resorted to scheduling film screenings and revues as part of the Royal Opera House programs. Both Stoll and Wanger offered Massine immediate engagements. The choreographer opted for Covent Garden and soon put together a small company whose nucleus was Savina, himself, and some of Diaghilev's dancers. During the 1921 Ballets Russes season in London, Diaghilev had produced a three-act *Sleeping Beauty* (entitled *The Sleeping Princess*) that had ended in financial disaster, making it easier now for Massine to recruit such dancers as Lopokova, Sokolova, Woizikowski, and Thadée Slavinsky. Ninette de Valois, not yet a member of Diaghilev's company, also signed on with Massine.

Massine settled himself and Savina in a flat at London's Phoenix Hotel and the couple rented a dance studio on New Oxford Street, where classes and rehearsals began immediately. With Lopokova and Massine billed as the "world's greatest Ballet Dancers," his newly formed group opened at Covent Garden on April 3. The repertory introduced London to some of the works created in South America, including *Ragtime*, to Stravinsky's music, as well as *The Fanatics of Pleasure*, a divertissement ballet to music by Johann Strauss the Younger. There were also popular excerpts from *Tricorne, Boutique,* and *Astuzie.* According to *The Times,* "the dancers were given a great welcome by a large audience, especially M. Massine and Mlle. Lopokova in their dance duets." *Ragtime* "seemed to amuse the house very much, in spite of the little invention shown in discovering movements," and the critic "soon tired of the simple, if not childish, idea of the mechanical figure." The Strauss dances, however, "were danced to a happier style."[15] Despite its divertissement quality, Ninette de Valois found the choreography interesting and some numbers full of invention.[16] The performances at Covent Garden were a success with the public, and the company was offered an immediate engagement at the Coliseum. A return to Covent Garden was arranged for July, after a provincial tour.

T. S. Eliot attended the performances at the Coliseum and was further impressed with Massine's artistry and stage presence. "I have been to see him," he wrote Mary Hutchinson, "and thought him more brilliant and beautiful than ever. . . . As I [had never been so close before], I quite fell in love with him. . . . He is a genius."[17] After meeting Massine later in June, Eliot wrote Hutchinson: "Do you think Massine likes me? And would he come to see me, do you think?"[18]

Massine's instinct was to remain aloof, but his career now required him to move in London's social and artistic circles. Renewing former ties, he began to get himself noticed and inquired after.

Lady Ottoline Morrell, the wife of Liberal M.P. Phillip Morrell, was one of England's most prominent hostesses of the day, an aristocrat whose glittering parties and salons at Bedford Square in London and at Garsington Manor, a few miles from Oxford, are part of the British cultural lore of the first three decades of the twentieth century. During the Great War, Garsington Manor became a refuge for pacifists and conscientious objectors, and here she played hostess to many of the era's most brilliant social, political, artistic, and literary personalities, including Raymond Asquith, Bertrand Russell, Maynard Keynes, D. H. Lawrence, Roger Fry, Virginia Woolf, T. S. Eliot, Aldous Huxley, and Lytton Strachey. The ambience at Garsington Manor was decidedly relaxed: sexual freedom was a matter of fact—among Her Ladyship's lovers was Russell—and homosexuality was openly accepted. Lady Ottoline was known for her eccentricities and her oddly striking physical appearance as much as for her kindness toward struggling talent. Massine described her as "dressed in fantastically-coloured satins and brocades," looking like "a majestic bird of prey."[19] She had championed Diaghilev, whom she met before the war, and during the 1918–20 Ballets Russes London seasons she befriended Massine. Their correspondence shows a sincere rapport. Now she aided him in every way that she could, introducing him to the right people, even recruiting wealthy students for his ballet school.[20] They frequently met in London, or the Massines would spend weekends in Garsington. "I come to see you Wednesday next week? . . . Shall we come to Bloomsbury?"[21] writes Lady Ottoline, or, "If you would care to come in on Thursday to tea you would find a *very* interesting man here—James Stephens."[22] Although Massine never had much inclination to entertain—he was also notoriously tightfisted—he would on occasion receive special visitors at his apartment. One of its biggest draws was the modernist paintings on display from his own collection: "I should very much like to come see your pictures, especially your Braque. Also to see you," writes Lady Ottoline from Garsington in April 1922.[23]

Also among Massine's close acquaintances at this time in London were Osbert and Sacheverell Sitwell.

By the beginning of 1923 Massine was actively working in the theater. He created incidental choreography for the play *Arlequin* (produced by Albert de Courville) and choreographed his first revue, *You'd Be Surprised,* starring George Robey, which opened at Covent Garden on January 22. For this, he staged the exotic ballet *Togo,* with music by Darius Milhaud and designs by Bloomsbury artist Duncan Grant, and several dances, including a Chinese dance to music by Johann Strauss the Younger. These may have been stimulating exercises for Massine; but Sokolova, for one, found most of the pieces quite uninspiring.[24]

Many London stage luminaries came to the Massines' studio for coaching: Viola Tree, Gladys Cooper (whom Massine coached in 1923 for *Peter Pan*), Tallulah Bankhead. Bankhead writes:

Facing my first London audience in The Dancers, *on the curtain's rise I was dancing for the supper in a British Columbia saloon, on its fall the toast of Paris, a ballerina! Actor-manager Sir Gerald du Maurier was a perfectionist. Feeling the demands of the part might be beyond my dancing range, he sent me to a ballet teacher. Reluctantly I went to the studio—a bleak, dark and empty room. There I was greeted by a rapt young man.*

The rapt young man was Léonide Massine, whose jetés and tournées and what-have-yous are discussed in hushed tones, wherever balletomanes engage in their rituals.[25]

Among his students were the young Frederick Ashton, who would become England's leading choreographer, and Eleonora Marra, who in 1924 would replace Savina in Massine's affections.

Massine surely enjoyed being drawn into London's theatrical whirl, but his professional future must have appeared quite uncertain. He had no guarantee of employment from one engagement to the next. Teaching helped financially but could not nourish him creatively; and in any case, it seems unlikely that Massine was an inspired teacher—he took far more pride in mastering ballet's theoretical problems than in refining the pedagogy of academic dance. (Years later he would develop his own theory of dance notation.) No doubt there were other frustrations as well. He must have sorely missed the Ballets Russes, a company organized and disciplined enough to execute his artistic ideas with poise and authority. But he kept his spirits up by constantly, almost compulsively, exploring possible future collaborations and projects, most of which, unfortunately, never got off the ground. He continued shuttling between England and the Continent, and Paris was soon a second hub of activity.

After the Great War, Paris again became Europe's mecca of illusions and aspirations, with Montparnasse as its artistic and intellectual center. The city was spellbound by the new artistic movements of dadaism and surrealism. Adding to the tumult were the free-spending international set, the "lost generation" of American expatriates, an unruly new dance called the Charleston, and widespread delirium over *le jazz hot*. Coco Chanel transformed the appearance of women, and avant-garde canvases shocked the bourgeoisie. Paris was the major battleground in the war between old and new values. In the forefront were the likes of Man Ray, Jean Cocteau, Tristan Tzara, André Breton, Gertrude Stein, André Gide, Constantin Brancusi, Nancy Cunard, and Cole Porter.

In the midst of this ferment, Massine saw the wisdom of renewing his artistic and social contacts in France. Among them were Ravel, Fauré, Satie, and Milhaud, four composers who in 1924 endorsed Massine's induction into the Société des Auteurs, Compositeurs et Editeurs de Musique to ensure his receipt of royalties for his works currently being performed by the Ballets Russes in France.[26] Picasso, Lucien Daudet, the Delaunays, Gontcharova, Larionov, and Derain were other artist friends Massine contacted. But of paramount importance was the Count Etienne de Beaumont.

Etienne and Edith de Beaumont were leading figures in the Parisian haut monde. The count's lineage could be traced to an aristocratic Touraine family dating from 1191. In 1907 he had married Edith de

Taisne, also of noble birth and a few years his senior. He was tall, flamboyant, possessed of exquisite manners, and homosexual. He had a penchant for lavish entertaining and for sponsoring young artists; he designed jewelry for Chanel and Schiaparelli, arranged charming *soirées musicales,* and had organized an ambulance service during the war. The countess was more reserved, with a serious interest in Greek poetry; her translation of Sappho was later published in an edition with designs by Marie Laurencin. The much-discussed couple's magnificent eighteenth-century *hôtel particulier* in the rue Daruc was a meeting place for Parisian society, artists, and writers. The setting was breathtaking, with salons as sumptuous as those in the Louvre and splendid gardens ornamented with neoclassical statues.

This palatial residence was also the setting for the count's most meticulously rendered social statements: his celebrated masquerade balls. Many of these spectacles were decorated by Picasso, Sert, or Laurencin. The costumes, designed by Picasso, Jean Hugo, or the count himself, blended flights of fancy with bizarre fantasy. Once Princess Soutzo appeared as a Christmas tree and the Maharanee of Kapurthala made a triumphant entrance as caviar, held aloft on a silver tray by four attendants. Every detail of these balls was carefully orchestrated by Beaumont. His guests sometimes had to wait for hours in a drawing room before making their precisely timed entrances, usually as a sort of tableau vivant accompanied by dance and song composed for the occasion. Dress rehearsals were required.

In 1923 Picasso, Satie, and Massine collaborated on a divertissement for a ball dedicated to "L'Antiquité sous Louis XIV." During preparations for this extravaganza Beaumont struck on the idea of organizing a series of performances centered around Massine. (According to Bernard Faÿ, "Beaumont did not hide . . . his cult for the dancer Massine, whom his admirers had renamed *le devin Léonide,* and his [Beaumont's] desire to have the Parisian public recognize the superiority of this artist's genius."[27] Soon Beaumont was gathering some of the most prestigious artists in Paris for the venture. By then he had also developed a sexual infatuation with Massine, but his yearning, the evidence suggests, remained entirely sublimated in their artistic collaboration. The two men established a close friendship that lasted until after World War II.

Preparations for Les Soirées de Paris, as the season was called (after Apollinaire's prewar journal), began early in 1924. It was to take place at the music hall La Cigale from May 17 through June 30 and would mainly consist of a series of ballets, with a few music-hall numbers included.

The count also planned two dramatic pieces: Tristan Tzara's *Mouchoir de nuages* (dedicated to the rebellious and fascinating English heiress Nancy Cunard) and Cocteau's adaptation of Shakespeare's *Romeo and Juliet*. According to Francis Steegmuller, Beaumont enlisted Cocteau to contribute something "in which there would not be a role for Massine, in order that the pro-Massine purpose of the *Soirées* be at least slightly disguised."[28] Steegmuller also notes how "Massine's absence from the cast, strategic though it was, resulted in Beaumont's taking little interest in *Romeo*."[29]

Massine choreographed seven works: *Salade* (book by Albert Flament, music by Milhaud, scenery and costumes by Georges Braque); *Mercure* (music by Satie, scenery and costumes by Picasso); *Les Roses* (a plotless ballet to music by Henri Sauguet); *Gigue* (a baroque piece to music by Bach and Handel, performed at the piano by Marcelle Meyer, with scenery and costumes by Derain); *Premier Amour* (a sketch about a girl who falls in love with a doll in her dreams, set to Satie's *Trois morceaux en forme de poire* as well as his polka from *Petites pièces montées,* interpreted at the piano by Satie and Meyer); *Le Beau Danube* (book by Massine, music by Johann Strauss the Younger, decor after Constantin Guys, and costumes by Beaumont), and *Divertissement* (a plotless *suite de danses*—waltz, variation, pas de deux, rigaudon, and mazurka—to *Chabrier* music, performed against color projections). The American dancer Loie Fuller oversaw the lighting design.

Rue Daruc became Massine's headquarters. He temporarily moved into an annex. Two large rooms in the house served as rehearsal studios, in one of which he taught a morning class to about thirty dancers. The company, recruited in London and Paris, included some Diaghilev defectors, the most important of whom was Idzikowski. Lopokova came to Paris from London to join the venture, but Savina remained in England.

Word of Massine's latest undertaking reached Diaghilev in Monte Carlo. He was furious. For one thing, Les Soirées would coincide with the Ballets Russes' forthcoming Paris season. Though several of the works of Beaumont's enterprise would prove rather amateurish in spite of all the prestigious artists involved, Diaghilev rightly feared that it could draw attention away from his own engagement. Massine and Beaumont's effrontery in competing with him so openly must have been unbearable. Equally galling was the participation of such artists as Satie, Picasso, and Derain, all associated with Diaghilev in the past; others, such as Braque and Milhaud, were collaborating with the Ballets Russes at that very moment. (Perhaps to dispel any hint of disloyalty to Diaghilev, Marie Laurencin, who had just come from designing the scenery and costumes for Diaghilev's *Les Biches,* appears credited as "N." in the program for *Les Roses.*) Diaghilev was both frightened and envious, and the gossip was that "Big Serge" was in "such a rage" that he was willing to engage "everyone possible with a contract forever."[30] Indeed, Diaghilev would not let matters rest, and before long he retaliated. He advised Poulenc and Auric, who had just contributed scores to two new Ballets Russes productions, *Les Biches* and *Les Fâcheux,* that if they participated in Les Soirées those ballets would not be presented in Paris. He also tried, unsuccessfully, to persuade Milhaud not to collaborate with Beaumont. Milhaud had just composed the score for Diaghilev's production of Cocteau's *Le Train bleu.* Cocteau, afraid of falling out of Diaghilev's favor, wrote the impresario:

> *I was so sorry not to have seen you to say goodbye. I wanted to explain to you about a Cigale project which I should think will please you as it changes the aspect of the whole enterprise.*
>
> *E. de Beaumont wants me to stage* Romeo et Juliette, *to alternate with his music-hall programme. I am working with Jean V. Hugo, and I am having some Scotch bagpipers sent over from England.*
>
> *So I am doing nothing that is in any way like your productions, and am confining myself to* theatre *theatre.*[31]

With Beaumont, Diaghilev employed a more gracious strategy. In the spirit of requesting a professional courtesy, he asked the count not to engage Idzikowski for the coming extravaganza. According to Lopokova, "The count promised, in the meantime Big Serge tried behind his back to destroy the count's season, so that now the count is furious and engages Stas [Idzikowski] for spite."[32]

The intensive rehearsal period began in February, with two or three sessions a day. The work must have been exhausting, but by April 26 Lopokova wrote to Maynard Keynes that "Massine looks well and seems pleasant to everybody."[33]

As opening night drew near, however, tempers flared. The relationship between Lopokova and Massine became particularly tense, and in her letters to Keynes she complained of not being paid proper attention and protested that her suggestions were not being considered. "I plead [with] Massine to have clear lights in the scene where the psychological moment develops [probably referring to *Le Beau Danube*], but he is difficult."[34] The sometimes open, sometimes buried rivalry between the two dancers was rearing its head: "My friends find as ever that Massine does everything to shadow me and not make me his equal," Lopokova wrote, adding that "we can't change the nature of Massine, it is always twisted in the wrong direction."[35] Contention between the two dated from the Ballets Russes' return to England in 1918, when, just as Karsavina and Nijinsky had done in Diaghilev's prewar seasons, Lopokova and Massine became the sensation and rage of London. After Massine left the Ballets Russes, his ensuing professional instability made him exceedingly wary of anyone he believed might threaten his position; thus the 1922 and 1923 collaborations between the two dancers at Covent Garden and the Coliseum had been marred by Massine's petty squabbling over money and his intrigues to monopolize the limelight. Now as then, Lopokova was fed up with his attempts to upstage her:

> I went to a rehearsal for that damnation ball tomorrow. Stas came into the dressing room with a newspaper . . . and it said how this charity ball included all the amateurs society and L. Massine. As it is a thing of charity I absolutely want my professional name, and as Count is very busy, I left the dirty theatre. . . . Besides my costume is the same as corps de ballet and they do not take least trouble to make it better. . . . The Count must not overlook these matters, and if he does, there is penalty for him; the announcement certainly comes out of his organisation. Tonight I shall tell him so.[36]

Lopokova also denounced Massine's rash treatment and incessant overworking of the dancers—a recurrent grievance over the years among his co-workers: "I still work like an elephant. . . . I told Massine that he must give us one free night before Saturday to come into a normal condition."[37] And the following day she wrote: "In the theatre from 2 till 8½ forever waiting, trying on costumes, and [have] not been able to dance with the orchestra except for 7–8 minutes. I told Massine that except [for] himself, he considered the other dancers as mud (in *The Roses* he does not dance), but the ballet with him he rehearsed for hours, so that musiciens [sic] when tired were logic[al] to stand up and depart."[38] Massine's obsessiveness could sometimes make him overlook the needs of other dancers, and his impersonal manner often made them feel that they were merely tools for his artistic advancement. His introverted personality did not help. He struck many as cold, insensitive, and untrustworthy. Keeping his distance, he invited suspicions that he harbored ulterior motives. Asked to justify his tyrannical demands, he would simply declare that "I did not ask of dancers what I did not ask of myself."[39] (The young generation of dancers in the 1930s would be devoted to Massine and accept his sometimes unreasonable demands out of respect for his unquestioned genius. Most of his contemporaries' admiration, however, had no cultlike reverence attached to it. They saw his despotism as utterly uncalled for.)

Les Soirées opened with a gala on May 17. Among the works created by Massine, only *Mercure, Salade,* and *Le Beau Danube* received the highest acclaim. *Mercure,* in fact, was mainly disliked by the press, but it was hailed in the artistic community as the high point of the season.

The idea of *Mercure* was credited to Massine in the program, but in a letter to Picasso dated February 21, 1924, Beaumont advanced the concept as his own, passing it on to Picasso to use as a point of reference for a series of designs on which the work was to be based.[40] In a letter to Satie written on the same day, Beaumont informed the composer of his letter to Picasso and proposed a working title for the ballet of *Mercure: Tableaux vivants.*[41] (This later was changed to *Les Aventures de Mercure,* and, finally—more in keeping with the original idea—to *Mercure: Poses plastiques.*)

The ballet consisted of three parts and twelve scenes,* some of which lasted only twenty to thirty seconds. The series of tableaux vivants included dancers and sculptural aids such as wooden silhouettes (made mobile by other, hidden dancers or by strings) and constructs of enmeshed wire. Gertrude Stein commented: "Calligraphy, as I understand it in him [Picasso], had perhaps its most intense moment in the decor of *Mercure.* That was written, so simply written, no painting, pure calligraphy."[42] Such stage sculpture in motion had antecedents in *Parade* and *Le Tricorne* and was an important device in turning these two ballets into what Ornella Volta has described as Picasso's "*Machines de guerre contre le ballet traditionnel.*"[43] The male and female costumes were modeled after classic Greek tunics—with the incongruous addition of long white evening gloves for everyone except Mercure himself (Massine). The gloves were not Picasso's idea—it has been credited to Beaumont—but he liked it.[44] Dancers who appeared as stagehands were dressed in black unitards with hoods. One of the most peculiar scenes in *Mercure* featured

---

* The twelve scenes were *La Nuit, Danse de tendresse, Entrée de Mercure, Danse des signes du Zodiaque; Les Trois Grâces, Le Bain de Grâces, Mercure vole les perles des trois Grâces et s'enfuit, Colère de Cerbère; La Fête chez Bacchus, La Polka des lettres, Entrée du Chaos,* and *Enlèvement de Proserpine.*

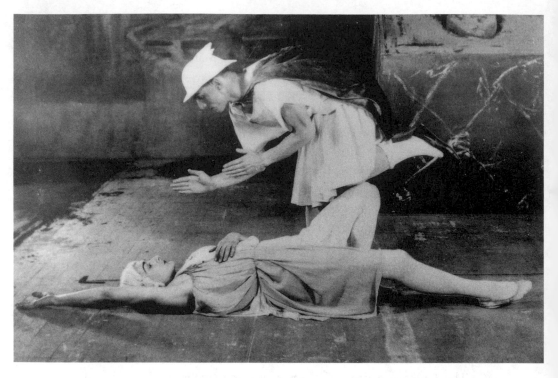

Massine as the title character in the Diaghilev revival of Mercure, 1927

figures of the three Graces, played by three muscular male dancers *en travesti*, all wearing large papier-mâché breasts and pictured in a vertical bathtub. W. H. Shaw wrote in the *Criterion*:

> Mercure *left one uncertain. The effect produced on the first night audience was indicative. The younger generation led by Louis Aragon became so excited that they leapt from their seats, running through the theatre to the loge of the Comte de Beaumont, screaming in menacing tones, "Vive Picasso! Vive Picasso!," as if uncertain whether to thank or damn him for presenting anything so thrilling. . . . The curtain rose on a tableau representing night in a manner entirely new to Picasso, an abstract composition made of canvas and wire. The three graces were done by three mechanical figures which were many times as large as the dancers who carried them across the stage. The dance of Chaos was executed by a group of dancers entirely covered by different colored tights, reaching even over their faces, crawling across the stage, supporting other dancers on their heads and backs.*[45]

Mercure gave Satie the happy opportunity to work with his admired friend Picasso—and without Cocteau, from whom he had broken off social and artistic relations for good by 1923. In an interview for the *Paris-Journal* on May 30, the composer described the ballet and its music: "I wanted my music to create a body, if you will, to go along with the actions and gestures of the characters. The poses are exactly similar to those that one can see in the fairs. The spectacle resembled the music hall, all together without stylization and not at all in rapport with that which is essentially artistic."[46]

Salade, described in the program as a "choreographic counterpoint in two acts," was a commedia dell'arte imbroglio in which two couples—Polichinelle and Rosetta, Cinzio and Isabelle—pursue all sorts of intrigues, only to end up marrying. But according to Madeleine Milhaud, the composer's wife, Massine did not treat the ballet in a light, commedia dell'arte style. He gave it a "tragic dimension, especially the scene in which the Polichinelle is beaten and which Massine performed heartbreakingly."[47] Although the critic Fernand Gregh described the work as "a rhythmic pantomime, a series of stylized gestures that, for a second, froze the actors in poses that became a tableau,"[48] according to Massine his intention was to show "what was essential to dance uncluttered by any sort of mime, thereby liberating it from anything that is foreign to its nature: dance should appear in its fundamental character. *Le Sacre* was a great monumental symphony; *Salade* would belong to the genre of chamber music. . . ."[49]

Lopokova, who did not dance in *Salade,* found Massine's performance "admirable" and the ballet "one of [his] best."[50] Its structure, she wrote, "develops like a building."[51] She found "the decor by Braque very attractive."[52] Noting the shallowness of the Cigale's stage, the critic Raymond Cogniat described the decor as a "line of arches which spread across the full length of the stage . . . dividing it in two parts or zones which were independently lit from one another and where the actions of the interpreters took place, thus creating at the same time the illusion of a space that would have been impossible to render by the use of perspective if the stage itself had been any deeper. Consequently, the arches did not allow the upstage to look empty."[53] Braque's costumes, with the exception of Massine's pale yellow, employed a color scheme of autumn leaves. As inspiration for the scene Massine gave Milhaud various themes of antique Italian music.[54] The critic Arthur Hoerée found the score one of the composer's best.[55]

Le Beau Danube returned to the demi-caractère divertissement genre

Massine had already explored in *La Boutique fantasque*. Its two scenes depicted a Hussar who, strolling in a Viennese park with his young bourgeois fiancée, encounters his old flame, a Street Dancer. The two women square off and the Hussar temporarily succumbs to the charms of his former lover. However, he is genuinely in love with his young intended, and they are reconciled at the end. The story had been conceived during Massine's difficult days in Rome after his breakup with Diaghilev. According to Massine, "*Le Beau Danube* came as a reaction from the intense seriousness of *Parade* and *Le Sacre du Printemps*. It was an absolute necessity for me to create it. Curiously enough, [it came about] during the very strongest period of jazz, before there was any thought of a return to the Vienna waltz."[56] Massine's selection of danceable tunes by Johann Strauss went against the current trend toward either jazzy or more serious ballet scores. (In the 1920s Strauss's reputation was not high. When Malipiero had arranged his music for *Fanatics of Pleasure*, he asked Massine not to include his own name in the program credits.) *Le Beau Danube* consisted of a series of polkas, mazurkas, waltzes, and marches. The dances—pas de deux, solos, and ensembles, danced by others in the park as well as the three leads—were intertwined with the narrative passages to advance the story line. And Massine employed some of his favorite storytelling techniques, such as simultaneous action and an apotheosis at the finale.

Polunin's decor depicted a tall carriage taking two gentlemen for a ride in the park, a scene inspired by the romantic engravings of Constantin Guys. Beaumont's period costumes relied on a muted color scheme of sepias, russets, dark greens, grays, and burgundies. Although Lopokova found the ballet a little long, she thought that the costumes were the most lavishly produced of the season, and asserted that while the other ballets were for an elite, *Le Beau Danube* was for "the grand public."[57] Indeed, the ballet was Massine's most popular of the season; it was performed seventeen times (*Gigue* was performed fifteen times, *Salade* fourteen).

All of Paris now gravitated toward the two sites where the battle of the impresarios would be played out: La Cigale and the Théâtre des Champs-Elysées. And no matter which side one might be on, with the Ballets Russes performing Massine's *Parade*, *Sacre*, *Cimarosiana*, and *Pulcinella* the choreographer was easily the celebrity of the season. The Diaghilev-Beaumont competition fueled tensions and intrigue between their supporting camps. Jean Hugo recalls that during one of Massine's appearances Beaumont shouted "Bravo! and applauded noisily. There was no echo. Misia had entered. She was the Ballets Russes incarnate, which

Massine had betrayed. She did not go unnoticed, and when the curtain fell, many hesitated to applaud."[58]

Diaghilev also came to La Cigale. Pointing to the poster for Les Soirées, he commented, "Only my name is missing."[59] At one performance he was accompanied by Bronislava Nijinska and Serge Lifar, and when Nijinska applauded Diaghilev seemed to become upset.[60] While he felt that *Le Beau Danube* was "pure trash,"[61] he thought that the lighting and choreography of *Salade* "had marked a definite step forward."[62] And he admired *Mercure*, a work he later added to his repertory—the only ballet he ever acquired from another producer.

One can see Massine in his creations for Les Soirées taking two quite distinct aesthetic approaches. The first, in modernist works like *Salade* and *Mercure*, is dominated by the collaboration of the painters, Braque and Picasso respectively. These works are almost experimental in their fragmentation of images and stylization of movement. In both, but especially in *Mercure*, the strictly visual aspects of painting and sculpture overshadow the dancing. In a May 1924 interview in *Candide*, Beaumont described this approach as one in which the function of the choreographer and leading dancer "takes the place of an instrument within the orchestra of dancers. Composition, optics, movement, lighting are some of the problems that this great artist [Massine] has strived to resolve, giving to himself in the whole ensemble just the importance of a dominating color in a painting."

Le Beau Danube, Divertissement, and *Les Roses* reveal the opposite tendency; here, dance is the predominant element. (According to critic Paul Ginistry, *Les Roses* was composed of "harmonious groupings" which served as a background for the virtuosity of Idzikowski.)[63] The fact that *Danube* was conceived by Massine without the collaboration of any other artist is one clear indication of his new preference for pure dance within a dramatic context. This was a crucial step in his development, but what we can only call an incomplete one. It had been clear for months that in working with Beaumont Massine would be unable to exercise much artistic independence: in a letter dated January 14, 1924, just after Massine had approached Lopokova to dance in Les Soirées, the ballerina told Maynard Keynes that Massine's "friends" and "associates have control over everything, he [Massine] employs his power only as a *maître de ballet*."[64] Thus one wonders whether had Massine had more freedom during the Soirées season, he would have produced even more dancing ballets instead of following the modernist formula of the 1920s, a course that was very much determined by Beaumont's aesthetics.

Massine's negotiations with theatrical producer Charles B. Cochran to bring Les Soirées to London—a move that incensed Diaghilev—came to nothing. So by the summer of 1924 he had to face his vanished hope to create his own repertory company.

After Les Soirées Massine returned to London, where his marriage ended. (He and Savina would divorce in 1925.) According to Massine's autobiography, Savina felt abandoned during their long separations when he was engaged by Beaumont in Paris. Yet their problems apparently predate Massine's involvement with Beaumont. Mostly, in fact, he writes, their breakup could be traced to her feeling "disillusioned" about the marriage.[65] In a letter to Keynes dated January 20, Lopokova hints that Savina had just returned to Massine after temporarily leaving him. Massine refused to answer Lopokova's inquiries about whether or not he and Vera "were in a state of partition" and declined to discuss his "domestic drama" with her.[66] The fact that Savina did not come to Paris to join Les Soirées was a clear sign that by the beginning of 1924 their relationship had badly deteriorated. Her absence was the beginning of the end.

Into the breach stepped Massine's London student Eleonora Marra, who would be his emotional mainstay for the next few years. She had come to Paris to create leading roles in the repertory. It is impossible to say precisely when their affair began, but it was only the first of many. Extramarital relationships would continue to checker Massine's emotional life. Despite his pleas for solitude, he was incapable of being alone, and one lover was quickly replaced by another. The sheer number of his involvements until the end of his life, coupled with his unending search for new sexual conquests, suggests that sex became a sort of safety valve for accumulated pressure, a mechanism to lower his anxiety. For a man so closed within himself and so detached from others by his inability to communicate on a more intimate level, sex—next to the aesthetic gratification of his creative work—became a primary source of pleasure. While through his art he could ascend to a higher self, it was sex that reconciled him with his human nature.

Since his return from South America in 1922, Massine had made several attempts to renew his artistic relationship with Diaghilev. On separate occasions he had asked Misia and Jacques Rouché, director of the Paris Opéra, to intercede on his behalf, but all such advances had come to nothing.[67] Now, in London, the two men effected something of a reconciliation. Massine writes that Maestro Cecchetti told him that "Diaghilev was in town and wanted to see me. I was surprised at this news, and perhaps a little curious, and readily agreed to Cecchetti's suggestion of a rendezvous at his studio a week later."[68] Diaghilev proposed that Massine return to the Ballets Russes to choreograph two new ballets. As usual, he had more than one motive. Since Massine's departure, Nijinska had been the company's choreographer. By 1924, however, Diaghilev had shown interest in the work of George Balanchine, who had been touring Western Europe with a group of dancers from St. Petersburg. He recruited Balanchine for the Ballets Russes—the reason usually cited for Nijinska's departure in January 1925. (Did she also know that Massine was about to be rehired?) With Nijinska gone and Balanchine not yet established as a choreographer, one can see why Diaghilev needed Massine. One can also see further Diaghilev's ploy to eliminate a competitor.

He was ready to take his onetime protégé back—even under Massine's exorbitant conditions. The art critic Michel Georges-Michel served as intermediary. From Italy, where he had just met with Massine, he wired to Diaghilev the choreographer's astronomical demands: 160,000 francs annually, a rehearsal schedule to be set by Massine himself, plus full casting authority, contingent only upon Diaghilev's approval.[69] Massine was adamant. Diaghilev acceded. (Balanchine, once he was established as a choreographer and principal dancer with Diaghilev, was paid only 2,500 francs a month.)[70]

The negotiations concluded, Massine took Marra to Italy for a long respite on the Isole dei Galli, which he had finally acquired in 1922.

The three tiny islands, lying three nautical miles off Positano in the Gulf of Salerno, are steeped in legend. In antiquity they formed a single island which in profile had the shape of a reclining woman; seamen called it Sirene. Homer immortalized the site as the home of the Sirens whose song had lured Ulysses. In the fourteenth century the islands served as a fortress and lookout for the king of Naples (Robert of Anjou) against Saracen invaders. Later they were used as a prison, and as a hideout for pirates in the seventeenth century.

When Massine bought them, the largest of the three, Isola Lunga (approximately eight hundred meters in length), held a fourteenth-century ruined tower. On the highest island, Brigante, stood the remnants of another tower and a water cistern probably built in the seventeenth century by a nobleman from Sorrento. The third island, Rotunda, slightly larger than Brigante, was empty. From Galli one has a magnificent view across the water to Capri, Amalfi, and, on a clear day, the mountains of Sicily.

During the summer of 1924 Massine ordered the first fleet of workmen and materials from the mainland to Isola Lunga.

Massine

The local people in Positano referred to me as the mad Russian who has bought a rocky island where only rabbits could live. Even my caretaker, Nicola Grassi, was pessimistic, pointing out one tiny fig tree growing among the rocks and telling me that nothing would ever thrive on the island. One day a priest from Capri came to visit me. When I asked him if he thought I should ever succeed in cultivating the land, he bent down, picked up a handful of soil, and said: "This soil is the same as we have on Capri. I see no reason why you should not cultivate your island as we have done." He was right, but it was not as easy as it sounded, and it was many years before I was able to plant the island with vines and trees.[71]

In the course of Massine's life, the mission of building his home on Galli took on pharaonic dimensions. Working against the deteriorating effects of salt, winter weather, and time, he poured unflagging energy and a huge portion of his earnings into creating a refuge from the world. Galli came to stand for his hermeticism; as an almost Nietzschean metaphor, it exalted the individual's isolation in his struggle to live a truly creative life. Over the years his efforts were rewarded. Isola Lunga eventually boasted a private radio station; four beaches built by Massine; an electrical plant generating thirty kilowatts of power; a port with boathouse; four 400-meter terraced gardens planted with fruits, including grapes (the island eventually undertook its own small wine production); a lighthouse (serviced by the Italian government); a two-story central villa—for whose design in the 1930s Massine received suggestions from Le Corbusier—and a terrace with a spectacular view of Capri. A second five-bedroom villa, with a view of Positano, served as the caretaker's quarters. The fourteenth-century tower was eventually restored and became Massine's residence in his last years. Its interior had a sober Florentine aura, with Carrara marble pillars carved after those in the cathedral at Ravenna. On the first floor (above the ground floor) the choreographer erected a large dance studio, floored with Siberian pine and including a mezzanine balcony to seat a string quartet. A kitchen, a dining room, a library, and bedrooms completed the accommodations.* On Isola Lunga Massine also built an open-air theater, which was destroyed in a mid-1960s storm that sent its columns crashing into the sea.

On Brigante Massine restored a boathouse, built a large dock for fishing and swimming, and at the top of the island dug out two terraces for cultivation. Rotunda, the third island, remained undeveloped. In 1924,

---

* During my stay in Galli in 1978 I was Massine's guest at the tower.

all three islands were only deserted rocks in the Mediterranean. As time passed they became an indispensable resting place in a vertiginous life.

By 1925 Massine was back at work for the Ballets Russes and "felt again the atmosphere of creative exhilaration."[72] He claimed that after his London meeting with Diaghilev their relationship "was quickly re-established on its old footing" and that in Monte Carlo Diaghilev "welcomed me warmly."[73] Others report that the relationship was polite but distant. Right at the start Diaghilev made it clear to Massine that resumption of any close, friendly contact between them was out of the question.[74] Also, Diaghilev had taken Savina back into the Ballets Russes since her separation from Massine. (Later, after Marra and Massine separated, Diaghilev took her, too, into the company.) Massine's position in the company was undoubtedly difficult. He kept to himself and maintained a calculated distance from his colleagues. According to Sokolova:

From the first day he appeared embarrassed and uncomfortable with the company. When he said, "How do you do?" he just pressed his lips together and curled up the corners of his mouth: that sufficed for a smile. At rehearsals he spoke to no one, except to give directions: he and Grigoriev exchanged civilities and that was all. . . . Savina was ignored as if she did not exist. She was deeply hurt. Diaghilev and Massine were never seen together, and we gathered there was little love lost on either side. If in the old days it had been impossible to get a glimpse of Massine's inner thoughts and feelings, now he seemed to exist in complete isolation. It would have been interesting to know his opinion of Dolin, Lifar and Balanchine. He was lonely, but refused to be friendly, and although some of our "old gang" were secretly glad to have him back it was clear that an earthquake would be needed to make him show any emotion.[75]

It seems, though, that Massine was more at ease with those who had not been part of the company during his previous tenure. To the young Russian composer Vladimir Dukelsky (who later became famous as a composer of popular songs and musical comedies in the United States under the name Vernon Duke), it was a "delightful surprise" when "this forbidding and admittedly difficult master, certainly the top choreographer of his time, took to me and my music immediately. He smiled repeatedly, nodding his head, and he sat directly opposite me while I played."[76] The composer and the choreographer spent most evenings together, "which annoyed Diaghilev, who insisted that Léonide had no soul, no heart and no taste and was only interested in money."[77] Dukelsky, on the other hand, found "Léonide stimulating company, although he detested crowds, organized gaiety," and "disorganized drinking."[78]

Those who encountered Massine for the first time found him handsome and decidedly aloof, yet with a captivating, effortlessly theatrical air, especially in the rehearsal room, where he wore his habitual costume of black alpaca flamenco pants. They were high-waisted with creases down the sides, and his full-sleeved white crêpe de chine rehearsal shirt had been designed especially for him by Bakst. Dukelsky described him thus: "Although of a small stature, [Massine] was an arresting figure; his head was of extraordinary beauty, the eyes flashing and hypnotic, the smile rare and therefore all the more beguiling. His movements were brusque and oddly, determinedly, virile, with none of the unmasculine grace and softness too often typical of male dancers. . . . His manner was distant, inaccessible and reserved in the extreme."[79]

Massine's two choreographic assignments were both to use libretti by Boris Kochno, who had been Diaghilev's secretary and artistic collaborator since 1921.

The first Massine work rehearsed and premiered in Monte Carlo was *Zéphire et Flore,* a modern adaptation in seven scenes of an eighteenth-century tale in which Boréas, madly in love with Flore, kills Zéphire with an arrow during a game of blindman's bluff and carries Flore off to his cave. As Flore struggles helplessly with her abductor, the Muses arrive with the corpse of Zéphire. The gods intervene and revive Zéphire, the lovers are reunited, and Boréas is punished forever.

This would be another production in the Diaghilev postwar mold of works inspired by the Grand Siècle. The libretto grew out of Kochno's interest in Russian poetry inspired by mythological themes from Greece. When he first brought the idea to Diaghilev, the impresario proposed to do it in the Russian style prevalent at the beginning of the nineteenth century, when princes' private theaters sponsored plays performed by their serfs.[80] The music was commissioned from young Dukelsky; the scenery and costumes from Georges Braque.

According to Kochno, *Zéphire et Flore* marked a return by Massine to lyricism that lent the work an impressionistic quality. He felt that the choreographer was especially successful in realizing a lyrical neoclassicism in the roles of Zéphire and Flore, danced by Anton Dolin and Alice Nikitina. They were juxtaposed with the roles of Boréas (danced by Lifar) and the Muses, rendered in Massine's characteristic angular style.[81] The ballet was not well received in 1925 in Monte Carlo or later that same year in Paris, but it met with greater acceptance in the autumn in London. Writing in the *Morning Post*, Francis Toye described it as "an essay in pseudo-classicism."[82] *The Times* called the choreography "vivid and ingenious. [Massine] does not use concerted movements, like Fokine, but gives to each dancer a separate part, so that the effect may be called, in the musical term, contrapuntal."[83] The ballet also scored a big success in 1926 in Berlin.

Les Matelots was a practically plotless ballet in five scenes. It had a lively score by Georges Auric as well as scenery and costumes by the young Spanish painter Pedro Pruna, an artist who would collaborate with Diaghilev twice more during the 1920s. The action revolves around the adventures of three sailors and two girls and shows what happens when one of the sailors tries to test his girlfriend's fidelity. The scenario was little more than a pretext for the five characters to perform a *suite de danses* consisting of solos, pas de deux, pas de trois, and ensembles. For Massine the highlight of the production was a "carefully synchronized pas de trois in which the sailors, standing on chairs, mime the playing of a game of cards."[84] For Cyril Beaumont, the sailors' "rolling gait, their quick alert movements, their ability to retain their balance in almost every position, their susceptibility to women and their passion for cards, were all admirably expressed in Massine's choreography."[85] Although Valerian Svetlov found its almost nonexistent plot difficult to make out,[86] the ballet was nevertheless a tremendous success in its Paris premiere in 1925. Later that same year in London Raymond Mortimer wrote in the *New Statesman*: "Every movement is unmistakably signed 'Massine.' There is in it wit, satire and good humour, superabundant vitality and continual formal beauty."[87] According to *The Times*, Massine had "shown a great wealth of imaginative invention, which is very welcome after the pale trivialities recently put before us."[88] Diaghilev himself declared in the *Morning Post* that *"Les Matelots* is the most definite success we have had since the war. . . . Massine has achieved nothing so astonishing since the *Boutique*. And the reason why it is so good is that he did it quickly, in one impetus . . . here he has no doubts, no hesitations."[89]

Soon after Massine finished these works, and before the season began in Monte Carlo, he returned to London. Nineteen twenty-five was to be a busy year for him. He collaborated with Cochran on two revues, *On With the Dance* and its sequel, *Still Dancing,* serving as choreographer and dancer for both.

On With the Dance was a revue by Noël Coward, in two parts and twenty-two scenes, with music by Coward and Philip Braham. It featured the beloved star Alice Delysia, all *diamantée* with ostrich feathers, gowned by Paris couturier Jean Patou. Massine contributed three ballets: *The Rake, Crescendo,* and *A Hungarian Wedding.*

The Rake, which had music by Roger Quilter, scenery and costumes by William Nicholson, and masks by Betty Mutz, was inspired by the art of William Hogarth. According to Massine, "to suggest the debauchery of eighteenth-century England I filled the stage with Hogarthian characters—obese women, grotesque musicians and deformed bedlamites. As the Rake, drunk and slouching in his chair, Terry Kendall gave an excellent performance."[90] Cochran considered *The Rake* a "complete success."[91]

Crescendo had scenery and costumes by Gladys Calthrop and a score filled with jazzy tunes. ("Pick Up Your Sins" was its most popular melody.) The program note touted the ballet as epitomizing the 1920s:

> *In an age when the romance of Machinery is superseding the lilies and languors of Victorianism, Art must of necessity reflect the angular tendencies of the time. Man becomes a puppet, and Beauty a slave to the new forms of the relentless progress of civilisation. Crescendo is an attempt to portray the transition from the ethereal to the material—the gentle tranquility of* Les Sylphides *is rudely shattered by the insistent clamour of modernity— contemporary types push aside the dim memories of yesterday—Massine as the spirit of the age dominates the scene, and his puppets jib to the tune of cocktails and jazz, until, willy-nilly, they are swept up to a frenzied climax of impressionistic movement.*

In an interview with the *Morning Post* Massine described his approach in *Crescendo:*

> *Every age has its own way to move and its own dancing modes, and we cannot continue to devise our choreography according to the precepts of the schools of the sixteenth, seventeenth and eighteenth centuries. . . . What we have to do today to make dancing vital is to learn all we can from the Italo-French School of three hundred years ago, and transpose it into terms of the best in modern jazz. We have to alter the direction of the ancient school, and, by adapting its conventions, its form and its steps, create a new spirit representative of the spirit of the age.*[92]

But *Crescendo* had problems from the beginning, and modifications had to be made along the way. Cochran's practical, show-biz assessment in a letter to Massine was that "the opening was splendid, but from that point all dances seem a little on the long side, with the exception perhaps of the three 'Nifty Nats.' The ballet drops badly with the entrance of the three couples after Delysia's and your exit."[93] Cochran suggested that Massine cut two minutes and recommended that the dancers in the closing number, "The Automobile Age," wear motor goggles to convey to the audience the intended parody. Despite weak spots, the ballet had its effective moments, especially Massine's role. Coward wrote: "There is something elegantly vicious in the strange extremities of it; a corruption half base, half spiritual, with the inevitable latent sorrowfulness of conscious, unreluctant sin. The ballet itself is more or less incoherent, and trivial; but it is enough that you have created that strange, half-lunar figure, reaching blindly out to a beauty beyond its own posturing; as though it mocked lightly at things hidden from and sacred to itself."[94]

The evening ended with *A Hungarian Wedding,* led by Delysia singing. Massine and Marra danced in all three ballets.

Collaborating with Cochran in *On With the Dance* taught Massine even more about the dynamics of a musical revue than he had picked up working on *You'd Be Surprised.* Unlike the ballet process, where carefully crafted movements were honed during the rehearsal period into a polished work, in a revue changes were constantly being made on the spot to sharpen the production. Sometimes numbers had to be shortened or additions made, and these changes were always subject to further overhaul based on their success with the audience. The correspondence between Cochran and Massine lays out in detail the working relationship between a theatrical producer and a choreographer. Massine declared it a pleasure to work with Cochran, "for he did everything with vitality and imagination, responding with alacrity to new ideas, and maintaining a wonderful harmony between all his collaborators." Schooled in the ballet, Massine found the challenge of *On With the Dance* an "exciting venture" that brought him "into close contact with a fresh facet of the London theatre." He enjoyed meeting and working with Noël Coward, and was "immediately attracted by his charm and crackling wit."[95]

While *On With the Dance* ran at the London Pavillion, the Ballets Russes presented *Zéphire* and *Les Matelots* in Monte Carlo and Paris, and Massine received congratulatory cables from Diaghilev, Kochno, and Dukelsky. When the company moved to the London Coliseum in the summer, Massine rejoined them as guest dancer. In addition to some of his old roles, his repertory included for the first time the French sailor in *Les Matelots.* His return was not easy for Savina. Diaghilev vindictively paired them in the pas de deux from *Cimarosiana* and again in the Blue-bird pas de deux.

When the London engagement ended, Massine and Marra returned to Galli.

> From time to time I received letters from Semenoff [sic] in Positano, telling me what was happening on Galli. In this way I learned that work on the vineyards was going well, but that more pine trees had been destroyed by the tramontana—the bitter north wind that sweeps down from the mountains. I had already realized that the only way to combat the tramontana, and the equally destructive sirocco, was to continue planting trees every autumn, but not until I had lost hundreds of pines did I discover that the best things to plant on Galli were cypresses, the local Southern pines, and rosemary bushes. Through trial and error I was gradually learning how to cultivate my island. I visited nurseries in Florence and Rome during my holiday in the autumn of 1925, buying hundreds of plants and bushes, and also ordered grape vines to be shipped over from Sicily.[96]

Upon his return to London from Italy, Massine started work on the revue *Still Dancing*, which opened on November 19, 1925, at the Pavillion. Although this time Coward was not to be involved, Delysia remained the star. Within two parts and twenty scenes, there were four ballets by Massine: revivals of the successful *Rake* and *Hungarian Wedding* from *On With the Dance*, and two new works, *Pompeii à la Massine* and *Pyjama Jazz*.

Pompeii à la Massine had scenery and costumes by Doris Sinkeisen and a potpourri of melodies, mainly by Louis Ganne. The program note read: "The fantasy represents an entertainment presided over by Ariadne. It commences with a dance of flowers and a caterpillar, followed by the repair of Ariadne's heart, broken by the flight of Theseus. After an incident between the Alchemist and his clients, there comes a Chinese visitor. The Pavane, danced by Ariadne, leads up to the finale." *Pyjama Jazz*, the revue's finale, was a 1920s extravaganza led by Delysia, with the whole cast in fashionable pajamas provided for the occasion by Selfridge and Company.

Cochran's association with Massine proved so successful that before 1925 ended he began to negotiate Massine's participation in his next revue, *Cochran's Revue 1926*, scheduled to open on April 29. He wanted Massine and Nicholson, who had collaborated so successfully on *The Rake,* to work together again in a ballet based on an episode from Boccaccio's *Decameron*. Massine in turn suggested that Cochran engage

Massine in costume for the Chinese number in Still Dancing, *1927*

Dukelsky as composer and hire the dancers Nicholas Zverev and Vera Nemtchinova, who were husband and wife, from Diaghilev's company. Diaghilev, his fury held in check, genteelly complained to Cochran:

> *You knew, of course, that Mme. Nemchinova was my pupil and that it was with me that she learned to dance in the past ten years . . . Allow me to add in a friendly spirit that I very much regret . . . the way you exploit the Russian artists whom I have discovered and trained. Dukelsky writing bad fox-trots for musicals is not doing what he is destined to do; Massine dancing in supper clubs and composing choreographies in the style of* Pompeii à la Massine *dangerously compromises himself; likewise, Nemchinova is not made for revues . . . I take the liberty of telling you this in view of our longstanding friendship. One must create works and artists and not exploit those created by others for purposes very different from yours and in an atmosphere having nothing in common with what you do, and what you often do very well.*[97]

For *Cochran's Revue 1926* Massine revived his *Gigue* from Les Soirées and created two new works: a pas de deux, *La Carmagnole,* with decor by Guy Arnox and music by Adolf Stanislas, and the Boccaccio ballet, *The Tub. The Tub,* to music by Haydn, with scenery and costumes by Nicholson, was based on the tale of Giannello Strignario and revolved around the exploits of an unfaithful wife, Peronella (Nemtchinova), her deceived husband, Piero (Zverev), and her lover, Giannello (Massine). While the husband is away, Peronella receives her lover, but to their surprise the husband returns home with a friend who wants to buy a wine barrel. Peronella hides Giannello in the barrel, then, after he emerges, makes her husband believe that he, too, has come to buy it, and all ends well. Less neatly, life was imitating art, or vice versa: the triangle on stage was being paralleled in the performers' lives. Since their collaboration in *Les Matelots,* Massine and Nemtchinova had embarked upon a short-lived love affair.

In January of 1926, Massine had received preliminary offers from Diaghilev to revive *Mercure* and to make two new ballets: *La Pastorale,* to a score by Georges Auric, and *Jack-in-the-Box,* to orchestrated piano music by Satie. For *Jack-in-the-Box,* Massine was to collaborate again with Picasso. But when Massine skipped the Ballets Russes season in order to keep his commitment to Cochran in the spring of 1926, Picasso dropped out of the project and showed little interest in working with Diaghilev on any other. As it happened, Beaumont owned the rights to *Jack-in-the-*

Box and did not hesitate to impose on Diaghilev his choices of Derain as designer and Milhaud as orchestrator. (Beaumont wanted *Jack-in-the-Box* and *Mercure* to coincide with the Satie festival he was organizing as an homage to the recently deceased composer.) Diaghilev then proposed having *Mercure* rechoreographed, since Massine was unavailable; but Picasso objected, and *Mercure* was not to be restaged for Diaghilev until 1927.[98]

For the next two years Massine's life followed a pattern: the summer he would spend in Galli, supervising works in progress; from autumn through spring he would join Diaghilev as guest choreographer and dancer. In 1927 he produced the revival of *Mercure,* a new version of *Les Fâcheux,* and the world premiere of *Le Pas d'acier.* In 1928 he created his last work for Diaghilev, *Ode.*

Les Fâcheux, premiered on May 3, 1927, was another modern adaptation of an earlier work, Molière's 1661 comedy-ballet of the same name. Diaghilev first had produced it in 1924 with music by Auric, choreography by Nijinska and scenery and costumes by Braque. According to Kochno, the 1924 version failed because his libretto concentrated on individual characterizations, a challenge Nijinska was rarely up to, since her abilities were more suited to ensemble work. Massine, on the other hand, was skilled at embellishing the personality of each role. Kochno has called him a "clockmaker" who was able "to translate words into dance movements, contrary to Fokine, who translated words into pantomime." To Kochno, a ballet by Massine was *"une conversation chantée."*[99] Nevertheless, Massine's version of *Les Fâcheux,* following in Nijinska's footsteps, was not very successful.

Without doubt, Massine's boldest venture for the Ballets Russes in 1927 was *Le Pas d'acier,* which was premiered in Paris on July 4. The ballet, in two scenes, depicted two facets of Soviet life: the fields and the factory. It had a score by Prokofiev and scenery and costumes by Georgy Yakulov. *Le Pas d'acier* was Diaghilev's attempt to align himself with the experimental aesthetics of the postrevolutionary art of Russia, the outgrowth of the country's radically transformed political, social, and economic structure. One of the new artistic movements was constructivism, which celebrated the perfection of technology and the era of the machine. *Le Pas d'acier* was to be the Ballets Russes' contribution to constructivism.

Diaghilev's enthusiasm for a Soviet-inspired ballet was born in March of 1923, during the visit to Paris of Alexander Tairov's Kamerny Theater. Initially he planned to engage a team of Soviet artists: Tairov or

Vsevolod Meyerhold as director; Yakulov, Tairov's scenic designer; and Soviet choreographer Kasian Goleizovsky. When only Yakulov accepted his invitation, Diaghilev offered the commission for the stage direction and choreography to Massine, believing him, according to Kochno, the only other appropriate choice.[100]

Prokofiev and Yakulov wanted "to show what was new in the Soviet Union, above all, its achievements in construction." They would propel the "action on stage with big and small hammers, rotating conveyors—belts and fly-wheels and flashing signals. All this encouraged a common creative impulse during which the choreographic groupings both worked at machines and choreographically represented machines in operation."[101] The constructivist elements were to be provided also by Massine's choreography and mise-en-scène.[102] Massine devised a new choreographic lexicon that pictured, through expressive mechanical movements, a world in which human emotion was stifled.[103]

Despite British reservations about a Soviet-inspired ballet, when the new work was presented in London in July *The Times* found the second scene "extraordinarily impressive, and even terrifying."[104] Wrote the *Daily Express*: "Massine has created new postures and steps, strange contortions and movements that give the impression of powerful, complicated machinery, pistons working, wheels turning, and intense labour. The effect is stimulating, exciting, at times comic, and on the whole interesting to the highest degree."[105] For Cyril Beaumont, the second scene "gave a masterly impression of rhythmic power and beauty of machines":

> There were isolated movements which gradually built up into one huge machine, now of this type, now of that. Arms weaved, swung, and revolved; feet pounded the floor; even bodies took part in the movement, swinging from the waist in different arcs and at varying angles. The dancers massed, divided, strung out into line, and, with arms outstretched sideways, sharply turned their hands up and down, flat to the audience, which action ingeniously suggested a flashing lamp; this flashing, arranged in changing patterns, was most effective. So the rhythmic force ceaselessly grew in intensity until there appeared on a central platform two figures bearing giant hammers, which they swung and wielded more and more strongly until, at the height of the tumult, the climax was reached with the constructivist elements adding their quota—signal discs snapping on and off, and wheels spinning faster and faster. At this point the curtain fell to the accompaniment of a frenzied outburst of applause.[106]

Massine with Alexandra Danilova
in Le Pas d'acier, *1927*

This scene renewed Beaumont's "admiration for Massine's rare ability to contrive movements appropriate both to the theme of the piece and to the rhythm of the music, and then to combine the component parts into one vast orchestration of sound and expressive action, ever increasing in intensity until the conclusion was attained." [107]

Yet as the Ballets Russes season ended, Massine began to feel that most of his possibilities for creative work in Europe had been exhausted. He had now produced five more works for Diaghilev, but he remained unhappy. In his autobiography he remembers worrying in 1927 that since by then "Balanchine was doing so much of his [Diaghilev's] choreography . . . there would not be enough work for the two of us." [108] What he does not say is that although Balanchine had created six works in three years (1925–27), two of them—*La Pastorale* and *Jack-in-the-Box*—first had been offered to Massine and turned down by him, or that in 1927 Massine produced three ballets for Diaghilev, Balanchine one. Still, there is reason to believe that Massine chafed at sharing the Ballets Russes with *anyone*, since he had never had to before. And certainly he must have been irritated when Diaghilev commissioned from Balanchine a new version of *Le Chant du rossignol* in 1925, at a point when Massine's own version was only five years old.

But beyond any rivalry with Balanchine, Massine probably felt stunted artistically. His strained personal relationship with Diaghilev rendered him powerless in setting the company's artistic course—that responsibility had been given to Kochno. Massine's chief contribution thus far had been to execute projects that had been conceived by others. He behaved like a competent craftsman: he came, did his job, and left.

So in the summer of 1927 he set his sights across the Atlantic. If the United States was not to offer him the creative outlet he longed for, it might at least provide more generous financial rewards. And there was no denying that money was desperately needed to continue the renovations on Galli. [109] By July he was writing to Otto Kahn in New York to explore the possibility of working at the Metropolitan Opera House. He also contacted three English theatrical agencies, Daniel Meyer Company, Foster's, and Ernest Edelstein, as well as any other London contact who might help him secure a job in the United States—if not at the Met, then perhaps on the Broadway stage, in Hollywood, or with the Chicago Civic Opera. On February 7, 1928, Massine sailed for New York on the *Mauretania*, clutching letters of introduction, including four from Cochran to theatrical tycoons Charles B. Dillingham, Florenz Ziegfeld, Morris Guest, and Max Hart. New York's Plaza Hotel became his center of operations.

By the time his frantic American sojourn ended in mid-March, the agent William Morris had negotiated for Massine a preliminary contract with S. L. Rothafel of the Roxy Theatre in New York. The six-month term of the agreement would begin in December 1928 and included first-class transportation from Europe as well as a weekly starting salary of $350.[110]

Back in Europe, Massine hectically began preparing repertory to bring to the United States. He sought performing rights to some of his works in the Ballets Russes repertory and to the segments he had created for Cochran's revues. He also found creative energy for two new ballets, *Perpetomobile* and *Ode.*

Unsatisfied with doing Ballets Russes work for hire, Massine now began to explore ideas independently. His inclination toward abstraction, which first had shown up in his 1920 *Sacre du printemps,* by 1927 had become nearly all-absorbing. By the end of that year, in search of collaborators for an uncompromising abstract ballet, he approached two old friends, Sonia and Robert Delaunay. In a carefully composed letter, Sonia responded ecstatically, congratulating Massine on his commitment to a new "regenerating and liberating movement" that was to signal the "beginning of a new era for ballet."[111] A sort of budding manifesto, her letter divided ballet into three periods: classicism; the analytical period, which she called the *"époque de nature morte"*; and modern ballet, or the "period of pure dance." Sonia believed that their collaboration could coax modern ballet to "wash off all that junk dealing [*brocante*] of false modernity, of mannerism and idiocy." The aim of their work together was to force ballet to align itself with the new contemporary art and produce "pure dance for the senses and the intellect, without tricks, naked."[112]

Such brave words make it all the more regrettable that even today the history of *Perpetomobile* remains largely unknown. Set to music by Schubert, it was described on a list of productions Massine intended to take to America as "visions of rhythm and colour by L. Massine with scenery and dresses by Sonia and Robert Delaunay."[113] We know that Massine began to rehearse the work in Paris after his return from the United States, and some of Sonia's costume sketches have survived; all other specific information about the work is lost. It is impossible to say whether it was completed and, if so, whether it may have been privately presented or was in fact never seen outside a rehearsal room.

Despite these uncertainties, *Perpetomobile* holds a prominent place in Massine's oeuvre. It marks the high point of his exploration of abstraction during the 1920s, and its conception is a precursor to his purely abstract symphonic ballets of the 1930s. One can see in the description of

Perpetomobile a clear point of departure for his 1933 collaboration with André Masson in *Les Présages,* and its influence is apparent again in his 1939 collaboration with Matisse in *Rouge et noir.*

The argument for *Perpetomobile*'s pivotal role in Massine's growth becomes even more tantalizing when one examines a work completed around the same time, his last for Diaghilev. *Ode: Meditation on the Majesty of God on the Occasion of an Apparition of Aurora Borealis* has long been regarded as one of the Ballets Russes' most elaborate and hypnotic productions. It was a ballet oratorio in three acts to a libretto by Kochno, with music by Nicolas Nabokov, scenery and costumes by Pavel Tchelitchev, and special lighting effects and projections by filmmaker Pierre Charbonnier. It had the barest of story lines: "Nature expands her mysteries to a pupil. She exhibits the stars, and a river, flowers and bacteria, and finally 'the master work, the end of all yet done'—man."[114] The oratorio was based on an ode by the eighteenth-century Russian writer Mikhail Lomonosov. Diaghilev first envisioned it as a period piece recalling imperial coronation festivities, and it is on this idea that Kochno based his libretto. But as work among Kochno, Tchelitchev, and Massine went forward, the original concept underwent drastic revision, and Tchelitchev's notion of building the ballet around "the seven days of creation culminating with the appearance of the Aurora Borealis—the northern lights" prevailed.[115] In the end, *Ode* became for Kochno an evocation of the sumptuousness of the tsarist court translated into modernist terms.[116] For his part, Diaghilev loathed the final conception and doubted that the collaborators could bring it off.[117]

Rehearsals for *Ode* began in Monte Carlo in the spring and continued in Paris. Diaghilev by this time had ceased to take much direct interest in Ballets Russes productions, but in this case he took control of final rehearsals to bring some order to what he considered the chaotic state of *Ode.* Above all, according to Haskell and Nouvel, Diaghilev wanted "to suppress a series of cinematographic projections that horrified him."[118]

Nevertheless, the final result was impressive. *Ode* was a multimedia work whose cosmic/microscopic effects were achieved with the help of slide and film projections on a giant backcloth, making the character of nature itself seem to float on clouds. Phosphorescent costumes and neon light projections heightened the effect. Cecil Beaton was especially taken by Tchelitchev's decor:

Ode *was remarkable for the fact that Tchelitchev had completely discarded painted scenery. The setting consisted of ropes and two lines, which mounted from either wing to meet high above the centre of the back of the stage, on which were hung small dolls. . . . Against a blue void the still, small dolls gave the scene vast size and depth, while the black, white and grey dancers formed triangles of rope, strange mechanical designs.*

There was no insistence on the reality of this geometrical immensity. The keynote was suggestion: when Lifar appeared as a cleric, he wore a curé's tabs, but retained the dancer's tights. All the dancers, their faces obliterated with flat masks, were black-gloved symbols in a nocturnal world. Behind gauze screens a man and a tall, thin woman, like a blade, gave an impression of nakedness, without conscious nudity. It seemed as if all humanity had been reduced to embryonic form.[119]

When first approached for *Ode*, Massine had felt that the poem, "a contemplative hymn to nature," was not appropriate for a ballet. But after studying it, he "found a series of images beginning to take shape" in his mind.[120] Together he and Tchelitchev mapped out a cohesive visual spectacle blending stage design and choreography in a totally unified effect. Massine hewed to classical ballet technique, relying for his effects on purity of line and elongated movements. Felia Doubrovska, who danced in the premiere, recalled that with the exception of some of the architectural and geometrical configurations for the corps de ballet and the role danced by Lifar, the choreography was poetic and classical, emphasizing long arabesques, développés, and a formal rhythmic beauty.[121] The classical line was accentuated by the female dancers' costumes: white unitards and headpieces like swimming caps. (Doubrovska's exquisite physical instrument probably served Massine's choreography beautifully.)

Ode was an important advance in the evolution of Massine's "new classicism." Even as early as the *Astuzie* divertissement of 1920, he was beginning to depart from the choreography he had produced under the influence of the neoprimitivist and modernist aesthetics of Gontcharova, Larionov, Picasso, and Falla. In 1926 he had begun to study in London with Nicholas Legat, former director of the Imperial Ballet School in St. Petersburg. Legat helped him to trust his emerging new feeling for flowing movement and openness, and to move beyond Cecchetti's more self-contained classical style and Massine's own deeply imbedded roots in folk dance. The elements of this new classicism stand out in several of Massine's works from the twenties, especially *Le Beau Danube, Divertissement, Les Roses, Zéphire et Flore,* and *Ode,* but it would find its most sublime expression in the symphonic ballets that he began to produce in 1933.

When *Ode* premiered on June 6, 1928, in Paris and on July 9 in London, its reception was mixed. The ballet was visually splendid, yet most critics were perplexed by the multimedia effects or by the work's overpowering surrealism—or both. In London, Edwin Evans reacted coolly to some of the lighting devices and film projections but admired the choreography, calling it "extraordinarily good" and finding in "its soft-hued background and the dancers in pure white before it [a scene] to be remembered long afterwards as a feast of beauty in movement."[122] Cyril Beaumont praised the choreography: "Massine displayed the greatest innovation and originality in the composition of his ever-changing groups, which were never symmetrical and yet harmonious. The actual movements were in the manner of the classical ballet whose linear beauty was here given its full value by reason of the bodies being, for all practical purposes, unclothed. But the lines had an unusually austere and chaste quality, a geometrical rather than an emotional beauty."[123] Beaumont described one of the pas de deux as an "elegy" in which

> the dancers jointly upheld, each with one upraised hand, a slender, horizontal pole, from the first and last third of which was suspended a length of gauze, a little higher than a man and about twice the breadth of his body. This device was like two straight curtains with a gap between them equal to the width of one. A number of beautiful effects were achieved when the dancers danced behind the gauze, which invested them with ectoplastic quality, or else appeared alternately in the open space, so that a solid form danced with a shadow in one; sometimes their arms alone curved and crossed in the intervening space.[124]

For Beaumont, *Ode* had a "strange character," a "celestial beauty," and an "intellectual appeal." A decade later, A. V. Coton called it "the 1928 grand experiment."[125] Lynn Garafola argues that *Ode*, like *Apollon Musagète*, another 1928 Diaghilev production (with choreography by Balanchine), anticipates the 1930s "in the appearance of dreams, romance, and fantasy elements . . . in the new importance assigned to dance in the overall ballet spectacle, and in the renewal of interest in the danse d'ecole."[126]

Before departing for the United States at the end of the year, Massine was engaged by Ida Rubinstein to choreograph two ballets for her newly organized company. They were not to be premiered until the following year.

The Russian-born Rubinstein had made her Paris debut with the Ballets Russes, dancing the leading roles in Fokine's *Cléopâtre* and

Schéhérazade. Her technique rose to amateur level at best, but she excelled in mimed parts where her enigmatic beauty could often be seen to great advantage. After her success with Diaghilev she sponsored seasons in Paris, presenting works created for her by some of the era's most prominent artists. In 1928 she founded her own company, producing ornate works in which she was regarded as the absolute embodiment of fin-de-siècle aesthetics. She held court in her Parisian *hôtel particulier* (decorated by Bakst), surrounded by a number of influential personalities from the worlds of society, the arts, and letters, including Gabriele d'Annunzio, Paul Valéry, Ravel, Gide, and Benois.

Massine's two productions for Rubinstein—conceived, as was customary, by the diva herself—were *David* (libretto by André Doderet, music by Henri Sauguet, and designs by Benois) and *Les Enchantements d'Alcine* (libretto by Louis Laloy after Ariosto, music by Auric, designs by Benois). Both works revolved around a hero's adventures and provided exotic backdrops for Rubinstein's striking presence. They exploited her penchant for playing male parts *en travesti*, a trademark of her productions since her unforgettable creation of the title role in the Debussy-d'Annunzio *Martyre de Saint Sébastien* in 1911. Rubinstein steeped these roles in decadent sexual ambiguity, which delighted her followers.

Massine, however, was not much inspired by her. For one thing, he was being asked merely to prop up, not to elevate, her lurid conceptions. The grande dame herself was yet another problem. "Rubinstein, who was really more of an actress than a dancer, was beautiful and statuesque, but though she had a striking stage presence it was difficult to get her to move gracefully." Since the ballets were "centered on her," Massine "had very little opportunity for original choreography."[127]

Despite this unfulfilling work, the months spent in Paris put Massine in high spirits. Already that spring Nabokov had found the choreographer "at moments even gay and smiling" instead of his usual "stern and taciturn" self.[128] There was good reason: he was in love with a beautiful twenty-year-old Russian dancer, Eugenia Delarova.

Delarova, born in 1907 in St. Petersburg, left the Soviet Union in 1926. She met Massine in Paris in the spring of 1928 in a class given by the Russian ballerina Lubov Egorova. One day after class he asked Delarova about the situation in Russia at the time of her departure. The conversation was brief, but provocative enough to make him go to see her dance at the Folies-Bergère. Later he showed up at a rehearsal of a troupe assembled by Nemtchinova and Dolin, where she was a recent recruit. Finally, he sent her a note at the Folies-Bergère asking her out. After several dates, the love affair grew passionate.[129]

Delarova, extroverted and easygoing, found Massine gloomy and too serious. His lifestyle seemed to her needlessly severe and austere, and she saw no reason for him to dress stuffily in dark clothes. He seemed aloof and guarded all the time. But Delarova had fallen in love, and decided to brighten him up, hoping her ability to enjoy life would prove contagious. And her lack of inhibition gradually rubbed off on him; he allowed for some spontaneity and became much more stylish.

During the summer, on their way to Galli, they motored through some of Massine's favorite Italian towns, lingering in Florence and Naples, where he showed her the paintings and architecture he had learned to love. In Positano they visited the Semenovs, who had become Massine's surrogate family. By then Massine's appearance had begun to show some moderating Delarova touches: sandals, shorts, brightly colored shirts. His inordinate jealousy didn't faze her, and their first few months together were idyllic. Caressed by the southern Italian sun, their days in Galli were filled with romance. By night they would sail in the moonlight, their favorite music pouring lushly from a portable gramophone. As soon as they arrived back in Paris from their holiday, they married, and days later they sailed for America.

PART FOUR

Years of Transition: The Symphonic Ballets

Only metaphor can provide us with evasion, and it creates out of real things imaginary reefs, the blossoming of illusory islands.

—ORTEGA Y GASSET

Massine's dancers in the fourth movement of Choreartium, 1933:
*Tatiana Riabouchinska, Tamara Toumanova, and
David Lichine in the foreground*

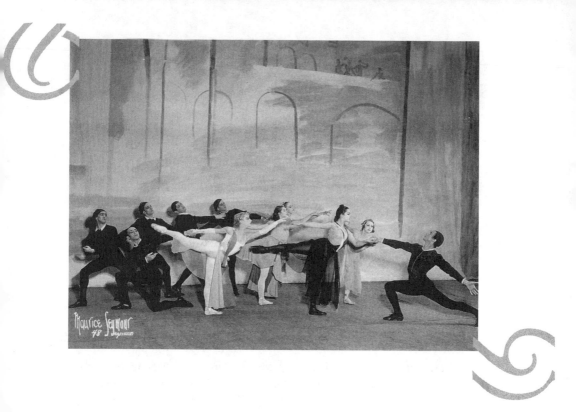

CHAPTER 10

New York, December 1928–London, June 1936

MASSINE'S ARRIVAL in New York was scarcely publicized. In the *New York Times* John Martin hinted that the Roxy management harbored some misgivings about just how well their new choreographer would adapt to working in the American theater. The Roxy's terse announcement had said only that Massine would assist Miss Ragge and Léon Leonidov in staging the theater's dance offerings. "Assistant" struck Martin as a surprisingly humble job description for one of the world's leading choreographers. But Rothafel was in fact hiring Massine on a trial basis. He had been warned not only that Massine was difficult and demanding but that his productions could be ruinously expensive.[1] In order to dispel just such doubts, Massine had asked Cochran to vouch for him personally with Rothafel.[2] He was fully aware of his predicament: "In Europe I had made something of a reputation, but in America I was just another dancer who had been vaguely associated with the Ballets Russes."[3]

The productions at the Roxy, I discovered, were vaudeville-type spectacles performed on a vast raked stage. I was amazed at the way the director, Léon Leonidov, managed to manoeuvre the interminable rows of sequined and high-kicking chorus girls on and off stage. When I was introduced to Leonidov he told me that I would be expected to provide a new ballet every week, with occasional solos and divertissements.

It was a staggering responsibility to have to create every week a ballet which would appeal to the enormous Roxy audience, particularly as my productions had to be coordinated with the weekly theme of the rest of the spectacle and in keeping with the seasons of the year. I composed Spring Ballets, Easter Ballets, Christmas Ballets, and ballets for such festivals as St. Valentine's Day, Halloween and Thanksgiving. The music was mostly Victor Herbert, Sigmund Romberg and Franz Lehár. As well as rehearsing the new ballet, which had to be ready by Thursday each week, I also danced four times a day, and five times on Saturday. I did not see much of New York. When I was not at the Roxy I was in my bed, asleep. Eugenia was in the corps de ballet, and she too danced four times a day and five on Saturday. It was a miserable life for her, but she realized we had no choice, and never complained.[4]

In May 1929 Massine and Delarova made a short trip to Paris to supervise the final rehearsals of *David* and *Alcine* for Rubinstein. Feeling as if they had just been "let out of prison,"[5] they rambled about Paris visiting old hangouts, shopping, strolling through galleries, or enjoying old friends, especially Gontcharova, Larionov, and the Delaunays. At Sonia Delaunay's boutique, Delarova bought new dresses. Then the couple returned to New York and toiling at the Roxy.

In August 1929, the Massines were on a short vacation in Virginia Beach. A member of the local press gave them the awful news: on the nineteenth, in Venice, Diaghilev had died. Massine "sat down on a bench and thought of all the years I had spent with him, all the ballets we had collaborated on, all the times I had danced for him. . . . Although I had twice left his company, I had the deepest affection and admiration for him, and knew too how much I owed him. . . . Having been so closely connected with him for so many years, I think I must have felt his loss more than anyone."[6]

In the years ahead, with the man of flesh and blood actually gone,

Massine's recollections of Diaghilev would gradually shift from memory to myth. Massine, Diaghilev's pupil turned antagonist, eventually became his most fervent apostle. The edge of their stormy relations dulled with time. For the moment, however, his present responsibilities called to Massine and, bewildered as he must have been at this paradoxical loss, he could deal with his sorrow only by quickly returning to New York—and to work.

Immediately after Diaghilev's death Massine wrote to Beaumont:

Etienne! Do you want to take over the direction of the Ballets Russes? I would leave everything here in order to help you—we would create masterpieces—Picasso will help us . . . I am full of enthusiasm—and if you believe that you would like to do it, cable me to come to Europe and I will leave immediately.

We will take another direction—there are so many beautiful things to be done—discuss all of this with Picasso . . . Etienne—you are the only person who could succeed.[7]

Tempting as this offer may have been, Beaumont was not interested in following in Diaghilev's footsteps.

Cole Porter introduced Massine to theatrical producer E. Ray Goetz, who hoped to reconstitute the Ballets Russes in America and present seasons in New York and on tour.[8] (Goetz had wanted to do the same thing in 1928, but no engagements materialized.) Now, with Massine as middleman, Goetz moved to secure the rights to the deceased impresario's properties; but in the United States of 1929 raising cash proved extremely difficult, and he had abandoned the idea by 1931. This was only one of many disappointments for Massine in the years from 1929 to 1931. He drove himself into a frenzy trying to resurrect Diaghilev's company. He talked up the idea continually with the Grigorievs, Woizikowski, Sokolova, Doubrovska, Balanchine, and Lifar, among other Ballets Russes alumni.[9] Looking for financial backing, he found two major prospects: Sir Thomas Beecham at Covent Garden and René Blum at the Casino de Monte Carlo. Negotiations with Beecham lasted until 1932, but nothing came of them. And in Monte Carlo, where at first there was no interest in reviving Diaghilev's company, by 1931 Blum was instead organizing a new permanent ballet company at the Casino in collaboration with Colonel Wassily de Basil of the Paris-based Opéra Russe. The spring of 1932 witnessed the triumphant debut of the Ballets Russes de Monte Carlo.[10]

Massine

Yet Massine stood apart from these developments, doggedly trying to keep his career afloat in hectic round trips between the United States and Europe. The artistic highlight of 1930 was a revival of his *Sacre du printemps* for the League of Composers. Nicholas Roerich was to collaborate on the design; Leopold Stokowski would conduct the Philadelphia Orchestra. Cast in the role of the Chosen Maiden was the American modern dancer Martha Graham, who later reminisced:

> It was a great turning point in my life, and it moved me into an area which fed me a very great deal. I had no sense of belonging to the ballet world at that time, and I was struggling to find a language which was, I felt, a little more true than what I had to do in the Follies and in vaudeville, when I was there, and in Denishawn. . . .
>
> The passionate Russian thing—whether it's Russian or whether it's primal doesn't matter, but the rite was a sacrificial one and it had nothing to do with the idiosyncrasies of ballet style or modern dance. You had to accommodate yourself to it, and the music is very, very powerful, as we all know. We go and hear somebody's new composition just this year, and we will say, "Well, that is just straight out of Stravinsky," because he has a lure for people which is very hard to resist. I met him once. I meant absolutely nothing to him. He was in a wrath at the moment—not at me, but just at the world in general.
>
> But Sacre meant spiritually a great deal to me and still does. . . . It's close to me emotionally and it was a turning point in my life.[11]

Stories about the edgy working relationship between Massine and Graham during *Le Sacre du printemps* abound.[12] How true are any of them? Two such volatile personalities would seem to provide ample material for combustion, but in fact there appears to have been only one minor flare-up: Graham refused to rehearse her solo in full force. Such holding back in rehearsal would indeed have been incomprehensible to Massine, who came from a deeply ingrained Russian tradition of zealous commitment to a role from day one. As a result, so the story goes, he threatened to replace her. But *did* he? Anna Sokolow, who danced in *Sacre*, suggested that Graham's decision not to dance full out in rehearsal was due to simple precaution, because she first "wanted to see what we were doing and how we were reacting to the direction of Massine."[13] Bessie Schönberg, another cast member, concluded that Graham "faithfully learned what Massine had to teach her, but then she took it to the studio by herself and made it her own, which I am sure meant that she stressed other things than Massine might have and changed certain things. I am sure she didn't want particularly to exhibit this every time at rehearsal and have Massine say, 'You're not doing it right.' "[14] Also, she cannot have been eager to appear a fool before the eleven members of her own company who were dancing in *Sacre*.

Others recall no temperamental exchanges at all between Graham and Massine. Lily Mehlman, also in the cast, remembered Graham as "very cooperative . . . and there was great respect shown to her by Stokowski and Massine."[15] Said Schönberg: "When she was needed, she was all there."[16] In conversations with the author, Delarova did not recall any particular friction. Massine, also in conversations with the author, described his work with Graham as unqualifiedly productive. In his memoirs he wrote: "Martha Graham's powerful performance as the Chosen Maiden added considerable strength to the production. I found her a most subtle and responsive dancer to work with, and her small stature and delicate movements gave the role an added poignancy."[17] Nor would Graham confirm stories about dissension between herself and Massine:

I'm sorry to disappoint you on that. I had made up my mind that I would follow direction completely, and I did. I never argued with any of them because I felt they were dealing with something which I was not ready to deal with choreographically or musically, and I remember the first time Massine came to my apartment. It was during the Depression, and I had an apartment that looked over Central Park which I got because nobody else wanted it. . . . It had no furniture. I had an army cot, and a chest of drawers, and a kitchen table, a grand piano, and a Victrola. So Massine came and we played the Sacre. He was very nostalgic. He said it was a very different way of hearing it, compared to the last time he had heard it, and it brought back memories which I'm sure didn't encompass a bare living room in the Depression facing Central Park with a small Victrola on the floor and no other furniture except the piano.

But I made up my mind that I would follow his choreography as nearly as I could, and his direction, and I did. There were certain things balletically that I changed a bit. But my style was beginning to develop at that time, and I would do the thing the way I would do it, you see, and usually Massine was very generous and he said, "We'll keep that." For instance a leap or something of that kind. And I remember rehearsing with him at Roseland because there were no studios available—this great big shiny room with all those mirrors. I was very thin in those days and I was in a

black dress. And he was very thin and he was in black, kind of Spanish
pants that he always had, and he looked at us in the mirror. He was teach-
ing and we were alone. He said, "We look enough alike to be brother and
sister." Well, we did in some strange way. . . .[18]

To say the least, stories about strife between Massine and Graham seem
to have been much exaggerated.

Massine's *Sacre* was a singular event in the development of American dance. One of the most prestigious ballet choreographers of the day
was working in the United States with *modern* dancers; thus it marked an
important moment of fusion between two apparently irreconcilable approaches. According to Sokolow, "It was a revelation in the world of
modern dance to have a Russian ballet artist come in, introduce us to another world, introduce us to Stravinsky . . . and then watching Massine
work, which we did when we stood on the side while he worked on
other things. . . . I couldn't help thinking that there was a connection between the approach to dance as Martha Graham had and Léonide Massine had."[19] Bessie Schönberg described Graham's daring solo: "She was
in the air practically all the time. They were complete splits in the air
with, of course, not her toes pointed, but her heels pointed and her
hands at an angle. And they were like little screams in the air, they were
like little yells; and it was frenetic, extraordinary; and deeply moving,
deeply moving."[20]

The ballet was presented in Philadelphia on April 11 and at the Metropolitan Opera in New York on April 22, sharing the program with the
American premiere of Schoenberg's opera *Die glückliche Hand.* The double bill, called the "most important dance event of the entire year"[21] by
the New York *Herald Tribune,* was ecstatically received by the press and
the intelligentsia. In the *Times* John Martin wrote:

There can be little question that it provided a landmark on the road to the
theatrical theatre, the theatre of synthesis, or "rhythm," as Mr. Stokowski
called it. . . .

Of Massine's choreography it is only possible to speak with enthusiasm.
Just as the music does not yield its fullness at one hearing, it is doubtful if
there is one pair of eyes in a thousand capable of seeing the full richness
and beauty of this dance setting. As has been noted already, it was extraor-
dinarily inventive. The movements of the individual dancers were colored
with hieratic suggestions and imbued with a tremendous muscular vigor
which at the same time seemed to be inhibited by the mental limitations of

a crude people. Through this combination of opposing ideas the choreographer conveyed without an instant's relief the overpowering influence of something not understood—the mystery, if you will, of nature in its vernal surging. In the mass designs were creations of surpassing beauty, ingenious to the last degree, but none the less stable for that. . . .

In the first part of the ballet there perhaps was the most impressive evidence of Massine's artistry. The dance of the adolescents, in which the men perform tremendous movements before a background of girls seated and moving with their arms; the mock abduction and the spring rounds that follow; the games of the rival tribes, and the intricate and extraordinary mass movement that closes the act, all these are choreography that ranks at the very top of modern dancing. Through its complicated visual counterpoint and its terrific energy, there shines the barbaric passion of elemental human beings. If it were not so near in the physical standards of savagery, akin to that of the animals themselves, it would be sensual and voluptuous beyond what we are accustomed to condone in the theatre. As it is, it is so young, so frank, so strong, that it seems a part of nature itself, a visualization of that rich depth which rolls through the music.

As the maiden chosen for sacrifice, Martha Graham proved once again her right to rank with the foremost of her art. The famous dance which brings the ballet to an end puts a terrific burden upon the dancer. After two acts of mass movement, keyed far higher than any single dancer could be expected to reach, she is called upon to touch the peak of performance. This is a problem for the choreographer as well, and Miss Graham in the movement designed for her by Massine succeeded in doing the seemingly impossible. . . .[22]

But even the complete triumph of *Sacre* could not guarantee Massine further employment. For the next two years the bustling between Europe and the United States continued. Except for commitments to the Roxy in the early spring and guest performances at the Arts Club of Chicago, by 1931 Europe was again the Massines' center of operations.

In April, Walter Nouvel had approached Massine on behalf of Ida Rubinstein to return to Paris the following month.[23] Rubinstein engaged Massine from May 1 through July 15 for her company's Parisian and Covent Garden seasons; he was to supervise revivals of *David* and *Alcine* and to stage a new production, *Amphion*.

The *mélodrame Amphion* revolved around the adventures of the mythical character who received a lyre from Mercury and whose music moved stones. It was based on a poem by Paul Valéry, set to music by

Arthur Honegger of Les Six, with scenery and costumes by Alexandre Benois. Valéry's idea for this pantomime-ballet was to demonstrate expressive parallels among music, mime, and gesture (for him gesture had the triple value of the symbolic, the significative, and the active). He wanted "words, song, orchestra, pantomime, dance, and theatrical design to all merge as a whole."[24]

Valéry's involvement created high anticipation in the Paris press. But *Amphion* opened on June 23 to mixed reviews. Instead of the promised coordination of voice, music, action, and dance, most reviewers found confusion on stage. Louis Schneider lauded Benois's sumptuous decor in the grand opera style as "nothing Greek, nothing classical; conceived, as the costumes, in that modern Russian style that opens the door to all fantasies."[25] André George, on the other hand, deplored its "dark heaviness."[26] Henri Malherbe lamented that the designs, though naturalistic in inspiration, contradicted the symbolic intention of the poet, which was to free himself from the pseudorealistic style.[27]

As always with Rubinstein, the choreography relied more on pantomime than dance. Yet Levinson felt that "Massine's choreography, though relegated to semidarkness since all the light was directed towards the protagonist and surrounded by all sorts of obstacles, manifested originality, although it was compressed by the uncalled-for tyrannical necessities of a paradoxical mise-en-scène."[28] The choreography's "counterpoint of movement" and "monumental gymnastics" were not "exempted of grandeur," and "Massine's Russian constructivism" was justified by the libretto.[29]

Once again, Rubinstein was lambasted for producing works that kept her own persona firmly at center stage. There would always be those who would succumb to her charms, Emile Vuillermoz acknowledged. Nevertheless, he bluntly asked, "Why does she persist in personally engaging in battles in the fields of choreography and diction out of which she would not be able to emerge victoriously?"[30] Levinson complained, "How sad that Mme Rubinstein, who stages so many important productions, persists in spoiling everything by becoming a star."[31]

The Rubinstein engagement ended in July, and the Massines spent the rest of their summer in Galli. The young composer Igor Markevitch—Diaghilev's last lover—was their guest. In the spring Massine had been approached by the British and Dominions Film Corporation to create a new ballet to be included in an English film based on the story of *Le Beau Danube*.[32] He had chosen Markevitch as composer, before having

met him, undoubtedly through the good offices of Alexandrine Troussevitch. Troussevitch, who had become a sort of secretary to Diaghilev
during the impresario's final years, had introduced him to Markevitch;
and after Diaghilev's death she backed Massine's efforts to revive the Ballets Russes. (An eccentric chain smoker, Troussevitch spent her last years
in a Greek Orthodox convent in Palestine.)

From their first meeting in Paris, relations between Massine and
Markevitch were friendly:

> *Massine and I met in Paris for the first time, and he was so moved by the
> memory of Diaghilev, which I embodied for him, that he could not hold
> back his tears. As for me, I remember the atmosphere of exceptional qual-
> ity which emanated from his personality, which was possessed by the
> power of his own creativity in a way that was both naive and willful. The
> more I have become acquainted with Massine at his work, as I saw him
> implement a choreography or give a course in classical or Spanish dance,
> and the more I have learned of the first works he created in conjunction
> with old collaborators such as Picasso or Cocteau, all the more I have
> reached the conviction that Massine will turn out to have been one of the
> greatest choreographers and dancers of all times; possibly the most com-
> plete of all. . . .*
>
> *Many artistic affinities brought us close to each other from the start.
> The Ballets Russes remained for Massine one of those rare subjects on
> which he would expound, and which seemed to touch him. One felt that
> they had brought him to himself and that he felt a deep need to keep them
> in his memory. The rest of the time, as he concentrated upon his work, he
> did not offer many possibilities for contact and was easily thought of as in-
> human.*[33]

Their second meeting took place in Naples, where they rented a vertical
piano to bring along to Galli. On the island, Markevitch was introduced
to Delarova and to Massine's father, Feodor, who had recently arrived
from the Soviet Union to visit his son in Italy.

Over the years Massine had maintained a steady correspondence
with his family in Russia, although he had not seen them since 1914. His
sister, Raissa, and brother Mikhail had both married, and Mikhail had
two children. His mother and brother Gregori had died, and Massine
now wanted Feodor to spend time with him in Galli. His father helped
with domestic chores, and "every evening at sunset he would stand out
on the patio, playing his French horn, and I shall always remember him,

sunburned, white-haired, but still erect, as he played us the lovely old Russian tunes which were part of my childhood."[34]

On the island Massine and Markevitch immersed themselves in the creation of the ballet score and libretto, and though the work was demanding, their days under the hot August sun were relaxing in all respects but one. Much to Markevitch's astonishment, Delarova—whom he described as "seductive" and "passionate"—began an open flirtation with him. Given Massine's jealous nature, it is easy to see why, according to Markevitch, the "atmosphere became tensed, the island seemed to shrink, Massine's handsome face became impenetrable, and I feared all the time a catastrophe."[35] Getting off the island may have been the only way to ease the strain. Thus, when work on the ballet score was complete, the party, with the exception of Massine's father, returned to the mainland. (Brigitte Helm, the star of the film, so disliked Markevitch's score that the ballet was dropped from the project before it was choreographed.)

Massine and his wife were given to exploring Italy's ruins, architectural sites, and museums. He took special delight in guiding her around a country he had learned to love through Diaghilev's eyes. On this particular excursion, they parted from Markevitch and traveled on their own to Sicily by car.

> From Taormina we drove via Syracuse, Agrigento and Segesta, to Selinus, where I was overwhelmed by the sheer immensity of the ruined Temple of the Giants. Wandering among these fragmentary columns and massive remains of statues of mighty gods, some with severed torsos over forty feet long, I was excited by the challenge which they presented. They immediately suggested to me vast harmonic groupings, and I wondered if it would be possible to create with human bodies a similar feeling of physical grandeur wedded to pure music. I realized that this could only be done by using the symphony of a great composer as the inspiration for my choreography, an idea which was to return to me later.[36]

That autumn and winter Massine pursued various projects that were set to debut the following year. First, he signed with Milan's Teatro alla Scala to choreograph two works to open the following January: a revival of Giuseppe Adami's *Vecchia Milano,* and *Belkis.* The latter, a grandiose pageant in six scenes to music by Respighi, featured the Persian princess-turned-dancer Leila Bederkhan. According to the *Dancing Times,* some of the numbers were successful, especially those performed by the rising Scala star Attilia Radice, but overall Massine's choreography was dull and repetitious.[37]

He was to fare better on the London theatrical stage. In September, Cochran approached him to create the dances for *Helen!*, a new production based on Offenbach's operetta *La Belle Hélène*.[38] It was to be directed by the renowned Max Reinhardt; Oliver Messel was hired as designer; and Evelyn Laye was to sing the lead role. Massine looked forward to collaborating with Reinhardt, whom Diaghilev had considered "a key figure in the development of realism in the theatre."[39] Massine found the Austrian director "a most interesting character, civilized, cultured and easy to talk to." And Reinhardt was astute when it came to stagecraft.

> *Once I had begun working for him I realized also that he was a complete man of the theatre, and one who well understood the value of simplicity in choreography. . . . While doing the choreography for the banqueting scene, the bacchanal, and the battle episodes, I learned some very valuable lessons from him, mainly concerned with the importance of rhythm in large ensemble scenes. He also had a wonderful way of integrating comic situations into large crowd scenes. Although he allowed me complete freedom as far as my own work on the production was concerned, I was always eager for his help and advice, and was flattered when he subtly intimated that he considered my participation in the production . . . almost as important as his own.*[40]

Helen! was rehearsed throughout November in Manchester, where it had its first run before moving to London's Adelphi Theatre on January 30, 1932.

In Manchester, shattering news arrived: Massine's father, who had remained in Galli with the caretakers, had died, like a mythical hero in exile, alone with his French horn and far from his native land. Heartbroken, but unable to leave England, Massine asked his wife to rush to Galli to arrange the funeral and oversee the burial of his father on a hill at the top of Positano.[41]

Flush with the success of *Helen!*, Cochran sought another collaboration with Reinhardt, Massine, and Messel. He wanted to revive a work he had produced in 1911 at the Olympia Theatre, *The Miracle*. Massine described *The Miracle* as "a wordless pageant in seven episodes based on the legend of a nun who breaks her vows for love of a knight, and returning to the convent after many years finds that her place has been taken by the Madonna and no one had missed her."[42]

The Spielmann in Max Reinhardt's The Miracle, *1932*

Cochran's 1911 extravaganza, under the direction of Reinhardt, required two thousand extras and featured a lavish cathedral decor whose rose window was three times larger than the one at Chartres. In 1923 Reinhardt had directed a grandiose production starring the English beauty and social luminary Lady Diana Cooper. It had toured the United States under the management of Morris Gest, who in many ways pushed Reinhardt out of the limelight. Now in 1932, Lady Diana, who had been adored in the U.S. tour, again was to appear as the Madonna; Tilly Losch, the Viennese dancer-actress, was cast as the nun. In addition to creating the dances, Massine was to play the role of the Spielmann, a trickster or minstrel who persuades the nun to abandon her duties. Except for some mild backstage intrigue between Lady Diana and Losch, the production went smoothly.[43]

The Miracle opened at the Lyceum on April 9 and had a considerable success. Lady Diana, as always, received excellent reviews. It was no triumph, however. According to *The Times,* Massine's choreography was "at its best when its mood has gaiety and light . . . before it takes on a tragic colour,"[44] and his performance as the Spielmann had "a genuine power to excite which fails only when, being used in excess, it is dissipated in violence."[45] Lady Diana found him as inventive as her 1923 Spielmann, Werner Krauss, and more reliable.[46] Reinhardt declared it a pleasure to work with Massine, and in a congratulatory letter before the run ended wrote that "the collaboration with you was a wonderful experience for me and I am firmly resolved to repeat it again in the coming future."[47]

Between his stints with *Helen!* and *The Miracle* Massine went to Monte Carlo to choreograph a new work for the debut season of the newly organized Ballets Russes de Monte Carlo under the direction of René Blum and Colonel de Basil. From its inception the new company had the potential to make ballet history. Blum and de Basil, with the artistic collaboration of Kochno as *conseiller artistique* and Balanchine as ballet master, launched the most important enterprise of its kind since Diaghilev's death in 1929. Also signed on were former Diaghilev collaborators Derain, Benois, Miró, and Auric; among the newcomers was the designer Christian Bérard. Serge Grigoriev, Diaghilev's régisseur for twenty years, assumed the same position in the new company, and his wife, Lubov Tchernicheva, was named ballet mistress. A number of Diaghilev dancers, led by Doubrovska and Woizikowski, also joined the effort. But it would be a new generation of young dancers who would define the company's style and personality. Mostly Russian-born, they had been trained in Paris in the strictest Russian tradition by the émigré Imperial Theater stars: Olga Preobrajenska, Mathilde Kchessinska, Lubov Egorova, Volinine. Though they were only in their teens, each possessed dazzling technique and a distinctive stage presence.

Massine had been asked to choreograph two ballets, only one of which materialized: *Jeux d'enfants,* to Bizet's twelve-part, four-handed piano suite, with scenery and costumes by Miró.[48] The ballet portrayed a little girl's dream of toys coming to life. There was no narrative line, only a series of episodes depicting the child's interactions with her toys. The little girl as spectator and participant gave the work its unity.

Massine's choreography blended classical balletic vocabulary with expressive idiosyncratic movement. With their mastery of classical technique as a solid base, the dancers were urged to make the toys recognizably human. A. V. Coton later compared the work to Massine's 1919 *La Boutique fantasque*: "Massine had abandoned all reference to the 'unnatural' toy movement idiom of *Boutique Fantasque* in composing this work. All the toys and games . . . danced perfectly balletic and athletic measures as against the entirely derivative movement idioms of the toys in *Boutique Fantasque*."[49]

Jeux d'enfants was crucial in spelling out the 1930s aesthetic of pure dance as the essential element of ballet. This new dance-music integration differed drastically from Diaghilev's 1920s productions, where dance was generally subordinated to narrative. Of *Jeux d'enfants* Coton wrote that "every phase of the plot's unfolding is continuous within the dancing sequences; neither a bar of music nor a single movement by any of the participants is wasted on action extraneous to the continuity and development of music and dance forms, from curtain to curtain."[50] Classical virtuosity reigned supreme. Here was a company whose ballerinas could perform breathtaking multiple pirouettes and grandes pirouettes on pointe. And thus the prominence of the ballerina was revitalized after her years of subordination to the male dancer in Diaghilev's company.

Although Massine's recent successes in London and New York had been rich learning experiences, collaborating again on a ballet with a major painter proved highly stimulating, helping him to catch up with advances in the plastic arts, most notably surrealism. As he had done with Picasso, Matisse, and the Delaunays, Massine worked closely with Miró to ensure visual coherence in the completed ballet. The design exploded a nursery into a playful jumble of surrealistic geometrical forms in vibrant primary colors. These forms and the still silhouettes of the dancers against the gray-blue backcloth gave an impression of children's paper cutouts. The backcloth set in motion gave the entire scene the magical effect of a moving canvas.

Massine's arrival in Monte Carlo had been eagerly awaited. The young dancers held him in awe but were also wary of his no-nonsense reputation: serious, aloof, and inaccessible. He completely disarmed them. Though he continued to keep to himself, remained earnest about work, and demanded total concentration, he formed a warm working rapport with the company. Tamara Toumanova found him "all kindness from the very beginning,"[51] and Tatiana Riabouchinska did not find him "intimidating at all. He was very reserved but was kind and even gentle; he was soft-spoken and inspiring."[52] Now that he seemed more at ease, his Diaghilev colleagues came to believe that his detachment in the past had likely been aggravated by his personal relationship with the volatile impresario. Also obvious to everyone was the change wrought by his sparkling and sociable wife. Soon Delarova had charmed everyone, and became a welcome member of the company sightseeing parties formed at the Café de Paris and seen strolling through Monte Carlo.

Jeux d'enfants was ideally suited to the young troupe. They had quickly caught on to Massine's style, and their roles suited them perfectly, especially the fifteen-year-old Riabouchinska as the Child and thirteen-year-old Toumanova as the Top. In 1932 the ballet triumphed in Monte Carlo and in Paris. When it was presented in London the following year, Ernest Newman wrote in the *Sunday Times*: "One's first impression is that Bizet's charming music does not lend itself to the action. . . . Yet in a very little while it becomes clear that Mr. Massine has achieved the almost impossible, by a boldness of translation that soon converts our first skepticism into willing belief. *Jeux d'enfants* is a delightful fantasy, in which action, miming, costumes and colors combine subtly to the one end."[53]

After Monte Carlo, the Massines returned to London for *The Miracle*. At the conclusion of its run on July 23 they left to spend their holidays in Galli, stopping over in Salzburg as Reinhardt's guests at his castle in Leopoldoskron.

The summer of 1932 was professionally unsettling. In July Massine had written to Rothafel and Jay Kaufman of the Roxy, inquiring about their plans for a Radio City ballet company. He wondered if he could be hired as ballet master and stage some of the full-length classics from the repertory of the Imperial Theaters. Massine regretted that during his tenure at the Roxy he had not been able to produce a full-length work and insisted that the moment was ripe to revive the classical style. He enclosed a list of twenty-two classics, including *Swan Lake*, *Sleeping Beauty*, *Nutcracker*, *Raymonda*, *Le Corsaire*, *Paquita*, *Coppélia*, and *La Fille mal gardée*.[54] It was a bold proposal, but something even grander was in store for Massine. By December he found himself in Paris as the new ballet master for the Ballets Russes de Monte Carlo.

After the first Monte Carlo season, sharp differences over the artistic direction of the company had arisen between Blum and de Basil on the one hand and Kochno and Balanchine on the other. The latter two departed at the end of the Paris summer season, their contracts having expired. With Balanchine gone, de Basil moved quickly to hire Massine. The director knew a valuable asset when he saw one: Massine was a bigger draw as a choreographer than Balanchine; he was in his prime as a performer; he maintained close ties with the English theatrical establishment (London was de Basil's next objective); and he was indispensable if de Basil was to obtain Diaghilev's scenery, costumes, and props, now owned—through Massine's intercession in the past—by E. Ray Goetz. What's more, hiring Massine eliminated a potential competitor, since up to the summer of 1932 the choreographer had been steadily negotiating with Sir Thomas Beecham about the possibility of founding a permanent ballet company at Covent Garden.

The Massines came to Paris in late autumn to start preparations for the Monte Carlo season, and by January 2, 1933, they had joined the company in the principality of Monaco. Following an exhausting rehearsal period of three and a half months, the landmark engagement at the Théâtre du Casino opened on April 13 with the world premiere of *Les Présages*, set to Tchaikovsky's Fifth Symphony, with scenery and costumes by the painter André Masson. (When Massine in late autumn had outlined for Blum his plans for new works, the director had found the notion of a ballet choreographed to a symphony quite disturbing. Hoping to dissuade Massine, he had enlisted the support of the great conductor Bruno Walter, to no avail.) The first ballet in Western Europe set to a symphony, *Les Présages* signaled a new creative phase for the choreographer and marked a turning point in the history of twentieth-century dance.

Massine's objective in *Les Présages* was to create an abstract ballet without any literal story or narrative line. Tchaikovsky, in his correspondence with his patroness, Nadezhda von Meck, had pondered at length the concept of man's struggle against the forces of destiny. Following their lead, Massine linked each movement of the symphony to a symbolic theme introduced by allegorical characters. The first movement dealt with man's desires, temptations, and diversions, with the main character, a female called Action, symbolizing man's progress. The second movement depicted love in conflict with the baser passions; its main characters were two lovers, who together represented Passion, and Fate. The third movement was an interlude of gaiety symbolized by the character of Frivolity. In the fourth movement man's passion for war is aroused; he struggles mightily against it and vanquishes it at the end. All the leading figures of the previous movements come together in the finale.

The creation of an abstract choreographic counterpart to the structure of the music had a precedent in Massine's *Perpetomobile* of 1928. Indeed, many of his earlier ballets contained the seeds that blossomed into *Les Présages*: choreographic counterpoint, asymmetry, juxtaposition of styles, contrast between the qualities of weight and lightness, mass movement, abstraction. In conversations with critic Arnold Haskell in 1933, Massine asserted that his artistic growth could be measured in the evolutionary process that produced *Les Femmes de bonne humeur* (1917), *Le Tricorne* (1919), and *Les Présages* (1933), a propensity that he described as "the start of a new development which should bring me back to pure choreography." [55]

As usual with Massine, he derived the choreography from his dissection of the score; musical themes found their complement in a solo dancer or group of dancers. Sometimes dancers would represent sections of the orchestra, such as woodwinds or strings. Massine's choreographic counterpoint was so intricate that at times not only the soloists but each dancer in the ensemble became an independent entity.

The masterly juxtaposition of styles began in the first movement, where Action and a male dancer danced to the first and second musical themes, respectively. Here Massine contrasted a freer choreographic idiom to classical ballet technique. The "modern" idiom was appropriate to the role of Action, brilliantly danced by Nina Verchinina. Though classically trained, Verchinina had an affinity for the freedom and expansiveness of Massine's approach; eventually she became its embodiment. [56] The French dance critic Pierre Michaut described Action's choreography as "a play of arms well defined and rich in expression, raised up, extended, soft or rigid, frequently disassociated." [57] Here the emphasis on the torso and arms became as relevant as the leg work.

Verchinina described Massine's method:
"He experimented with movements. First he would create a varia-

tion that was more technical and classical in style, sort of a *pas de valse* with piqués and so forth. Then he would start working with me, and the movements began to evolve into something different and much more expressive." (This is reminiscent of Massine's description of Picasso's method.) "We would work until I was able to feel the movements as if the music was passing through my whole body—fingers, hands, head. The objective was to be able to feel Massine's movements inside of me and to understand what he wanted to achieve and to express. He was very responsive, and I was able to see immediately when he was happy, when he was able to transfer into my body his idea of the movement he wanted. He would not explain much, but he would show his basic idea. He mainly strove for me as the interpreter to grasp what he wanted so I could give the movement my own feeling and individual expression. My choreography for Action was a warrior dance, an ode to life, and every movement had a meaning: when I had both palms facing in front of me and I pushed one back, it would mean that I was creating fire; when I would move my rigid straight arms around me—as if I was cutting the air—they were swords; or I would make circular movements as if I was making designs in the space."[58]

The use of space was one of Massine's key principles. Verchinina explained: "Space exists and one must feel it as a presence, and every movement is executed inside (within) the space. Massine would show a circular movement, for example, and after I would perform it he would say, 'Now push through space, feel the pressure of the space around you, feel your body in friction with the space,' and so on until my movement would achieve the corporeal expression that he visualized in it. It was force against the space, my body cutting, piercing through the space, moving through space, whether being pushed by it or pushing it, designing movements within the space. Otherwise there was no dynamics, movement is dead, there is no expression. That is why even when there was no movement one would still project and transmit, because there is a dynamic relationship between the figure and the space."[59]

Massine fixed the dancer in relation to space, symbolizing the individual and the universe. Instead of a vacuum, Massine's space became a medium through which the dancer moved. This dynamics of space imposed on the dancer a dialectic of pressure and void which determined the quality of the movement: tensed, relaxed; flexible, rigid. The dancer's constant friction in space brought along an emotional impulse that gave expressivity to movement.

Massine's regard for the utilization of space and its dynamic relationship to the physical body placed a new emphasis on how a mass was formed and deployed. When he considered "the ancient ruins of Selinus, Agrigento and Paestum, it was the mass and volume of these structures which offered a challenge."[60] In *Les Présages* he "decided to avoid all symmetrical compositions and to render the flow of the music by fluctuating lines and forms both static and mobile. I deliberately chose to follow the movements of the symphony in a logical evolution of choreographic phrases, successively applying the regroupings themselves into new shapes and patterns."[61] Groups emerged and broke up before the audience fully realized that they had been formed. The spontaneity (automatism, according to the surrealist concept) of the fleeting entrances and exits was enhanced by the asymmetry of the corps patterns and the distorted spatial relations.

In the second-scene adagio, Massine created perhaps the first modern romantic pas de deux. Unlike the Petipa classical pas de deux (adagio, variations, coda), or the romantic and neoromantic Fokine pas de deux (a dramatic incitement in the development of the action), the pas de deux in *Les Présages* became its own raison d'être. Massine's creation of a self-contained, self-sufficient pas de deux (which at times became a pas de trois with the appearance of Fate) set a precedent for the many works that were later devised by other choreographers for slower movements of other symphonic or concerto ballets.

Though an all-female corps made brief entrances, the third movement was a solo for Frivolity. Here Massine reached the peak thus far of his new classicism. Riabouchinska explained the ardent connection she felt to the work:

"The rhythm of the choreographic phrase had a great degree of subtlety in the way Massine would join smaller steps as a preparation for bigger, more brilliant ones, to reach some spectacularly difficult ones in a sort of choreographic crescendo. Other times he would invert this order in a sort of decrescendo—always with a great emphasis on the torso and arms. This approach would make certain steps stand out more and enhance their aesthetic value—like when I finish an *enchaînement* in an attitude back in a *cambré* position. It made the technicality of the dance less mechanical, and you were swept away by the phrasing. The choreographic construction was such that you felt part of a grandiose conception. At the time there was nothing as grandiose in contemporary ballet."[62]

This movement employed a strict classical technique, free of any obvious symbolism. For André Levinson, who did not care for the philo-

Les Présages, *1933: fourth movement, the Rockets*

sophical connotations of the work, the audience became euphoric "at the moment of the waltz-scherzo, which defends itself victoriously against all implicit metaphysics."[63]

The finale was an apotheosis in which all the figures from the previous movements reappear—a Massine innovation that subsequent choreographers freely appropriated. The acrobatics of the ballet, especially in the spectacular finale, were novel in the West. By coincidence, they resembled the pyrotechnic style developed in the Soviet Union in the 1930s.

As designer for Les Présages Massine had wanted Matisse, with whom he collaborated in 1920 on Le Chant du rossignol. The painter declined (though they would work together again six years later). Matisse, who later attended many of the rehearsals in Monte Carlo, recommended Masson.

Preliminary discussions took place in Paris during the winter of 1932. Working together, Massine and Masson eventually conceived the ballet as a painting in motion. *Les Présages,* we can now see, operated on a deep level of symbolism and in a style reminiscent of German expressionism. As Massine explored and developed his symphonic ballet genre, his treatment of the figure/space relationship became a venue for his cosmic interpretation of the world.

Masson's interest in expressionism had begun in 1929 when he broke with André Breton and the surrealist movement. Although his work remained largely surrealistic in character, by 1932 he had begun painting expressionistic scenes of ritual killings. In his work of this period, color, line, figure, and background were united in a dynamic whole, and there are striking similarities between the color scheme of Masson's 1933 *Massacre in the Field* and that of *Les Présages*: bright reds, greens, yellows, purples, blues. All the female costumes were modeled on the classical Greek tunic, probably owing to Masson's recent interest in Greek mythology. The backdrop was a multicolored array of comets, shooting stars, rainbows, tongues of flame, spouting hearts, and other emblems of an apocalyptic vision.

The premiere in Monte Carlo on April 13 was a triumph with the public and the press. But it was the Paris premiere at the Théâtre de Châtelet two months later that launched the "symphonic ballet" controversy that was to rage in full force for years. There, *Les Présages* found vociferous supporters and equally adamant detractors. Some musicians deemed the use of a symphony to bolster a ballet nothing less than a sacrilege (although Isadora Duncan had already had symphonies performed to accompany her dances); and from the artistic community, the design drew outraged objections. Up until then, painters working with choreographers had confined themselves to suggesting an appropriate atmosphere within a realistic ambience. Masson's approach was purely painterly. Even the surrealist *Jeux d'enfants* stayed within the realistic boundaries of the premise, which was, after all, a surrealistic nursery. In *Les Présages* Masson avoided poetry as well as realism, fastening on pure abstraction and symbolism. He had two related aims: to capture the flow of the music in the arrangement of color and, more importantly, to link the movements of the dancers to the design of his backcloth, to suggest color parallels to the music. In the face of the controversy, the ballet was performed without decor and in practice clothes in London in 1935. The critics were nonplussed, and ended up agreeing that Masson's contribution was vital to the work's total effect.

Factions for and against the ballet immediately sprung up. Some people, such as Balanchine and Lifar, argued that a symphony required no choreographic elucidation—though in the 1940s, they themselves would use symphonies and concerti for their ballets.[64] Massine's supporters contended that he was breaking new ground. The two camps couldn't agree on a number of questions: (1) Was it right to superimpose a philosophical allegory on a ballet? (2) Was it fusion or only a mishmash to juxtapose classical ballet technique and an idiom closer to the Central European modern dance movement? (3) Did the innovative, self-sufficient pas de deux in fact stand on its own? (4) What was intended by the use of asymmetrical and almost automatic mass movement? (5) Were the acrobatics justified artistically? (6) Was the abstract choreographic treatment of the music aesthetically satisfying or only a riddle for the audience to puzzle over ad infinitum? It has turned out, of course, that this work was ballet's turning point, ushering in the currently accepted aesthetic of abstraction and nonrepresentational dance.

The controversy was not confined to artistic circles. In the midst of the frightening European economic and political upheavals of 1933 (depression, the burning of the Reichstag, the victory of the Nazi party, the establishment of the "National Revolution," the exodus of German intellectuals and artists), a minority of liberal intellectuals and artists objected to the militaristic tone of Massine's fourth movement with its strong reference to war.

Though opinion was divided, the ballet was an immense success. For Pierre Michaut it "had an imposing sensation as much for its intensity as for its originality. . . . Some passages remain in one's memory: the scintillating, luminous entrance of Frivolity (Mlle Riabouchinska) and the grandiose final movement, a vast composition of ensemble, a true orchestration of masses, where movement, full of force and magnitude, sustains itself by a continuity and dimension truly powerful."[65]

The roles were milestones in the careers of the dancers, who, much like the "symphonic ballet" itself, were seen as representatives of a new generation and style. Nina Verchinina as Action, in her own eclectic way, welded the music to the choreography with unusually angular movements. As Passion, the fourteen-year-old Irina Baronova combined poetry with brilliant attack, suggesting the extraordinary classical-modern ballerina she was to become. As Frivolity, the fifteen-year-old Riabouchinska stamped the role with her speed, lightness, elevation, and ethereal presence. (Along with Toumanova, Baronova and Riabouchinska were the legendary "baby ballerinas.") David Lichine, the male dancer who with Massine was to dominate the international spotlight in the

1930s, was all virility and barbaric exuberance in the roles of Passion and Hero. In his powerfully dramatic appearance as Fate, Leon Woizikowski met the high standards set in his Diaghilev performances.

That July in London, the ballet caused a sensation. Its most ardent advocate, Ernest Newman, dean of British music critics, found that "it is really the music of the symphony that [Massine] has translated into a ballet, and this in such a way that, incredible as it may appear to anyone who has not seen *Les Présages,* the inner life of the work, as an organic piece of musical thinking, is not diminished but actually enhanced. There are points, indeed, at which none of us will henceforth be able to listen to the music in the concert room without seeing it in terms of this ballet. . . ."[66]

The second new work of the Monte Carlo season was a revival of the 1924 *Beau Danube.* Massine eliminated its heavily narrative scenes and modified the choreography to capitalize on the flair and technique of his young cast. The ballet—led by Alexandra Danilova, Riabouchinska, Baronova, and Massine himself—became one of the company's signature pieces. According to Coton: "Of all works in the de Basil repertory this is probably the most popular; certainly no other work except possibly *Boutique Fantasque* has an equal appeal as purely romantic choreography in Massine's own special idiom. . . . It dispenses with formal balletics, and achieves perfection of pattern between dance and musical line."[67] During the company's first London season, Coton noted, *Le Beau Danube* and *Les Présages* "drew people to watch ballet . . . who otherwise might never have been attracted to the ballet theatre."[68]

Beach, the third new work, was an homage to the principality of Monaco. The ballet had an original score by the young composer Jean Françaix (a protégé of Nadia Boulanger), a libretto by René Kerdyk, and scenery and costumes by the French artist Raoul Dufy, who had started as a fauve. *Beach* gently satirized topical characters from the Riviera's smart set. A prologue, two scenes, and an epilogue showed the world of Nereus, with its Nereids and Tritons, being transformed into a collection of fashionable Monte Carlo types, who after an outing at the resort return to their mythological kingdom in the sea.

André Levinson likened the spirit of the piece to a spectacular music hall revue. Massine's choreography, he found, took its inspiration from the Jazz Age and the open-air culture, utilizing tap and the fox-trot as well as stylized sports movements. No doubt Massine was influenced by his years at the Roxy. At the same time, the lyrical pas de deux between Baronova and Lichine was danced in a pure balletic idiom. Dufy's designs consisted of beautiful seascapes that gave a fish-tank look to the stage, and the costumes were witty and chic (Dufy designed textiles for Paul Poiret's prestigious *maison de couture*). The evening gowns were by couturière Jeanne Lanvin, who also launched the soon-to-be-fashionable navy-blue dinner jacket.

The final work premiered in Monte Carlo was *Scuola di ballo,* based on a comedy by Goldoni that exposed the intrigues of a teacher, his students, their parents, and an impresario in a dance school. The ballet was set to music by Boccherini as orchestrated by Françaix, with scenery and costumes by Etienne de Beaumont, whose most recent collaboration with Massine had been back in 1924. The choreography took its style from commedia dell'arte, in which the hands, arms, and torso were used to tell the story. However, unlike *Les Femmes de bonne humeur,* which emphasized Massine's *cantinella*-like pantomime, *Scuola di ballo* employed a great degree of technical virtuosity and choreography packed with flowing variations that lacked the flickering quality of the 1917 work.[69]

The ballet required precisely what Massine could call forth from his dancers with ease: idiosyncratic characterizations which gave them an opportunity to excel technically and dramatically. Massine shaped characters to suit his dancers' personalities yet left enough room for them to make the roles their own. Said Baronova: "To penetrate into Massine's roles, dancers had to work on their own and approach the parts as actors do. We had to explore the characters in order to obtain their mannerisms. For Massine, two things were of utmost importance: expressivity in the body and fluency of movement, both subordinated to the music."[70] Riabouchinska added: "After he gave them the basic idea, the dancers had to work on their own. They had to digest and build their interpretations as long as they were consistent with the overall approach."[71] (This was a lingering influence from Massine's early exposure to the Moscow stage.) Every role depended on a strong personality: Massine, Baronova, Riabouchinska, Woizikowski, Yurek Shabelevsky. Delarova made her Ballets Russes debut as Felicita, the inept pupil. Massine described her solo as "a wonderfully droll take-off of an inadequate dancer clumsily caricaturing classical steps blended with grotesque leaps."[72] Her performance was praised as a "real piece of farce."[73]

The ballet was mostly well received in Paris. Emile Vuillermoz wrote: "The lessons, the entrances, the exits are arranged with an astonishing freshness of invention. Never had Massine discovered effects so youthful and so alive, devoid of all that angular trepidation."[74] Only Levinson found it inferior to *Les Femmes* and *Pulcinella.*[75] Haskell, on the

Massine with Tatiana Riabouchinska in Scuola di ballo, *1933*

other hand, declared it in "perfect harmony with the music and the thought of the time."[76] Toumanova, who was not in the cast, called it a gem.[77] Ernest Newman observed:

> *Over all the production there is that sense of "nothing too much" that is always one of the best features of the ballet school that has arisen out of the old Italian comedy: never for a moment does the grotesquerie overshoot the mark. And once more one is astounded at Mr. Massine's genius for translating music into action. Only the musicians in the audience can fully appreciate what he does in this respect; there are a hundred subtleties in the way of capturing the very essence of a rhythm, of an accent, even of a splash of orchestral colour . . . to make them clear to the reader one would*

have to quote this or that bar of the music with a section from a film of the ballet.[78]

"When the de Basil company launched its first big-scale English season," Coton wrote, "the item of news of equal importance with that of the resurrection of ballet was the promised return of Massine to London."[79] That promise was fulfilled in the summer of 1933, in Massine's double triumph as choreographer and lead dancer of a brilliant company. For Haskell it was "a company of extraordinary training and versatility, and, from that point of view at least," it was "the finest and the most complete" the critic had seen.[80] The Ballets Russes de Monte Carlo's historic engagement at the Alhambra Theatre opened on July 4. The three weeks initially scheduled were extended to nineteen. The company took London by storm and throughout a meltingly hot summer performed nightly to sold-out houses. Now, joining the elitist audiences that had supported Diaghilev, a new public was making its way to the ballet. During the 1930s, ballet became the rage in London, and Massine its undisputed star. His new repertory, as well as the older works, earned him even greater critical acclaim than he had received with Diaghilev. Coton tried to put his achievement in perspective: "No other choreographer has experimented in so many forms to produce always interesting, occasionally vivid and beautiful, and never shoddy, work. Out of the living corpus of his work we can construct a document of every phase of experiment of any value since Fokine's heyday; what Massine has done, other choreographers have done—later."[81] He added that in his twenty-eight works Massine had "evolved a richer and wider catalogue of mixed miniatures and grand-scale projections of movement such as neither Fokine, nor any other living choreographer, has achieved."[82]

A Massine ballet created an instant cult. Agnes de Mille recalled how "the furor evoked by the baby ballerinas and the love commanded by Danilova were not in a class with the adulation accorded to the master of all, Léonide Massine. Seeing a Massine ballet had become one of the erotic pleasures of the London season. The expensive spectators in the stalls contented themselves with 'Bravos' and gush. The devotees upstairs gave themselves unrestrainedly to screaming, jumping up and down, beating the railing, hugging one another, slathering at the mouth."[83]

And it was not only Massine the choreographer who was praised; Massine the performer proved irresistible. Haskell summed up the opinion of public and critics alike:

Massine today is at the very height of his powers, both as a creator and as a dancer. There are obviously greater technical performers, but no one who is even nearly his equal as an artist. It is in his case that I have felt the same concrete audience contact as with Pavlova. I once watched Le Beau Danube from the wings. At the moment where Massine stands motionless, centre stage, remembering as he hears the strains of the famous waltz, and then very slowly raises his arm above his head as the crowd of idlers and midinettes passes him by in scorn, I looked into the auditorium by chance. Like some big wave the audience had risen in their seats, craning forward, as if his hand had pulled some unseen string. There is no one else who could achieve such a result by standing almost completely still. It is quite another thing to whip an audience into excitement by a complicated technical feat.[84]

For Haskell, Massine ranked with the masters of movement. "As a mime, Massine could only be compared to Chaplin. His characters were round; they had pathos and humour. The Barman in the otherwise trivial *Union Pacific* [of 1934] was a masterly study, a splendid distillation of the comedy of the silent film. When one adds such varied roles as the Can-Can Dancer in *La Boutique Fantasque* and the Miller in *Le Tricorne*, we have a performer of rare quality, especially in his early days, when the *buffo* dancers were so often stereotypes."[85]

Scheduled to close the Alhambra engagement was the world premiere of *Choreartium*, to Brahms's Fourth Symphony. Tchaikovsky's Fifth had imposed upon the choreographer a dense, specific psychological mood. Brahms's Fourth, not in the strictly academic sonata form, summoned from Massine a resolutely abstract ballet sans theme, symbolic idea, or reference to allegorical characters. He wanted instead a choreographic rendition of the music's structure through continuous sequences of movement. The soloists, couples, trios, and ensembles, interwoven into intricate patterns, mirrored the fluctuations and climaxes of the music. Even more so than in *Les Présages*, the dancers here were tied to musical themes or groups of instruments. Massine particularly wanted to use "women dancers to accentuate the delicate phrases, while the men interpreted the heavier, more robust passages. The music with its rich orchestration and its many contrasts, lent itself admirably to this kind of interplay between masculine and feminine movements."[86]

The opening movement highlights this gender contrast. The principal couple's pas de deux (one critic called it the first allegro pas de deux) becomes a dialogue between the female (Toumanova), dancing to the

Rehearsal of the first movement of Choreartium, *1933*

strings, and the male (Lichine), dancing to the woodwinds. This movement, said Massine, was composed of "airy patterns of moving figures, continually forming and reforming in evanescent designs" through which the principal couple "moved like waves, undulating through the shifting groups."[87]

The first, third, and fourth movements were examples of Massine's new classicism, where intricate pointe combinations were followed by large, open, flowing movements for the women, and pirouettes, *tours en l'air*, jumps, and *batterie* for the men. The second movement was a return to his modern idiom: a solo for Verchinina before an all-female corps de ballet in architectural formation.

> *I had been told that Brahms had visualized this Second Movement as an afternoon in Sorrento, but I could not see it that way. To me there was a spiritual quality in it which suggested medieval Italy, and reminded me of a fresco I had seen in the Palazzo Campanile in Siena. Most of it had become blurred with the passage of time, but there was a group of women in deep burgundy red robes which was still visible. I made these women the*

leitmotiv *of the movement, threading the image of them through the en-*
sembles, in which the weaving dancers, with their arms extended, formed
a succession of harmonic choreographic progressions and dynamic
evolutions.[88]

Unlike her forceful Action in *Les Présages*, in *Choreartium* Verchinina had
to dance introspectively, as it were, differentiating fluid from tensed
movements, meticulously contrasting weight and lightness, tension and
relaxation.[89] Massine called it "a mystical dance."[90]

Massine's mastery of figure/space relationships let the audience
perceive stage movement in three dimensions. His theory of movement
at this point was essentially architectural. *Choreartium*'s mass configurations—a dialectic between motion and stasis, arrest and movement—
turned the theory into practice.[91]

Coton traced this approach to Massine's final work for Diaghilev.

Choreartium, 1933: first movement

"That Massine had not forgotten his devices of architecturing the choreography of *Ode* when he began to create part of *Les Présages* and, later, most of the fourth movement in *Choreartium*, is obvious."[92] (In fact his interest in architectural formations began as far back as *Le Chant du rossignol* and reappeared later in *Amphion*.)

Choreartium was first presented to a select London audience in a midnight dress rehearsal, the night before its premiere. Osbert Sitwell provided the introduction, to an assembly that included political, social, and artistic luminaries. The ballet immediately became the talk of the town. Massine was accused of blasphemous arrogance in daring to use a symphony (especially one by Brahms) as background music for a ballet, of presumptuousness in trying to interpret a self-sufficient musical work in terms of dance, and of selling out to modern dance in the second movement. London critics divided into two factions. The opposition was headed by composer, conductor, and critic Constant Lambert. The proponents, or Massinists, were led by Ernest Newman. The controversy was played out for a full year in their respective newspapers, the *Sunday Times* (Newman) and the *London Referee* (Lambert). Readers in both camps passionately followed the war of words. Newman wrote:

> *Massine showed the common sense we might have expected of him when he put aside all thought of reading a story into Brahms's symphony and decided to approach it as music pure and simple. . . . If music is to be ruled out from ballet when it is "pure" music, what justification is there for* Les Sylphides, *for example? There is no more programme in Chopin's music than there is in Brahms's; yet the enduring success of* Les Sylphides *proves that choreographic figures can be devised that are felt to be not in the least alien to the spirit and the build of this music. We are bound to grant, I think, that there is nothing a priori incongruous in the mating of "pure" music, whether that of Brahms or of any other composer, with the lines and masses and movements of the ballet. . . . The only question is to what extent the choreographer has succeeded. . . .*
>
> *What has Massine done with the remainder of the symphony? Here I can only wonder at the lack of imagination that prevents some people from seeing the points of genius with which Massine's choreographic score, so to call it, positively bristles. There can, of course, be no question of a translation of the "meaning" of this music as a whole into terms of another art: this kind of music is just itself, the expression of something to which there is no real equivalent in any other art. But if there is no equivalent, surely there can be parallelisms; surely certain elements in the musical design,*

certain gestures of the music, certain softenings and hardenings of the colours, can be suggested quite well in the more objective medium. I found myself profoundly interested in watching these correspondences, many of which gave me a fresh respect for Massine's genius. Unfortunately, as I have remarked before in a similar connection, there is no way of making these correspondences clear to the reader without quoting the musical passages in question side by side with photographs of the particular moments of the ballet with which they are associated. But how any musical listener in the audience who knows the Brahms score and has any imagination at all could fail to perceive these extraordinary parallelisms I confess myself unable to understand.

The opening entry of these two figures for instance, with their curious gliding, undulating motion, seemed to me as perfect a translation into visible motion of the well-known dip and rise of the first phrase in the violins as could possibly be conceived. I could cite similar felicities of parallelism by the hundred; the sense of the musical design conveyed for instance by the entry of the same two figures each time the first subject of the symphony assumed a leading part in the structure, the subtle distinctions invariably made in choreography between the basic elements in the music and the transitional passages—between the bones as it were and the cartilages—the curious correspondence between harshness in the harmonies and musical colors and angularities or violences in the gestures, and so on. In the finale, which, as the reader no doubt knows, is in passacaglia form—a series of variations upon a ground fugue—Massine seems to me to have done wonders. He typifies the commanding main theme by six black figures that persist through the whole movement as the ground bass itself persists in the music; and he intensifies or thins out the action and the groupings in accordance with the changing texture of the variations.[93]

Repeatedly in the years-long debate Newman compared the choreographer to Wagner: "If, it was said, Wagner was allowed to go on as he was doing, it would be the end of true art, just as it is now said that if the nefarious activities of Massine are not checked it will mean the ruin of both the symphony and the ballet. But Wagner quietly went on doing what he had set himself to do, and the public ranged itself on his side, let the critics foam at the mouth as they liked—another parallel with the Massine case."[94]

For Haskell, *Choreartium* was "forty minutes of individual and group movement, always beautiful, logical, and yet surprising, with every member of the huge cast an individual and at the same time part of a fresco."[95] He was certain that "such a feat on this scale has never before been attempted in choreography. It is the birth and triumph of pure dancing and shows that in the hands of a master its possibilities are inexhaustible."[96] Coton argued that in *Choreartium* "Massine had completed the most important experiment in balletic reorientation since the day of Fokine."[97] He traced Massine's accomplishments in *Choreartium* to earlier attempts in *Le Soleil de nuit*, *Cimarosiana*, *Ode*, and *Les Présages* (he could have added *Sacre*).[98] Coton felt that "by discarding all scenaric complications and working with no other guide than the musical score he had produced the most complete pattern of 'meaningless' [meaning abstract] movement, absolute and satisfying in itself, in the history of ballet."[99]

Les Présages and, especially, *Choreartium* proclaimed the autonomy of a choreographer freed from the conceptual limitations of scenarist and designer. This was a bold departure not only from the Diaghilev ballet but from the Ballets Russes de Monte Carlo's 1932 productions. The symphonic ballet provided a new, purely reflective pleasure, which found value and aesthetic satisfaction in the choreography alone. Leading world conductors of the time (Beecham, Stokowski, Monteux, Eugene Goossens, Eugene Ormandy) conducted performances of *Choreartium* in England and the United States throughout the decade.

As the season drew to a close, the Ballets Russes de Monte Carlo savored a triumph that was broader and deeper than any under Diaghilev. Their unprecedented success permitted de Basil—aided by Massine's contacts—to set up an impressive sponsoring committee that won the company the Royal Opera House at Covent Garden as its London home base, an arrangement that lasted from 1934 until the outbreak of war in 1939.

The impresario Sol Hurok brought the company to the United States for the first time in December 1933. The first engagement, in New York, had no general support (after the brilliant opening night, the ballet public proved so meager that the houses were practically empty). But by the end of its United States tour the company, led by Massine, the legendary baby ballerinas, Danilova, Verchinina, and Lichine, had achieved financial success and become a vital force on the American artistic scene. Thereafter the troupe toured North America, including Mexico, Cuba, and Canada, for six to seven months a year. The balance of their engagements were in Europe. In grueling one-night stands and in longer engagements in the larger cities, Massine became a household name and built an international following unmatched by any of his predecessors.

Yet, once again, alongside Massine's professional triumph his apparent marital bliss was undergoing a steady erosion. His five-year marriage was being shaken. This time the object of Massine's affection was the beautiful young dancer Vera Zorina. As it happened, the German-Norwegian Zorina, née Eva Brigitta Hartwig, was brought to Massine's attention in 1933 by Delarova herself. Brigitta was appearing in London opposite Anton Dolin in *Ballerina,* a play with ballet interludes. Massine, who rarely attended the theater, was in the habit of sending his wife to new shows to scout young dance talent. After attending a performance of *Ballerina,* she urged Massine to snap up two gifted members of the cast: Brigitta and the Englishman Frederic Franklin.[100] Massine wasted no time (it is uncertain whether or not he attended later performances of *Ballerina*), enlisting the critic Arnold Haskell as middleman in the negotiations with Brigitta. She joined the roster of the Ballets Russes de Monte Carlo during the 1934 Covent Garden summer season under the name Vera Zorina. (Franklin did not join Massine until 1938.)

Massine and Zorina began their affair during the North American tour that followed the London season. Privacy in a touring ballet company is generally hard to come by, but Massine and Zorina were obviously in love. Risks were taken. Delarova, in what seems a last-ditch attempt to save her marriage, accepted Zorina into the life she shared with her husband.

Throughout the American tours, the Massines traveled in a trailer attached to the choreographer's Lincoln. A Lithuanian couple, Alexander and Elizabeth Drevinskas, served them as chauffeur and cook, an arrangement that allowed Massine to bypass the inconvenient schedules of the Pullman trains arranged by Hurok, and thus to live a more regulated life during arduous series of one-night stands. Zorina became a member of Massine's caravan, as it was called, which required a strenuous adjustment.

When the company returned to England in the spring of 1935, the traveling threesome continued. On April 30 in Nice the party of five (including the Drevinskases) obtained a collective Spanish visa to proceed to Barcelona for the company's season at the Gran Teatre del Liceu.[101] After the Barcelona season (the Massines and Zorina stayed at the same hotel), Massine and Zorina made plans to meet secretly in Piešťany, a spa in Czechoslovakia that he frequently visited. According to Zorina, the days spent there "were reassuring, peaceful, and an oasis of peace during those turbulent two years."[102]

Massine was a man with a divided nature. One side was suspicious, aloof, and distant. The other, which predominated only when he was in love, was passionate, romantic, and possessive—as long as the love object yielded to him. He poured out his feelings for Zorina in heartfelt letters after she had left him in Pieštany:

> *The day you left—Never in my life, I haven't thought that I could love like I love you—Never nobody can tear from me what I acquired with you here. The feeling and the memory of us close heart to heart will be indefinitely vivid in me—Remember suddenly that huge dark cloud with wonderful light ribbon which appeared almost above our heads and sent the dark cloud away as though giving us to understand that the dark stormy cloud of our life might soon be gone too.*
>
> *The next day—Some force dragged me to the place where we have met the sunset. It is about the same moment now. Coming here I stopped every place we stopped with you. I looked on the ground trying to find the trace of your feet—every place reminds me of you, I feel your breath. Now I am standing there and sun is going almost hidden behind the mountains. "You are like out of gold," you said to me looking in my face—Once you said "I love you—at least you are a true person"—and you sat on the couch, it was almost dark. I looked at you and expression of your face overwhelmed me—you were like some Leonardo da Vinci paintings, so soft and so mysterious lighting was on you.*[103]

After the Czechoslovakian interlude, the company reassembled in London for another successful season at Covent Garden. Zorina writes:

> *After our London season, Léonide invited me to spend my vacation on the Isola dei Galli, the private island he owned off the coast of southern Italy, near Positano. I am unable now to understand how I could have agreed to travel once more in a triangular fashion, but then I am not eighteen any more. I don't believe one can ever again re-experience the ferocious passion, the longing, the hope—ah yes, the hope that things will change. I had no capacity for self-denial—nor could I give up hope—nor was I ready to admit defeat.*
>
> *We motored through Italy, stopping at Ravenna to admire the pure ivory throne and sarcophagus of the Byzantine Empress Theodora and the wonderful mosaics showing the Empress and her entourage. How mysterious their large-eyed, direct gaze seemed, and how perfect the splendor of their attire, which in spite of the opulence of cascading pearls, emeralds, and rubies, coupled with the utmost regal bearing, nevertheless gave the impression of an austerity. We remained for a few days in Abano, near*

Venice, so that Léonide could take mud baths for his ailing knee. From there, we visited Padua and Vicenza.

The Giottos in the chapel in Padua made a deep impression on me. For a dancer, who cannot express anything except through the movement of her body, there was a great deal to be learned. In the physical expression of lamentation, in the hands turned upward like birds in flight, in the raised arms, in the manifestation of sorrow of the spirit expressed silently but powerfully through the body. We stood there and looked and looked, absorbing and trying to remember every detail. The magnificent Palladian villas, and the perfection of the Teatro Olimpico in Vicenza, tiny but with the most miraculously deep perspective of the small stage—what treasures for an eighteen-year-old to see for the first time.[104]

After a visit to Ravello and Positano, the threesome headed for Galli to spend the summer holidays. But though there were delectable moments of swimming, sunbathing, and boating, the atmosphere was thick with tension. Years later, in her autobiography, Zorina wondered "why a man would want to subject two women who loved him to such an unhappy arrangement—both of whom complied in the hope that they would be left alone with him one day."[105]

The next United States tour was more exhausting than the two previous ones had been. It included a more rigorous string of one-night stands; moreover, Massine had openly retained counsel to get him a divorce from Delarova so he could marry Zorina. But this could not be arranged; according to the French courts, the "status and capacity to sue are governed by the law of the nationality of the parties."[106] The marital tensions escalated. Trying another tack, Massine directed New York attorney George Boochever to explore the possibility of obtaining a divorce in the Mexican courts on grounds of incompatibility, hoping that it would be recognized in France.[107] Massine wanted to have everything in order by the time the company arrived in El Paso; from there he would travel to Mexico to initiate the proceedings.[108] But this gambit failed.

De Basil ordered Zorina not to travel in the Massines' caravan. Yet even after she went back to traveling with the other dancers, the anguish did not stop. In Orlando, Florida, Zorina cut her wrists with a razor blade. She later wrote that she "had no intention of committing suicide or any thought of death. It seemed that by inflicting physical pain I might stop the mental pain I was no longer able to endure."[109] Massine, the ardent lover, showed no sympathy. She accused him of simply becoming "annoyed and angry."[110] The resolution of the crisis came during the 1936

Covent Garden season. Massine, writes Zorina, "solved his dilemma by bringing another woman into his life, a woman who was to become his third wife."[111] After the London season ended, Zorina left the Ballets Russes de Monte Carlo and went on to a successful career in musical comedies and films.

Massine and Tamara Toumanova as the Poor Couple in
Jardin public, *1935*

CHAPTER 11

London, June 1936–Paris, June 1939

BY 1936 the professional relationship between de Basil and Massine had seriously deteriorated. The strain had begun in 1934 during the first Covent Garden season. The year before, the two men had jointly acquired from E. Ray Goetz most of the scenery, costumes, and props of the Diaghilev organization—an extraordinarily rich cache. But in May 1934, a Ballets Russes press release asserted that de Basil was sole owner and proprietor: "Since the appearance of Colonel de Basil's company at the Alhambra Theatre last year, a group of English admirers have acquired the scenery and costumes belonging to the Diaghilev organization and presented them to Col. de Basil."[1] Massine's solicitors, J. D. Langton and Passmore, immediately demanded that the managing director of the Royal Opera publicly retract the statement and pledge that none of the scenery and costumes would be removed from the theater without Massine's consent.[2] After months of litigation, Massine and de Basil agreed that by August 1934 de Basil would purchase Massine's portion of the properties for 143,000 francs, to be paid over a period of one year.[3]

But the quarreling was not over; the prize of the artistic director-ship of the company continued to loom between them. Massine had wanted to be named Artistic Director back in 1933, but de Basil had con-sistently turned him down, deeming his artistic hold on the company al-ready too strong. He had a point. Danilova observed: "With Diaghilev, we had always felt that the success of a new production rested on the col-laboration of everyone involved, but with de Basil, we had the sense that the weight of the entire company had fallen on one man's shoulders—our success depended on Massine."[4] To loosen Massine's grip, in 1935 de Basil, always wary of a possible Massine defection, hired Bronislava Ni-jinska as guest choreographer; she produced a new work, *Les Cent Bai-sers,* and the following year revived her 1922 Stravinsky ballet, *Les Noces.* De Basil also continued to nurture David Lichine as a choreographer.

Massine's complaints kept piling up. He wanted his name, title (in a compromise de Basil in 1934 had appointed him "maître de ballet and artistic collaborator"), photo, and biographical note included in pro-grams and press releases. He wanted for himself and his wife the same first-class steamship accommodations provided to the de Basils. The régisseur was to notify him of the company's schedules and repertoires at the same time de Basil was informed. He objected to not being con-sulted about the hiring of Nijinska and several new dancers, or the com-missioning of *Le Pavillon* from Lichine in 1936. And he protested that since 1934 he had not been able to win approval for a revival of his *Sacre du printemps* with Verchinina (Nijinska's *Noces* must have been a slap in the face).[5]

By March 1936, while the company was touring the United States, Massine had secretly begun to explore the possibility of leaving de Basil and organizing his own company. He contacted René Blum in Monte Carlo (by 1935 Blum had severed his association with de Basil and gone on to organize the Ballets de Monte Carlo) and Sir Oswald Stoll in Lon-don as potential backers.[6] He then approached Lifar, Woizikowski, and Balanchine about joining the venture.[7] These bold moves were like tremors before the quake, which was not to occur for another year.

During the 1936 Covent Garden summer season, de Basil decided to organize a second company to tour Australia while the nucleus performed in Germany and later in America. Massine refused to have his ballets included in the repertory of the Australian company since he could not be there to supervise the performances, and sought a restraining order from Justice Bucknill in London. But when it became apparent that the petition would not be granted before the new company sailed, Massine personally rehearsed his works so that they could be presented to Australian audiences in authentic form.[8]

In the midst of these disputes, Massine created one of his most monumental works, to Berlioz's *Symphonie fantastique*. It would be his last production for de Basil's company.

Since *Choreartium* in 1933, Massine had produced three minor works to fulfill the company's need (and Hurok's demand) for novelties: *Union Pacific* (1934), *Jardin public* (1935), and *Le Bal* (1935). The first was the most successful. Based on the building of America's Union Pacific Railroad, it had a scenario by the poet Archibald MacLeish, music by Nicolas Nabokov, decor by Albert Johnson, and costumes by Irene Sharaff. As the first ballet by an international company based on an American theme and dance idiom, it was designed to bolster the Ballets Russes' publicity campaign in the United States. The general public liked the ballet, but it

The Barman in
Union Pacific, *1934*

stirred artistic controversy, especially in the dance community, where the Russians were resented by those burgeoning elements struggling to create an American ballet school and company. As Grace Robert noted, "It was not greeted with any particular acclaim by the critics, who seemed to think that the Russians were carrying their invasion of the United States too far."[9] *Union Pacific* gave the company's leading dancers some outstanding roles, especially the Barman and Lady Gay, created by Massine and Delarova. Massine's dance always stopped the show, and later the role of Lady Gay became identified with Baronova, who would take it over after the premiere.

Jardin public, based on a passage from André Gide's novel *The Counterfeiters,* had scenery and costumes by Jean Lurçat and a score by Vladimir Dukelsky. It was an attempt at a social ballet where various alienated characters, including a rich and a poor couple, as well as a man who commits suicide, meet in a public park. The ballet was a failure in the United States and England. However, as with *Union Pacific,* there were memorable performances, especially by Toumanova and Massine as the poor couple and Delarova as the woman who rented the chairs. Haskell wrote of her performance: "She has created a character that can be placed beside Massine's barman."[10] In spite of its indifferent reception, Massine remained attached to *Jardin public,* and in 1936 he revised it, with new decor and costumes by the Polish artist Alice Halicka. This new version, however, did not fare any better.

Nineteen thirty-five also saw the premiere of *Le Bal,* a new version by Massine of a ballet originally choreographed by Balanchine for Diaghilev in 1929. Massine chafed at having to rechoreograph an already existing work (this was to become the fashion with de Basil in order to take advantage of the Diaghilev properties he owned). *Le Bal* was a minor addition to the company's repertory and was dropped from it soon after.

These three ballets were created, rehearsed, and produced under strenuous, almost catastrophic conditions during the long and exhausting American tours. In a preunion era, rehearsals were held in any space available, from hotel basements to train station lobbies, and many times would not begin until after an evening performance and go on until three a.m. Only the dancers' dedication and their devotion to Massine enabled them to accept the almost inhuman working conditions. Toumanova recalls: "During our first years with de Basil there was no limitation to our working capacity. There was a collective fervor in the company, and we lived to see those performances come through. Our only concern was to give our very best on stage and to make it happen. It was almost a religious feeling that we had been chosen to keep this art and tradition alive. And of course we worshiped Massine, who was our inspiration. I do not think any of us would have said no to any of his requests. We admired his genius, and each one of his ballets was a revelation—even the ones that were not a great success had something special. Working with him was a constant learning experience and a process of exploring unimaginable possibilities of new movement."[11]

MASSINE HAD FIRST CONSIDERED Berlioz's *Symphonie fantastique* as early as January 1933, probably in lieu of Tchaikovsky's Fifth.[12] However, it was not until 1934 that he began to plan it, and by 1935 he was seriously immersed in the work. In August of that year he wrote to Etienne de Beaumont, who was taking a two-month cure in Germany, soliciting advice about a designer.[13] After a lengthy preparation period, rehearsals began in the late spring of 1936, when the company arrived in Barcelona for its May season at the Gran Teatre del Liceu, and continued in full force at Covent Garden. The rehearsal schedule was demanding, and, as was typical, Massine engaged himself compulsively in the creative process. No other work the Ballets Russes had produced was as rigorously demanding as the Berlioz. The entire company, including soloists and corps, was utilized, and to realize Massine's grandiose conception, extra, day-long rehearsals were scheduled on weekends. After one of these rehearsals Ernest Newman wrote to his wife, Vera:

> They all looked worn out this morning. Riabouchinska looked like a wraith with galloping consumption, and was coughing all the time and Baronova is sick. How they stand this life is a mystery to me. Ballet dancing must be a hard life. They have two more rehearsals and the performance tomorrow. How any girl can take up ballet dancing as a career is beyond my comprehension. And what skinny creatures they mostly are. They remind me of worker bees who work . . . to make money for goodness knows who—for they don't—they get precious little out of it for themselves.[14]

Symphonie fantastique was perhaps Massine's greatest statement of his idea of the dance-drama, and although the work followed the narrative idea set down in the composer's synopsis, the ballet was not dominated by its narrative element. On the contrary, the narrative was minimal, and, with the exception of the fourth scene, dance predominated within the episodic structure of the music. For the five movements Massine devised five independent tableaux, given continuity by the external elements of the main characters, the Musician and the Beloved (who appears only when her musical idée fixe is played). An internal element also provided continuity: the ballet's pervasive mood, which depicted the world as a metaphor for the Musician's tormented soul, the emotional state of mind emanating from the romantic first-person narrator.[15]

In *Symphonie fantastique,* Massine found a point at which to fuse the symbolic as well as the purely abstract approaches of *Les Présages* and *Choreartium.* At the same time, the fourth movement allowed him to

Symphonie fantastique, *1936, third movement: left to right, Paul Platoff, George Zoritch, Tamara Toumanova, Massine; decor by Christian Bérard*

conceive a scene of spectacular realism set to music. As Newman commented: "Nothing so pungently realistic has yet been seen in ballet as the March to the Scaffold and the Witches' Sabbath."[16]

Massine's monumental conception for *Symphonie fantastique* contains the various techniques characteristic of his previous work: an emphasis on mass configurations and pyramid constructions to achieve the illusion of three-dimensional movement through space; counterpoint choreography; contrast between weight and lightness; and the contrast of action and tempo. The fusion of all of these effects and devices enhanced the neoromantic expressionism of the ballet, which was linked to the romantic musical qualities of Berlioz's composition.

Symphonie fantastique marked a turning point in Massine's oeuvre. For the first time there is a glimmer of the self through the exaltation of the romantic ego, a dimension that had been absent from his ballets up to this time. Contrary to his tendency in his comic, *demi-caractère* ballets, in which the hero is integrated into his environment, here Massine moves toward a tragic tradition in which the isolated hero drifts into solitude. This new expression of the self was undoubtedly the result of a subconscious desire for self-expression, and coincided with the two-year period of emotional turmoil over his frustrated relationship with Zorina. In Massine's enactment of the role of the Musician, every movement was imbued with a personal dimension. As with his Joseph two decades earlier, he used parallels with his own character to build his interpretation:

> I was fascinated also by the morbid personality of the chief character, and as I began to interpret the role, which I danced myself, I found it called for a good deal of dramatic action. Here once again my early experiences as an actor at the Maly proved invaluable. In the process of choreographing this ballet I found myself increasingly caught up in the part. This, I think, was inevitable, for if I had not been able to identify myself with the young Musician, my dancing would have been meaningless.[17]

But something else was at work, too. Despite its symbolism and its grandeur, *Symphonie fantastique,* with its connotations of emotional craving and guilt, is one of Massine's most intimate works, and seems to take its cue from the choreographer's personal experience. The choreography also becomes at times the expression of an idea. The second scene is a case in point. As the waltzing grows madder and more frenzied, the Musician is spun about in a confused whirl of dancing couples, the visualization of his inner turmoil. Probably no other ballet has matched the Ball scene in its expression of the romantic sensibility. If the aesthetic creative process was for Massine a means of transcendence, the larger-than-life quality of *Symphonie fantastique* was, almost in a Schopenhauerian manner, the ultimate expression of the artist's will.

At the time of the creation of *Symphonie fantastique,* the symphonic ballet controversy was still very much alive. Just prior to the work's premiere on July 24, Ernest Newman wrote four articles on the subject for the *Sunday Times,* again crossing swords with a colleague, this time J. A. Westrup of the *Daily Telegraph.*[18] Although the new work aroused the ire of some, the ballet was for the most part highly praised, even by those who had not been proponents of Massine's earlier experiments. Nevertheless, one of the staunchest admirers of *Choreartium,* A. V. Coton, complained that with *Symphonie fantastique* "Massine had abandoned further research into the potentialities of absolute movement—pattern-building, divorced from story-telling, character building and commentary. . . ."[19] Newman, on the other hand, gave the choreographer what was for him his highest praise: "One feels, indeed, that had Berlioz had a choreographer like Massine ready to his hand it would have been in some such form as this that he would have planned to have his work presented."[20]

Critics were divided in their appreciation of one or another movement. The reviewer for *The Times* felt that the second, the waltz, was most successful because it was most appropriate for choreographic treatment.[21] Coton described the fifth movement as "a scene which, divorced from the rest of the work, might be Massine's best purely inventive choreography since 1928 [probably referring to *Ode*]: as daring a realignment of choreographic material as the first movement of *Choreartium.*"[22] In general, the third movement was considered the strongest. Constant Lambert, a fervent antagonist of the symphonic ballets, conceded Massine's triumph in this instance: "It was surprising to discover how successfully the pastoral scene 'came off,' for on paper one would have said it was an impossible task. . . . [The designer Christian] Bérard, of course, is more static than dynamic, and Massine more classical than romantic, so when both are treating the most serene and classical music in the symphony we get a closer fusion of three minds than we get elsewhere in this ballet."[23] Newman wrote: "The result has been as convincing a demonstration of [Massine's] genius as he has ever given us, an idyll of the first order, with a new miming and a new translation of music into terms of dance. So skillfully and imaginatively has it all been done that there is soon an end of our first fears of an intrusive realism when we catch sight of the deer in the background; even this animal is woven harmoniously into the general texture of the idyll."[24] The critic W. J. Turner wrote in a congratulatory letter to Massine after the premiere: "I consider the third movement . . . an absolute masterpiece and the finest piece of plastic imagination I have ever seen in choreography."[25] And on the other side of the Atlantic, W. J. Henderson wrote in the *New York Sun*: "The third movement, the pastoral, in which Berlioz essayed to make so much [of] the woodwind dialogue, is the best of Mr. Massine's conceptions. Here the choreography is imaginative, poetic and subtly suggestive, while the series of pictures evolved by the action is not only delightful to the eye, but filled with sentiment and fitness to the study and the music. Mr. Massine found himself quite as much at home here as he did in a similar situation in *Choreartium*."[26]

Edwin Denby, on the other hand, disliked the ballet's "nervousness," its lack of "human feeling," and concluded that "the characters are intellectual references to types; they do not take a mysterious life of their own."[27] No admirer (with rare exceptions) of Massine's work, Denby nevertheless acknowledged that

> Massine is without doubt the master choreographer of today. He has the most astonishing inventiveness and the most painstaking constructivity. He is an encyclopedia of ballet, character, specialty, period, and even of formulas from modern German dancing. . . . Besides this gift of detail he has a passion for visual discipline, a very good sense of dramatic variety and climax, and one watches the whole Fantastique—except perhaps the last finale—with a breathless attention. The prison scene in particular moves as fast as a movie thriller. In the Fantastique Massine uses even more successfully than in Présages or Choreartium the device of a number of simultaneous entrées, giving an effect like a number of voices in music; and his gift for following the details as well as the main line of a score is remarkable.[28]

Denby found the sets and costumes nothing short of "miraculous." Christian Bérard brilliantly captured the feeling of a romantic mise-en-scène: the mythical landscape in the first scene, the mysterious ballroom, the ruins of the pastoral scene, and the somber, cavernous subworlds of the two final movements. The romantic devices included the illusion of the disappearance of walls and, in the third scene, the flying entrance of the Beloved. The visual impact was enhanced by

Kochno's intricate chiaroscuro lighting design. Each contribution helped to make *Symphonie fantastique* a great theatrical event.

Massine looked for his next challenge. There was much to choose from: a Mozart or Beethoven symphony, a lively Viennese divertissement ballet in collaboration with Etienne de Beaumont, as well as the ever-present possibilities of reviving *Le Sacre* or resurrecting *Liturgie,* his first, unfinished choreographic essay. For the new *Liturgie* he was planning to draw inspiration from a series of Mantegna friezes in the National Gallery and set them to music from the fifteenth and sixteenth centuries, to create a series of rhythmic tableaux on religious themes.[29] He hoped to persuade Nadia Boulanger to consult with him on the score. He also considered staging Zoltán Kodály's *Háry János.*[30]

At the end of the Covent Garden season, the Massines first visited Piešťany, then, en route to Galli, stopped in Salzburg to visit their friends Alice and Hugo von Hofmannsthal. In September Le Corbusier visited the Massines in Galli.

Nineteen thirty-seven would mark Massine's definitive break with de Basil. The 1936 petition for a restraining order was followed by a famous 1937 copyright suit. Massine's patience was wearing thin. He was already irritated that he had been forced to go to court to stop de Basil from using his ballets in the Australian repertory. Now, more inclined than ever to break away, form his own company, and establish sole ownership of his ballets, he filed suit against the Colonel when the company returned to London in the summer of 1937. The case stirred a great deal of talk in artistic circles and was thoroughly raked over by the international press, especially in England and the United States.

The ballets to which Massine laid claim fell into three categories: eight works that he had choreographed before he and de Basil signed a contract on June 1, 1932; the six he created under that contract; and the three works executed after they made a new agreement in August 1934. On February 23, 1938, Lord Justice Greer ruled that four ballets in the first group would go to Massine and four to de Basil. To Massine's dismay, the other nine ballets, including the three symphonic ballets, would go to de Basil, who had paid for them. By the time of this ruling, however, Massine had already defected, having performed for the last time with de Basil's company in San Francisco on January 30.

As it happened, during the American tour in the spring of 1937, Massine had found in Julius Fleischmann, a Cincinnati industrialist (of a yeast, liquor, and coffee fortune), the financial support needed to create his own company. When the loss of Massine became imminent in 1937, de Basil hired Michel Fokine as guest choreographer. Fokine's departure from Blum's Ballets de Monte Carlo opened the way for Massine to re-contact Blum and to propose reorganizing his company with American capital. The troupe would be sponsored by World Art, Inc. (a name taken from Diaghilev's journal *The World of Art*), with Hurok as its American manager, Fleischmann as president of the board, and Serge Denham, a Russian-born banker, as vice-president. Since Massine was ballet's most prestigious international figure, he of course became the operation's driving force. On January 2, 1937, he promised Denham that he would leave de Basil in order to become the new company's artistic di-rector, choreographer, and premier danseur. Massine also guaranteed the participation of famous artists such as Hindemith and Matisse, both of whom wrote letters of intent to Denham—all of this in order to secure the backing for the enterprise.[31] To Hurok, Massine agreed to extend his expiring contract with de Basil until the 1937–38 American tour, with the crucial proviso that Hurok would sign a "proper" contract with Denham before May 15, 1937.[32] Blum's company, renamed the Ballet Russe de Monte Carlo, was to have headquarters in both Monte Carlo and the United States. On November 19, 1937, Blum sold the Ballets de Monte Carlo to World Art, Inc. (later to be called Universal Art), with the pur-chase to take effect on February 1, 1938.[33]

Massine's Ballet Russe de Monte Carlo would gather an impressive roster of dancers: Toumanova, Danilova, Delarova, Alicia Markova, Mia Slavenska, Lubov Rostova, Nini Theilade, Nina Tarakanova, Nathalie Krassovska, Lifar, George Zoritch, Michel Panaiev, Igor Youskevitch, Frederic Franklin, and Roland Guérard. Efrem Kurtz left de Basil's com-pany to become its leading conductor. The rival companies attracted the attention of the international press early in 1938, and the Battle of the Ballets, as it was known, became an artistic and social war that involved some of the most important personalities of the time in Europe and the United States. But in the long run, the outcome of this crisis would prove detrimental to Massine. After five years of work, he possessed an out-standing and versatile company trained, coached, and molded to give body to his choreographic ideas. As Haskell had observed the previous year: "Massine's departure will not only damage the company as a whole, but Massine himself perhaps even more. It has taken all of five years, hard work and sacrifice to build up this magnificent ensemble. . . . It would take more than five . . . to create another such."[34]

In January 1938 Massine returned to Europe to organize the new en-terprise. He approached old collaborators and friends such as Count

Etienne de Beaumont, who once again took an active part in his projects. After Massine settled in Monte Carlo, preparations could begin for the company's spring debut in Monaco. With complete control of his own company, he tried to establish a creative atmosphere reminiscent of his early days with Diaghilev. The whole company was overtaken by an almost frenzied mood of artistic collaboration. Monte Carlo became a feeding ground for dancers, composers, painters, and prominent supporters; there were Dalí, Chanel, Kochno, Bérard, Beaumont, Hindemith, Tchelitchev, all enraptured by the creative process. Even Massine's relationship with the dancers grew closer; during the day-long rehearsals, the leading members of the company would gather at his villa outside Monte Carlo for sandwiches and relaxation.

Massine's return to France put him back in touch with the artistic trends prevailing in Paris. He recontacted friends, especially painters, some of whom (Masson, Miró, Dalí, Duchamp, Ernst, Man Ray) had enjoyed a rousing success during January and February with the famous surrealist exhibition at the Galerie Beaux-Arts. His return to the Continent also exposed the choreographer to the darkening political, social, and economic reality of Europe. His previous five years had been spent mostly within the sheltered milieu of the Ballets Russes, in England and America. England throughout the 1930s had tried to remain insulated from the ominous events unfolding in continental Europe; and in America the approaching cataclysm was dulled by distance. Massine was never acutely political, but in Paris he could not avoid reality. Days were somber. The "May crisis" that followed the Anschluss, Hitler's annexation of Austria, made it evident that he also had designs on Czechoslovakia, and signaled Germany's plans for territorial expansion.

The spring engagement at Monte Carlo's Théâtre du Casino was to include only one premiere by the company's choreographer: *Gaîté parisienne*. (Massine was not appointed artistic director until March 23, 1939.)

Gaîté parisienne probably had as its point of departure the divertissement ballet on a Viennese theme that Massine was discussing with Beaumont in 1936. But, undoubtedly in reaction to the frightening events in Austria, Beaumont changed the setting to Tortoni's, a fashionable Parisian café of the Second Empire, to which came various characters in pursuit of love and pleasure: a Glove Seller, a Flower Girl, a Peruvian, a Baron, an Officer, a Duke, and other topical characters mingled with dandies, cancan dancers, and brilliantly uniformed soldiers. The score consisted of excerpts chosen by Boulanger from a number of Offenbach works,[35] orchestrated by Manuel Rosenthal in collaboration with Jacques

Monte Carlo, 1938. Standing: Eugenia Delarova, Igor Youskevitch, Christian
Bérard, Massine. Seated: Barbara Karinska, Alicia Markova, Boris Kochno,
Etienne de Beaumont, and the Countess de Beaumont

Brindejonc-Offenbach, the composer's nephew. The scenery and costumes were designed by Beaumont. *Gaîté parisienne* followed in the tradition of *La Boutique fantasque* and *Le Beau Danube.* Here the slight plot of
flirtations, amorous intrigues, and conquests unfolded as a series of
solos, pas de deux, and ensembles, including a climactic cancan. (According to Frederic Franklin, Massine intended to end the ballet with the cancan, and it was Kochno's suggestion to add the final scene.[36]) Less balletic
than *Boutique* and *Beau Danube,* the Offenbach piece was fashioned more
in a glorified music-hall style.

A sensational hit with the public, this piece of sheer escapism met
with a mixed reception from the European press. In London, Newman
found it "lovable,"[37] and Fernau Hall, writing for the *Dancing Times,* compared it favorably to *Boutique, Beau Danube,* and *Union Pacific:*

> *The dance of the soldiers, for example, is much more clean-cut and vital*
> *than the corresponding dance of the Cossack toys in* Boutique, *and it has*
> *a gloriously impudent quality which sets the atmosphere of the whole bal-*

let. As for the fight, it is incomparably better than the fight in Union Pacific, *and one of the finest scenes Massine has ever arranged. No actual
fighting takes place, but the effect given by the complex dancing movements
is far more real than the real thing could ever be. All the experience Massine has gained in handling large groups in his symphonic ballets is brilliantly applied in this scene, so that although the whole stage is filled with
dancers, all of whom constantly remain "in character," the general effect is
always clear and definite. As for the Peruvian himself, he is a pure joy, and
quite unlike any other Massine role.*

*The Can-Can dances are built up to a fine climax, with some very effec-
tive virtuoso effects on the way.*[38]

Haskell and Cyril Beaumont, however, did not fall under its spell. Beaumont found it inferior to *Le Beau Danube* and lacking the latter's "homo-
geneity" and "charm."[39] In the United States, the ballet won praise from
public and press alike. John Martin in the *New York Times* found it superior to *Le Beau Danube* and "fresh as a daisy, extraordinarily skillful and inventive."[40]

In America, the ballet became the company's signature piece, as *Le
Beau Danube* had been de Basil's. It was an ideal piece to end a performance, and much of its success depended on the brilliant, unforgettable,
and (even in their own day) legendary performances of Danilova as the
Glove Seller, Massine as the Peruvian, and Franklin as the Baron.

In March there was an unexpected development: a scheme to
merge the warring Ballets Russes factions.[41] The idea was Hurok's. He
envisioned managing what he called "the finest ballet company that . . .
ever existed."[42] His ploy had a double aim: to merge the companies and
to oust de Basil in the process. Agreements were signed and repudiated.
Lawsuits and counterclaims were filed. The merger failed to materialize.

For the upcoming summer season at the Drury Lane Theatre in
London, Massine's company would face direct competition from de
Basil's under the artistic guidance of Fokine. Counterprogramming, Massine premiered two new ballets: *Seventh Symphony* (Beethoven's) on July 12
and *Nobilissima Visione,* set to an original score by Hindemith, on July 21.

Massine had first considered the symphony as early as 1936, after
Symphonie fantastique. (He no doubt had been encouraged to do so by
some words of Newman's published that year in the *Sunday Times:* "Les
Présages *and* Choreartium . . . draw full houses at Covent Garden; and we
unregenerates now hope that Massine, having at last got the Berlioz ballet off his hands, will turn his genius to the Beethoven No. 7.")[43] Without

The Peruvian in Gaîté parisienne,
1938

the abstraction that had characterized *Choreartium*, and closer in mood to *Les Présages*, *Seventh Symphony* was Massine's depiction of the creation and destruction of the world, utilizing universal archetypes derived from the Bible and classical mythology. He wrote:

> *I had for some time been intrigued by the problem of interpreting this monumental work, whose powerful chords in the First Movement suggested the formation of the earth, with moving masses of soil and water creating rivers, hills and valleys. The clarinet theme which follows seemed to me to represent the evolution of plant life, while the chords of the next passage conjured up in my mind the flight of birds and the running of small animals through the forest. Standing on Galli one summer afternoon, watching the waves, whipped up by a sudden storm, pounding the unyielding rocks, I found the theme of the ballet clarifying itself in my imagination. I saw in the first scene the basic forces of nature, Earth, Air, and Water, assembled by the Spirit of Creation. Plants, birds and animals appear. Finally, Man, Woman, and the Serpent emerge from the living rock. The second scene I conceived as the story of man's guilt and despair, symbolized by Cain and Abel and the introduction of death with man's first murder. The third scene introduced the gods of Olympus. Beginning in a mood of gaiety, I created a choreographic movement which led on to the debauched bacchanal of the Fourth Movement, concluding with the destruction of the world by fire.*[44]

Although relying less on counterpoint than in his first three symphonic ballets, Massine drew on all his characteristic techniques for *Seventh Symphony*. However, whereas in *Choreartium* and, especially, *Symphonie fantastique* he had achieved an architectural quality by emphasizing the construction of moving masses on stage, *Seventh Symphony* produced a sculptural effect. Here, apparently amorphous groups would begin to fall into formations representing air, water, earth, and fire. These visual images were essential to the mise-en-scène and stood in contrast to the actual formal dancing of the other characters. Forty years later Massine observed: "The richness and beauty of the human body lays in its manifold possibilities of movement, whether it is classical technique, folk dance, or simply visual images that can be created through corporeal rhythmic movement. In the *Seventh Symphony* I wanted to expand the possibility of body movement to the utmost, not just through dancing, but exploring the potentialities of rhythmic corporeal movement as well."[45]

Seventh Symphony, *1938: Fourth movement, final moment of the bacchanale*

However, the corporeal movement in *Seventh Symphony* could be called plastic only insofar as it caught and expressed a visual image inspired by painting or sculpture. Even as it captured such an image, the movement quickened. Massine avoided the trap awaiting any choreographer who tries to re-create visual images in movement: his plasticity kept the work from feeling static. On the contrary, the film of the ballet shows, as Jack Anderson noted, that the dancing is characterized by a kinetic dynamism. Albertina Vitak, writing in 1940, said that the ballet had "more straight dancing with less theatricalities than Massine's previous symphonic works." [46]

Like those predecessors, *Seventh Symphony* provoked a great deal of controversy. Some critics admired the result; others were skeptical about the use of a Beethoven symphony; and still others felt that Massine simply hadn't succeeded, whether a viewer thought his goal worthy or not. Some looked back to *Les Présages* and *Choreartium* as models and regretted that he had departed from them. Francis Toye wrote in the *Daily Telegraph*: "We have had enough of the symphony ballets. Not because of their lack of reverence for Beethoven . . . but because they are a bore."[47] But Newman, though he felt that the scherzo movement did "not lend itself well to choreographical parallelism,"[48] again championed Massine, comparing him favorably to Fokine:

> *What I cannot understand is why Massine should be censured for doing well what other choreographers aim at doing but do not succeed in. Examine certain of Fokine's ballets from L'Oiseau de Feu onwards, and you will see that he too has constantly aimed at finding choreographic equivalents for features of the music that in themselves have no connection to external reality. . . .*
>
> *Now Fokine is constantly "pointing" to this or that feature of the music in his choreography; the trouble, so far as I am concerned, is that too often the pointing is almost unbelievably naive. I do not mind so much when, in L'Epreuve d'Amour, he adopts the very obvious device of making his dancers stamp when Mozart's cellos and basses seem to stamp: it is not very brilliant invention, but it may pass. But when, in those long woodwind chords in the Midsummer Night's Dream overture, he makes his elves do a jerk of now head, now body, on each chord in turn, I feel that the limit has been reached of my tolerance of naiveté. When Massine points a phrase in this fashion—take, as an example, the movements of the Spirit of Creation at the commencement of the Beethoven—the dancer's movements and gestures not only mean something in themselves but form an organic part of a large design.*[49]

In New York the second scene, with its possible reference to Christ's Descent from the Cross, created a bit of an uproar and was even found sacrilegious by some. As Jack Anderson expressed it in 1981, "In this day of rock musicals based upon the Bible, it is hard to imagine such a scene causing any hullabaloo."[50] Denby was scornful of the entire enterprise:

> *Like a cigarette company, he is using famous names to advertise his wares. But I cannot help resenting it, because they are names of living things I have loved. It is hardest to bear in the case of his Seventh, where the orchestra is constantly reminding me of the Beethoven original.*
>
> *Trying, however, to put aside this private resentment, I still am disappointed. . . . I could see a kaleidoscopic succession of clever arrangements, but there was no thrill in the order in which they came. There was no sequence in the movement that awakened some kind of special feeling, some*

kind of urgency. It all occupied the eye as long as it lasted, and left no reality, no secret emotion behind. I missed the sense of growth and interplay, of shifting kinds of tensions, the feeling of drama, almost, that makes the best choreography mean much more than a string of effects. As a pictorial arranger Massine is inexhaustible. But dancing is less pictorial than plastic, and pictures in dancing leave a void in the imagination. . . .

Because Massine's tension is static he can never make us feel the curious unfolding that is like tenderness. Like a Hollywood director, he gives us no sense of human growth (there isn't time), he keeps everything at a constant level of finish; everything is over as soon as it starts. He has no equivalent for mystery except to bring down the lights.[51]

The ballet received some of its most eloquent reviews when it reached Paris in 1939. Vuillermoz was a firm admirer:

It is fashionable to be dynamic, and in this regard we must grant that Massine is a full embodiment of that restless ideal of his time. Once the curtain falls at the end of each of his creations, the interpreters are all out of breath, but so too are the spectators. . . . Massine excels in architectural combinations, in which he utilizes the different parts of his dancers' bodies simply as construction materials, obtaining thereby arabesques of new and unforeseen interest. This all happens, of course, in the midst of violent, carried-away motions which infuse his rhythms with the power of a hurricane. . . .

There are some purists . . . who have deemed it proper to cover their faces and to cry out against the sacrilege of someone daring to translate into choreographic terms the rhythmical indications of a Beethoven symphony! Allow me to smile at such prudish qualms!

. . . There is never any sacrilege in attempting to uphold in the synesthetic creation of a plastic medium, the grandeur of a rhythmic creation. . . .

The fact is, the beautiful images which accompanied the four movements of the Seventh Symphony—the Creation, the Earth, the Heavens, and Destruction—are a most respectful, noble, and, I dare say, Beethovenlike embodiment of the clear and legible tempo indications appearing in a score that is not at all esoteric.[52]

Of special interest were the reactions of leading French composers. Florent Schmitt, among those who had called the adaptation of a symphony into dance a "sacrilege," succumbed once he saw the work itself, describing it as "a spectacle full of great pathos that owed its birthright to music itself."[53] And Henri Sauguet in *Le Jour* noted that the ballet "does not shock the musician who sees come to life with intelligence the different voices of the symphony." He felt that the ballet was full of "boldness, fire, invention, and real grandeur."[54]

The second premiere of the Drury Lane season, *Nobilissima Visione*, was inspired by the *Little Flowers of Saint Francis*. Massine had considered collaborating with Hindemith as early as 1935, and in the summer of 1936 the Hindemiths and the Massines went sightseeing together in Italy. From Poverello they proceeded to Florence. Massine wrote: "The idea for this work came to me from Paul Hindemith. . . . He had just come from the great church of Santa Croce [in Florence], which contains the frescoes by Giotto depicting the life of St. Francis of Assisi. He had been deeply impressed by them; taking me by the arm he hurried me back to the church to see them. I too was struck by their spiritual beauty and could well understand why they had so profoundly moved Hindemith."[55]

After much thought, Massine was still hesitant about the idea, and he approached the writer François Mauriac for advice. Although Mauriac was also unconvinced, by then the idea had so intensely fired Massine's imagination that there was no turning back. (Later Mauriac commented: "I must admit that when Léonide Massine spoke to me for the first time of his project for St. Francis, the idea seemed to me worse than bold—it was even sacrilegious. This is because I had not realized that the dance, as this great artist has conceived of it, can express what is most beautiful and sacred in this world: the love of God taking possession of the soul of a young man.")[56] At the end of the summer of 1937 Massine invited the Hindemiths to Galli to work on the new ballet. In fact, however, most of the preliminary planning had already taken place earlier in the summer in correspondence between the two. In its embryonic stage the scenario was to concentrate on Saint Francis's miracles. But in a letter dated August 12, 1937, Massine suggested to Hindemith that they focus instead on the character of Saint Francis himself, structuring the action on "three distinct periods, that is to say, his life before the conversion, the period of the conversion and the miracles." Massine continued: "It seems to me that this idea is superior to the first one. It allows for a greater episodic variety, a strong contrast between the first and the third parts and a very beautiful moment, that of the conversion. It also brings to the fore the character of Saint Francis, an aspect that seems interesting to me due to his profound and rich spirituality and his reactions to all the events of his life." Massine proceeded to list the eight episodes that he found most remarkable in the saint's life and which, in fact, were incorporated into the final scenario.[57]

The rehearsals for *Nobilissima Visione*, as well as those for *Seventh Symphony*, took place during the spring of 1938 in Monte Carlo. During the rehearsal period Hindemith played the score at the piano and advised Massine on "the structure of some of his musical phrases, which were extremely complex and difficult."[58] Pavel Tchelitchev, with whom Massine had worked previously on *Ode*, was commissioned to design scenery and costumes in medieval style.

Nobilissima visione, later better known as *Saint Francis*, had five scenes:

First Scene: The Shop of Pietro Bernadone. Francis and his companions are spending time at his father's shop. Motivated by the arrival of a knight, Francis departs for war, dreaming of military honor and glory.

Second Scene: A Country Road. Francis is disappointed by the knights' greed and abusive behavior when they attack an unarmed group, carrying off the women and whatever loot they find. Francis prays for guidance, whereupon Poverty, Obedience, and Chastity appear as allegorical figures. The latter two vanish and Francis follows Poverty.

Third Scene: The House of Pietro Bernadone. At a banquet celebrating Francis's return, a group of beggars show up, and Francis gives them the gold vessels from the table. His father is furious and strikes his son. Francis takes off his rich clothes and, laying them at his father's feet, leaves the house.

Fourth Scene: Francis Finds Happiness as a Hermit. He meets a wolf. His three companions join him. As Francis sleeps, Poverty appears to him in a dream. As he awakens, he welcomes her as a bride. They exchange sashes and the companions celebrate their marriage with bread and water.

Fifth Scene: A Landscape with a Great Rock in the Distance. Surrounded by nuns and monks, Poverty leads Francis to the summit of the rock against a blazing sky.

Choreographically, the ballet was rooted in the *terre à terre*, nonvirtuosic modern idiom that had characterized the second movement of *Choreartium*. The steps were stylized, with an Oriental Byzantine touch derived from Italian primitive painting, especially from the works of Giotto. Some of the phrases were reminiscent of martial art. For Massine, *Nobilissima Visione* "was not a ballet at all. It was a dramatic and

Massine as Saint Francis, with the three Companions and with Nini Theilade as Poverty, in Nobilissima Visione, 1938

choreographic interpretation of the life of St. Francis in which Hindemith, Tchelitchev and I tried to create and sustain throughout a mood of mystic exaltation."[59] The ballet, possessing great sobriety of style, had very effective and ingenious movements. For example, in their pas de deux Saint Francis (Massine) and Poverty (Nini Theilade) "danced an adagio which was more like a slow allegro. There was not one lift. They danced a lot of the same movements together, facing each other."[60] And in the final scene the alleluia was sung silently by the hands of the Franciscan monks and nuns.

Opening night had all the excitement of a traditional Massine premiere. In attendance were Lady Cunard, Lady Juliet Duff, Sir Kenneth Clark, Lord Berners, Baron Gunzbourg, Alice von Hofmannstal, Edward James, and the Sitwells. In a letter to Massine after the premiere Hindemith wrote: "We have admired your devoted art and the sublime passion with which you capture the spirit and the heart at the same time." The composer acknowledged that "the birth of this work has marked a period full of happy and productive discoveries."[61] Although the ballet was greeted with twenty-one curtain calls, its critical reception was mixed. Haskell felt that the music sounded "like so much unpleasant noise, signifying nothing," and that the choreography was "dull."[62] Francis Toye strongly disagreed with the suitability of the subject and added, "I have no desire to see Massine impersonate St. Francis, who after all is one of the major saints in the calendar. It would be a pity if he were now encouraged to try his hand at St. Paul or one of the apostles."[63] When the ballet was presented in the United States, it found admirers in press and audience alike. According to Grace Robert, this was in part because the public had grown accustomed to the seriousness of modern dance works, especially those by artists such as Martha Graham, and "welcomed an appeal to more adult emotions."[64] Denby, predictably, disliked it: "St. Francis seems a slinky posturing, a Sakharoff-Kreutzberg parody of illuminated Books of Hours and Minnelieder, with a grand finale of anthroposophic chorus girls.

"No one but Massine could have got any theatrical effect out of this hodgepodge of minor pictorial devices, no one but he could have held the stage with a solo only half executed—but everyone acknowledges his stupendous gift of showmanship, and eminence, for that matter."[65] By 1940, however, he admitted that St. Francis had been the "last time Massine took a chance with novel choreography."[66]

John Martin, on the other hand, praised the ballet in the New York

Massine

Times as "one of the most memorable and beautiful dance works of our day." He added:

> Unorthodox in subject matter, elevated in tone, and revolutionary in its choreographic procedure, it is one of those creations which, like Bronislava Nijinska's Les Noces, grew out of boldness of conception without regard for precedent or consequences.
>
> Massine has caught not alone the particular development of Francis "so little and simple and rude of speech," but has evoked a masterly picture of the Middle Ages in which he moved. It is perhaps not so much thirteenth century Italy in detail as the entire medieval period he has sketched in little, with its sumptuousness and its misery, its cruelty and its vision . . .
>
> The movement, though it does not deny its ballet premises, is touched in an extravagant style definitely influenced by medieval illuminations and those painters we have come to call "primitive" and richly evocative. If it is designedly naive, it is never merely quaint or whimsical, but eminently dignified and honest. For all its distortions and inhibitions, it has great pace and flow, and proves itself in every way fitted to convey feeling in eloquent terms. Like St. Francis himself, it is both ascetic and joyful; sparing and full of color.[67]

Hurok called it "one of Massine's greatest triumphs and one of his very finest works. The ballet, unfortunately, was not popular with mass audiences; but it was a work of deep and moving beauty."[68] Similarly, George Amberg wrote: "The work was a rejection of the prevailing realistic tendency in the ballet and an affirmation of true spirituality. . . . In no other ballet did Massine seem so totally absorbed in the world of his creation. In no other ballet did the limited realms of stage space and stage time seem to expand into such unlimited poetic dimensions. . . . As the story unfolded, the actual events appeared as symbolic stations of human inspiration progressing toward ultimate transfiguration."[69]

In Paris the following year the work aroused special interest in the musical world (Hindemith's music was forbidden in Germany during the Third Reich). While Schmitt found the score monotonous, except for the scene of the wolf,[70] and Sauguet felt that it lacked definition and color,[71] Milhaud praised it warmly. For him it had "great loftiness of thought and it was all imbued with an extremely mystical feeling."[72] In general, the choreography was praised, and Sauguet singled out the last scene when "the hands of the dancers seem to leave their bodies, mute, like birds taking flight toward the heavens with St. Francis's soul."[73] Even dancers who were not in the cast found the ballet moving, plastically beautiful, and extremely spiritual. Danilova today considers it her favorite work by Massine.[74]

BEFORE THE COMPANY left Europe in the fall of 1938 to tour the United States for the first time, Massine finally divorced Eugenia Delarova. The last months of the marital breakup were stressful and dramatic, as was the postdivorce period, since Delarova remained on the roster of the Ballet Russe for the next two years. There was no divorce settlement. Most dancers were saddened by the separation, since for them Massine and Delarova had become an institution, and she in particular was highly esteemed not only for her charm and friendliness but for her kindness to everyone, and her undisputed devotion to Massine and his career. "She was behind it all," declared Franklin. "She watched rehearsals; she brought to Massine's attention those dancers who had talent and special qualities and could be made into soloists. Delarova was always part of the creative process, and she was there as a sort of diplomat trying to orchestrate everything for Massine, and when anyone had a problem she was always there to take care of it."[75]

During the United States tour Massine produced one new ballet, based on Slavic mythology. The idea for a Russian ballet had been proposed to Massine by Hurok, who wanted to emulate the tremendous success the de Basil company had enjoyed the previous year with Fokine's *Le Coq d'or*. The impresario demanded that the American tour include a world premiere, so *Bogatyri* was rehearsed during the hectic London season, and premiered in October 1938 at the New York Metropolitan Opera House. It revolved around the adventures of the half-historic, half-legendary hero who had defended Prince Vladimir, the first Christian ruler of Russia. In the ballet, the handsome Bogatyri Dobryna Nikitich (Panaiev) sets out to rescue Princess Anastachiuska (Mia Slavenska), the daughter of Prince Vladimir, from the clutches of the twelve-headed snake dragon. In the course of the Bogatyri's search, a battle takes place with a Tartan tribe after which the tribeswomen seduce the Bogatyri, causing them to forget their mission. In the meantime Alyosha (Frederic Franklin) discovers the dragon's garden and saves the princess. When they return safely home, a huge wedding celebration takes place. The ballet was set to Borodin's Second Symphony, the two movements of his unfinished Third Symphony as orchestrated by Alexander

Glazounov, and the Nocturne from his String Quartet No. 2 as orchestrated by Nicolas Tcherepnine. Perhaps the most noteworthy aspect of the production was Nathalie Gontcharova's magnificent scenery and costumes.

At the end of the United States tour, the company returned to Europe. On March 14, 1939, Massine married his third wife, the statuesque and strong-willed Tatiana Orlova, née Milishnikova. They had met a few years before when she took some Spanish character-dance classes he was teaching at Egorova's studio in Paris. In the interim, Orlova was in and out of Massine's sight until the relationship suddenly blossomed.

In the spring of 1939, the deterioration of the political situation was immediately evident. In September 1938, England, France, and Italy had surrendered Czechoslovakia to Hitler in Munich, allowing his armies to march into that country on October 1, and now Europe slid inexorably towards war. On March 15, 1939, German troops marched into Bohemia and Monrovia; that evening Hitler himself made his entry into Prague. Clearly Poland was his next objective.

The Monte Carlo spring season introduced two new works by Massine: *Capriccio espagnol* (May 4) and *L'Etrange farandole* (May 11), later better known as *Rouge et noir.*

Massine had invited to Monte Carlo the renowned Spanish dancer Argentinita as guest artist to take over the role of the Miller's Wife in *Le Tricorne.* The choreographer came up with the idea of co-creating with her another ballet based on Spanish folklore. The choice of music was Rimsky-Korsakov's *Capriccio espagnol*, a dance suite that "portrayed a country fair, with gypsies dancing in a rousing *bulería* until the dancing becomes general and the watching couples swing into a frenzied *jota.*"[76] *Capriccio espagnol* became a flashy vehicle for Massine and Argentinita. Later Denby wrote:

> Capriccio Espagnol *has the benefit of Argentinita's exhaustless repertoire of regional steps, and of Massine's equally exhaustless repertoire of effective theater. Most of it is pleasant to watch and the end is one of those bang-up finales that are indispensable to ring the curtain down if you have a lethargic audience. Massine has a solo, and in it he makes the other men look like little boys. The showmanship, the bite of his stage presence is superlative; look at the slow curling of his hands as his dance begins. It is inaccurate to call such a dance as his Spanish in the specific sense . . . and foolish to compare him with a real gypsy, who would probably have no gift*

*for dominating a crowded stage and would hardly be visible at that mo-
ment to an ordinary audience.*[77]

  Rouge et noir was the second and final collaboration between Massine and Matisse. The idea had arisen when Massine visited the painter's
studio while the painter was at work on a huge panel decoration commissioned for the Barnes Foundation in Pennsylvania. Massine was so
taken by the sense of movement and rhythm in Matisse's work that he
asked his old friend to collaborate with him again on a ballet.[78] But it was
not until 1939 that this joint creative effort materialized.

  For the music Massine selected Dmitri Shostakovich's First Symphony, which Matisse then visualized in five basic colors, taking the great
arches of his decoration for the Barnes Foundation as a point of departure for the decor. Matisse recalled that he "divided the background in
four colors, blue, red, black and yellow, with white arches. I dressed the
dancers in the same colors of the decor in blue, red, black, yellow and
white unitights. . . . I was satisfied with the idea because I managed to
free myself from all those insignificant accessories that had no direct relation with the plastic element and the dynamism of ballet."[79] In a letter to
Massine dated May 18, 1938, he wrote:

> *I should tell you I believe that in order to facilitate your choreographic
> composition of the First Symphony it seems to me to be indispensable to
> dress your male and female dancers in colored tights or work costumes for
> the torso and the legs—and even the arms since the volumes of color which
> you will have to move around should not be hacked down and cut up into
> small pieces by having the arms and the legs dressed in any old colors. The
> extra cost will be really insignificant if you compare it with the benefits
> you will obtain.*[80]

Massine was not completely satisfied with Matisse's initial idea for the
front curtain, however, and suggested that the painter change it. Matisse
replied: "You have made a just observation regarding the curtain and it
has set my brain in motion, so that since your arrival I have worked on it
and have come up finally with a new curtain which I hope will please you
entirely."[81]

  Massine gave allegorical meaning to the colors: white (man and
woman), yellow (wickedness), blue (nature), red (materialism), and black
(violence). (Massine told Danilova that white stood for Russia, black for

fascism, and red for communism.)[82] Though more abstract than *Les Présages*, *Rouge et noir* was a sequel to the Tchaikovsky ballet, and as in *Les Présages* each movement was given a symbolic theme.

First Movement (Aggression). Man, symbolizing the poetic spirit, is pursued and overtaken by brutal forces.

Second Movement (Field and City). The men of the city encounter the men of the field and drive them off.

Third Movement (Solitude). Woman parted from Man is tormented in her solitude by an evil spirit.

Fourth Movement (Destiny). Man eludes the brutal forces and finds Woman again. But their joy is short-lived, for in freeing himself from his worldly enemies he is conquered by destiny.

While in *Les Présages* the hero triumphed over fate and the adverse forces of war, paralleling the European reality of 1933, *Rouge et noir* presented a pessimistic finale of wretchedness and disillusionment. In his treatment of it Massine summoned the anguish of the age, its overwhelming feelings of alienation, despair, failure, and the angst of loneliness, stressing a cosmic level of identification outside the self. In this ballet he proved his ability to conceive emotional ideas in terms of forms. *Rouge et noir* was a personal metaphoric expression of the philosophical and political ideas that permeated the historical moment. The political connotations of the ballet did not escape audiences or critics. Pierre Michaut commented that for some the ballet's "abstraction hid an esoteric meaning . . . a political allegory: the dramatic crushing of helpless nations, victims of the violence and brutality of victimizing nations—Abyssinia, Austria, Czechoslovakia. . . . Woman . . . who survives, symbolizes the spirit that prevails and cannot be defeated."[83] However, Michaut felt that although the symbolic theme did not impose any action or narrative development and the work was purely an abstract ballet, it nonetheless produced in the spectator "a dramatic impression quite oppressive, a clear sign that its agitation is not pointless."[84] Jack Anderson later pointed out that "one of its most effective moments, a solo lamentation for Markova, symbolized to some audiences the grief of Czechoslovakia overcome by Germany."[85] Danilova described Markova's solo as "a cry—she *bourréed* all around the stage, changing the positions of her arms, of her body. She was weeping without tears, with her soul."[86]

Rouge et noir was a visualization of music in absolute dance terms, but Massine resorted less than in his four previous symphonic ballets to architectural constructions and to counterpoint. Here his objectives were abstraction of content (despite the symbolic theme) and abstrac-

Rouge et noir, *1938*

tion of line (linear development). While in *Les Présages* and *Choreartium* the choreographic line is clearly defined as geometrical, with each image contoured and modeled, the line in *Rouge et noir* fuses abstract formations, achieving, in part through its fluctuating velocity, a galvanic power. Abstraction not only serves the thematic structure but is at the heart of the choreographic impulse, showing a greater degree of introspection than ever before from Massine. In its handling of mass formations that were constantly shifting and regrouping, the choreography became a device to manipulate the audience's visual field. As Grace Robert commented: "It was extraordinarily effective scenically, though best seen from a distance. . . . The groups formed and came apart, making wonderful blocks of color like an abstract painting set in motion."[87]

The opinions of the Paris critics were mixed, the majority preferring *Seventh Symphony* and *Nobilissima Visione* to the pessimistic *Rouge et noir*. But Pierre Michaut nevertheless admired the result, describing the choreography as "various groups that form, scatter, and re-form. It is a simple handling of lines and formations in movement. The handling of forms is accompanied by a play of colors; the various leading characters detach themselves from the large background figures, by which they are reabsorbed. A visual symphony of forms and colors in movement is superimposed on the musical symphony." [88]

In the United States, too, notices were mixed. Denby disliked it:

> *The set and underwear costumes, effective for a while, become rather professorially meager long before the piece is over (and rather unpleasantly indecent). . . . The choreography I am at a loss to describe because it does not seem to relate itself to anything I feel. I will gladly accept it as my fault that it all seems to me to happen in a vacuum. I can see ingenious arrangements and good technique, a touching opening in the third scene, and an odd feeling of a conventional anecdote at the very end. When I like something I am sure I am right; when I don't, I'm not. I should like to read a sympathetic criticism of this ballet to help me get interested.* [89]

John Martin's reservations centered on the fact that the ballet was "partly abstract, partly programmatic, partly dominated by a color symbolism that is far from clear. Another is the ground of the willful mysticism of the theme." [90] Grace Robert admired the group formations: "Massine had taken a lot of criticism of previous symphonic ballets on the subject of the unballetic scurrying of dancers on their way to form one of his famous architectural tableaux. To a certain extent this criticism was justified, and he answered it superbly in *Rouge et noir,* where the groups (many and fascinating) click into position as though placed there by a gigantic hand working a jigsaw puzzle." [91] Robert Lawrence thought it was one of Massine's finest efforts: "Although [he] provided a philosophic program, *Rouge et noir* is—as its title implies—an abstract play of color and line which may be enjoyed without any recourse to a deeper meaning. Massine's patterns are self-sufficient; and in few other ballets by any master is emotional content so compellingly wedded to formal design." [92] For George Beiswanger it was Massine's "best constructed and most poetic ballet." [93]

Massine's symphonic ballets of 1938 and 1939 reflect in their themes the historical context as well as the aesthetics of the time that produced them. *Seventh Symphony* and *Rouge et noir* were very much concerned with cosmic events, with conflict, violence, loss of love, sacrifice, destruction, and death—a corollary to the anxiety of a continent facing depression, civil war, fascism, Nazism, and the portent of holocaust. The themes of these ballets were recurrent in the works of other European artists of the immediate prewar years, especially those associated with surrealism. For Michaut, *Seventh Symphony*, with its "apocalyptic destruction of humanity," and *Rouge et noir*, a "symbolic drama of the condition of man," hinted that "Massine was probably suffering a mystical crisis as he had in the past." He compared the choreographer's crisis with Stravinsky's and added that "when we think of the situation of these great spirits, living in exile, separated from the land of their ancestors and their first masters . . . Massine has imprinted on his ballets a pessimistic and desperate accent. More and more he distances himself from futility. And his worry about these immeasurable questions reveals an anxiety of the soul."[94] Nonetheless, to counterbalance the devastating *Seventh Symphony* and *Rouge et noir*, there were *Gaîté parisienne* and *Capriccio espagnol*, two pieces of theatrical escapism, and *Nobilissima Visione*, a work that reiterates spiritual values and wherein man finds salvation. The Saint Francis ballet was Massine's return to the mysticism and religious fervor that from childhood had given him a vision of transcendence. On the edge of a world catastrophe, *Nobilissima Visione* was a reiteration of the Dostoyevskian perception that man must not become alienated from his spiritual world, otherwise human existence can only tilt toward tragedy.

PART FIVE

The War Years

*Being essentially the instrument of his work, he [the artist]
is subordinate to it. . . . He has done the best that there is in
him by giving it form. . . .* — JUNG

*It is not others' hopes that you have to fulfill. You're going
nowhere, they say? Whatever you offer of yourself, it will
be your all and not what others would expect from you.
. . . Let them study you or let them leave you. You ought not
to lower your soul to their lack of understanding.*

— UNAMUNO

*Michel Larionov
and Massine on stage
in front of Dalí's decor
for* Bacchanale, *1939*

CHAPTER 12

Paris, June 1939–New York, August 1946

AFTER THE 1939 Paris season ended in late June, the members of
the Ballet Russe de Monte Carlo scattered on holiday, planning to reassemble for a Covent Garden engagement on September 4. The opening never took place. On September 1 Nazi troops invaded Poland. As
Hitler's armies marched into Warsaw, German war planes bombarded
the Polish capital in the first of hundreds of air strikes that would devas-
tate Europe over the next six years. On September 3 England and France
declared war on Germany.

Paris grew frantic. Massine's and de Basil's dancers found themselves stranded there, unable to leave Europe. Life was immediately con-
ditioned by war. Restaurants and shops were boarded up or closed. Some
Parisians quickly joined an exodus toward the south. Those who re-

mained behind sometimes had to carry gas masks or make their way to bomb shelters during air raid drills.

The first transatlantic passage that Massine was able to book he turned over to Delarova. She was now, since their divorce, quite alone and a source of great anxiety to Massine, who wanted her safely out of Europe as soon as possible.[1] Fortunately, Massine and Orlova were also able to leave soon afterward, on the *Rotterdam.* They arrived in the United States on September 14. The difficulties of transporting a ballet company across the Atlantic during wartime (especially given the variety of the dancers' nationalities) caused the scheduled Metropolitan Opera engagement to be moved back from October 10 to October 26. To be certain of making the new date, Massine trained a second ensemble in case members of his company were unable to leave Europe.

On October 26, the Ballet Russe opened its revised schedule at the Met (most of the dancers having arrived only that morning). On November 9 Massine's *Bacchanale* received its world premiere. A surrealistic outing with scenario, decor, and costumes by Dalí, it was set to excerpts from Wagner's *Tannhäuser* (including the Venusberg music and, as the finale, the Pilgrims' chorus).

The first planned collaboration between Dalí and Massine went back at least as far as 1937, when the two artists discussed a ballet called *Tristan fou,* with a scenario by Dalí based on Wagner's *Tristan und Isolde.*[2] Besides excerpts from *Tristan,* the music was to include jazz and traditional Spanish *pasos dobles.* Elsa Schiaparelli was to contribute the costumes.[3] Dalí signed a contract with Denham on November 11, 1937,[4] but *Tristan fou* did not materialize until 1944. By the spring of 1939, Dalí and Massine had instead begun work on *Bacchanale,* first in Paris and later in Monte Carlo.

Massine's friendship with Dalí (they met in the mid-1930s) and genuine admiration for his painting cemented the collaboration. And Massine's choice of the flamboyant designer was firmly endorsed by the Ballet Russe management. A master of self-promotion, Dalí by the end of the 1930s had a high profile in the United States as well as Europe. His work had been exhibited in America since 1932, and he had first visited in 1934. By 1939 he was notorious in New York, especially after the uproar that year over his designs for Bonwit Teller's windows. When the store's management altered them, the painter, in a fury, destroyed his own work. The fracas ended with him smashing the windows themselves.

The scenario for *Bacchanale* traced the mounting delirium and eventual suicide of King Ludwig II of Bavaria, Wagner's patron. It was Dalí's attempt at a psychoanalytic ballet, a tribute to Freud, who, he claimed, had allowed him to understand Wagner.[5] He painted a harrowing picture of a man in the grip of despair: "The subject represents the Bacchanalia of Tannhäuser as it develops in the imaginative and delirious confusion of Ludwig II of Bavaria's brain. He will remain until the end of the performance the *sole and unique* protagonist, the action being executed only by a Bacchanalia of mythological hallucinations, of images and sentiments to which he is prey."[6] Among the characters that appeared were Venus (stepping out of a Botticelli-like seashell), Lola Montez, Sacher-Masoch (accompanied by his wife), two satyrs who observed the performance while knitting red socks, and an assortment of other mythological creatures. Massine's description of the action further catalogued some of its bizarre details:

> In this mingling of symbolism, psychology, fantasy, and reality, we showed Ludwig, imagining himself to be Tannhäuser, approaching Venus (danced by Nini Theilade), and being almost blinded by the effulgent vision. She becomes a dragon, and as Lohengrin Ludwig kills it. But his sight grows worse, and his last vision, as he dies wearing Lohengrin's helmet with Tannhäuser's pilgrim robe, is of Leda embracing the swan—"the symbol," to quote Dalí, "of heterosexual love." The final symbols of Ludwig's death were the parasol and Lola Montez emerging from the belly of the swan.[7]

Bacchanale's theme reflected the surrealist preoccupation with the dark, irrational motives buried in the unconscious. Ever since the movement's 1929 manifesto, a credo strongly influenced by the psychoanalytic study of dreams, a generation of artists had searched the hidden corners of the psyche for images too ghastly to embrace yet too powerful to disown. Dalí's designs had utilized the same illusionist dream imagery that tantalized other surrealists of the 1930s, such as Magritte and Tanguy. (The designs Miró had produced in 1932 for Massine's *Jeux d'enfants* were closer to the ideas of the first surrealist wave of 1924, whose manifesto emphasized automatism and improvisation.) Working in the style of his oil-painted dream photographs, Dalí centered the decor on an enormous swan, wings spread, with a large hole in its breast through which the dancers made their entrances. The background depicted Spain's Emporda Valley (Dalí's birthplace); and center stage, above the swan, the temple from Raphael's *Betrothal of the Virgin* was visible. The costumes, with highly charged sexual overtones, were a riot of imagination: one fe-

Backdrop by Salvador Dalí for Bacchanale, *1939*

male dancer had a large rose-colored fish head; Lola Montez wore a hoop skirt over harem trousers; some male dancers' tights were festooned with large red lobsters symbolizing their sexual organs; Venus wore a long blond wig as well as full-body pink tights to give the illusion of total nudity; and the three Graces wore absurdly large breasts. (Many of these "obscene" motifs were modified in later performances, sanitizing the production.) Chanel had built the costumes in Paris, but during the war they couldn't be transported across the Atlantic, so when the production opened in the United States they were reproduced there by Karinska.

Bacchanale was such an elaborate visual spectacle that its dance elements were overshadowed by Dalí's paraphernalia. Massine himself acknowledged that his work was circumscribed by the painter's conception: "As I had to sustain in my choreography Dalí's bizarre atmosphere, without intruding on his scenic creations, I did not have in this ballet the scope for choreographic invention which I had had in *Symphonie Fantastique*; this was a more demented dream world. Also I found myself somewhat inhibited by the surrealist setting and costumes."[8] In league with Dalí's allusive imagery, Massine's choreography and mise-en-scène aimed at creating a dreamlike aura. He put classical vocabulary at the service of unusually distorted and grotesque steps. Sensational plastic and visual images, such as the striking entrance of Venus, became ends in themselves. According to Danilova, the goddess's appearance "was erotic and quite beautiful—a Botticelli-like scene with Nini Theilade, as Venus, dressed in pink leotard, with white [sic] long hair, posed like a pearl on a shell at the rear of the stage."[9] Another eye-popping moment came in Ludwig's death scene, in which a series of umbrellas sprung open on stage. Jack Anderson, writing about the film of the ballet (preserved in the New York Public Library's Dance Collection), was spellbound by the scene with Sacher-Masoch and his wife, "she forcing him to the floor and kicking him while he cringes with delight and degradation," and the portrayal of death as a dancing umbrella: "His mincing, fidgety steps are ludicrous, yet unsettling." Anderson called this character a descendant of the grotesque managers in *Parade*.[10]

The ballet, as expected, was a *succès de snobbisme*. John Martin in the *New York Times* found that Dalí's "fantasies benefit greatly by the addition of the time element, for they can develop to climaxes with a degree of shock and surprise that static presentation . . . cannot hope to approximate."[11] Robert Lawrence, chiding Massine, concluded that *Bacchanale* marked "a lamentable point in the evolution of Léonide Massine. . . . Massine abdicated as a generative force, contributing instead a danced framework for a pictorial background."[12] Not everyone was quite so disappointed. Alfred Frankenstein declared that:

> For all the grandeur of its architecture [the music] belongs in the same bracket with the nymphs of Bouguereau and other Victorian purveyors of sweetness and light. It also extols that hefty, Germanic, cymbal-and-drum vulgarity of which Wagner was sometimes guilty. . . .
>
> Dalí, it seems to me, thoroughly appreciates this, and embodies it in his figure of the mad King Ludwig, whose attitudinizing is almost the ultimate satire on inflated, rhetorical grandiosity. At the opposite pole to Ludwig are the two imps soberly tending to their knitting. These are the imperturbable answer of common sense to Ludwig's soaring, Olympian ambitions. . . . They are a kind of choreographic Bronx cheer.[13]

For George Amberg,

> *its significance . . . was much broader than its insistent and ostentatious*
> *Freudian symbolism, for it was revealing evidence of our artists' ceaseless*
> *endeavor to articulate the processes of the subconscious. Massine's method*
> *was debatable, but not his intentions. The cryptic symbols and mystifica-*
> *tion he used are as irritating in the theatre as in any other medium and*
> *they ultimately condemn* Bacchanale *as a repertory piece. The essential*
> *motivation, however, is perfectly valid. If we find Tudor's sensitive probing*
> *into the subconscious more convincing and powerful, we still cannot deny*
> *the theatrical magnificence of Dalí's terrifying images and grandeur of*
> *vision.*[14]

During 1940 and 1941 four new Massine works were produced: *The New Yorker, Vienna 1814, Labyrinth,* and *Saratoga.* None of them proved successful.

The New Yorker (October 18, 1940) and *Saratoga* (October 19, 1941) were, of course, based on American themes. By 1940 the emergence and establishment of American ballet was a fact, further exacerbating the hostility that the dance community had felt since the 1930s toward the various manifestations of the Franco-Russian ballet. With Europe at war and the Ballet Russe forced to operate solely and indefinitely in the western hemisphere, the company decided to align its programming with local taste, so Massine was coaxed into producing ballets on American subjects and at the same time all but ordered by Denham to discontinue his work on symphonic ballets. (In November 1940 he expressed to the press his "patient regret that he had not been permitted to continue his work on creating large dance works to the great symphonies."[15] By then he had "advanced very far in a Mozart work" and had been planning to choreograph a Schubert symphony in collaboration with Bérard, who as Massine spoke was in occupied France.[16])

The idea for *The New Yorker* was suggested to Massine by one of the magazine's writers, Rea Irwin, and was inspired by cartoons from its pages by Peter Arno, Helen Hokinson, William Steig, and Otto Soglow. The score was selections from George Gershwin made with the assistance of his brother, Ira. They included a collection of hit songs, the *Cuban Overture,* a small segment of *An American in Paris,* and excerpts from the Concerto in F.

The New Yorker did not have a propitious beginning. Massine, utterly uninspired, suggested to Denham that he hire an American choreographer for the project, perhaps Eugene Loring. But Denham declined to follow the advice,[17] and the work was prepared in correspondence between Denham in New York and Massine as he toured with the company in South America. Through July and August of 1940 Massine struggled, in sometimes bitter exchanges, to come to an agreement with Denham about scenario, designer, music, and orchestration. He thought the libretto "not a brilliant one"[18] and "far from . . . satisfactory."[19] He had suggested either Peter Arno or James Thurber as the designer, feeling that Irwin, "who in two years had designed only one page in *The New Yorker*,"[20] did not qualify. This correspondence was filled with Massine's complaints that his artistic advice "did not get any attention and contrary action has been taken."[21] Denham's thoughtless insistence on the dismissal of dancers from the corps had, Massine charged, forced "the principal artists" to take part "in the ensemble, which never happened since Diaghilev's time."[22] What irked him most was the "lack of someone capable to organize our work on the new productions normally, so that they should be decided upon and completed during nine months instead of rushing them through three months, which is a real tour de force."[23]

Massine's comments on *The New Yorker* after its creation reveal his obvious reservations and lack of enthusiasm. "It was not easy finding a style for this comic ballet. . . . The Gershwin music which has real melodic quality is really either too close to some of us or too outdated for present swing enthusiasts. In a hundred years such a ballet would be very easy to formulate." About the characters he added: "It may not provide stock characters as profound as the traditional *commedia dell'arte* of the Italians, but everyone recognizes the Hokinson lady, the Peter Arno clubman, the petty flappers, Soglow's Little King. Unfortunately, for a ballet, these characters are perhaps too familiar. Everyone has his own idea. . . ."[24]

The New Yorker followed the divertissement structure of *Gaîté parisienne*, and the choreography integrated various American dance idioms, including tap. The ballet was pleasant entertainment but not a success. Denby acknowledged that the work was "entertaining, with many excellent caricatures,"[25] and John Martin found Massine's own interpretation of the Timid Man "funny, inventive and completely off the beaten track."[26] On the road it was generally well liked. But Irving Kolodin wrote that "all of Massine's good intentions and wit did not compensate for the orientation that might have been supplied by an American choreographer."[27]

The gestation of *Vienna 1814* (October 28, 1940) goes back to Massine and Count Etienne de Beaumont's 1936 plan to create a ballet on a Viennese theme.[28] *Concert d'Europe,* as the ballet originally had been titled,[29] was to be set to piano music by Carl Maria von Weber as orchestrated by Hindemith, with scenery and costumes by Bérard. By 1940 Denham had resurrected the idea, insisting on "a lively ballet."[30] Massine devised a divertissement that attempted to "recreate the splendour and gaiety of a ball given to the diplomatic corps in Vienna by Prince Metternich to celebrate the defeat of Napoleon."[31] The ballet ends with the news of the emperor's escape from Elba. Some of Weber's piano pieces, his Siciliana, and his *Turandot* Overture were arranged by Broadway's Robert Russell Bennett, and the scenery and costumes were by Stewart Chaney. The ballet offered some good dancing opportunities for the cast but passed without praise.

Before Massine began work on his second ballet on an American theme, he collaborated with Dalí on *Labyrinth,* another surrealist extravaganza. This time they agreed on Schubert's Seventh, which Massine once had hoped to adapt in collaboration with Bérard. But Bérard was in Europe, so Massine decided to work instead with Masson, who had arrived in the United States in the summer of 1941.[32] However, this arrangement, which Denham opposed, did not materialize. This seems a pity when one considers Masson's important creative American phase from 1941 to 1945 and his influence on the younger generation of artists, especially Jackson Pollock.

Dalí's scenario for *Labyrinth* was based on the myth of Theseus and Ariadne in the labyrinth. The labyrinth and the minotaur were recurring images among the surrealists of the 1930s. According to Massine, Dalí "envisaged the uninterrupted continuity of Schubert's melody as a musical parallel to the ball of thread which Ariadne gave to Theseus to guide him out of the Labyrinth. His idea was to employ a blend of choreographic and surrealist images to suggest the turmoil aroused in Theseus's mind by his encounter with the Minotaur."[33] At first, the choreographer was not much moved by the idea, but:

Dalí was a persuasive talker, and I found myself carried away by his bizarre symbolism. As we discussed the individual scenes, I was both amused and revolted by the images he invented. For the episode in which Theseus kills the Minotaur, he wanted to use a real calf's head to be followed by a scene in which the dancers would ceremoniously cut chunks from the head and eat them. One evening, after we had begun rehearsals, Dalí and I took a taxi to Sixth Avenue, where we visited one restaurant

after another in search of a calf's head. The waiters were stunned, but po-
lite; the best they could offer us was a veal sandwich!

There were times when Dalí's imagination got completely out of hand.
When he suggested that, as a symbol of destruction, we should drop a
Steinway onto the stage, I drew the line.[34]

Massine found certain scenes effective, however, singling out one
that showed "a girl in a transparent tunic lying motionless on the stage.
Several dancers were suspended above her, hidden by the backcloth,
except for their feet, to which we attached live white pigeons. In this
way we created the illusion of a nude girl with doves fluttering above
her."[35]

As he had done with *Bacchanale,* Dalí again stole the show. According to Robert Lawrence, "isolated moments of Massine's genius managed to filter through this mass of philosophic double talk and scenic
weightiness. Certain passages of the scene within the labyrinth, the jovial
cockfight of the scherzo, the excellent pas de deux for Castor and Pollux
in the finale, indicated that the choreographer could rise above his scenario."[36] Denby was put off by Dalí's grandstanding: "Dalí hogs the show
so completely he won't let you see Massine's part of it, or hear Schubert.
. . . He focuses your eye at a spot so high on the drop that every time you
pull it down to look at the dancers below you feel acutely uncomfortable.
Besides dwarfing the dancers he dresses them in incredibly bad taste."[37]
Walter Terry, on the other hand, found the painter's work "more significant than any that ballet has disclosed before. Strangely enough, they are
not silly, and although the opening scene reveals a tremendous cracked
skull and a chest with a doorway in it, the effect is one of archaic
grandeur."[38]

Massine's final ballet of 1941, *Saratoga,* had from its beginning little
possibility of success. The project had been imposed on Massine as a fait
accompli, part of the company's new policy. Massine writes: "I was disappointed to be told that the directors had decided in the future to produce only ballets directly sponsored by individual backers. . . . It was
therefore no surprise to me to be asked to produce *Saratoga.*"[39] The action of the ballet took place at the fashionable racing resort at the turn of
the century. The scenario and the music were by Jaromír Weinberger, the
decor and costumes by Oliver Smith. In 1949 George Amberg wrote: "It
was an ambitious, not to say pretentious, production with a pleasant
theme, attractive decor and costumes and some lovely dancing. Poten-
tially, *Saratoga* may have had some of the ingredients of an American

Gaîté Parisienne, but it turned out to be an uninspired piece of no particular description or spirit. The score was especially poor."[40]

Massine's final productions for the Ballet Russe de Monte Carlo were not successful, but the choreographer took consolation from the rapturous reception his other works in the repertory were enjoying, especially *Le Beau Danube, La Boutique fantasque, Gaîté parisienne, Capriccio espagnol,* and *Le Tricorne.* Also, when de Basil's company, now renamed the Original Ballet Russe, returned to the United States in September 1940, its Massine ballets were a resounding success. Anatole Chujoy, writing in *Dance,* voiced the consensus about the first symphonic ballets. *Les Présages,* he maintained, "holds the interest of the audience as much as it did before. The pas de deux . . . in the second movement . . . is the finest example of a modern adagio found anywhere." Reassessing *Les Présages* in retrospect, he concluded that "only now, having seen all of Massine's other symphonic ballets, can one appreciate how much the choreographer put into *Destiny (Les Présages).* It served as a source of material for a number of sequences in his later work." Chujoy found *Choreartium* "still one of the finest Massine ever did," and claimed that *Symphonie fantastique* "remains as exciting a composition as it was when it was first presented here."[41] These ballets were given outstanding performances by an impressive roster that included most of the original dancers: Baronova, Riabouchinska, Toumanova, Verchinina, Lichine. *Scuola di ballo* was presented with Delarova as Felicita, the role she created.

The four unsuccessful productions for the Monte Carlo company—*The New Yorker, Vienna 1814, Labyrinth,* and *Saratoga*—made Massine an easy target for critics. "The current weakness of the Ballet Russe de Monte Carlo," wrote Walter Terry about the 1942 season, "is not a sudden occurrence. The process of enervation commenced months, perhaps years ago, and a good share of the blame must be laid to its artistic director Léonide Massine. . . . Every creator needs a rest, and Massine has needed one for the last two years."[42] But Massine was being asked to shoulder the blame for all of the company's ills, whether he had been responsible or not. For instance, the choice of the season's opening-night program—*Saratoga, Labyrinth,* and *Gaîté parisienne*—was lambasted by Terry. In fact, the selections had been made not by Massine but by Hurok, who, according to his rival Denham, was making a "deliberate attempt to undermine" the Ballet Russe.[43] (It is interesting to note that during Massine's tenure as artistic director he expanded the repertory of the company to include works by Ivanov and Petipa [*The Nutcracker* and Acts II and III of *Swan Lake*], Fokine, Nijinsky, Ashton, Lifar, and Nini

Theilade, as well as the full-length *Coppélia* and *Giselle*.) For some time it had been evident that the working relationship between Denham and Massine had turned edgy and tense; these harsh criticisms of Massine further disturbed the delicate balance between them.

During the 1938–39 season, the Ballet Russe de Monte Carlo had been in every way a choreographer's company: Massine's. He was ballet's superstar, and his reputation had been indispensable in attracting sponsors to back the creation of a new company. His international prestige was such that by 1938 his name alone could draw money from investors on both sides of the Atlantic. This, of course, gave him a great deal of power over the company's artistic policies. Still, from the beginning Denham had been inclined to insert himself into the decision-making process. In a letter dated August 26, 1937, he advised Massine to ignore the opinions of his "pederastic friends" concerning *Gaîté parisienne*, declared that there was no need for an orchestrator for Offenbach's music, and suggested that the choreographer completely rework the libretto of *Seventh Symphony*.[44] A year later, in a letter dated August 13, 1938, Massine was finding it necessary to curb Denham's meddling:

> I would urge you to refrain from interfering in my department, as we are already paying heavy punishment for your interference with the artists. . . .
>
> I would therefore again ask you not to have anything to do with the artists individually or in group, not to interfere in the artistic advice of it or make any remarks which may result in financial and moral losses to the company. If you have any complaint or defects to register you could ask me or tell me.
>
> I hope it will not be necessary for me again to call your attention to these matters as I have so much to do—preparing new productions, watching the old productions and rehearsing the company—[and] should not have to give my valuable time on unnecessary evils.[45]

When the Ballet Russe returned to the United States in 1939, the relationship between the two men was showing pronounced cracks. With the company stranded indefinitely, far from its home base in Monte Carlo, Denham tried to restrict Massine's artistic control. (It is possible that Denham had already realized that in the United States Massine was becoming ballet's bête noire; the local critical and financial establishments were increasingly shifting their support to American ballet and to Balanchine.) In 1940—before Massine had made any of his unsuccessful ballets—Denham commissioned Balanchine to mount on the Ballet Russe two works he had created for Lincoln Kirstein's American Ballet: *Le Baiser de la fée* for Denham's spring season and *Poker Game* for the fall. By 1941 rumors, obviously unsettling to Massine, abounded that Balanchine was set to replace him at the Monte Carlo company.[46] (Denham's invitation to Balanchine must have given Massine a chilling sense of déjà vu; he had only to recall the invitation de Basil extended to Nijinska back in 1935–36.)

By 1940 Massine was astonished that he was being prevented from choreographing any new symphonies, which, he told an interviewer for *Dance* magazine, was what "most of all interests me."[47] (It is clear that at least as early as 1939 Denham had lost interest in Massine's symphonic genre. When Massine had proposed that year to create a second ballet with libretto and designs by Matisse, Denham bluntly informed him that such an artistic decision rested solely with the company's directors. In a letter to Fleischmann Denham worried: "I am somewhat afraid that by force of gravity, but perhaps against his own wish, Léonide will fall into his usual 'symphonical choreography.' ")[48]

If all of this artistic haggling weren't demoralizing enough, Massine's years in exile were also taking their toll. He felt "separated from Europe" and from his "most trusted collaborators."[49] By 1942 his grievances were multiplying. He quarreled heatedly with Denham over rehearsal time for *Mysteria,* another Dalí-Massine ballet (set to music by Bach), which never materialized. He angrily pointed out that his title of artistic director was omitted from posters, that his salary was slow in arriving, and that he was receiving neither royalties nor traveling expenses.[50] Sensing that his authority was ebbing, he specifically "spoke against further attempts to acquire repertoire or personnel from the . . . American Ballet," writes Jack Anderson. "Yet he did not oppose guest choreographers in principle. He suggested that forthcoming seasons offer two new productions by himself and two by someone else: Fokine, Balanchine, or any other appropriate choreographer."[51]

At the same time, despite all the turmoil, Massine in 1942 was eagerly trying to salvage his association with "his" company. In January, perhaps in an attempt to boost his own confidence, he sent Denham a list of twenty ballets he was prepared to undertake over the next few years.[52] In 1941 Massine had contacted Manuel de Falla, who was living in Argentina, having fled his beloved Spain after Franco's takeover and the assassination of his dear friend Federico García Lorca. Massine had proposed four Spanish literary works to Falla as possibilities for collaboration; they eventually settled on Cervantes's *Don Quixote,* but Falla died in Argentina in 1946, still at work on the score.[53]

Yet it is clear that by 1942 Denham was ready to sharply curtail Massine's influence within the company. Early that year Denham had begun negotiating with Lincoln Kirstein for performance rights to twelve ballets from the American Ballet repertory. In his correspondence with Fleischmann on this subject, Denham revealed a complete lack of interest in Massine as company choreographer, having concluded that "as a matter of policy, we will have to curb him [Massine] and let him do something where he can display his ability and his wit."[54] By April of that year Massine, quite aware of Denham's intentions, had bowed to the inevitable, openly talking about a "friendly discontinuation" with the Ballet Russe, a proposition that Denham saw as a "great relief of our finances."[55] Massine's services had never come cheap.

The wild card in the Massine-Denham crisis was the rivalry between Denham and Hurok. In the 1930s and 1940s Hurok was synonymous with the ballet establishment in the United States. He had begun his career as a dance impresario in the 1920s; in December 1933 he took a major risk by bringing de Basil's Ballets Russes to America for the first time. At first the company was mainly a success with "café society" opening-night audiences, but by the end of its 1934–35 tour it had become a coast-to-coast artistic and financial success. Throughout the rest of the thirties the company performed six to seven months a year throughout the United States, bringing ballet not only to large cities but to small and mid-sized communities in a series of one-night stands. By 1936 *Time* magazine was reporting that "ballet has suddenly become a rage not only in Manhattan but in 100 other U.S. cities visited by the Monte Carlo dancers since last October. The fever began in earnest last season when the company toured 20,000 miles. . . . It played to capacity audiences . . . [in] houses in Little Rock, Ark.; El Paso, Tex.; Portland, Me. In Brockton, Mass., a leading citizen was impressed because the ballet's appearance there was one of the rare occasions when he had known his townsfolk to turn out in formal evening clothes."[56] In the heyday of the Ballet Russe, its Russian dancers were household names. Massine, Danilova, Baronova, Riabouchinska, Toumanova, and Lichine became as popular as movie stars and in the process transformed ballet into a full-fledged commercial enterprise. Hurok the impresario dominated the scene, for in addition to his far-reaching booking apparatus, until 1946 he held the exclusive lease for ballet at the Met. He exerted wide influence over the internal affairs of the companies he sponsored.

From 1940 on, Hurok launched a series of outright attacks on Denham, claiming that he had become "infected with Diaghileffitis" and that "with the 1940–41 season, deterioration had set in in the vitals of the Monte Carlo Ballet Russe." [57] (Indeed, by then Denham had grown completely intractable in his artistic directives.) Hurok observed:

> *I could not be other than sad, for Massine had given of his best to create and maintain a fine organization. He had been a shining example to the others. The company had started on a high plane of accomplishments; but it was impossible for Massine to continue under the conditions that daily became less and less bearable. Heaven knows, the "Colonel" had been difficult. But he had an instinct for the theatre, a serious love for ballet, a broad experience, was a first-class organizer, and an untiring, never ceasing, dynamic worker.*
>
> *Sergei Denham, by comparison, was a mere tyro at ballet direction, but, amateur or not, he was convinced he had inherited the talent, the knowledge, the taste of the late Serge Diaghileff.* [58]

Wanting "to be free to experiment" [59]—actually, hoping to mastermind the entire ballet explosion singlehandedly—Hurok in 1941 dropped his exclusive contract with Denham's company and signed on with Lucia Chase's fledgling Ballet Theatre as manager.

The struggle between Denham and Hurok necessarily involved Massine. With no further interest in Denham's company, Hurok naturally wanted to secure Massine's services; he was fully aware that to the general American ballet-going public, ballet was *Russian* ballet, which meant Massine. The three men were soon craftily double crossing one another. In the spring of 1942 Massine was given permission to create two ballets as guest choreographer for Ballet Theatre later that year, a temporary break that Denham took as a welcome financial boost, "so that we may be able to save his two and one-half months' salary." [60] By November Massine's permanent departure from the Monte Carlo company was imminent; on the sixth he signed a new agreement with Universal Art that annulled his old contract (due to expire in 1948) as the organization's artistic director. Massine writes:

> *I was informed that my ten-year contract with Universal Art Inc. had not been ratified by the Board of Directors. After working for them for three years, I was summarily dismissed. It was a bitter blow, which left me feeling bereft and disillusioned. Although I protested vehemently, there was*

nothing I could do. Ever since I had been appointed Artistic Director to the Company, I had devoted all my time to it, thinking I was building on a sure foundation. I had gathered together and trained a superlative group of dancers, and through my own efforts, and my artistic contacts, I had brought distinguished artists to work for it, among them Bérard, Dalí, Derain, de Beaumont, and Matisse. I felt that I had more than fulfilled the original aims of the Board by reviving traditional ballets and creating new ones with both American and European participation.[61]

In a recurrent nightmare, Massine once again initiated litigation over the ownership of his ballets. But unlike the outcome with de Basil back in 1938, the decision was now rendered in the choreographer's favor. The case was heard by the American Arbitration Association, and arbitrator James Gifford ruled that "the scenic properties and costumes for most of my own ballets, including *Le Tricorne, La Boutique fantasque,* and *Capriccio Espagnol,* should be assigned to me without fail. He also established my legal right to perform all or any of my own works anywhere I chose, and to make copies of the costumes and scenic material which had been used in the productions which I had done for the Ballet Russe de Monte Carlo." When the ordeal ended, Massine was "moved" by the decision, and "after everything had been settled I went to thank him [Gifford]. As we shook hands at farewell he smiled and said 'Just remember that bankers must not have the right to dismiss artists so easily.' "[62]

On November 10 Massine joined Ballet Theatre. His departure from the Ballet Russe de Monte Carlo marked the last time that he would be affiliated with a ballet company in the role of resident choreographer. From his breakup with Diaghilev in 1921 he had tried to establish his own company. When he finally succeeded, it was to last only four years, of which the final two were marked by his diminished authority and gnawing uncertainty. Beginning in 1942 he embarked on a long international career as guest choreographer and performer—though in 1960 he would make one last attempt to realize his dream: a company of his own.

DURING MASSINE'S GUEST ENGAGEMENT with Ballet Theatre in the summer of 1942, he created two new works, *Aleko* (September 8) and *Don Domingo* (September 16); both ballets were premiered in Mexico City.

Aleko was based on Pushkin's dramatic poem *Gypsies* and was set to

Tchaikovsky's Trio in A minor (orchestrated by Erno Rapee). The idea for the ballet had been in Massine's mind since 1941 (it had been called *Gypsies* on the list of potential productions he had sent to Denham in January 1942). The work had spectacular decor and costumes by Marc Chagall, who was also waiting out the war in New York. Massine and Chagall had met briefly in Paris, but upon Chagall's arrival in New York German Sevastianov, Ballet Theatre's general manager, reintroduced the two men. (Sevastianov, husband of ballerina Irina Baronova, previously had been associated with de Basil during Massine's tenure.) While working on *Aleko,* Massine and Chagall, two Russians in exile, forged a bond that would rise to a special level of intimacy. In his memoirs, Massine reminisced that Chagall "never forgot that he was a disappointment to his family. His mother, who had intended him to become a photographer, had had ambitions for her son, wanting him to settle down in a suburban house with a wife, a family, and a lot of good solid furniture." [63]

Aleko was Massine's first Russian ballet since *Bogatyri* (1938) and his most important since *Le Pas d'acier* (1927). It came at a time of professional uncertainty and personal anxiety for both artists, who, "meeting in the world of Tchaikovsky and Pushkin," according to the Chagall biographer Franz Meyer, "looked upon it as a fragment of their homeland brought to life by their joint efforts out of a common 'memory.' " [64] Working with Chagall must have provided a respite for Massine after the pressures he had recently endured with Denham. For the painter, too, the experience was consoling: "For Chagall and his wife the months spent working with Massine were among the happiest of their stay in America and years later a few bars of the Tchaikovsky Trio sufficed to evoke the wonderful unison of the period." [65]

Aleko took shape in a spirit of teamwork. In their adaptation of the poem, each artist tried in his own medium to bring the richness of Pushkin's imagery to life. The preparation took several months, during which Massine and Chagall met regularly at the painter's Manhattan apartment. Massine would bring his record player so that they could talk out the conception of the ballet as they listened to the score. One sign of their close collaboration can be found in Chagall's sketches, which include detailed notations on the choreography and the action. [66]

The ballet was divided into four scenes, the first and second of which were set to the first movement of the trio. In the first scene Aleko abandons city life and arrives with the Gypsy Zemphira at her camp. Other main characters are introduced: Zemphira's father (the Chieftain), the Young Gypsy, who also falls in love with her, and the Fortuneteller.

The second scene presents a carnival with a picturesque assortment of acrobats, street dancers, and clowns. As Zemphira dances, she is swept up in the collective euphoria. In the third scene a group of youths go bathing on a bright summer afternoon. A love interlude between Zemphira and the Young Gypsy is interrupted by the arrival of Aleko, who pleads with Zemphira to return to him. She rejects him in favor of her new lover. In the finale Aleko in his delirium confronts visions from his past. The line between reality and fantasy disappears, and in a moment of despair he murders the lovers. Zemphira's father banishes him from the camp and he is condemned to wandering.

The planning and groundwork were accomplished in New York, and in Mexico City, where the company had been invited for a five-month period as guests of the government, the choreography was worked out and the scenery and costumes took shape. Over Massine's objections, Chagall had not been allowed on the stage of the Metropolitan Opera House because he was not a member of the American Trade Union, so Massine invited him to Mexico City, where he would have no interference in executing the backdrops.[67] The Chagalls and the Massines settled in the San Angel district, an artistic colony on the outskirts of the city; but as the work on *Aleko* grew more intensive, they took lodgings at a hotel close to the Palacio de Bellas Artes, where Ballet Theatre's season was to take place. Although free time was hard to come by, Massine managed to lead the Chagalls on brief excursions and to introduce them to several Mexican luminaries as well as some of the other European artists and intellectuals who had found refuge in Mexico City. Massine remembered the capital well from his first tour there with de Basil's company in 1934. On that occasion the company had inaugurated the newly built Palacio de Bellas Artes with its dazzling Tiffany proscenium.

While Chagall and his wife, Valentine, who was in charge of costume construction, worked at the theater, Massine rehearsed the company in the Hotel Reforma. Fokine, who was also in town as guest choreographer for Ballet Theatre, shared a dressing room with Massine. It was to be their last encounter:

He was as withdrawn and uncommunicative as ever, as aloof as when I had gone to his room in St. Petersburg for my first audition in 1914. He was always polite, but formal, and I could never relax in his presence. I had always had the greatest admiration for him as a choreographer, and I found it puzzling that a man who had created such rich, flowing movements should be, as an individual, so cold and inflexible. I remember noticing in Mexico City that he wore a shirt and tie and a tightly buttoned-up suit for rehearsals, and when he had finished I could see the sweat rolling down his face. I wanted to suggest that he would be more comfortable in a rehearsal costume, but of course I never dared to do so.[68]

Staging *Aleko* with the new company meant that Massine had to introduce his unorthodox working habits, which took some getting used to. Dancers such as Markova and George Skibine, who had worked with him before, easily adapted to his rehearsal style. Others had difficulty. Two aspects of Massine's method were especially disconcerting. One was his penchant for devising different choreography for the same musical phrase, then asking the dancers to perform all the versions, from which he would choose the one that he felt was most appropriate. The other was his routine lack of verbal communication with the dancers. As Skibine explained: "He would show the steps to you and then just sit and look. He wanted you to improvise; he showed you the steps so fast that you never really caught exactly what he did. You worked on it yourself— he let you create the parts."[69] Dolin, who had been cast as Aleko, dropped out of the ballet during rehearsals; he explained in his autobiography that he could not endure Massine's way of proceeding. (Massine was not happy with the choice of Dolin for the male lead and thought that Skibine could more convincingly portray the young and temperamental Aleko. This probably contributed to the wary working relationship between Dolin and Massine which led to Dolin's walkout.)

Chagall's contribution to *Aleko* consisted of four backdrops and more than seventy costumes. Leland Windreich described the backdrops:

For the opening scene Chagall created a troubled cobalt sky at nightfall, dominated by Pushkin's pearly-white, uncanny moon and its reflection in a lake, with a brilliant red cock flying to reach it. Sidney Alexander, a Chagall biographer, notes the phallic symbolism in this image, which is repeated in a motif painted on Zemphira's costumes for this scene. Two lovers embrace in a cluster of clouds. The second scene shows a fiddle-playing bear floating over a tilted village, a couple drifting in space, and a monkey dangling from a branch of lilacs. A golden wheat field dominates the third painting, with two huge blood-red suns: one has jagged rays, and the other is a bull's eye encompassed in rings. A fish head and a peasant's sickle emerge from the tall grass, and an inverted birch branch floats earthward. In the finale a doe-eyed white pony with hind quarters which melt into the wheels of a carriage streaks across a black sky lit by a gold chandelier.[70]

According to Meyer, there was a close relationship between the back-cloths and the artist's earlier works—"Act I with the lovers in the sky, a fantastic scene of 1938; that for Act III with the scythe in the tall grass, one of the *Fables*"—but the stage provided Chagall with a new ambience that was "more spacious and flowing."[71]

The costumes were built by Mme Chagall under the close supervision of the painter, who personally decorated them. For Chagall, said one art critic, "a stage costume is not a garment but the means by which the character who is represented physically and morally can participate in the life of a whole."[72] The lighting design, directed by Chagall, was an important element in creating the visual poetic imagery: "The 'poem' is born of the blue night, grows in the cool light of morning, becomes radiant color in the bright noontide and finally dwindles away in the lonely distance of a starry night."[73] According to Windreich, "spotlights behind the first and last backdrops effectively accentuated the figures depicted as charging into the sky and gave the moons the effect of having been painted on stained glass."[74]

It was typical of Massine's eclecticism that the choreography was composed of the various techniques that had characterized his *demi-caractère* and symphonic ballets. For instance, in the fortune-telling episode in the first tableau and in the ballet's fourth scene, he juxtaposed different kinds of action, with many activities occurring simultaneously on stage. Action montage was the means by which Massine expanded the physical space into a series of subspaces—an appropriate treatment of a story in which the external reality and the hero's inner world cohabited. Another choreographic technique was the juxtaposition of styles, about which Grace Robert noted: "It joins classical with free plastic dancing in a manner that does violence to neither style. The wild dances of the gypsies in the first scene, the stylized Russian dances in the third, are exhilarating. The pas de trois is a strictly classical exposition of line . . . the spirited mazurka performed in the third scene by Zemphira and the Young Gypsy is an interesting elaboration of a folk-dance form for balletic purposes."[75]

Massine's most recent symphonic ballet had been *Rouge et noir* (*Labyrinth* had been completely dominated by Dalí's conception); *Aleko* pointed to the new direction he was taking in the genre. In it he focused less on massive vertical formations, such as pyramids, and more on elaborate horizontal configurations, and an incredible wealth of choreographic detail that signaled a new "baroquism," to some extent a return to that of his early Diaghilev years.

In mood, *Aleko* represented the neoromantic expressionism of the 1930s and was related more to *Symphonie fantastique* than to any other work. Both depicted the romantic introspection of the hero, manifested in his delirium. Choreographically, both emphasized sweeping ensembles and the employment of dancers as part of the mise-en-scène. A case in point was the fourth scene in *Aleko,* which Grace Robert described as "rich in plastic groupings." Robert declared a moment in the work where "girls wearing black gloves, with arms extended in the form of a Latin cross, are held high in the air to make a background for the drama . . . especially memorable."[76] This image was reminiscent of the crosses created by the walking monks in *Symphonie fantastique.*

Alicia Alonso, whose performance as Zemphira (the role created by Markova) was highly acclaimed when the ballet was presented in London and Paris in 1953, still had vivid recollections of the choreography in 1988: "[It] was imbued with a dramatic style which was very characteristic of Massine. There was a great richness of movement: a classical step or position would be stylized in a sort of demi-caractère sense. There was a great deal of contrast between the leg work, torso and head movements, all subject to the musical rhythm. The whole choreography was a question of style; even the development of a character was a question of style, all marked by Massine's own personality. There was a multiplicity and variety of movements, angles, positions. This style is very much in contrast to the choreography that prevails today: dynamic, dry, in a straight line, the dancing taking place with the dancer facing or with his back to the audience. Today's choreography is like modern constructions—cutting, geometrical. On the contrary, Massine's choreography had innumerable nuances of body movement." About the group configurations she added: "Sometimes a specific block or group of dancers did not mean much by itself until it would be seen within the context of the whole picture effect as each group was integrated to another. The aesthetic balance depended on the composition of the various groups in their collective formation. It was a fascinating clockwork mechanism."[77]

The choreography was extremely difficult, and the lifts were murderous. Skibine withdrew with a back injury after the Mexico City premiere. Markova later was reported to have fainted twice during performances of the ballet, and "panicked at the thought of doing it"; in 1943 she underwent surgery for a hernia which, she said, was "aggravated" by the choreography in *Aleko*.[78] The ballet ended with one of those grand Massine finales, the stage swirling with movement, the work exerting its seductive power over audiences. Marcia Siegel described Massine's ballets as "busy, explosive, full of great rushes and changes of energy. They must have been enormously appealing to the audiences' emotions—you can sense a kind of Broadway programming of the sensibilities, the great sweeps of emotion and the long pregnant pauses, the melodramatic multiple pirouettes. Massine was fond of large choral groups, which he designed in harmonizing or contrapuntal masses, in the manner of the modern dancers."[79]

With nineteen curtain calls, the premiere on September 8 was a thunderous success with the cosmopolitan Bellas Artes audience (which included Diego Rivera). The Mexican press reported that Massine had brought to *Aleko* "a humanity, an emotional and poetic depth which he has never before achieved."[80] The work was introduced at the Metropolitan in New York with Skibine as Aleko, Markova as Zemphira, Hugh Laing as the Young Gypsy, and Antony Tudor as the father, and proved to be Massine's greatest success since the outbreak of the war. Robert Lawrence wrote in the *Herald Tribune* that "the double murder of the gypsy girl and her lover by Aleko is one of the most shattering experiences not only in the dance, but in the whole world of theatre."[81] For Denby the work was "Massine's finest since *Fantastic Symphony*. It has lots of his expert stylization of local color (in this case, Russian gypsies and peasants), lots of his stylized dance-pantomime, lots of his ballet counterpoint. . . . It has as prize plum a long last scene with the breathless melodramatic thriller rush that Massine does better than anyone else."[82] Of course Denby, an admirer of very little of Massine's work, also pointed out the qualities of *Aleko* that he disliked: "an agitation that seems senseless, a piling up of scraps of movement and bits of character like so much junk from Woolworth's, patterns but no room for them, accent and meter but no rhythm and flower of phrase. The duets are bizarre without intimacy; the man has to jerk from one position to another by turning his back awkwardly on his partner."[83]

But when Massine took over the role of Aleko several months later, Denby felt that the whole ballet became more intelligible and delineated:

The title part of Aleko *is difficult because the character, who stands in opposition to the entire company, is at the center of the action only at the beginning and at the very end. At other times when he appears, he seems to express a sort of self-pity that is not especially communicative, and his ges-*

ture is "inward." Other stars do not hold the attention in these portions. Massine, however, dominated the stage with ease. He also gave the story a lively beginning by showing convincingly how pleased a city youth would be to be accepted by gypsies as one of their alien world.

Though Massine avoided a few technical feats Dolin adds to the role, his superior understanding of the story, and of its specifically Russian aspects, made the ballet itself clear.[84]

Alfred Frankenstein wrote in the *San Francisco Chronicle*: "*Aleko* is a hyper-romantic, rhetorical subject, and if you accept that as its premise, it follows that the dance Massine has created for it is perfectly in keeping. It is rich in pattern and pace, inventive within the framework of Massine's well established style, fervent and vivid both as dance and as dramatic expression."[85] And four years after it was first seen in New York, Grace Robert wrote: "*Aleko* is a brilliant montage of a gypsy life that never existed out of the realm of poetry. When a realistic touch appears, it is only for the purpose of pointing up the fantasy. One must see this ballet many times before the wealth of detail may be absorbed."[86]

Massine's second Mexico City premiere was *Don Domingo de Don Blas,* created in collaboration with the Mexican composer Silvestre Revueltas and the Mexican artist Julio Castellanos. Based on a seventeenth-century drama by the Spanish playwright Juan Ruiz de Alarcón y Mendoza, the ballet revolved around the rivalry between Don Domingo and Don Juan, the rich and poor suitors of Doña Leonor, Don Ramiro's daughter. The action was transferred to Mexico; according to Charles Payne, "The ballet was designed as a flattering tribute to Mexico, which Sevastianov hoped would persuade its government officials to make the Palacio de Bellas Artes available to the Ballet Theatre as its summer residence; it at least accomplished this purpose."[87] Although Massine employed a team of teachers from the Mexican Ministry of Education to coach the cast in Mexican dances, the ballet was an uninspired work whose tepid reception, especially in the United States, made its stay in the repertory a brief one.

ONCE MASSINE JOINED Ballet Theatre in the summer of 1942, his family life became more normal. From the moment of their arrival in the United States in 1939, the Massines had constantly been on the go, in part because the Ballet Russe de Monte Carlo was primarily a touring company. To make life easier during these peripatetic years, Massine had bought

> a large Lincoln, with a trailer fitted with a modern kitchen and a comfortable bed-sitting room. This was driven by a Russian chauffeur, Georgi Lanbourinsky, who came of an old Cossack family. Since Tatiana and I both disliked hotel cooking, we also engaged an Italian cook, who travelled with us, hundreds of miles, from one engagement to another, usually by night. It was not a very satisfactory way of living, but at least it spared us the monotony of long train journeys and the anonymity of a different hotel each night too.[88]

In 1941, while Massine was in Los Angeles filming *Gaîté parisienne* and *Capriccio espagnol* (now retitled *The Gay Parisian* and *Spanish Fiesta*) for Warner Bros. under the direction of Jean Negulesco, the couple's first child was born. They named her Tatiana, after her mother. As a father Massine found that "day to day life seemed to have a deeper meaning, and I even found myself dancing with renewed energy." However, it did not take long before they had to "face the problem of trying to fit Tatiana into our hectic and nomadic life. It became too much of a strain to travel with both of us, a small baby, a nurse, a cook and a chauffeur crammed into the Lincoln, even with the space provided by the trailer. We decided that as soon as possible we must find a permanent home."[89] In the spring of 1943, with a reduced touring schedule to fulfill with Ballet Theatre, they decided that they "could not endure another oppressive summer in the city, and so we bought a house at Long Beach, on Long Island. Built in the 1930's, it had a pseudo-Gothic tower and a large garden, which I enlarged by buying several adjoining lots to safeguard our privacy. . . . Tatiana swore [it] was the ugliest house in Long Island, though she admitted that it was a pleasant and comfortable one to live in and bring up our family . . ."[90]

Now that he "seemed to be permanently settled on Long Island, Massine had a large dance studio built onto the house, and was able to practice there every morning before going into New York for rehearsals."[91] He "began work on another production for Ballet Theatre, a companion piece, in a way, to *Gaîté parisienne*, a light-hearted evocation of Paris during the 1790s. I discussed the project with Efrem Kurtz, and we agreed that Le Cocq's [sic] *opéra-bouffe*, *La Fille de Madame Angot*, which was based on a vaudeville of 1796, would provide suitable material for it. He helped me to select extracts from that and operettas by Le Cocq, which were orchestrated for us by Richard Mohaupt."[92]

To make the plot of the Lecocq work more amenable to dance, Massine modified the identity of the characters. The ballet was divided into three scenes. As the program synopsis described it:

> *Soubrette, betrothed to a barber, falls in love with an artist. He caricatures an old official and his aristocratic mistress, whose beauty so entrances the artist that he loses all thought of Soubrette.*
>
> *The artist, fleeing the Hussars sent to arrest him for his damaging cartoons, crashes a party given by the aristocratic lady. She conceals him and diverts his pursuers. During the ball the artist is discovered and ordered to prison by the minister, a scene witnessed by the lovelorn Soubrette, who arrives with her equally unhappy barber. The artist, however, snatches this of all moments to declare his love to the titled lady.*
>
> *Soubrette retaliates by arranging a masque to which she invites her friends, the lady, the official and the released artist. The love affair between the lady and the artist is exposed to the duped old official, and Soubrette, healthily disillusioned, returns to her barber.*[93]

The four leading roles were taken by Nora Kaye, Rosella Hightower, Massine, and André Eglevsky.

Mademoiselle Angot, which premiered at the Met on October 10, 1943, marked Massine's return to his comic-narrative *demi-caractère* ballets. As always with his works in this genre, the commedia dell'arte interpretive style kept the piece light and the dancing nimble. The characters were stock theatrical types, which meant that there was virtually no development. Each character was relevant to the others only within the boundaries of their shared theatrical truth. Making a connection with the audience wasn't the main goal; making a blatantly theatrical impression was. T. S. Eliot had honored Massine's characters by calling them "impersonal," since according to Eliot a work of art was relevant only within its own terms; not even its relationship to its creator should mediate in order to explain or illuminate it. It could remain impersonal insofar as its objectivity (Eliot's theory of the objective-correlative) served to keep the work's emotional content at a distance. As Eliot would express it: "The progress of an artist is a continual self-sacrifice, a continual extinction of personality."[94] But while Massine's characters indeed remained impersonal with respect to any relations outside their theatrical selves, they throbbed with personal vitality within the terms of their aesthetic truth.

It's not surprising that Massine's personages were criticized as stereotypical and shallow at a time when psychological characterizations were becoming more usual in ballet. But this subjective mode didn't fit with Massine's objective theatrical realism. Massine's characters were given coherence by plot development, not by internal conflict. His character types, in other words, did not leave room for speculation.

Of course, in his symbolic symphonic ballets Massine did permit himself a more subjective emotionalism. These works expressed (albeit metaphorically) an inner turmoil, an inner vision. He sometimes could be at his most personal only when his posture was loftiest—indeed, cosmic. This is the gem to be found at the core of his symphonic ballets. Working at this high-minded level, where he could resort to symbol and myth, Massine was free to let his feelings of alienation, anguish, rejection, fear, and despair, as well as his experience of the angst of loneliness, pour out. *Rouge et noir* is a good example: through abstraction and symbolism he transcends the personal and particular in favor of the poetic and universal.

As produced by Ballet Theatre (there was a subsequent, revised version in Europe), *Mademoiselle Angot,* according to the critics, had two major handicaps. While it offered some excellent dancing opportunities for the cast, it lacked a cohesive narrative structure. The critics discerned no clear plot development, and they were not prepared to let the choreographer off the hook by labeling the work a dance suite. Furthermore, Massine's stylistic and choreographic "baroquism" (a quality very much rooted in his earlier immersion in the rhythms and counterrhythms of flamenco, maintained by the feet, waist, arms, *épaulement,* and head) departed from the openness of movement, simplification of detail, and clear definition of line that he had embraced from *Le Beau Danube* onward.

Some found "baroquism" oppressive in its lack of expansion and pointless in its excess. Denby was disturbed by so much "superactivity," complaining that "as dancing it is a constant jumping about, fluttering of dresses and arms and legs that has no cumulative effect. . . . The plot of Massine's ballet disappears in fact under a load of separate dance numbers that have neither logical connection nor dramatic destination. . . ."[95] In a later review he added: "The trouble with *Mademoiselle Angot* is simply that for all its constant commotion it seems endless and pointless; the

successive dances seem to flounder around without either a steady subject or any consecutive form." [96]

But perhaps it is more reasonable to see *Mademoiselle Angot*'s busy
and intricate choreography and stylistic embellishment—well-known
characteristics of Massine's early ballets—as a return to a more familiar
way of working. This was, after all, a time when his personal and artistic
fortunes were highly uncertain, in fact quite unknowable. The disloca-
tion of the war, the loss of his company, hostile criticism, professional instability, artistic isolation—these forces would contribute to his
introversion, and were reflected artistically in his choreography and personally in his Long Beach refuge with its Gothic tower.

Over the next three years Massine produced only two new works.
November 27, 1944, saw the premiere of Beethoven's *Moonlight Sonata*, a
rather sentimental pas de deux for Toumanova and himself, both appearing as guest artists with Ballet Theatre. On December 15 *Mad Tristan* was
presented by the newly organized Ballet International under the sponsor-
ship of the Marquis George de Cuevas.

Originally planned in 1937 as *Tristan fou*, *Mad Tristan* was a two-
scene piece set to excerpts from Wagner's *Tristan und Isolde* arranged by
Ivan Boutnikoff. The libretto was hallucinogenic:

> *The first [scene] opens with Isolde waving the fatal scarf and proceeds to a
> horridly confused acrobatic love duet with Spirits of Death like shivering
> maniacs and Spirits of Love like enormous dandelions in seed milling
> about. It ends with the revelation of two Isoldes, both equally fascinating
> and differently horrid; King Mark with two soldiers wondrously armed
> enters.*
>
> *The second scene shows Tristan on a version of Böcklin's Isle of the
> Dead, plagued by a sardonic Shepherd, plagued by a beautiful bouncing
> ship, plagued by the Isoldes and the Spirits and other faceless figures. It
> ends with Tristan dying for love as upstage his own repulsive mummy is
> lowered into a vault caressed by white wormlike dismembered living
> arms.* [97]

As expected, *Mad Tristan* was Dalí's show. Denby called it

> *a masquerade that only a genius could invent. Dalí takes Wagner's music
> and Massine's choreography and uses them as props for a spectacle, and
> what a show he puts on. . . .*

Mad Tristan *is nothing like a classic ballet, it is not something to be seen over and over. It is fascinating as a contradiction of classicism. It is fascinating too for its imaginative abundance, for the largeness of its pictorial presence. And it is wonderful how Dalí turns whatever pictorial reference he offers into an immediate insignia of the unconscious world within us. To put it more simply, as a show and the first time you see* Mad Tristan *there isn't a dull moment in it.*[98]

Grace Robert commented:

The symbolism employed in Mad Tristan *has become obscure, and is less related to the textbooks of abnormal psychology than in the two former [Dalí/Massine] ballets. Dalí seemed to have become obsessed with wheelbarrows, which were pushed about the scene by a group of dancers realistically pantomiming the tics of spastic paralysis. There were several female dancers dressed in what looked like white tulle evening dresses, their heads concealed by globe-shaped arrangements of flowers or dandelion seeds.*[99]

For George Amberg the "controversial" *Mad Tristan* was Ballet International's artistic event of the season. "This 'paranoiac ballet,'" he wrote,

*was a surrealist masterpiece. It was a thoroughly serious and valid piece of operating visualization which proceeded with the haunting and compelling irrational consistency of a dream. As ballet it was disastrous, and it must have been the despair of choreographer and dancers. But it was frank and legitimate theatre and, incidentally, the first notable attempt in many seasons at an imaginative use of the stage illusion as a creative medium. . . . * Mad Tristan *has probably not furthered the cause of ballet, but it has revived faith in "theatrical" theatre. Eventually the ballet may benefit.*[100]

With *Mad Tristan*, Dalí and Massine completed their surrealistic triptych. "All three productions were cerebral works," observed Amberg, "the freezing point of emotion, and their shock effects were carefully planned."[101]

BY 1944 MASSINE'S professional life had become more unstable. The relationship between Hurok and Ballet Theatre had deteriorated considerably; the company resented his employment of a roster of Russian guest stars that justified the promotion tag: "The greatest in Russian

Ballet by Ballet Theatre." In 1945, with the appointment of Lucia Chase and Oliver Smith as administrative directors, Ballet Theatre embarked on a campaign of de-Russianization. With Denham's company no longer a viable option, the future for Massine in the United States grew increasingly uncertain. Moreover, the arrival of his second child, Léonide Jr. (later known as Lorca), rendered his financial responsibilities more pressing. In 1945, capitalizing on the Ballet Russe's reputation and his own popularity, he organized a performing group called the Ballet Russe Highlights, with the participation of leading dancers including Baronova, Eglevsky, Yurek Lazowsky, and Anna Istomina. Under the management of Fortune Gallo, the group toured from coast to coast with a divertissement program. A second tour took place the following year, without Baronova but with Igor Youskevitch, Rosella Hightower, and Komarova added to the roster. But as Massine explains:

> *While we were on tour Tatiana and I and the children again travelled in the Lincoln and the trailer. We visited about twenty cities, including Chicago, Boston and Philadelphia. But although the performances were well received by audiences and press alike, I soon found that expenses were eating up all the profits. It was a hectic life, too, for every evening we performed about twenty dances from our repertoire, with only one interval. This meant quick changes and perfect coordination between cast, stagehands and orchestra, for each dance lasted only a few minutes. It was impossible to use any scenery, and our costumes and makeup had to be kept very simple. In the end Ballet Russe Highlights, though highly gratifying artistically, proved to be a very strenuous and unprofitable affair.[102]*

In the spring of 1946 Massine received an offer from England to appear in a murder mystery play, *A Bullet in the Ballet*. Deferring to his wife's judgment that the tours were "impractical" and "a strain on the whole family,"[103] he accepted. In August, after an absence of seven years, the Massines and their two children sailed for Europe.

Massine's years in the United States during the war marked the lowest ebb of his artistic reputation. The combination of two factors—the conditions that prevented him from further exploring his interest in symphonic ballets, and the emergence of a new American art whose triumph was consolidated by the end of World War II—contributed immeasurably to this decline.

In the early 1940s, Massine was highly admired by the general public, and his name was undoubtedly one of the biggest box-office draws.

Each production of his ballets was an event. As a performer he was a star; although he was nearly fifty, even those critics most antagonistic toward him as a choreographer continued to find him a titanic stage presence. About his performance in *Le Tricorne* Denby wrote: "He still dances all of it, and especially the farruca, to great effect, though he dominates the stage more by his matchless stage presence than by technical virtuosity. He almost alone of ballet dancers seemed formerly to have something of the edge of the great Spanish dancers, something of their brilliant attack and unpredictable rhythm."[104] And about his *Petrouchka* the critic said: "Massine . . . is by far the most intelligible Petrouchka we have. He throws himself in despair through the paper wall. When he reappears on the roof he is eerily derisive; and his final collapse is scary."[105] In 1941 Massine and the Ballet Russe brought twenty-five thousand people to the Hollywood Bowl. That same year, thirty-six thousand New Yorkers made their way to Lewisohn Stadium to see him, despite temperatures in the mid-nineties "on two of the most humid evenings of the summer."[106] In 1945 his Ballet Russe Highlights brought twenty-five thousand people to Lewisohn Stadium and fifteen thousand to Philadelphia's Robin Hood Dell.

But despite his popularity, the war years were a period of creative stagnation for Massine. He remained insulated from the germinating and fermenting American artistic scene; his spiritual headquarters were always in Europe. His aesthetic and personal maturity had been channeled into his symphonic ballets, a genre he longed to extend and amplify. When he was not allowed to do so—and was actually obliged by the Ballet Russe management to produce works that were of little interest to him—much of his creative momentum was dissipated. This meant heavy reliance on collaborators like Dalí to provide him with scenarios, a situation unlike that during his highly fruitful period of 1933–39, when he did the job singlehandedly. So it was not surprising that, in a 1940 interview, he voiced a rather unusual public complaint that he was forbidden by his employers to choreograph symphonies.[107] Also detrimental to his unstable personal and professional circumstances was the strong anti-Massine bias of the cognoscenti. Unfortunately, his presence in the United States led neither to a new phase of artistic re-evaluation within the dance community nor to any significant redefinition or reorientation. Yet he himself was chastised for not moving on to a new style. Possibly his greatest fault, at the age of fifty, was his loyalty to his own aesthetic vision—and to little else. Amberg wondered why "none of Massine's contacts with American life and art show in his work, since his art had so thoroughly and easily assimilated the indigenous qualities of other peoples and he had so keenly reflected the temper of his time and environment and so sharply caught the essence of human types and characters. But nothing in his creation or performance indicates that he was touched at all by the folk or society, the countryside or the climate, the thought or the feeling of America." [108]

The 1930s had seen the awakening of a consciousness that fostered an indigenous expression that once and for all would end European domination of America's artistic life. In ballet the aesthetic principles of Lincoln Kirstein—the driving force behind the creation of the School of American Ballet—were an adaptation of the Diaghilev formula, with the crucial accent on Americanism. "With the Depression," writes Marcia Siegel, "came a period of introspection and patriotism in all the arts and by the mid-1930s the idea of finding an American dance had become institutionalized." [109]

Resentment against Europe gave birth to a new nationalism and the writing of belligerent letters of protest, pamphlets, and manifestos which turned the cause of an American Art into an intellectual battle cry. These writings were mainly aimed at overturning the aesthetic judgment of the establishment, represented in the art world by museums (especially the Museum of Modern Art) that supported the European modernist tradition and served a highly functional purpose within the dealer-critic system, and in the ballet world by Sol Hurok. The general feeling of the American dance community was expressed by Agnes de Mille: "[In 1933] Hurok imported de Basil's Ballet Russe de Monte Carlo and the craze that was to endure seventeen years and sweep everything else to corners." [110] And according to George Amberg: "The Ballets Russes became synonymous with ballet for the uninitiated American public, a misunderstanding which hindered the development of a native ballet." [111]

Kirstein, the champion of George Balanchine and of American ballet, directed his censure—though it also touched Martha Graham and the American modern dance movement—against the Franco-Russian ballet and Massine. A glance at his titles reveals his journalistic militancy: *Blast at Ballet,* "Let's Go Native," "Stardom: Slave and Native," "Lincoln Kirstein Smacks at the Ballet Russe," "Ballet Blitz"—all were crafted to attract attention and alert the audience to his mission. His attacks on the Franco-Russian ballet were incessant: "Ballet is in a bad time in America today because the blackmail of the Russian organization primed by publicity and patronage still works." He described the Franco-Russian reper-

tory as "vitiated" and a "dying formula."[112] Massine did not fare any better. As noted by Jack Anderson: "Massine may also have been used as a
pawn in an ideological battle. He found himself domiciled because of
the war in America during a period when it was necessary to demonstrate the viability of American ballet. Because he failed to produce the
kind of American ballet certain advocates demanded, Massine, the per-
sonification of Ballet Russe, was open to attack, and some critics attacked ferociously."[113] Kirstein dismissed his symphonic ballets as "silly"[114]
and, in a frontal assault, noted that "Massine has a right to embellish the
old music-masters, but it is scarcely a creative act when he does so. It is,
pure and simple, an inferior art; the art of illustration."[115]

The disruption caused by the war and the lack of encouragement
must have been debilitating indeed. Massine must have nearly suffocated
from demands that he align himself with a cause that had nothing to do
with his own artistic values. The prevailing judgment of the time coincided with Amberg's: "Massine's American career contributed immensely to the ballet education of this country but, for all its brilliance
and fecundity, did little to further the growth of a native tradition."[116] But
it was precisely the new American ballet that had produced the change in
aesthetic taste, to which taste Massine's work was now anathema. Balanchine, Tudor, and de Mille were the new pacesetters. Interestingly, Eugene Loring, more than forty years after his seminal ballet *Billy the Kid,*
suggested that the time had come for a reassessment of Massine's influence, and described Massine's ballets as models against which American
choreographers of the 1930s and 1940s reacted in search of their own
style, or from which they assimilated new ideas. Specifically, Loring drew
attention to the influence of the cinematographic technique of *Union Pacific* and *Symphonie fantastique.*[117]

Edwin Denby was the apologist for the new aesthetics, especially
the dogma of neoclassicism. Although he approved of Massine's Diaghilev pieces, he took exception to the symphonic ballets, and his criticism, when not generally negative, appeared to question Massine's artistic integrity. "If one took him seriously," Denby wrote, "he would be
guilty of murdering the Beethoven Seventh, the Scarlatti, and even tender little Offenbach. . . . There is of course no reason for taking Massine
seriously; he doesn't mean to be, he doesn't mean to murder."[118] If art, as
some would have it, is the illusion that provides an aesthetic truth,
Denby's incompatibility with Massine's art never allowed him to gain a
closer glimpse of that truth. Even when it came to his best work of the
time, the most that Denby could muster was a nod toward the achieve-

ment of a master craftsman who, like a prestidigitator, always had a good, effective trick up his sleeve.

As Amberg wrote, "Massine's serious substantial compositions did not touch the general American public in a profound, emotional sense."[119] And the negative attitude of tastemakers Kirstein and Denby further debased Massine's artistic reputation, especially in subsequent decades when his symphonic ballets were not in the active repertory and thus could not speak for themselves.

With the coming of war, patriotism swelled. Walter Terry wrote in "Recipe for American Ballet" that "the days of our national inferiority complexes are over, and the United States is feeling proud of its governmental system, its industries and its culture. Relegated to the dimming past are the beliefs that only exotic names can produce art and the 'Dubinskayas' are discovering that the Patsy Bowmans and the Eugene Lorings are of no mean ability."[120] After the war, the triumph of the economy and the liberal ideology of the United States also marked the apogee of American ballet, modern dance, and painting (the New York school).

Massine was profoundly affected by these events—artistically and physically uprooted, denied the chance to explore his full creative potential through his symphonic ballets, and made the target of savage criticism. Throughout his long career and despite its ups and downs, he had been accorded respect by critics and artists who were themselves, in their respective fields, luminaries—Apollinaire, Clive Bell, Roger Fry, T. S. Eliot, Ernest Newman. By 1939 and the outbreak of World War II the choreographer seemed at his zenith, permanently fixed in the firmament like a glorious star. Only a decade later, after sixteen years (including his Roxy period) of advancing and contributing to the cause of dance in America, he now found himself the ballet establishment's persona non grata.

PART SIX

Europe and the Postwar Years

*The poet begins where man ends. The
destiny of the latter is to live his human
itinerary, the mission of the former is to
invent what does not exist.*

—ORTEGA Y GASSET

Massine with Moira Shearer
in The Red Shoes, *1947*

CHAPTER 13

London, September 1946–Edinburgh, September 1960

A BULLET IN THE BALLET was a dramatization of a mystery novel by Caryl Brahms[1] and S. J. Simon, revolving around the backstage intrigue in a ballet company where every dancer cast as Petrouchka is murdered. The play included Fokine's *Petrouchka*, revived by Massine with the assistance of Idzikowski, *Gaîté parisienne,* and a new *ballet blanc, Reverie classique,* choreographed by Massine to the music of Chopin and led by Massine and Irina Baronova. The musical was rehearsed in London, opened in Edinburgh on October 1, 1946, then proceeded to engagements in Glasgow, Manchester, Leeds, Blackpool, and Liverpool. It had considerable success during its provincial tour; but backing for a London engagement was never found, and the show closed after its final performance in Liverpool.

Massine's presence in England for the first time since the onset of war was in itself an event in the ballet community and fed speculation about his future. Discussions were held about his joining the Ballet Rambert,[2] but nothing came of them. During the tour of *A Bullet in the Ballet,* Ninette de Valois, founder-director of the Sadler's Wells Ballet (later to become the Royal Ballet), invited Massine to revive *Le Tricorne* and *La Boutique fantasque* and to act as guest choreographer and dancer early in 1947.[3]

De Valois, a *demi-caractère* dancer and choreographer much influenced by Massine, profoundly admired him. By 1946 her company was a well-organized institution that had achieved artistic excellence during the war years by relying on the choreographers Frederick Ashton, Robert Helpmann, and de Valois herself. Now de Valois wanted Massine as the company's first guest choreographer. She believed that his introduction to ballet of "the character and demi-caractère technique, always supported by classicism," was already vitally important to her troupe's artistic development. She saw no "other master choreographer who could really bring to classical ballet the techniques of character and demi-caractère. His knowledge in this field was tremendous, and he alone had the capacity to make it belong to the classical school—character ballets of the classical school, not character ballets on their own."[4] De Valois realized how important it was for her dancers to get to know his work, for "he had a definite style of his own. It was a character style underneath it all, imposed on classicism. Also he was a long-term pupil of Cecchetti, and a lot of the Cecchetti background work and the Italian style was strongly felt in his work, and this was indispensable if the dancers were to grasp a better understanding of the demi-caractère style."[5] De Valois valued Massine's *demi-caractère* ballets not only for their dancing opportunities but also for their sharp, universally recognizable characterizations. His ballets such as *Mam'zelle Angot,* remarked Alexander Bland, "abounded in character roles of the type which de Valois, following in Massine's footsteps, liked to create and which deployed the dramatic abilities that she encouraged in her artists."[6] De Valois also felt that exposure to Massine's sense of musicality and rhythm would benefit the company. One of her chief concerns was the development of the male dancers, for whom Massine was especially important.

But hiring Massine was also a political ploy, for despite the hiatus of the war years the choreographer and the Ballets Russes still had a strong following. As Bland noted: "It was a shrewd move, for it brought back those members of the Russian ballet audience who had been reluctant to transfer their allegiance to the home-grown Company."[7] And in revival the two Diaghilev works "with their imaginative Ecole de Paris designs and their nostalgic echoes of pre-war triumphs amply fulfilled their function—to set the mantle of the Ballets Russes firmly on the shoulders of the Sadler's Wells troupe."[8]

By the beginning of 1947 the Massines were settled in a four-room flat in Kensington High Street near Kensington Gardens, where the children played in the afternoons accompanied by their nanny. The flat was decorated in the austere English manner with Chippendale furniture from shops in Chelsea and Kensington. Other pieces were acquired at Sotheby's and Christie's.

Massine's first contact with de Valois's troupe took place one Sunday morning when she assembled the company for a special class on the old Sadler's Wells stage. It was Massine's chance to decide whether he wanted to work with her company. Only days afterwards rehearsals began for the spring season revivals of Le Tricorne and La Boutique fantasque.

Working again at Covent Garden, the site of so many triumphs, Massine felt "as happy there as in my early years with the Diaghilev company."[9] As usual, the schedule was exhausting, but as the dancer Alexander Grant recalled, working with him was "a learning experience, because we took a lot by watching him demonstrate during rehearsals and especially watching him perform his roles on stage."[10]

For most of the dancers, Massine still had the aura of his prewar eminence. Margot Fonteyn, who danced the role of the Miller's Wife, described him this way: "The great Massine was already a legend; a strange, quiet man, with those marvelous eyes that fascinated yet also had the effect of a closed door. Occasionally a quick smile lit up the impassive face, and the door opened briefly. But even then I felt at a great distance from him."[11] Although she felt that she was not "particularly good in the role . . . the exhilaration of swirling about in the fandango opposite the intense face of Massine, and then watching him stand absolutely motionless at the end of the Miller's dance while the audience cheered wildly for five minutes, was so overwhelming. . . ."[12] But despite the success of the revivals, especially Le Tricorne (the ballerina Moira Shearer, in a secondary role, found it fresh and inspiring to dance),[13] the company had trouble grasping the proper style, phrasing, and sweep of movement of these ballets. The leading female roles in particular failed to come to life. Fonteyn was beautiful to look at in Le Tricorne, but her movements were not convincing. As for La Boutique fantasque, "the inability of the Wells to produce a Danilova robbed the can-can of a climax."[14]

Massine with Margot Fonteyn in Le Tricorne, *1947*

Although de Valois considered the works to be masterpieces of twentieth-century ballet, she also felt that with the war an era dating back to Diaghilev had come to a close. However, it was still too soon to fashion a proper method of reinterpretation. She cited Lopokova, who observed that "it is easier to revive a work whose style [is] a hundred years old than one that is twenty."[15] Grant believed that the difficulty in Massine's ballets was that they required a unique type of actor-dancer. "In the 1930s the Ballets Russes artists were able to convey character through movement. The choreography was the movement that gave them the key to characterization, and they were able to convey what they were, and who they were, through their dancing because they were actor-dancers. They were incredible artists to be able to do that, and they were an inspiration at the time for all of us who saw them. These Massine ballets require artists who are such dynamic and charismatic people that they can hold the attention of a whole audience with a single movement."[16] In the postwar generation, said Grant, such actor-dancers were almost nonexistent.

Massine returned to the London stage as a performer when he was already past fifty. He was still slim and agile and possessed a commanding theatrical presence, but some younger members of the audience had not seen him before. While they found him charismatic, some of the impact of his dancing, about which so much had been written, was missing from his performances. P. W. Manchester commented: "It's very difficult to watch a dancer in his middle forties if you never saw him when he was thirty-five . . . because . . . when we watch dancers over a period of twenty or thirty years, we don't really notice the erosion. It is very gradual. But if they are great artists they will still, for us, have something. But to be presented with somebody whom you never saw before, to suddenly see Massine in 1947 . . . how could you possibly have really seen him? You know he never taught anybody that great slide at the end of his dance [in Le Tricorne], where he had a slide across the stage and then leaped to his feet and stood absolutely still. By [1947] . . . he wasn't able to do that."[17]

As the successful Sadler's Wells ballet season drew to a close, Massine was approached by the British film director Michael Powell to participate in his next picture, The Red Shoes, which was to include a ballet based on the Hans Christian Andersen story of the same name.[18]

The team of director Powell and writer Emeric Pressburger had by 1947 achieved international recognition for a series of outstanding films, especially A Matter of Life and Death (Stairway to Heaven in the United States; 1946) and Black Narcissus (1947). Pressburger had written The Red Shoes back in 1937 at the request of producer Alexander Korda as a vehicle for Merle Oberon, soon to become Mrs. Korda. The film did not materialize, and almost a decade later Powell and Pressburger bought the script back from Korda and persuaded Arthur Rank to produce it. Powell had agreed to participate with Pressburger on two conditions: (1) the leading role of the ballerina Victoria Page must be taken by a dancer, and (2) the film would include a twenty-minute ballet. This was a risky proposition, one that even Pressburger feared; he suggested cutting the ballet to ten minutes. "In the end," Powell recalled in his memoirs, "and mainly through Emeric's pressure, the ballet ran seventeen minutes."[19]

Powell felt that his exposure to ballet and his knowledge of the form were indispensable to the making of the film. During the 1920s he had lived on the French Riviera, where he attended Ballets Russes seasons in Monte Carlo, met some of the dancers and even, once, Diaghilev himself. He had thrilling memories of Massine's performances. During the 1930s he had followed the Ballets Russes de Monte Carlo seasons in London and was very much impressed by the symphonic ballets.[20]

The story of *The Red Shoes* revolved around a ballet company and its impresario, Lermontov, a character patterned after Diaghilev (and played in the film by Anton Walbrook). The impresario demands from his artists complete dedication and devotion to art. When his prima ballerina, Victoria Page, falls in love with the company's musical director, Julian Craster, Lermontov turns vengeful and implacable. Linked to the story of Victoria Page, who is faced with the dilemma of choosing between art and life, is the actual creative process and performance of *The Red Shoes,* a ballet about a girl who cannot stop dancing until she is driven by her red shoes to her own death. The ballet itself, as a dramatic device, is inextricable from the context of the film story and becomes a symbol for the main plot. To quote Pressburger: "The gem of the whole thing, in one sense, does lie in Andersen's story, for the ballet grew out of that story, and the main plot out of the ballet. One stage followed another. Above all, I wanted to have a film in which a work of art would not merely be discussed, but in which it would appear. That was my aim."[21]

Powell's choice of choreographer and leading dancer for the film was Robert Helpmann of the Sadler's Wells company, a personal friend of Powell's who had worked on his 1942 film *One of Our Aircraft Is Missing.* The leading female role was given to the marvelously young, striking-looking Moira Shearer, also from Sadler's Wells, whom Powell had recently seen in Helpmann's ballet *Miracle in the Gorbals.* The role of the prima ballerina was taken by the French dancer Ludmilla Tcherina, and the dual role of the choreographer Ljubov in the film and the Shoemaker in the ballet *The Red Shoes* was given to Massine. Powell admired Massine tremendously and was convinced that he was the right choice for the part. When the director "heard that he had arrived in London just when I was casting for *The Red Shoes* I felt that fate had brought us together just when I needed for the film all the genius of the world."[22]

Powell had briefly met Massine during the Diaghilev years, but it was not until their collaboration in *The Red Shoes* that a very special friendship evolved that united the two men for the rest of their lives. Powell "worshipped him as an artist for twenty-five years of his brilliant career, and loved him as a friend for the next thirty years. We loved to work together and together we created magic."[23] He described Massine as "intensely musical, a superb mime and a good actor. He could pass from dignity to buffoonery in a flash, one moment a monk, the next a monkey."[24]

However, asking Massine to dance another choreographer's work made Powell hesitant. He writes about their first meeting:

He had taken an apartment in one of those tall stone and red brick Kensington houses, just around the corner from Barker's department store, and we met there. He was preternaturally solemn and stared at me with a look that was centuries old. I explained what we were up to and that Grischa Ljubov was based, perhaps, partly upon himself. He bowed. Then I mentioned the ballet, spoke of Brian Easdale [who was composing the film's score] and Sir Thomas Beecham [who would conduct the Red Shoes ballet], and explained Bobby Helpmann's part in the proceedings. The temperature of the room went down perceptibly. Massine picked his words carefully. He had nothing against the Sadler's Wells Ballet and its leading male dancer, and of course it was my privilege to appoint whom I wished as choreographer. But if he were to dance the Shoemaker in the Hans Andersen story, he would obviously create the part himself, and would want credit for doing so. I was so mad about him by now—he brought half a dozen qualities to the film which had been sadly lacking—that I strode over this minor obstacle, merely saying that I was sure Robert Helpmann would agree to this.[25]

Shooting began in June 1947 on location in France. The ballet itself was filmed later at Pinewood Studios outside of London. From the beginning Powell was fascinated with Massine's interpretation and his intuitive understanding of the camera. Powell described him as a "genius" who developed his own relationship with the lens and its power.[26] That is probably why, according to the essayist Monk Gibbon,

Again and again through the ballet, Massine furnishes the film with some of its most striking visual effects. Powell has given not only some wonderful close-ups of the great Russian, which for colour and animation have never, I believe, been equaled on the screen, but he has used him to reconcile us to the whole macabre and magical aspect of the story. Massine contemplating his victim, Massine leaping forward to pour ink over a little bit of rag and so turn day into night, Massine crouching forward upon the church steps quite indifferent to the threat of the knife upheld in the girl's hands, all these moments are unforgettable. They are unforgettable because the personality of the dancer is as colourful as his costume or the setting.[27]

Robert Helpmann, Moira Shearer, and Massine in The Red Shoes, *1947*

Gibbon goes on to praise Massine's openness to the camera, especially when

> *at one point in the ballet, when a close-up of Massine, the cobbler, shows him either as renewing the spell which he has cast over the dancing girl or perhaps merely contemplating her with cynical detachment, his whole expression seemed to me such a masterpiece of inspired facial control that I almost cried out with pleasure. Powell has seized on a particular gesture, a sudden twist upwards of the palm, with the hand extended, accompanied by a facial expression full of such subtle implications as to be almost indescribable.*[28]

The working relationship between Powell and Massine was one of tacit understanding and complicity. Shearer remembers that Powell never gave him any direction.[29] Powell found him such a "formidable actor" that he gave him complete freedom to interpret his role. "I simply used to tell him, 'This is the shot, Léonide, you only have one and a half seconds to do it, and we are shooting from here. Let's run it.' "[30] The rapport between director and actor was so strong that Massine did not hesitate to make his own suggestions. Gibbon writes:

> He [Powell] takes the occasion when the cobbler shuts up his shop and proceeds to turn day into night. "In the original sketch the Shoemaker in his role as Magician appeared with his hat on and stood in the foreground with his arms wildly extended and the girl dancing away in the background." I said to [Hein] Heckroth [the designer of the film], "This is static and obvious. How about bringing his hands together, and having a close-up of the hands and letting the audience see the girl beyond them?" . . . But when it came to taking the shot the musical score had been refined down to leave only twelve seconds for Moira to leave her home and come right across the square dashing into the crowd, as well as for the business of the Shoemaker and his hands. I said to Helpmann, "You can have eight seconds for Moira. I want four seconds for Massine." Helpmann speeded Moira up still more, so that she spun across the set like a whirlwind. She became a teetotum. Massine was standing with his back to the audience and with upraised arms watching her. The camera had been following Moira. Massine said, "Why don't I turn and come up to the camera and blot the girl out?" Later he [Massine] added the touch of coming up and looking through his suddenly vibrating hands.[31]

According to Powell, it was also Massine's idea to leave Shearer alone on stage while she took her curtain-call bows.[32]

The Shoemaker should be added to the impressive gallery of portraits that Massine created throughout his career. He himself called the Shoemaker a rather "shady character, a mixture of magician and charlatan."[33] But the shadiness had broader dimensions. For Gibbon, the Shoemaker was "the apotheosis as it were of all human puppetry."[34] To allow Massine greater opportunity for characterization, Brian Easdale studied Massine's dancing in order to bring to the Shoemaker's music a compatible style and mood.[35]

That he created the role of the Shoemaker within the terms of Helpmann's choreography testifies to Massine's theatrical craftsmanship.

Shearer herself was unaware at the time that he was doing his own choreography.[36] While his solo scenes may not have presented much of a problem, Massine's perceptive understanding must have been tested in the scenes where his character interacts with others. There, his immersion in the collective dynamics is brilliant; but in addition these scenes become a fully realized study-in-movement of the protagonists' relationships. Together with Shearer's solos, any scene in which Massine appears lights up *The Red Shoes*. His impact is doubled, in fact, by the ballet's circular structure: it opens and closes with the Shoemaker performing "macabre antics outside his cobbler's shop."[37]

In the Shoemaker Gibbon saw reminders of other famous Massine characters, such as those in *Pulcinella* and *Les Femmes de bonne humeur*. In *The Red Shoes*, says Gibbon, Massine gives the spectator

> the very quintessence of his specific talent. . . . Massine's intense vitality shows itself at every stage. Though the whole of the Fun Fare is a vortex of hectic activity, the Shoemaker moving with "a cat-like elegance and sinuousness" stands out nevertheless as far more highly energized than anyone at the fair. He is a dynamic force behind all, not demonic, not even suggesting evil very strongly, but so highly magnetized and magnetizing, so charged with an electric force which is evident in every gesture, that he seems to control everything. It is the force of his character which makes the fairy tale side of the ballet so realistic for us. He "steals the show," but it is not a deliberate theft, nor does he take from anyone else. He steals it simply because the part he plays is the axis on which everything else turns, and because without the whimsical, capricious, sinister cobbler there would be no ballet at all. . . . His energy is revealed not merely in that terrific leap seen in one of the "stills," but it is implicit in every movement and every gesture, implicit most of all perhaps when he is not stirring at all.[38]

According to Powell, Massine had a "dramatic and human tension that became an integral part of his acting or dancing."[39] The director found a combination of these qualities in all of his scenes. He pointed out the facial expressions in his scene with Lermontov while they are backstage watching the excerpt from the second act of *Giselle*, when Massine delivers the line, "That is all very fine, very pure and fine, but you cannot alter human nature." Powell also commended the scene on stage, also with Lermontov, before the *Red Shoes* ballet begins, when Massine cries out, "Chaos, chaos, chaos!" while he clings to Lermontov, and then suddenly goes limp in Lermontov's arms for a fraction of a second, like a lifeless puppet, only to spring back to life with overwhelming vitality. (It is impossible to watch this scene without Petrouchka coming to mind.) For Powell, the final sequence of the ballet, just before the girl dies, illustrates Massine's impressive acting ability and his intuitive understanding of the theater. Powell was particularly impressed because a lot of the ballet, particularly Massine's scene here, "was simply made up on the spot, improvised to bring the whole thing down to storytelling. In this scene Massine had twenty to thirty seconds which I broke down into ten shots."[40]

Massine found filmmaking absorbing (he felt quite comfortable working with Powell) and

> *infinitely more complex than working in the theatre. The day-to-day work was repetitious, for if a single detail in a scene was not quite right, we had to take it over and over again. This was very exhausting, and I found it a great strain to repeat my scenes with the same conviction and intensity each time. Meticulous preparation was essential, and I had to sketch out the choreography in detail before each day's filming. While I was dancing I was always acutely aware of the camera, picking up and magnifying the most minute detail. I had to be careful to avoid excessively fast rhythms, which would have come out merely as a succession of jerky movements.*[41]

Despite Massine's reserve and distance throughout the making of the film—he never mixed with other members of the cast or the crew, appeared on the set only when he was needed, and always lunched alone in his dressing room—he developed a friendly rapport with Moira Shearer. At Covent Garden, the stunning redhead had appeared in *Le Tricorne* and had danced the *Boutique* cancan opposite Massine. From the beginning of the shooting they spent a good deal of time together. (Location scenes on the Continent were shot first, and on the morning of their flight there Shearer's eyes widened as she watched Massine consume three substantial breakfasts: one before boarding, one on the plane, and yet another on arrival.) She found him courteous, friendly, and charming, but he never struck up a conversation without prodding. She was fascinated by his personality and tantalized by the air of mystery about him, the hints of a deeper, more cryptic, and quite unreachable level. At the same time, she wondered how a man so enigmatic and withdrawn could seem to be the force behind almost everything happening in the course of the filming. She detected a great "sense of humor just with his eyes, and felt that if he had let himself be, he would have said a lot of wicked and funny things every five minutes about everyone and everything."[42]

When they began to shoot the ballet segments at Pinewood Studios, she got to know him even better. They often shared a cab to the studio and, later, to the rehearsals for the Sadler's Wells *Mam'zelle Angot*. By then he had relaxed a bit and did not seem to mind when she asked questions, especially about the Diaghilev days. But he never talked about current work or any aspects of the film, and never offered his opinion about their work together. "His attitude at work was practical. He wasn't troubled about anything and he stood back very dispassionately. He never showed emotion at any time of any variety."[43]

When the film was completed, it was £200,000 over budget and dismayed the producers. According to Powell:

> *When the Rank organization saw it they thought they were sunk. I didn't show it to Rank and John Davis, but Emeric did . . . When the film finished, they got up and left the theatre without a word because they thought they had lost their shirts. They couldn't understand one word of it. Universal were their partners and as soon as they could get a print they showed it to some executives . . . An executive stood up and said, "This film will not make a penny."*[44]

In addition, "most of them shared the opinion of [co-producer] Arthur Krim that it was an art film, and would require tough selling."[45] The film, however, became an immediate hit; in New York it ran for two years and seven weeks at the Bijou Cinema on Fifty-fifth Street and Broadway. Powell wrote: "I think that the real reason why *The Red Shoes* was such a success was that we had been told for years to go out and die for freedom and democracy, for this and for that, and now that the war was over, *The Red Shoes* told us to go and die for art."[46]

TOWARDS THE END of the summer Massine began to rehearse (atop the Stoll Theatre) his new production for the Sadler's Wells company, *Mam'zelle Angot*, a revised version of *Mademoiselle Angot*, his 1943 ballet for Ballet Theatre. This was his first "new" ballet work for Sadler's Wells and the first Massine premiere in London since 1939. The ballet remained close to the 1943 original, and although there were no major changes in structure, the story was clarified and the choreography varied to capitalize on the technique and personality of his new cast. The English cast featured four of the company's most brilliant dancers: Fonteyn in the title role, Shearer as the Aristocrat, Michael Somes as the Caricaturist, and Grant as the Barber. (Of these dancers, Fonteyn in her soubrette role was the least suitable.)

Working with Massine on a third ballet, the company by now better understood his idiosyncratic style. His emphasis on characterization was "all through dancing," recalled de Valois. "There was no mime, but the characters came through the movements he had choreographed. Everything was in the choreography and in the attitude of the character. In the case of the aristocratic lady the movements were elegant, in legato, regal, as a character sort of detached in contrast to the others. But all these characters were achieved through the painting of broad strokes, to show certain types of behavior through movement."[47] The ballet resorted to Massine's customary *demi-caractère* techniques: juxtaposition of action (one example is the pas de deux of Mam'zelle Angot and the Caricaturist against a pas de quatre for four male dancers), and quick, staccato steps with a great deal of rhythmic movement of the torso and arms.

True to himself, Massine exhausted and dismayed everyone during the rehearsal period. De Valois remembers that "some of the dancers could not take the strain in his work,"[48] and Grant felt that "he took for granted that no one got tired."[49] But, amazingly, he himself was able to keep pace and continue his practice of demonstrating each role. As usual there was very little verbal communication. Shearer discovered that "he expected the dancers to understand their characters through the movements. He was able to show and demonstrate when he wanted—especially specific visual images. He gave the straight choreography, no trial-and-error approach; there was very little experimentation. He never praised nor criticized, and when he pressed on to something else, dancers guessed that he was happy."[50] According to Grant, "He would work you until you would get it right to his satisfaction and so in the process you understood your character. A very important aspect of working with him was that he demonstrated each role and that he was extremely musical. But this was not a disconcerting approach for the company because Ashton was the same way—the more you did a movement, the more you understood what it was. There was very little explanation."[51]

Mam'zelle Angot marked the reunion of Massine with his friend André Derain, who designed new scenery and costumes. Derain came to London to supervise the execution of his designs and himself painted the flowers and vegetables on the backcloth.

Massine

Mam'zelle Angot premiered on November 26, 1947, and was an unqualified success. Mary Clarke called the press's reception of the work "ecstatic."[52] The reviewer for *Dancing Times* wrote: "The choreography bears all the hallmarks of Massine's genius and his demands are great. . . . Once the market is open they must be ready for all kinds of intricate *enchaînements* and lifts for unusual hand and arm movements which are a vital part of the roles he has created, . . . The thing that strikes one most is the contrast he draws between the dances."

While regretting the work's overreliance on atmosphere—especially in Mam'zelle Angot's waltz, where the "charm" and "purpose" of various actions were lost—the reviewer saw the "many deft touches of humour" as "evidence of Massine's close study of human nature and its foibles, proving that everyday life still plays a large part in artistic designs of all kinds. Perhaps the greatest compliment one can pay to Massine is to say that one must see this work many times before discovering all these delightful human touches, and their correct place in the setting to be fully valued."[53]

In a *Dance Magazine* article titled "Massine in England and America," Mary Clarke suggested some of the possible reasons Massine's ballets, notably *Mam'zelle Angot*, worked better for the English dancers than the Americans. Admitting that "neither English nor Americans approach Massine's choreography in the same manner as the Russians used to, [because] they lack the complete unselfconsciousness and personality that seems to be the birthright of every Russian dancer," Clarke argued that

> [the reason] Sadler's Wells has taken happily to Massine's style is doubtless due to their having been previously trained in Ninette de Valois's ballets, which are often period evocations . . . and which are based on movement which at its worst is fidgety but at its best sets the whole stage alive with vigorous character dancing. . . . De Valois has emphasized the importance of acting in ballet and has demanded neat characterization from her dancers rather than strong dance ability, leaving the creation of pure dancing to her leading choreographer, Frederick Ashton. . . . The division, however, has tended to become rather too marked and Massine's first complaint in England was that there were no true character dancers here: they either acted or they danced but not both.[54]

Mam'zelle Angot remained in the repertory of the Royal Ballet until 1968; it was revived in the spring of 1980 as a tribute to Massine.

324

BY 1948 MASSINE was operating on an extensive international circuit, for his works were in great demand. During the next few years he staged his ballets for La Scala, the Royal Danish Ballet, the Teatro Colón, the Opéra-Comique, the London Festival Ballet, the International Ballet, the Rome Opera Ballet, the Teatro Municipal in Rio de Janeiro, the Royal Swedish Ballet, the Paris Opéra, and many more. The revivals were mainly his classics from the Diaghilev repertory and de Basil's *Le Beau Danube.* Perhaps the ones that were best able to recapture the stylistic mood and the nuances of the period were those by the de Cuevas Company, where Massine's guest appearances found him performing opposite his Ballets Russes stars Riabouchinska, Toumanova, and Lichine.[55] He also staged several opera ballets, mostly in Italy. Until well into the 1950s Massine's wife acted as his assistant, bustling all over the world to supervise the preliminary rehearsals of his ballets for various companies while he worked on others. Massine would then arrive for the final rehearsals.

Nineteen forty-eight saw two new works. *Capriccio* was presented at La Scala on a gala Stravinsky program that also included a revival of Massine's *Sacre du printemps.* A more ambitious production than *Capriccio* was *Clock Symphony* (to Haydn) for the Sadler's Wells company, with scenery and costumes by Christian Bérard, his first collaboration with Massine since *Seventh Symphony* in 1939. Massine found that "the persistent rhythm of the *Clock Symphony* had reminded me of the revolving figures in delicate porcelain often found on baroque clocks, and I conceived the new ballet as an animation of these figures, modeling them on the delicate Meissen figurines I had seen in Dresden in 1927."[56] He

> devised a fairy-tale plot about a young Clockmaker and a Princess living in the Kingdom of Insects. When the king announced that he was taking a suitor for his daughter the poor young Clockmaker brought him an elaborate and intricate clock which he had designed and made himself. The other suitors, seeing that the Princess was attracted to the Clockmaker, secretly hid one of their pages inside the clockcase to dislocate its mechanism. In the final scene the hands of the clock go in reverse, but when the page has been extracted and the suitors banished from the kingdom, the Clockmaker is able to repair it and so wins the Princess in marriage.[57]

The complicated production, with a huge cast, featured a giant clock that opened up to allow the many dancing figures to emerge from it. The opening was dazzling: the curtain rose on Shearer, in a black and night-blue tutu, seated commandingly on a throne under a white canopy. The role of the Clockmaker was danced with gusto by Alexander Grant.

Even though this was Massine's fourth staging for Sadler's Wells, and the company had grown familiar with his style, the choreography for *Clock Symphony* presented them with a new degree of difficulty, a return to Massine's overemphatic baroquism of the earlier 1940s. The staccato leg work, with arm, torso, and head movements, was, according to Grant, "exhausting and very Massinesque . . . a type of technique that demands an extensive quick allegro footwork that is not used today in the same manner."[58] Shearer was afraid that "he was beginning to overchoreograph—to put too many steps per musical bar that gave the impression that the choreography was too full."[59] In his earlier works, Shearer thought, his choreography had a longer line, with more flowing movements; *Clock Symphony* was so packed with choreography that it became frenetic. The allegro technique demanded by the role of the Princess presented a painful test for Shearer. Throughout the first and second movements she remained sitting without moving, but when the third movement began she had to "leap into action, by this time stiff, stiff, but straight into the most tremendous quick jumping, leaping movements."[60]

Premiered on June 26, *Clock Symphony* was not a success. The story was difficult to follow without reference to the program notes; moreover, the reviewer of *Dancing Times* felt as Shearer did, that the piece was handicapped in that "Massine appears to have so overloaded his choreography with exceedingly intricate dances that in many instances there is no clear pattern."[61]

BY 1949 THE MASSINES had settled in Paris. Work commitments on the Continent, particularly in France and Italy, motivated the move. In Paris, the family bought a large four-story house at Neuilly-sur-Seine, where a great many of their belongings from London and Long Island found a new home. The decoration of the house was left to Tatiana, always the organizer, who created an elegant but sober environment, taking into consideration Massine's dislike of furniture that was not essential.

Although many of the works in Massine's impressive art collection had been kept in storage in New York since before the war, the walls at Neuilly were soon hung with Derains, Légers, Mirós, and Picassos, including the latter's series of zodiac signs. A photograph of Diaghilev radiated a strongly felt spiritual presence. The library contained an important collection of art and dance books, musical scores, and books by Russian authors. On the top floor Massine built a dance studio, so that he could avoid the crowded and badly heated Parisian ateliers. This studio also made it possible for his children to take ballet instruction at home from Maria Gourileva, a Cecchetti-trained teacher whom Massine thought outstanding.

From his early morning class, which he held alone in the studio, until night, life at Neuilly revolved around the master's work and needs. A butler, a governess for the children, a cook, a chauffeur, and maids were on hand, all subject to Massine's strict discipline and meticulously planned daily schedule. He was most relaxed during his leisurely luncheons with his family. Even here, however, talk of present and future work dominated the conversation. Massine apparently had little else to talk about. Surely the children were bored; as Lorca remembered, "He did not leave much room for anyone. We listened while he talked about his work, laughed when he laughed, and stopped when he stopped."[62]

Still, life in Paris was less nomadic for the family and a bit more sociable. Some of Massine's artist friends were frequent visitors. Also, Tatiana tried to arrange dinners and parties for guests from the worlds of art and dance. Her efforts sometimes aggravated her husband, who disliked social life and entertaining (with exceptions made for those few friends he enjoyed unreservedly, such as Derain, who always managed to arrive accompanied by a beautiful woman) and hated to waste time away from his work.

The family's summer residence was the Isole dei Galli. They returned for the first time after the war to find that the caretakers had kept everything in the best possible condition given the circumstances. It was a pleasant surprise to discover that the vineyards had produced six hundred liters of wine. Work resumed to refurbish and improve the islands, and the crucial construction of the main villa got under way.

For holidays the family would leave Paris in their Buick, suitcases tacked on the roof, and travel caravanlike through Italy. Frequently their destination was Positano, where they would board the boat to Galli. Each journey of this kind was designed as a learning experience; Massine organized visits to museums, cathedrals, churches, and historical monuments, in the course of which he would lecture his family about painting, sculpture, architecture, and music. The islands of Galli were a refuge for rest and work, from which strangers were banned. Only a few friends

visited, including the Stravinskys, the Hindemiths, Powell, and Markevitch, and it was common for them to spend most of their time sightseeing on the mainland, in particular Naples and environs, which Massine
loved. (Once when the Stravinskys and the Massines were visiting Pres-
tum, Vera Stravinsky heard that there was a case of cholera in the vicin-
ity and the group had to leave immediately for Galli.)[63] Guests' stays on
Galli were always kept brief.

In 1949, in a burst of activity, Massine returned to La Scala. In February he choreographed the ballets for *Carmen* and *Khovanshchina* and
produced a minor new work, *Quattro stagione*. Set to Vivaldi's score, with
scenery and costumes by Pierre Roy, the ballet was a series of vignettes
that captured the mood of each of the four seasons. Winter was in the
style of a *ballet blanc*, ending in a pas de deux by a poor couple in the rain.
Spring depicted a shepherd's dream of unrequited love and his awakening to reality. Summer was in the style of a *ballet de cour*. Autumn presented a series of episodes related to harvest rituals, ending in a
bacchanale. One Italian critic reported, "In the choreography, imaginative, noble and comic scenes alternate with one another."[64]

For most of the year, however, Massine was busy reviving works for
various companies and performing as a guest with the Marquis de
Cuevas Ballet. While with de Cuevas he choreographed a pas de deux for
Toumanova and Skibine set to Debussy's "Clair de lune." (It was never
performed due to Toumanova's departure from the company.)[65]

At the end of 1949 Boris Kochno commissioned a pas de deux from
Massine for his Ballets des Champs-Elysées. The work was based on an
idea by Kochno about the allegorical relationship between an artist and
his model, which disintegrates into a victim/victimizer relationship. A
struggle ensues in which the artist attempts to possess his model but is
destroyed by her in the end. The creation of *Le Peintre et son modèle* was
an experiment. Massine worked without a score, devising movements to
rhythms and tempi that he provided to the rehearsal pianist. Only after
the pas de deux was completed did Georges Auric compose a score based
on the movements.

The choreography departed from Massine's staccato style; it was
long of line and acrobatic. Irene Skorik, who danced the model opposite
Youly Algeroff's artist, found it remarkable, with an aspect of violence,
cruelty, and dramatic power that made a welcome change from the lyrical roles with which she was identified.[66] The scenery and costumes were
by Balthus.

In April 1950 Massine created two new works for Les Fêtes d'Avènement in Monaco, which were performed in the palace courtyard in the presence of Prince Rainier III. These were *Concertino,* an abstract ballet set to Françaix's 1932 work for piano and orchestra, and *Platée,* set to music from Rameau's *ballet bouffon,* a suite of dances—*musette, tambourin, passepied, rigaudon, contredanse*—in the style of Feuillet and Blasis.

In 1950 and 1951 Massine supervised various revivals for the Opéra-Comique and created two new works, *La Valse* and *Le Bal du Pont du Nord.* Set to Ravel's score and with scenery and costumes by Derain, *La Valse* was adapted from Mikhail Lermontov's play *Maskerad,* a story of jealousy, passion, and murder involving an officer, his best friend, and the officer's wife, with all of the action taking place during a ball. But aside from some "effective moments" Massine considered it "a failure, partly because the music was too repetitive. I had hoped to overcome this problem through the dramatic elements in the libretto, but the choreography was defeated by the monotony of the music."[67]

Le Bal du Pont du Nord had a libretto by Hubert Deviellez based on a dramatic Flemish tale, music by Jacques Dupont, and scenery and costumes by André Masson. In the ballet Adèle, daughter of the town's bell-ringer, steals away from her father's appointed watch to meet her lover at the fair, where she finds the swain flirting with her friend Marion. Adèle commits suicide by throwing herself from the Pont du Nord. To re-create the feeling of the story, the ballet was designed in the style of a Flemish painting. At its premiere in Lille it was titled *Meure flamande.*

Before returning to London to work again with Michael Powell on his film *The Tales of Hoffmann,* Massine was approached by Henri Sauguet to choreograph *Les Saisons (Symphonie allégorique)* for the de Cuevas company for the Bordeaux International Music Festival of 1951. Sauguet collaborated with Jacques Dupont on the music and libretto; Dupont designed the scenery and costumes. The choreography consisted of a suite of *tableaux vivants* illustrating man's relationship with nature as the four seasons follow one another.

Sir Thomas Beecham was the force behind *The Tales of Hoffmann.* After conducting the score to the *Red Shoes* ballet, he had offered to participate in any opera film Powell wanted to make. When Powell eventually took up the offer, Beecham suggested Offenbach's opera, a work dear to the conductor ever since he first brought it to Covent Garden in 1911.[68]

The new film reconvened most of the creative team that had produced *The Red Shoes:* Powell, Pressburger, Beecham, designer Hein Heckroth, Shearer, Tcherina, Helpmann, Massine. A major addition was

Frederick Ashton, who was to choreograph the balletic passages and appear in the film as well. Massine, as in the previous film, created his own roles.[69]

Hoffmann was shot in nine weeks at Shepperton Studios in London. The filming went smoothly, much more so, according to Shearer, than that of *The Red Shoes,* because the dancing passages were designed to run longer and the dancers could become even more engrossed in their performances.[70] Powell combined actors and dancers who lip-synched, singers who sang off-camera, and other singers who appeared on camera, singing and acting their roles. The various casts meshed flawlessly, giving brilliant performances in a visually striking film.

Massine played three roles: Spalanzani in the balletic first act, Schlemil in the dramatic second, and Franz in the operatic third. He brought an original interpretation to all of them, and played each with such conviction that Powell felt fully vindicated in his belief that Massine was a truly gifted actor.[71] Monk Gibbon, in his book on the film, discusses each Massine characterization, beginning with Spalanzani:

> a light, plausible, perfumed creature, taking an immense pride in his mere showmanship. Though the costume and makeup for the part are a shade bizarre, the face of Massine as Spalanzani, when he is not acting but sitting in his chair near the set, has a strange, graven beauty which might also be Egyptian. . . . He is light as a feather, he might be blown thistledown.[72]

The role of Schlemil—"the man without a shadow—is in itself the mere shadow of a part," for Gibbon.

> His face expresses a profound sadness; he is the battered old soldier, the indomitable failure, the man who has had his heart broken in the cruellest fashion. . . . [His face] is a deathly white, and, but for the two huge and immensely wistful and melancholy eyes, it might almost be a skull and not a face. It suggests sorrow and disillusion and despair but it is the stoicism of despair rather than its desperation.[73]

And in Schlemil's death scene Massine's "body turns slowly on its own axis, the black train winds itself round his legs, the mouth gapes open, the deep-set eyes seem for a moment to attain an unnatural brightness, and the body, run through by his opponent's sword, tilts tragically in an excessively difficult and uncomfortable pose, which he is able to hold

Massine as Spalanzani with Moira Shearer as Olympia in
The Tales of Hoffmann, *1951*

rigidly for a matter of seconds. Finally, just before he drops, the eyes widen into a grim stare and almost make us believe that they are about to slowly glaze."[74]

Powell agreed with Gibbon that Massine's performance of Franz is the film's masterpiece.[75] Gibbon writes:

> *Massine brings a lovely innocence into his characterization of Franz. He makes it unforgettable. It is built up by innumerable small touches. He nibbles his fingertips, he cocks his head on one side, he screws up his mouth and makes his eyes as round as O's; he rubs his hands in his apron to clean them or merely to occupy them. . . . Every expression of Franz's face is inimitable. . . . He is normal with the normality of peasant earth and of a lifetime of normal labour; he is immutable; he is the soil; he is, as Powell put it one day, "something that has been in that spot for 3,000 years, something that might almost have the pointed tips of the horns of a faun. . . ."*[76]

Gibbon regarded Massine's dance segment as Franz as

> *an improvisation in which the dancer seems conscious of the stiffness of his joints but indifferent to it. In it the old man liberates all his repressed aspirations and ambitions. Little by little he reveals an agility surprising in view of his years but which is in entire accord with his temperament. Massine has taken the rather obvious burlesque which Offenbach probably had in mind and turned it into something much more subtle, human and universal.*[77]

The Tales of Hoffmann instantly joined that special group of films that have become unclassifiable, and many historians consider it a masterpiece. Yet it was not a big success. Although it was awarded the Special Jury Prize at the 1951 Cannes Film Festival, Powell believed it could have won the Grand Prix if the final sequence had been deleted (a suggestion, probably made by the producers, that he had rejected).[78]

The ballet press found the film somewhat disconcerting. Though Shearer's dancing was widely praised, the choreography was judged formal, unimaginative, and predictable. According to Fernau Hall: "At no point in the film did Ashton create dance images expressive of the characters and moods of the personages involved, and this made the film as a whole into a bewildering succession of shots with little or no relation to the singing or each other. . . . Massine's superb acting in one of the cen-

Franz in The Tales of Hoffmann, *1951*

tral roles, with his professional assurance and complete grasp of the film medium, showed very clearly what was wrong with Ashton's choreography."[79]

Today Michael Powell is considered among the most important auteurs of English cinema, and *Tales of Hoffmann* is regarded by some as a film that was in many respects ahead of its time. In 1968 Thomas Elsaesser wrote:

Tales of Hoffmann *is no doubt seriously flawed, over-ambitious and uneven. It creates a confusing complexity, in which images of startling force are side by side with a rather too obtrusive, mechanical symbolism. But it is a film which is genuinely disturbing, not least by its uncompromising pessimism. Its importance derives from its partial failure; made in 1951, it foreshadows the decline of the great American cinema, and very accurately feels its way towards the modern "continental" cinema, haunted as the latter is by an often paralyzing self-consciousness about the limits of the cinematic medium. Powell's unresolved formal problems stem directly from his themes, which seem to belong more to the 1960's. The almost prophetic urgency of his themes has, as it were, wrecked the traditional narrative form and, today, one is inclined to view the fragments with singular affection and admiration.*[80]

WHEN FILMING CONCLUDED on the *Tales of Hoffmann*, Massine joined the Sadler's Wells Ballet to start work on *Donald of the Burthens*, which had been in its planning stages for more than two years and was to be his last new work for the English company.

Donald of the Burthens was based on a Scottish legend about a woodcutter who makes a pact with Death. In return for the gift of healing, he agrees never to pray and to make his fortune only under Death's banner. If Death is seen at the foot of a patient's bed, the patient will live, but if Death appears at the head of the bed, the patient must die. When Donald is asked to heal a dying king, he arrives to find Death already positioned at the head of the bed. To fool Death, Donald instructs the servants to turn the bed around; thus he heals the king and sends Death into a rage. But in celebrating the king's recovery, Donald forgets his vow and teaches a group of children a prayer; the pact is broken, and he is compelled to dance to his death.

The ballet was set to an original score by the Scottish composer Ian Whyte, with scenery and costumes by the Scottish artists Robert MacBryde and Robert Colquhoun. Rehearsals began at Covent Garden in September and lasted until December. The elaborate production required special coaching for the company in Scottish folk dances, such as the sword dance and the reel, which already had been integrated into Massine's choreography. According to Alexander Grant, who danced the role of Donald, the rehearsals, during which certain passages had to be drilled over and over, were taxing; but the company took heart from Massine's creativity and his unflagging energy, especially when he demonstrated movements himself—everyone agreed that no one else danced his choreography with quite his panache.[81] For the ballerina Beryl Grey, who danced the demanding role of Death, working with Massine was "exhilarating" and a revelation. Her biographer Pigeon Crowle wrote:

No detail was too small to be worked on again and again until [Massine] had achieved the desired effect, from corps de ballet upwards, and he was able to dance each movement himself—and so much better than anyone else. [Grey] learned much from watching him dance—he was so swift and light, able to draw with immediate ease a complete and clear picture, with every movement full of meaning and character. He was quiet and of few words, but had a fine sense of humor which was often reflected in his pene-trating brown eyes. His rare praise meant a great deal. [82]

Donald of the Burthens marked Massine's return to character ballet aesthetics, as exemplified in *Le Tricorne*. Only Grey's allegorical role of Death remained within the bounds of strict classical technique, and she alone danced on point. Her difficult and intricate choreography was "full of short, sharp, crisp movement," [83] in contrast to the Scottish folk idiom. The second scene featured a divertissement performed for the monarch, and after Donald's death, the ballet culminated in a characteristic, grandiose Massine finale with the whole cast (minus Donald), led by Death, performing a stylized reel.

At its premiere on December 12, 1951, *Donald of the Burthens* re-ceived seventeen curtain calls and, according to *Dance and Dancers*, "the loudest reception accorded to any new ballet since the war." [84] But its suc-cess was not lasting; like *Clock Symphony*, it was handicapped by a plot too intricate to unfold with clarity. While the Scottish press heralded *Donald* as a landmark, the more specialized London press was consider-ably less receptive. *Dancing Times* praised the cast and the folk-inspired dances, especially the opening, a sword dance superbly led

by Brian Shaw and eight men, whose performance is an object lesson in precision. Then comes a delightful Country Dance in which the manipula-tion of the four Danseuses' skirts stress their lilting movements and pat-terning. Alexander Grant then has a brilliant solo in which Massine exploits to the full the niceties of capers, high-cuts, turns and shakes, until Grant as Donald the woodcutter seems to be possessed of the very Devil. The finale is tremendously exciting, for Death compels everyone to dance her bidding after she has taken Donald's life, and here Beryl Grey domi-nates the stage and although this role is confined to eccentric movements, her tremendously forceful personality makes her dance stand out above all.

But the reviewer also had reservations:

> *Despite Massine's flair for revealing the subtleties and qualities of every*
> *kind of folk dance, the real essence of Scottish dance, with its rugged char-*
> *acterization of the Scottish people, has eluded him. He has caught its won-*
> *derful patterning, lilting quality, impetuous and neatly complicated*
> *footwork, but he has failed to express the strange mystical belief of the*
> *Scottish people in the supernatural, their pawky humor, lyricism, and*
> *above all their romanticism and love of clear-cut statement.*[85]

Clive Barnes in *Dance and Dancers* agreed that "any ballet by Massine
could never be less than competent" but nevertheless complained that
the two-scene ballet was "poorly constructed," since the first scene, consisting of two episodes, was "hardly more than half the length of the
final scene." He also noted that the narrative was obscure and that "by
the time the ballet had got going, in the divertissement danced before the
resuscitated King leading to the excellent and exciting Highland-fling finale, it is nearly finished." Still, he praised "the floor-patterns, with their
ingenious use of obliquely-placed blocks of dancers and the circular finale." He also thought that the best choreography in the ballet had been
given to "a group of children. Their 'prayer scene' had a pathos that the
rest of the ballet conspicuously lacked, and their 'follow the leader'
jumping entry into the finale was a fine piece of choreographic craftsmanship."[86] The critic in *Ballet Annual,* too, singled out the "superb
ground patterns." In addition, "the dancers are brought on and off in a
way one rarely sees today, and the finale is a masterpiece."[87]

Fernau Hall suggested that the work's fundamental flaw was Massine's inability to realize the incompatibility of the folktale with his expressionistic treatment, which ended with a puzzling "cheerful climax."
(But Hall seems not to take into consideration the fact that throughout
history subjects have been reinterpreted in the particular style of a period or according to the personal stylistic preferences of an artist. It is not
so much a question of the incompatibility of subject and treatment as,
rather, of whether or not the work of art is fully realized.) According to
Hall, Massine's myopia could be explained by "the fact that to a choreographer of his generation expressionism is not a style of art: it is art itself."
He concluded:

> *In 1919, in the heyday of expressionism, Massine had gaily satirized the*
> *moribund Petipa-style of ballets of the nineteenth century in La Boutique*
> *Fantasque. He was now faced with a situation in which his natural style*
> *offered no further possibilities of development and had lost its appeal to the*

*public, whereas the Petipa-style ballets popularized by Diaghilev and
Pavlova had become more reliable box office attractions than most types of
modern ballet. It is therefore easily understandable that he should attempt
to ensure the success of* Donald of the Burthens *(his most ambitious production for over a decade) by giving it the shape of a Petipa ballet—even
though this shape was completely unsuitable to the theme and represented
the most violent possible departure from the aesthetic ideals of his youth.*[88]

Alexander Grant agreed with the *Dancing Times* reviewer, who
found the music unsuitable and thought it suffered from a "lack of drama
and emotional content."[89] Grant remembered being fascinated by the
choreography but also recalled the story as unduly complicated. Ninette
de Valois, too, found the choreography "very interesting. . . . There were
some lovely passages and Massine, a very thorough person, did tremendous research on Scottish dance."[90] Grant concluded that *Donald of the
Burthens* had happened at the wrong time, when dance was moving towards abstraction and neoclassicism, and a folk ballet with "a complicated story seemed to be no longer part of the balletic scene, when all
the new contemporary abstract ballets were becoming the rage."[91]
Though Massine had made a profound impression with his abstract ballets in the 1930s, Grant noted, he now fiercely championed his character
and *demi-caractère* ballets, sensing perhaps that these genres were in dan-
ger of extinction.

Alexander Bland wrote in 1981: "There were, in fact, some moving
passages, but . . . uncertain translations of folk-dance into ballet bogged
the piece down."[92]

IN 1952, during Massine's association with the Maggio Musicale
Fiorentino, for which he staged the dances in Cavalli's *Didone* and
Rossini's *William Tell* and *Armida* (with Maria Callas in the title role), the
festival's director, Francesco Siciliani, introduced the choreographer to
Laudes dramaticae Umbriae, "a thirteenth-century Italian version of a
Latin liturgical play dealing with the life of Christ. I was much moved by
the simplicity and sincerity of the dialogue, and began to wonder
whether in using it as the basis for a ballet I might not at last accomplish
what I had set out to do so many years before in *Liturgie*. Here, surely,
was a genuinely primitive treatment of the subject which lent itself admirably to the kind of simplified choreography I had been trying to
evolve then with Larionov."[93]

Massine found the adaptation of the *Laudes* the most inspiring project he had undertaken in years. Siciliani offered to have the new ballet produced in the autumn for the Sacra Musicale Umbria, of which he was the artistic director. *Laudes evangelii,* as the work was titled, was to be produced in the fourteenth-century church of Santo Domenico in Perugia. The scenario, based on the life and Passion of Christ, was by Giorgio Signorini; the music, based on *laudes* by Jacopone da Todi and other thirteenth-century composers, was orchestrated and adapted by Valentino Bucchi. The scenery and costumes were by Ezio Rossi.

Working on a "sacred drama" reminded Massine of his first unfinished ballet. "It seemed strange, after so long, to be working on something so similar to *Liturgie*. Everything—text, music, the possibility of production—had fallen into place so easily that it seemed almost as if Diaghilev himself were giving me back my lost opportunity."[94] (Actually, in the summer of 1952, in Galli, Massine made copious notes on the choreography of *Liturgie*.)

Laudes had seven scenes: the Annunciation and the Visitation; the Nativity and the Flight into Egypt; the Entrance into Jerusalem; the Garden of Olives (Gethsemane); the Flagellation and the Via Crucis; the Crucifixion and Deposition; and the Resurrection and the Ascension. The spirit of the work derived from the ancient Umbrian *laudatori*. Massine recounts that in order "to evoke the atmosphere of the pre-Giotto *Laudi* I had based my choreography on the attitudes depicted in Byzantine mosaics, and on the paintings of the primitive Lucca and Pisa school."[95] A painting by Giotto, an artist whom Massine had always found fascinating, was the inspiration for the scene of the kiss of Judas. However, Massine's purpose was not archaeological reconstruction but the creation of a style of dramatic choreography that would require a personal vocabulary of symbolic gesture. The burden of the production in Massine's mind was to transform the spirit of the *laudatori* into a new theatrical language. Giorgio Signorini commented:

> *The* Laudes, *in fact, is not a miracle play or a sequence of dramatized hymns of praise; nor does it imitate the original Umbrian and Tuscan theatrical productions of the fourteenth century. But while it is no "imitation" as far as faithfulness to those dramatic forms is concerned, it nevertheless aims at a close correspondence with their narrative content, in which "narration" is indeed both chronicle and drama, a vein of pure, profoundly popular, poetry. The intention behind* Laudes Evangelii *was*

to translate a story reconstructed from old manuscripts into a new form of theater; to create a contemporary vision of that language.[96]

Valentino Bucchi added: "Regarding the musical text of this work, we followed, with very few exceptions, the old *Laudi,* remaining faithful, as far as language went, to the original harmonized melody according to the canons of the *ars antiqua.* Having made this musical language our base, however, we felt we could use the utmost freedom in the arrangement of the individual components, the instrumentation and the tonality."[97]

For the performance of *Laudes evangelii* Massine assembled a fifty-member company, with dancers from La Scala and from other troupes he had already employed for the Maggio Musicale. Rehearsals began in the summer in the Villa Romana at the top of a hill above Positano—a special arrangement made to allow Massine to commute daily from Galli. The rehearsal period was strenuous; dancers working with Massine for the first time came face to face with his compulsive work ethic. All needs save those of work had to be set aside. The final rehearsal ran twenty-four hours. Massine himself recalled that by then his "nervous system was so overstrained that in the middle of the night I woke up and found myself on the floor."[98]

A drama-ballet about the life and Passion of Christ did not go unnoticed by Perugian church officials, who doubted the religious integrity of the project. When a photograph of the French ballerina Geneviève Lespagnol (cast as the Virgin Mary) in rehearsal tights and leotard appeared in Roman newspapers, a delegation of priests was dispatched to oversee rehearsals and to certify that appropriate precautions were being taken with sacred matters.

The two-hour *Laudes evangelii* premiered on September 20, 1952, at the church of Santo Domenico. It was a spectacular production. The music employed four soloists, a chorus of ninety-two, and a fifty-five-piece orchestra. The stage was set at the head of the central nave, and a steel-supported ramp running the length of the church accommodated twenty-five hundred spectators. The tri-level stage was built in two sections, one of which floated to allow for the changes of scene. The first three scenes took place at stage level. The next two, the Garden of Olives and the Via Crucis, took place on a double ramp with all of the action going uphill. The final two, the Crucifixion/Deposition and the Resurrection/Ascension, unfolded on the highest level. A gold mosaic backdrop created an arch beneath the seventy-five-foot stained glass rose window, which was lit from the outside. As for the scenery, there was a chapel in the first scene, a grotto in the second, and a palm tree and fountain at the entrance to Jerusalem in the third.

The success of *Laudes evangelii* was tremendous. The Italian press raved, calling Massine a magician. (Despite the ballet's success, a Vatican spokesman would only go so far as to say that church authorities had taken no position on the matter. He did, however, permit himself to wonder aloud whether a church should be turned into a theater.) The work was also hailed by the international press. Arnold Haskell considered it a "masterwork: it is religious in feeling and scholarly in its understanding of liturgy and of the spirit and movement of the period from which it derives. Massine alone could have created it."[99] The work was such a success that for the next decade it toured cathedrals and festivals in Europe, including Nantes and Edinburgh. In 1959 it was presented at La Scala, where a scene called "Massacre of the Innocents" was added. In 1961 it was filmed by Associated Television with the Glyndebourne Festival Chorus; the production featured the younger Tatiana Massine as Mary, the elder Tatiana as Elizabeth, and Lorca Massine as Saint John. It was shown on television throughout England, Holland, Denmark, Canada, and Italy; and on April 8, 1962, it was aired in the United States. Jack Iams of the *New York Herald Tribune* thought it "splendid": "I know of no single word to describe the combination of ballet, mime, background music and voices through which the story was told. Perhaps it could be called a pageant—certainly the production was rich in pageantry, with its splendidly garbed figures moving against equally splendid, and effectively stylized, settings. The choreography by Léonide Massine was breathtaking, and the music, based on old canticles, was solemnly majestic."[100] Jack Gould of the *Times* hailed it as "stunning":

> *Through his exquisite design of movement, Massine achieved an uncanny blend of forms; at times the presentation almost seemed to be a succession of religious tableaux coming to life out of a stained window. The delicacy and inventiveness of the choreography, complemented by the soloists and chorus, imparted a mood of sustained awe mixed with the excitement of unfolding creativity.*
>
> *In the Ascension scene there was a grandeur of pictorial composition and a majesty of dimension rarely seen [on television]. Similarly, the scene of the Crucifixion was unforgettable, a visual tour de force of Christ towering in agony above the boisterous soldiers fighting over his garments.*[101]

Until the end of his life Massine would regard *Laudes evangelii* as one of his most important postwar achievements.

IN 1953 MASSINE created no new ballets. During the summer, however, Ballet Theatre included *Aleko* in its repertory for a European tour. The eleven-year-old Chagall-Massine ballet was brilliantly led by Alicia Alonso and Igor Youskevitch and enjoyed a triumphant reception. London and Paris were warm in their praise:

> *The choreography is a masterpiece. The four tableaux are held together by one single emotion that does not pause while drawing the spectator inside. There are no holes; no weaknesses. The action never falters. Although the piece takes place over a long period of time, we are never made to feel it. That is only made possible by the richness of Massine's perpetual choreographic invention, backed up by his enormous experience, which enable him to draw upon a repertory of forms and motions accounting for his constant renewal. . . .*
>
> *His expertise shows in the fast pas de deux full of dramatic élan and never falling into meaningless "expressiveness," which can be of such dire consequences to dance as an art form. As everyone knows, Massine's specialty lies in the arrangement of ensembles seemingly disconnected and free-flowing, as if they had arisen spontaneously yet following a rigorous pattern that obeys the strict logic of the composition. That is . . . a sign of the great masters. The entire choreography provides constant fulfillment.*[102]

The year's creative work was confined to choreographing the Dance of the Hours in *La Gioconda* for La Scala and staging and choreographing *The Snow Maiden* for the Rome Opera. But the year also brought Massine back to films, this time for *Carosello napolitano,* directed by Ettore Giannini.

Carosello napolitano was Giannini's only commercial film as a director. He had enjoyed a distinguished theater career as a writer and director and had produced some of the best Pirandello, Shaw, and O'Neill in Italy. He was also one of the first theater directors to work for the Italian operatic stage. His production of *The Abduction from the Seraglio* with Maria Callas for La Scala was an artistic highpoint of 1952.

Carosello napolitano—a history of Naples through song, dance, and pantomime—had been in Giannini's mind since the late 1940s, but backing for the project had proven difficult to obtain. Giannini explained:

"After the war there was a vogue in Italy for American cinema and neo-realism. Any subject dealing with folk was associated with fascism, and Neapolitan folk especially was at a very low ebb."[103] So in order to raise money for the film, Giannini first produced *Carosello napolitano* as a musical show. It had its premiere in Florence in April 1950, then successfully went on the road in Italy and later in South America.

When preparations at last got under way, Giannini wanted Massine for both his international prestige—essential for the financial backing—and his experience in film. The two men had met the year before at La Scala, where Massine was reviving *Le Tricorne* with the renowned Spanish dancers Antonio and Mariemma. When discussions about the film began, a close rapport developed between them. From the beginning Giannini felt as if they had worked and known each other for many years. He particularly appreciated Massine's economy with words, and they both seemed to have an aptitude for sustained concentration.[104]

The film depicted the history of Naples from medieval invasions through World War II. It was an allegory of the spirit of the Neapolitan people and their capacity for survival as seen through the experiences of a poor family of carnival players. Giannini's intention was to create a portrait of the city through various episodes that cohesively combined dance, song, pantomime, and acting. The spoken drama would fluidly link one passage to the next, allowing story, dance, fantasy, and reality to flow into one another. The episode of Margherita, for example, begins as a straight dramatic scene with spoken words, then develops into dance. Giannini called his approach "*realismo magico*: the method was realist, the reality was magical."[105] He aimed to diversify a cinema that he felt was completely dominated in content and practice by a realism tied to a strong social and political message.

Carosello departed from the traditional musical or ballet film in that it gave the dancers no opportunity to show off at center stage. With few exceptions, dancers in each scene were part of a collective whole, and many of them complained that they were not being given a place commensurate with their star status. According to Giannini, their protest eventually waned thanks to the example set by Massine, whose only concern was for the work and the realization of his artistic vision.[106]

Massine was to stage several pantomime scenes and choreograph four of the five dance episodes: the Pulcinella ballet, danced by himself and Rosella Hightower (the role of Pulcinella was originally conceived for an actor, but Giannini wanted Massine to appear in the film); the music hall cancan; the tale of Margherita (danced by Yvette Chauviré);

and the final tarantella, led by Antonio and Rosiata Segovia. (A statuesque, pre-Hollywood Sophia Loren was featured in a nondancing role.)

Giannini began by describing to Massine the action of a scene, which the latter then choreographed or staged. If Giannini approved, the scene was shot. The collaboration was so close-knit that the result was seamless; it was hard to determine where the work of the choreographer ended and that of the director began.

The fifteen weeks of shooting on *Carosello napolitano* took place in Theater 5 (Fellini's favorite) at Cinecittà. However, the ballet's climactic scene, the tarantella, was shot on location in Naples, as Giannini wanted to break the monotony of studio shooting and, above all, to end the film showing the real face of the city.[107]

Appearing in the heyday of neorealist cinema, *Carosello* sparked controversy among Italian critics, who found it difficult to categorize. Yet its international success was absolute. *Le Figaro* called it "something completely new that does not belong to any known genre, a sort of *suite chantée et dansée* . . . that never bores, though it is not aided by a story or characters to follow and has as its only theme the streets of Naples."[108] Ernest Borneman in *Ballet Today* felt that it was

> in many ways the most remarkable musical film to be made anywhere the world over. . . . Here is a fascinating, ingenious, provocative film—but a film which is bound to remain almost wholly unintelligible to the vast majority of filmgoers. . . . The idea is simple. . . . But the execution is fantastically complex. Since there is no continuity of plot, all continuity is either optical or acoustical. Visual metaphors, sound similes, musical allusions abound. Choreographed movements are used to carry one action through time and space. . . . This is Massine at his best. . . . This isn't dancing, this is an allegory. And it is beautifully done, . . . taking bits from the damnedest places and blending them all with an astounding degree of style.[109]

In 1954 *Carosello*, having been applauded continually throughout the screening, was awarded the Grand Prix at the Cannes Film Festival by a jury presided over by Jean Cocteau. Film historian Gian Piero Brunetta re-evaluated it in 1980: "Of all the Italian musical films made in the 1950's it is the only one that deserves to be compared with the great American musicals, because of its stage inventiveness, its close connection with the national tradition, the richness of its costume designs, and its awareness of the complete possibilities of spectacle. . . ." Yet Giannini's *realismo magico* did not fail to dig beneath the surface of postwar Italy. As Brunetta noted: "Beyond the colors, the dances, and the songs, one perceives throughout the whole film the feeling of a painful path, the telling of a story of hunger and misery never overcome and never vanquished by a journey destined to continue."[110]

While working on *Carosello napolitano* Massine was asked by the Rome Opera Ballet to create a *pièce d'occasion* for guest artist Yvette Chauviré. Very much an *hommage* to Fokine's *Les Sylphides, Les Dryades* was an abstract ballet in the neoromantic classical style, with symmetrical ensembles and soloists in the foreground. The score was made up of thirteen Chopin pieces, including preludes, waltzes, one mazurka, one étude, and a fantasie, all orchestrated by Vieri Tosatti. The scenery and costumes were by Dimitri Bonchiere.

The tremendous success of *Laudes evangelii*, which was still being performed around Europe, led the philanthropist Count Vittorio Cini in 1953 to invite Massine to produce another "sacred drama," this one to inaugurate the Teatro Verde on the Venetian island of San Giorgio Maggiore. Until the end of the 1940s the island had belonged to the Italian army; then, under Cini's supervision, it was converted into an impressive international cultural and artistic center that housed schools of navigation and the arts and crafts, as well as the open-air theater. These institutions were named the Giorgio Cini Foundation after the count's son, who had died in a plane crash a few years earlier.

The inaugural program of the Teatro Verde in July 1953 consisted of a revival of Benedetto Marcello's opera *Arianna,* with baroque dances choreographed by Massine, and the "sacred drama" *Resurrezione e vita,* with a scenario by Orazio Costa from Christ's words "Ego sum resurrectio et vita." The score employed music by the sixteenth- and seventeenth-century Venetian composers Monteverdi and Gabrieli, orchestrated and arranged by Virgilio Mortari. The scenery and costumes were by Virgilio Marchi, Valeria Costa, and Veniero Colasanti.

Rehearsals took place throughout the summer at the Teatro Verde. The Massine family stayed at the Villa Korompay on the Lido.

Massine's approach to *Resurrezione e vita* differed from his method on his previous "sacred drama":

> *I soon realized that this spectacle would have to be presented in an entirely different style from that of* Laudes Evangelii, *where the influence of the Umbrian text and music had inspired a portrayal of Christ's Passion in a*

primitive Italian pre-Giotto style. For Resurrezione e Vita . . . *we decided on a broader, more animated approach. It was to be in two parts, with a prologue portraying the Nativity, the Massacre of the Holy Innocents and the Presentation in the Temple. The first part embraced the episodes of the Christ-Child in the Temple, the parable of the Wise and Foolish Virgins, the Woman Taken in Adultery, the Prodigal Son, the Raising of Lazarus and the Temptation in the Wilderness. Part Two included the Entry into Jerusalem, the scene of the Mount of Olives, the Trial of Jesus, the Crucifixion and the Resurrection. The movements and groupings in my choreography were based on the paintings of Titian and Veronese.*[111]

At this time Massine's wife and children began to play an important role in his work—an arrangement that not only would expand with time but would eventually disrupt a family that had always been dominated by one personality. In *Resurrezione e vita,* the elder Tatiana played Mary Magdalene, the younger Tatiana an angel, and Lorca the child Jesus in the temple.

Anticipation ran high in Venice, but the day of the premiere, July 11, did not pass without complications. A fleet of vedettes and gondolas carrying the elegantly attired opening-night audience, which included Greta Garbo, made its way to the island that evening—but so did a tornado. Everyone was forced to take cover in the Palladio cloister, whence they later were rescued by the *vaporetti,* Venice's motorboat buses. The next night the same ritual took place, but this time among the passengers' minks and ermines one could also see raincoats and umbrellas with mother-of-pearl inlaid handles. Garbo arrived under a wide-brimmed, rainproof sailor's hat. As Count Cini addressed the audience with his message of welcome, a storm broke, again driving the guests to the cloister. They waited out the deluge until midnight, soothing their nerves with champagne. On Wednesday the thirteenth, in a third procession of gondolas and vedettes, Garbo and company made their way yet again to San Giorgio Maggiore, where the premiere finally took place.

Resurrezione e vita was an impressive artistic spectacle. The stage was composed of three revolving levels that allowed the life of Christ to emerge into view as if seen through frescoes, the scenes brought to life by Massine's expressive dance vocabulary. The press hailed the work. *Le Monde* wrote: "Let us repeat it again: the success was complete. . . . [Massine] did not try to be intellectual or even mystical. What he wanted was to give a new look, or, better, a new youth, to a centuries-old glory. He bowed low before the Italian Renaissance and in this way he resurrected it in all its luxurious effervescence." The reviewer added: "Among the most successful scenes I shall mention is the majestic arrival of Gasparus, king of the Magi, in front of the crèche, on which the swinging incense lamps converge, and the flagellation, in which Massine had mustered for the seasoned soldiers of Pilate a *variation grotesque* to poignant effect." [112]

Resurrezione e vita completed the sacred triptych Massine began with *Saint Francis* and *Laudes evangelii*.

AFTER FULFILLING HIS COMMITMENT to Count Cini, Massine returned to Galli to rest and prepare himself for his return to the United States. He and Denham had buried the hatchet to the extent of negotiating for a new work for the Ballet Russe de Monte Carlo. [113] Massine suggested a revival of *Laudes evangelii* with new scenery and costumes by Georges Rouault, [114] but although Denham was very interested in the idea (he pursued it until 1955), he came to realize that the demands of the production made it impractical. Instead, he proposed the creation of a new ballet set to Berlioz's *Harold in Italy*. [115] Denham's invitation was not unwelcome; not only was the idea attractive financially, it came at a most opportune time, when the Massines, naturalized American citizens, had to fulfill their obligation to return to the United States every five years to comply with immigration law. At the same time Massine was also interested in organizing a series of talks for Columbia Concerts at which he would lecture and demonstrate his theory of choreography, which he had been working on for some time. [116]

Harold in Italy was set to the four movements of the Berlioz work, which the composer called "Harold in the Mountains," "March of the Pilgrims," "Serenade," and "Orgy of the Brigands." The action revolved around the Italian sojourns of the poet Childe Harold, from Byron's poem. Like the Musician in *Symphonie fantastique*, Harold was a rather static first-person narrator.

When rehearsals started in autumn, Massine must have been delighted to find that Frederic Franklin, one of his favorite dancers during his tenure with the Ballet Russe, was now the company's ballet master. But despite this piece of luck, the rehearsal period was difficult and frustrating, and the work advanced slowly. The scrupulous choreographer would pursue a problem to its limits, then find it difficult to admit that what was clear to him might not be clear to others. Franklin remembers the whole process as "a struggle. . . . After so many years of absence, his choreography had become alien, especially considering that since 1944 the Balanchine era of the Ballet Russe had begun. [Massine] demanded artists who could express, who could act, who could feel stuff to come out of them, but by then dancers were getting away and away from this sort of ballet."[117] Some members of the company found Massine "very manic" and "out of another age."[118]

When *Harold in Italy* was premiered, certain critics dismissed it; Doris Hering in *Dance Magazine,* for example, called it outmoded.[119] But P. W. Manchester felt that despite some weak spots (a "poetic" blowing of leaves and yet another lyrical impression of deer, both stale holdovers from earlier Massine ballets), the "choreography for the ensembles is masterly, with its strongly marked masculine and feminine characteristics. How beautifully, too, he uses the upper part of the dancers' bodies, with a fluid grace that ripples to the fingertips." She especially praised the pas de deux of the happy couple and a country dance for the moutaineers led by shepherds who "discover their love for each other with an awestruck, simple wonderment which Massine transcribes beautifully into a folk dance idiom."[120] And Ann Barzel wrote: "Massine's reaction to the music is entirely emotional and his choreography is concerned with evoking emotion rather than with making formal design."[121] She agreed with Manchester that the final movement was the weakest: "The first three movements are epic in poetry and grandeur and epitomize the Symphonic Ballet at its best. The fourth movement, The Brigands, is a letdown. The episode is confusing and choreographically underdone. If Massine could be recalled to give *Harold in Italy* a worthy concluding movement it might be the summation of his credo on symphonic ballet, a truly monumental work."[122]

Seeing a rehearsal film of *Harold in Italy* thirty years after its creation, Jack Anderson commented on the "impressive ensemble movement. But," he added, "on first viewing, the principal trouble seems to be Harold himself"—a role to which perhaps only Massine himself could have done justice. "Not only does he appear to be the stock Romantic poet, and a rather droopy, soggy one at that; choreographically speaking, he has little to do except make overblown gestures. However, if one adjusts to such attitudinizing, then the presence of Harold becomes not only dramatically, but kinetically interesting. For with his slow, steady, meditative gestures and his periods of immobility, he becomes the ballet's focal point, the weight of his presence serving as a contrast to the ensemble's restlessness."[123]

Denham regarded his renewed collaboration with Massine as a success, and offered to make him the company's permanent artistic consultant, which would require that he "make one or more trips abroad for the purpose of collecting artistic materials for new productions, rehearsing our company, creating new productions for us, etc."[124] But Massine longed to remain in Italy, his spiritual home.

In 1955, however, Massine again crossed the sea, this time to South America as guest choreographer for the ballets of the Teatro Colón in Buenos Aires and the Teatro Municipal in Rio de Janeiro. His affiliation with the Teatro Colón had a tremendous impact on the Argentine ballet world, which considered him the greatest living dance personality. As the prestigious critic Fernando Emery wrote in 1955: "It is true that Europe and America have other creators. Balanchine, Lifar, Robbins, Lander, Christensen. . . . But for those who know and remember, Léonide Massine, through the years . . . still represents the unreachable zenith of classical dance."[125]

Between 1948 and 1955 Massine had revived eight works for the Colón: *Le Tricorne, Capriccio espagnol, Symphonie fantastique, Rouge et noir, Seventh Symphony, Gaîté parisienne, Jeux d'enfants,* and *Choreartium.* Now he was to create his first original production for the company, *Usher,* based on Edgar Allan Poe's *The Fall of the House of Usher.* Its score, by the Argentinean Roberto García Morillo, had been composed for the Colón but never had been used.

Usher was a return to a highly expressionistic neoromanticism reminiscent of *Symphonie fantastique.* However, despite several phantasmagoric scenes, *Usher* centered on three human protagonists: Roderick; his sister, Madeleine; and the Poet, who served as narrator. The group scenes appear and recede as brief visions in the protagonists' hallucinatory drama. Consequently the memorable choreographic qualities of *Usher* were to be found not in the ensemble groups (which in *Symphonie fantastique* were organically linked to the allegorical main characters) but in the long solos and pas de deux of the three principals, who most of the time were alone on stage. The highlights were the lengthy and acrobatic pas de deux: one with Roderick and the Poet (in which Massine anticipated the male pas de deux of the 1960s and 1970s), and two featuring Roderick and Madeleine, which disturbed both audience and critics by their implied incestuous eroticism. According to the critic Dora Kriner:

The combination of two techniques, classical and modern, provokes unexpected tension. Technically the use of elongation, that is to say beginning a choreographic combination with the torso excessively bent instead of straight and then developing the body into a classical figure . . . demands a calculated effort different from the customary. This play of imbalance that must be performed in an abrupt way creates in the space an angular and severe design that surprises us and which can produce various states of anguish.[126]

The technical as well as the expressive and interpretive demands of the roles were tremendous and were brilliantly met by José Neglia (as Roderick), Jorge Tomin, and Maria Ruanova. (When the Teatro Colón Ballet presented the work in Paris in 1960, Neglia was awarded a special prize from the city for his interpretation.) After the premiere, Fernando Emery wrote:

In his untiring search for new possibilities, Massine gives us moments of great pathetic intensity: Roderick's first three poses as he lies on his bed, his body tensed up like a bow that is being violently stretched; the convulsive, epilepticlike gait of the servant who opens the doors of the castle to him; the flowing duet of the two friends, in which the two premiers danseurs perform real acrobatic feats with a show of outlandish gestures; Roderick's and Madeleine's pas de deux; . . . the great frightening epileptic scene, so reminiscent of the sacred trembling of the Chosen Maiden in The Rite of Spring; *and the last grand scene in* Usher—*all of these combine to make out of Massine's new choreography a very vivid, tremendously dramatic and suggestive ballet. . . .*

Among the possible objections which one could bring up are the excessive complexity of the choreography and that the pantomime gestures do not always seem accessible to the public's understanding.[127]

For most dancers who performed the ballet, the pas de deux and the solos were bona fide choreographic challenges.[128]

FROM BUENOS AIRES MASSINE went to Rio de Janeiro, where he revived six old works (*Boutique, Tricorne, Gaîté, Présages, Capriccio espagnol,* and *Beau Danube*) with an impressive roster of guest stars (Franklin, Chauviré, Eglevsky, Maria Tallchief, Lupe Serrano, Michael Lland) and created a rather uninspiring *Hymn à la Beauté,* "based on a poem by Baudelaire, with a score by the Brazilian composer Francisco Mignone, and scenery by Georges Wakhevitch. The spirit of Baudelaire's beautiful poem evoked a stream of dramatic images, which took the form of scenes portraying Faith, Murder, and First Love. Each episode was chore-ographed within the context of the poem."[129]

ALTHOUGH IN THE SECOND HALF of the 1950s Massine contin-ued to revive earlier ballets, requests for original works declined signifi-cantly. More and more companies were launching, or associating themselves with, their own choreographers, and the generation of new talent that had begun to emerge in the 1950s was impressive. Other trends were also becoming apparent. The taste of the public was moving away from Massine's stylized, overly detailed, and distinctly personal story ballets and toward neoclassicism. Moreover, an elaborate Massine production could be mounted only by major opera houses, many of which were experiencing fiscal difficulties. And not only was Massine himself an expensive acquisition, so were his chosen collaborators—a matter in which he expected carte blanche. Most insidiously of all, Massine's unsuccessful works had begun to create for him a dubious rep-utation. In his advancing years he was looked upon as an artist who stood for an outdated aesthetic. His name might still bring prestige to a ballet company, but the demand was more and more fulfilled by revivals; in undertaking these, a troupe could offer its audience not only the great Massine—a legend who was still performing—but also the mas-terly accomplishments of such artists as Picasso, Derain, Stravinsky, and Falla.

The last four years of the 1950s saw only two new Massine produc-tions, *Mario e il mago* and *Don Juan. Mario,* which was premiered at La Scala on February 25, 1956, brought Massine together with the Italian the-ater and film director Luchino Visconti. The gestation of the ballet dates back to 1951, when Visconti met Thomas Mann, one of his idols, at the home of the writer Alba de Céspedes. Visconti already had the idea of adapting Mann's novella *Mario and the Magician*—whose theme was the psychology of fascism and the failure of willpower—into a two-act opera-ballet. He discussed his concept with Mann, who welcomed the idea; and upon Mann's agreement that the project was properly de-scribed as a "choreographical action," a contract was signed on August 27, 1951.[130]

The music for the new work was commissioned from Franco Man-nino, Visconti's brother-in-law, the scenery and costumes from Lila de Nobili, and the choreography from Massine.

Mario e il mago had first been scheduled to premiere at La Scala in

1954 but was canceled due to Visconti's wish to crowd the stage with bicycles in one scene. In a recent production of the opera *La città in cam-
pagna,* the La Scala audience had booed the appearance of a car on
stage,[131] and the management felt it prudent to postpone the production
until Visconti agreed to reduce the number of bicycles.

Mario e il mago was a hybrid of dance, mime, song, and pure dramatic speech, a grandiose spectacle that from the moment it began took
the audience's breath away. As the curtain went up on the first scene, a
railroad gate came down; soon a train passed through, emerging from
the right wing, and Mario, played by the French dancer Jean Babilée,
rushed to the gate looking for a girl. Placing one leg over the gate, he
suddenly flew off on it and disappeared through the sky, only to reappear
moments later, flying on a bicycle, which eventually landed on stage.

Babilée, one of the most fascinating male dancers of the postwar
era, had met Massine briefly in London in 1949 when both artists participated in a gala in honor of Nijinsky. Babilée had been surprised back then
to learn that Massine, who he thought had retired long before, was still
dancing. Watching him perform the Miller's dance from *Le Tricorne,* Babilée was overwhelmed; Massine was "magical, especially his sense and
control of the stage whether he was moving or still."[132] When he was
asked in 1954 to create the role of Mario, Babilée eagerly accepted the invitation to collaborate with "this legendary master,"[133] and when work
began at La Scala he was constantly astonished: "Massine was prodigious," he recalled. "Very intelligent, and every movement he created
was not only interesting but new, unusual. Gestures were at times stylized, unnatural, and there was always this quality of surprise in what he
did, because nothing was evident or obvious. This of course made the
choreography very difficult, because one had to really understand the
movement process."[134]

Babilée found Massine's originality and richness of gesture and
movement a wonder: "In *Mario e il mago* there was a sort of world tour—
India, China, etc.—and the movements that Massine created for these
pastiche dances were fascinating, as if he had been able to extract the
essence to produce his own personal evocation that was poetic, magical,
and at times mysterious. It was like a modern *Thousand and One Nights.*
He was extremely clever with gesture. Even the choreography that utilized simple daily gestures had a very strong theatrical value, and could,
when needed, sustain an emotional and symbolic content."[135] Discussing
the choreography of *Mario e il mago* more than thirty years after its creation, Babilée still remembered it as something "extremely personal,

beautiful, and unique—something that today would be striking and contemporary. Beauty and true art are never dated."[136]

Babilée found working with Massine deeply inspiring, and even, at moments, charmingly impromptu. At age sixty-one Massine "showed everything himself, and that had an incredible force. Although he always seemed very distant, and he valued the quality of silence while working, he also developed a special working rapport. Once he showed this variation which was extremely difficult technically and interpretation-wise, for it depicted all the essence of Mario's character. I was astounded. I worked very hard to master it, and when I finally did assimilate and understand it, I could see that it gave him as great a pleasure as it did me. Once during a rehearsal of his *Pulcinella,* which was staged for La Scala after Mario, I was dancing Massine's original role, and he made me repeat various times the same difficult variation. When I ended I was so exhausted and pale that I thought I was going to faint. He looked at me and like a robot gave me a shot of whiskey from a flask which he had in his pocket."[137]

Babilée, enthralled, felt that he and Massine had developed a solid working relationship. But their communication stopped there. "He was a solitary character. He was always in complete control, did not show emotions, and never wasted a minute on anything superfluous to work.

"Once, after we had already worked in *Mario,* I was on the La Scala stage rehearsing one of my ballets when I saw Massine enter with his black suitcase. I stepped out of the rehearsal to greet him and he explained that he was on his way to Paris from Rome, but had a few hours in Milan before catching the train. He wanted to work! I gave him the keys to my dressing room. He changed into his practice clothes and came to a corner of the stage to do his barre. While he was doing his demi-pliés and battements he was completely immersed in reading a book. When he finished, everyone on stage applauded. He simply left."[138]

Lila de Nobili, the designer of *Mario,* admired Massine's "exceptional capacity for work, his incredible concentration on his choreography, his complete control of the company—something that gave me the impression that I was having a chance to experience to a small degree the working spirit of Diaghilev's Ballets Russes."[139]

The working relationship between Visconti and Massine seemed to be based on mutual artistic respect. The *Mario* concept was in many ways similar to that of *Carosello napolitano* in its eclectic mixture of pure theater, rhythmic pantomime, song, cinematic technique, and choreography, all set to music except for the spoken dialogue of Cipolla, the Magician, played by the renowned actor Salvo Randone. (Babilée, as Mario, spoke only one word: "Sylvia.") The scenes without spoken dialogue or dance, set at the café or the beach, were completely cinematographic, filled with Visconti's beautiful, evocative, and languid images as well as the eloquent rhythm characteristic of his later films, particularly *Death in Venice.*

The collaboration between Visconti and Massine went very smoothly. According to Babilée, they discussed the concept of the scenes that Massine was to arrange, but Visconti never became involved with the dances in any way. Visconti's aesthetic, a sort of supra-realism, blended well with Massine's idiosyncratic movements to produce a stylized, multilevel story in which symbolism played a major role. For Lila de Nobili, achieving harmony in Visconti's realist mise-en-scène was not easy, but observing Massine and Visconti work together was "the privilege of witnessing the encounter of two heavenly stars."[140] The charismatic Babilée gave a performance that "was remarkable for its psychological penetration, telling mime and outstanding vigorous dancing."[141] The production won La Scala's coveted Diaghilev Prize.

Before Massine rejoined La Scala in 1959, he was approached by Michael Powell to collaborate with him on an English-Spanish co-production, *Luna de miel (Honeymoon).* The film, which was shot entirely in Spain, revolved around a ballerina's honeymoon journey through the Iberian Peninsula, with the leading roles taken by Ludmilla Tcherina and Antonio. Besides various vignettes featuring Spanish folk dancing, the film included two main dance numbers: Falla's *El amor brujo,* with choreography by Antonio, in which Massine appeared in his own creation of the role of the Spectre, and *Los amantes de Teruel,* led by Tcherina and Antonio as the tragic lovers, with choreography by Massine to the music of Mikis Theodorakis. (In this ballet most of the crowd scenes were staged by Powell; Massine was responsible mainly for the solos and pas de deux.) At the 1959 Cannes Film Festival the film was awarded the Special Prize of the Commission Supérieure Technique. Yet despite excellent performances (which aficionados still enjoy), the film has never been regarded by dance or film critics as more than a colorful travelogue.

In early 1959 Massine was once more associated with La Scala, where he staged *Laudes evangelii* and the dances for Glinka's *A Life for the Tsar* and also produced a new ballet, *Don Juan.*

Gluck's original score of *Don Juan* was first choreographed by Gasparo Angiolini, a master of eighteenth-century *ballet d'action,* in Vienna in 1761. While Angiolini's scenario derived from both Molière and a version of the story by Tirso de Molina, Massine's adaptation had primarily Molière as its literary source. Massine writes:

> *I wanted to present Don Juan not simply as a romantic adventurer, but as a man in conflict with himself. In the ballroom scene I had the advantage of working to some of Gluck's finest music. After the guests had left I made Don Juan and Doña Elvira linger together in the deserted ballroom. The ghost of Doña Elvira's father had already appeared to Don Juan, and the lovers were intensely aware of the hopelessness of their situation. At this point I created a pas de deux which expressed both Doña Elvira's sadness and the insoluble conflicts within Don Juan's character. In the final scene, where Don Juan is driven to desperation by the tormenting furies and demons, the ghost of Doña Elvira appeared, holding a skull, and danced round him as he lay distraught on the ground. For this dance I used the haunting strains of the Siciliana, played on the oboe, with which Don Juan had serenaded her in the opening scene. This heightened the pathos of Don Juan's final condemnation and made a dramatic and ironic conclusion to the ballet. It was a complex work to choreograph.*[142]

The favorable reception of *Don Juan* by the press testifies that though Massine's work of the 1950s was at times inconclusive and uneven, he could still produce ballets of arresting quality. Although Robert Laurence, writing in the *Saturday Review* of May 16, 1959, found the final scene relatively weak,* he thought the ballet in general

> *a triumph of theatrical invention, extraordinarily vivid, dramatically, and cohesive architecturally. . . . [Massine's] wonderful treatment of the central character, both in motion and repose, is quite the equal—in another sphere—of da Ponte's, or perhaps even superior. This Don Juan of Massine is no mere philanderer, gripped by a last-minute terror, but a poetic spirit constantly at war with himself. . . . The pathos of [Doña Elvira], the tragic conflict in the soul of Don Juan, have been here projected incandescently by Massine in a pas de deux which is the legitimate, tragic heir of the brilliant grand duo in Gaîté. I had thought this kind of enkindling*

---

* By now the last scenes in Massine's ballets had become generally the weakest. During his later years he became so extremely meticulous and detailed in his choreography that by the time rehearsals for a ballet reached its last scene, the dancers were exhausted, the time schedule was very limited, and the rehearsals became a literal tour de force.

*emotion lost forever to theatrical dance; but there it is, burning up the stage
and the audience unashamed, elemental, imaginative in the highest. . . .
Massine the creator, like the Phoenix, has risen from his own ashes.*[143]

Don Juan was Massine's first ballet with La Scala's rising star Carla
Fracci, the Doña Elvira. They would work together in three more productions the following year, the first of which, the one-act *Fantasmi al
Grand Hotel,* premiered at La Scala on February 11, 1960, with Fracci and
Mario Pistoni in the leading roles. The scenario, by Dino Buzzati (who
also designed the costumes and scenery), was the story of a country girl
who arrives in the big city in search of fortune and is trapped instead by a
group of gangsters headquartered in the hotel. She is accused of the
murder of a gang leader but is saved from death by a mysterious man. At
the end they both escape as the hotel collapses.

Although *Fantasmi al Grand Hotel* was an important production,
Massine's time and energy were by then being taken up by the planning
and organization of his most ambitious undertaking in many years. In
1959 he had been approached by the industrialist Ariodante Borelli to act
as artistic director of the Fifth International Festival of Ballet at Nervi in
Genoa the following year. Previously, the festival had been composed of
international guest companies, but this year Massine was asked to put together a ballet company from scratch, with a guarantee of complete
artistic control over roster and repertory. With substantial financial backing from the festival, the municipality of Genoa, and various industrial-
ists, including Borelli himself, Massine was to embark on his last truly
spectacular project.

At a press conference held at Maxim's in Paris, Massine declared
that the Nervi Festival was nothing less than a "resurrection of the Diaghilev era."[144] Certainly it represented his own attempt to return to the
Diaghilev aesthetic of total theater—of ballet as a fusion of all the arts,
of literature, music, and painting—and to reproduce the creative momentum of the artistic teamwork that the impresario had fostered. Massine believed himself to be the last bastion of a form of theater he feared
was on the brink of extinction, and Nervi was to be a reiteration of his
own aesthetic.

The festival repertory included a revival of Fokine's *Schéhérazade;*
two ballets by young choreographers (Maurice Béjart's *Alta tensione* and
Jack Carter's *Señor de Manara*); and five Massine works: three new productions—*La commedia umana, Bal des voleurs,* and *Il barbiere di Siviglia*—
and revivals of *Choreartium* and *Le Beau Danube.* The variety of the

Massine

Massine repertory testifies to his eclecticism, a survey of the broad range of genres he had explored throughout his career. Of primary importance was *Choreartium,* his earliest example of purely abstract choreography. However, it would be a mistake to regard Nervi as an act of nostalgia, for at its heart nostalgia is an attempt to recapture a fantasy, a feeling or event that never took place. Massine acknowledged the past but never ceased to keep the future firmly in his sights.

Rehearsals began in April. The fifty-five-member company assembled in Nervi was the cream of a new generation of talented dancers from all over Europe: Carla Fracci, Ethery Pagava, Duska Sifnios, Yvonne Meyer, Tessa Beaumont, Milorad Miskovitch, Paolo Bortoluzzi, Vasili Sulich. The roster also included Lorca and Tatiana Massine and five ballet masters: Leon Woizikowski, Tatiana Leskova, René Bon, Harry Haythorne, and Massine's wife. *Ballet Annual* in London dubbed the new company the "Italian Renaissance."[145]

Nervi instantly became an international art center reminiscent of Monte Carlo in the days of the Ballets Russes. The list of personalities arriving in Genoa was impressive: Georges and Nora Auric, Alfred Manessier, Jean Anouilh, the theatrical designer Jean-Denis Malclès, the *costumière* Barbara Karinska, and the French critic Irène Lidova were among them. The designer André Beaurepaire, who previously had collaborated with Bérard, Kochno, Cocteau, Petit, and Ashton, had never experienced "such a collaboration of artists, enthusiasm, collective energy and extravagance in spending in such elaborate productions and lavish designs."[146]

Massine's work reached new levels of compulsion. According to Vladimir Augenblick, his personal assistant, the choreographer worked obsessively and kept everyone else going at his pace. He drove himself to an almost frenetic degree and expected the same level of commitment from the others. He would arise at 5:00 a.m. to prepare his work; company classes began at 8:45, and rehearsals went on until midnight. When exhaustion overcame him during the long sessions, he would take a short nap in the studio, on a cot behind a screen. Augenblick saw him imposing his "iron willpower" on everyone. "Once, with a 40-degree [centigrade] fever he did his customary barre and then called his technical assistant, Carlo Faraboni, to give him instructions about the ballets."[147]

If the dancers could hardly believe how hard they were being driven, they were even more astonished by Massine's own Promethean determination. Sulich felt that for any choreographer the creation of one major work such as *La commedia umana* was sufficient for a season; but

Massine was not only producing *three* new works, he was responsible for the entire enterprise. He displayed incredible physical energy for a man in his mid-sixties. Sulich remembers that Massine once performed the Hussar's waltz in *Le Beau Danube* with full force to show Miskovitch how it should be danced. The dancers looking on were duly impressed but a little anxious, fearing that he might not make it through the demonstration.[148]

Although he was extremely patient with the dancers, Massine remained aloof. He was becoming even more distant, disconnected from those around him, more impenetrable and isolated. Lorca summed up his experience working with his father as "sweat and steps—little human contact."[149] Lidova, too, observed how detached and hermetic he was, and his almost inhuman disregard for the needs and limits of others. She was astounded by his habit of working eighteen hours a day.[150]

Nevertheless, the Massine mystique was unquestionably in full force. Beaurepaire saw him as almost mythical, an artist whose "attitude about work, his complete immersion in himself, and his aura of inaccessibility enhanced the dimension of a legendary personality." Moreover, he sensed that Massine was conscious of the effect that he had on others. Obsessive and distant as he found Massine, collaborating with him was a fascinating lesson in theater art. "Especially one was in awe of his culture," said Beaurepaire, "of his knowledge about painting and art and history."[151]

The first ballet premiered at Nervi was *La commedia umana,* the idea for which dated back to 1954, when Massine had planned to collaborate with the writer Curcio Malaporte on a new ballet for the Maggio Musicale Fiorentino. That project did not materialize; but when preparations for Nervi began in 1959, Massine, through the good offices of Francesco Siciliani, asked the Italian scholar and Boccaccio specialist Vittore Branca to assist him in adapting eight episodes from the *Decameron* for a ballet scenario.

La commedia umana was intended to be the festival's magnum opus and the most monumental undertaking of Massine's career. It would run more than two hours and boast forty-seven solo roles plus corps de ballet. Inspired by Massine's beloved Quattrocento, it was to be a study/dance fresco depicting the universal human condition and celebrating the choreographer's bond with Italy's humanist tradition.

Massine's interpretation of the *Decameron* followed Boccaccio's idea that, as Branca explains in the program notes, the lives of men are governed by forces of Fortune, Love, and Ingenuity, and that the power of

Virtue—the force that will guide man towards self-realization—is greater than all three together. The ballet incorporated eight episodes in three acts, with a prologue and an epilogue. Act One, "The Triumph of Fortune," included the tales of Andreuccio and Ginevra. Act Two, "The Triumph of Love," featured the tales of Guardistagno and Nastagio. Act Three, "The Triumph of Ingenuity," told the stories of Peronella, Elena, and Calandrino. In the epilogue, "The Triumph of Virtue," the tale of Griselda preceded the ballet's finale.

To adapt such detailed narratives for dance was a daunting task. Massine made use of many of his choreographic techniques and styles— angularity, a contrast between flowing and staccato movements, ensemble counterpoint. He described the range of his choreography: from "varied and vigorous ensemble movements like those in the prologue to the tragic and comic dances of the second and third parts and the light, gay ensembles of the third and fourth."[152] *La commedia umana* was a study in form, language, and style. It was an indulgence in choreographic detail, a reaffirmation of his choreographic "baroquism." At a time in dance history when the choreographic line had been simplified and ballets had a more melodic physical allure and an easy sensuality, appreciating Massine's overwhelmingly rich choreography required a vigilant and attentive eye as well as the sustained collaboration of the viewer.

Owing in part to its longueurs and to its uneven quality, the work had a perplexing and disconcerting impact. According to Lidova, it possessed novel and brilliant moments but was too long, too scholarly an adaptation, and needed to be cut.[153] Sulich felt that the story was too detailed and complicated and the choreography too intricate, despite the fact that it was the work of an experienced craftsman; with the exception of some beautiful passages, such as Fracci and Adolfo Andrade's pas de deux, it lacked inspiration.[154] The reviewer for *Le Figaro* said of *Commedia*:

> *A grandiose medieval fresco takes place in a frame of greenery, a spectacle composed of dancing, sound, and lighting, of a vastness never before equaled. . . .*
>
> *The principal fault of the choreography is, without doubt, a relative disproportion among the various episodes; but Massine, besides possessing an innate theatrical sense, a very sure taste, knows how to direct the ensembles, how to juxtapose the feminine qualities to the virile dances, and to evoke, without the slightest trace of vulgarity, the farce or the cruel games of love set to fourteenth-century music.*[155]

A more negative review came from Clive Barnes (who saw the company later on, in Edinburgh, where, he felt that, in addition to the work's inherent problems, the dancers were underrehearsed):

> *In his vintage years Massine, in such a work as* The Three-Cornered Hat, *based on an Alarcón fable, showed an almost unbelievable ability to make a complicated story clear in ballet terms. But what he could do once, it appears he can now do no more, and certainly his* Commedia Umana *was quite incomprehensible without constant reference to the printed scenario. . . .*
>
> *The choreography . . . had a sort of competence in that it at least never quite petered out, yet it was so full of padding, so loaded down with triviality, so lacking in any real inspiration or originality that the total effect was crushingly dispiriting. In fairness there were a few patches of quality among some of the solos and pas de deux. . . .*
>
> *The one real quality of the ballet was in its suggestion of a genuinely medieval atmosphere, and this Massine sustained moderately well throughout the evening. In this he was helped by the music, which while in itself monotonous and unsuitable for choreographic purposes, had been based on authentic medieval airs. He was also assisted by the curiously stylized settings and costumes of Alfred Manessier. These designs—and there were dozens of sets and well over two hundred costumes—succeeded in conveying an appropriate sense of period while being in themselves quite modern.*[156]

In a later evaluation of *La commedia umana,* Alfio Agostini wrote: "Massine's choreography was now as far removed from the brilliant historical and folk characterizations of his youthful works as from the severe classicism of his symphonic ballets or the dense gestural symbolism of his mystical creations. In this late work it achieved a perfect balance between dance and mime, classical style and modern influences, choreographic substance and narrative clarity."[157]

Massine's second new production for the Nervi Festival was a one-act ballet based on Jean Anouilh's *Bal des voleurs,* a comedy with musical interludes that had first been produced in 1938, with decor and mise-en-scène by André Barsacq and incidental music by Darius Milhaud. The new production had music by Massine's old friend Georges Auric, and the scenery and costumes were by Jean-Denis Malclès, who had been proposed for the assignment by Anouilh. In his autobiography, Massine described the gestation of the ballet:

I was also anxious to include in my programme something French, original and contemporary, so I asked my daughter, who was well read in modern French literature, to find something suitable for me. When she suggested Anouilh's Bal des Voleurs *I read it at once, and was delighted by the iridescent wit of the dialogue and the delightfully satiric and amusing characters, immediately feeling that the play would offer me the right ingredients for a lighthearted but highly polished ballet. I wrote to Anouilh, who invited me to visit him in his charming apartment situated in one of the old squares of Paris. He was not at all what I expected. A slight, bespectacled man, his manner was precise and businesslike, quite unlike his light, witty plays. He was pleased to hear that I wanted to make* Bal des Voleurs *into a ballet; in fact, he told me, he had originally conceived it as a* comédie-ballet. *But he wanted to be sure that his characterizations would not be lost in adaptation, so we went carefully through the text together, discussing each character scene by scene. Many months later, when most of the programme for Nervi was already taking shape, there were still a number of questions in my mind about* Bal des Voleurs, *so I went to see Anouilh at Lausanne, where he was staying at the time, and we had another long talk. He made it clear that the choreography must emphasize the basic situation of the rich Englishwoman so bored by her idle life that she invites into her home three obvious thieves.*[158]

Although an elaborate production, *Bal des voleurs* was an ephemeral ballet, although it was revived by the Royal Ballet in 1963 when Carla Fracci (who created the role of the Englishwoman) made her company debut as a guest artist.

The third new Massine work presented at the festival was *Il barbiere di Siviglia*, the choreographer's homage to Rossini. Following the concept of Diaghilev's 1914 staging of Rimsky-Korsakov's *Le Coq d'or*, *Il barbiere* was danced on stage while the singers sang in the orchestra pit. Besides admiring Rossini's music and especially *Il barbiere*, Massine also wanted to produce this work because he

always felt that in the operatic version much of Beaumarchais's wit and humor evaporated because of the physical demands of the singing. In many scenes where the text obviously demanded movement, the singers had to stand perfectly still while rendering their arias. In our production the opera was sung from the orchestra pit, which meant that I was free to create movements and gestures which fully exploited the comic situations inherent in the dialogue. It was, however, an unusually heavy task for me

. . . since the method chosen for the production called for continual dancing and no pantomime.[159]

According to Beaurepaire, the opera's designer, Massine's concept was "that of a *fête du théâtre* as a sort of apotheosis of the opera buffa."[160] *Il barbiere* was a sumptuous production styled after the eighteenth century; one costume was more elaborate than the next. (All of them were executed by Lydia Douboujinsky, who, as she had done for *La commedia umana*, supervised most of the shopping for fabrics in France, England, Switzerland, and Italy.) The production was a luxurious theatrical pageant.

Once the festival ended, the Ballets Européens de Nervi, as the company was called, appeared at the Edinburgh Festival, where they presented *Schéhérazade*, *Le Beau Danube*, *La commedia umana*, and *Choreartium*. Even though there were other attempts to book the company, it soon disbanded.

According to Lidova, the whole enterprise was "an extravaganza that was proof that Massine had lost touch with reality and had lost his ability to organize and manage a company's finances. The working schedules were exhausting and draining, and he showed no regard for the expenditures. Besides a large company, there was a full orchestra and chorus from the Genoa opera; some of the leading singers came from La Scala, and there were three conductors. He brought designers and composers to Nervi, and even Madame Karinska had settled there for three months, where she opened an atelier especially to execute the costumes for some of the works. The productions were outrageously lavish and cost a fortune. After the festival ended it went into bankruptcy, and the following year there was no festival. Massine's ideas were so impractical that he hoped to keep it as a company without realizing that most dancers were under contract to other companies, such as La Scala, and had been on leave just for the summer. The scale of the productions and the expenses of the enterprise made it prohibitive for any producer to undertake the project."[161]

Nervi was Massine's last adventure as a choreographer and artistic director of any company. The mixed critical reception of the works presented at Nervi dealt the final blow to his already faded reputation. Clive Barnes wrote:

Unquestionably the slump in Massine's reputation from its pre-war pinnacle has been among the truly remarkable aspects of post-war ballet. Once, and only a few years ago at that, regarded as the world's leading choreographer, Massine has now slid so far down the slippery pole of fashion that to the young generation of balletgoers he is rapidly becoming little more than a name. A few of his ballets are still regularly performed in the repertoires of the world, yet I cannot help feeling that his fame is slowly diminishing into that of an historically important, but nevertheless comparatively minor figure. Such an assessment I feel does Massine a grave injustice. Although he occasionally was overestimated in his heyday, fashionable ballet opinion today tends to neglect him.

Looking at Commedia Umana *and also recalling Massine's other creations over the past twenty years or so, I cannot but regretfully record my opinion that creatively his powers have now dwindled away to little more than competence.*[162]

Thus, the grandiosity of Nervi inspired a chorus of fatal whispers that Massine had become hopelessly extravagant and self-indulgent, out of touch and perhaps permanently off his stride. After the festival he began to withdraw from the ballet world into self-imposed seclusion.

PART SEVEN

The Late Years

I want to make things as hard for myself
as they have been for anybody: only under
this pressure do I have a clear enough
conscience *to possess something few*
men have ever had—wings, so to speak.

—NIETZSCHE

Massine in rehearsal during the 1960s

CHAPTER 14

Moscow, June 1961–Borken, West Germany, March 1979

FOR MASSINE the following year, 1961, was one of homecoming and touching roots. Asked by the Soviet Export Film Company to produce a number of his ballets in the Soviet Union for distribution to American television, he returned to Russia, in June, after an absence of forty-seven years. Massine traveled by train with Lorca—he avoided planes whenever possible—while his wife flew ahead to Moscow. (Tatiana remained in France.)[1]

The sight of Moscow filled Massine with long-buried passions, sensations, and memories. The Massines stayed at the Metropole Hotel, the very place the eighteen-year-old dancer had first met Diaghilev in 1913. But its splendor was no more. "Its nineteenth-century grandeur had faded; the carpets were threadbare, the walls flaking, the porters had discarded their gold braid, the lobby was no longer thronged with princes and grand dukes but with American businessmen carrying briefcases, European diplomats, young Russian technocrats, and other workers obviously content with the present conditions of life."[2] Yet at first it seemed that the city of his youth had not changed as much as he had expected:

As I looked at the towers and walls of the Kremlin, the vast Red Square, and the gay onion domes of St. Basil's Cathedral, it was as if my childhood and youth were unrolling before my eyes like a film. When we passed the Theatre School I recognized the massive door through which I had been taken, nearly half a century before, for my first physical examination by Dr. Kazansky. A flood of memories came back to me: my first appearances in ballet, the Gogol and Ostrovsky plays, my painting classes with Anatoli Petrovich Bolchakov. . . .

I remembered that afternoon in 1914, and my uncertainty and confusion before making the great decision to leave Russia. I felt it was indeed written in my stars that I should meet Diaghilev. Destiny had played a big part in the pattern of my life. I thought of some of the curious circumstances that had affected the course of my career. If Nijinsky had not broken away from Diaghilev's company, if he had danced the role intended for him in La Légende de Joseph, *then Diaghilev would not have come in search of a new young dancer to create this part. If I had remained in Moscow I would perhaps have become a competent actor at the Maly instead of a choreographer. I might even have been killed in the Revolution. Then, for no reason, I found myself thinking of Galli, of my first view of it in 1917, of my decision to buy it. It seemed to me that it had always been more than just a place of refuge; it represented something in my life which I had yet to discover.*[3]

The first obligatory visit was to the Theater School, where arrangements had been made for Massine to practice each day in a rehearsal room that once had served as the school's dining room. Massine found it "strange to walk through my old school and find it so unchanged. I went from room to room, remembering the games we played and my classmates calling me 'the gypsy,' my first teacher, Domachov, in his crumpled dinner jacket, instructing us in the first five positions, and our visits to the Bolshoi for rehearsals."[4]

Of course the most emotional event of his Russian sojourn was the family reunion at Zvenigorod-Moskovsky. His brother Mikhail, now retired, had moved with his wife, Sophie, back into the old family dacha about forty miles from Moscow. Massine's sister, Raissa, now a widow living in southern Russia, had returned to the dacha to embrace her celebrated brother once again, and Mikhail and Sophie's two grown daughters, Helena and Eugenia, were there with their husbands and children. Massine's childhood took hold of him again and offered him a welcome solace.

> From the garden I could still see the lovely monastery of St. Saavo across the river, its lime-washed walls and cupola looking just as I remembered them; I was sad to hear that the bell tower had long been silent, the silver and brass bells having been melted down for ammunition in the last war. Also a row of suburban houses had been built in the village, ruining the atmosphere of our wooded hilltop. But our house remained unchanged, and everything was as I had left it: the dark red walls, the green roof, the little square sitting room with its comfortable chairs and its birchwood cupboard. I was thrilled to see the brass samovar on the table and the old-fashioned sink with its pump handle where as a child I had so often washed my hands and face. . . .
>
> After a quiet hour in the garden, I walked in the cool of the evening to put flowers on the graves of my parents* and of my brother Konstantin. I could hardly find their tombstones, the graveyard was so overgrown with long grass and weeds.[5]

Reunited for the first time in nearly half a century, the family indulged in unrestrained Slavic expansiveness. Over the years, and despite the distances, Massine had preserved his emotional ties to his kin. He had confided in them when he was in distress, especially in his youth, and during his years in the West he had helped them materially whenever possible. So the bonds were solid. But forty-seven years of separation had inevitably planted doubts in their minds as well, and Mrs. Massine noted with tenderness how very eager he was to be accepted by them again.[6]

Upon his return to Moscow, Massine was invited to sit in on classes at the Theater School. He also visited the Stanislavsky Museum as well as the Theater Museum, escorted by its founder's son, Yuri Bakhrushin.

> The framed pictures of actors at the Maly in Ostrovsky's and Gogol's plays brought back memories of playing juvenile roles with Rybakov, Sadovsky and Padarin, and I realized what a great influence these men had had on my career. From them I had learned the fundamentals of expressive gesture

---

* Of course Massine means his mother's grave; his father had been buried in Positano.

*and mimicry and a strong technique which later applied to my dancing
and choreography. I was very interested to see Petipa's original notebook.
Although his sketches were somewhat primitive, I had no difficulty in interpreting them, and could easily follow the patterns he had set down for
the pas seuls and pas de deux and for the intricate ensemble movements
with which he had so deftly filled the stage.*[7]

From Moscow the Massines went to Leningrad (the once and future St. Petersburg), a city Massine had visited only twice before, with
Diaghilev. He was delighted to find on the walls of the Hermitage Museum works by his friends Derain, Picasso, and Matisse which previously
had belonged to the private collections of the country's prerevolutionary
merchants.

Professionally, the trip home was not successful; contracts to make
the ballet films failed to materialize. Massine returned again in 1963, accompanied by his daughter. This second trip was not a business success,
either; and it was marred by the sudden death of Mikhail. Massine and
Tatiana attended the funeral in Zvenigorod-Moskovsky, which was like a
vignette of old Russia. Mikhail was buried with full military honors, and
as the cortege slowly made its way to the cemetery, family and friends
followed the open black casket with its red velvet interior. Snow fell on
Mikhail's corpse and the procession of uniformed men and women
wrapped in black fur.[8]

Undaunted, Massine next tried Western Europe, where he plunged
into an exhaustive work schedule. But aside from a 1966 *Nutcracker* for
French television and various opera ballets for La Scala (where he also
staged his own version of *Les Noces* at the Piccola Scala),[9] new Massine
productions were rare throughout the remainder of the 1960s. (Among
the La Scala productions, however, was a joint choreographic effort with
Lorca of Rousseau's opera-ballet *Le Devin du village*.) Mostly, Massine
mounted Diaghilev revivals—for the Royal Ballet, La Scala, the Cologne
State Opera Ballet, the Vienna Opera Ballet, and the Ballet du XXE Siècle.
These revivals sometimes provoked decidedly mixed reactions, partly because contemporary dancers had trouble understanding and immersing
themselves in Massine's style, in mastering the dramatic and interpretive
demands of a Massine role. But even more troublesome was the conflict
that had arisen among dance writers, as historical sensibility clashed
head-on with critical response. Some critics, such as Mary Clarke and
Richard Buckle in England, appreciated these works within their historical context; others dismissed them as hopelessly dated. Massine's early

aesthetics and idiosyncratic choreography differed so drastically from the predominant trends of the day that a generation of dance critics had sprung up who were indifferent or hostile to works that only a few years earlier had been hailed as groundbreaking. Some critics charged that even in his prime he had been "overestimated" by his contemporaries—a judgment often voiced by Clive Barnes, among others.

Although offers for Massine's services had fallen off considerably, he was a compulsive worker who could not remain idle. Two new projects absorbed his time: he began to work more systematically on his theory of choreography, a project he had been mulling over for decades, and he began to dream of converting Galli into an international art center.

Massine's fascination with dance notation, which he believed was essential to preserve choreography, had been born at the Moscow Theater School, where he was the best pupil in the notation class of Maria Gorshkova. Back in 1917, though he was excited by the idea of filming his ballets for posterity, Massine had confided to Anatoli Petrovich his hope that "cinema will not replace choreographic notation."[10] Now, in the deep autumn of his career, he returned to the search for a scientific method. Relying on Stepanov's notation, fully aware of the rules that govern the motion of the body, he concentrated on developing a theory that would serve not only as a method to record dance but as an aid in composition. As he painstakingly reviewed all of his choreographic notes since 1920, one question drove him:

What is choreography? And I had no answer to it. I was like a child designing pages and pages, volumes and volumes, lines and lines, but nothing, you see. Until I met Paul Hindemith. It is from Hindemith that I first put my foot on the ground. I saw that what is in music must also exist in dance. So I tried that, and from there on I had no difficulty. Just work, work, work until I get sort of a possibility to make it concrete. What it represents, how it moves, what is the result of postures. From there on I felt much better. No more hesitation. I can write and continue my research work. No more discouragement to find out what it is all about.

*And then I discovered Stepanov. It was [Nicholas] Sergeyev who gave me that book. He said look at it and maybe you will be interested. I knew the book and had even had it in school, but I had never really studied it.**

---

* It is conceivable that Massine's notation textbook at Theater School was Gorsky's fairly simplified version of Stepanov's work. This might explain why he could get by brilliantly in school without having studied it closely.

Now I grab at the book and read it. This is a brilliant work. Where Stepanov stops, I now continue. But it is he who invented it. The good of it is not just that it is a recording system—it is a system that permits you vertically to compose and see what we have in every bar. It has a magic effect. By that, you see at once what the time signature is, you see at once whether it fits contrapuntally or not, and you see if in your body you get something to look at, whether it be dynamics, melody, dance or harmonic posture. And you get your posture in the right place, like in music, where the melody often needs heavy support and where the chords appear. The same process in composing the choreography. It is immense what Stepanov invented, you see.[11]

In the course of expanding his own thinking, Massine reabsorbed the theories of Pecour, Rameau, and Blasis, theoreticians he had encountered earlier in his career. He now had to see them afresh as he delved deeper "into the realm of harmonic and dynamic progression in choreography."[12]

Most of the actual writing of his theory of choreography was accomplished on Galli. Life on the islands was austere, with an almost spartan, ascetic quality. By the 1960s Massine was living in the renovated fourteenth-century tower. He believed in physical discipline, rising early in the morning, taking his customary daily barre, swimming twice a day, walking, hiking, working most of the day, then retiring early. Vladimir Augenblick recalls an episode that attests to the physical fitness of the seventy-one-year-old Massine. One day, as the boat to Galli sailed toward the islands, a storm rose up that was so violent the two men feared for their lives, but it subsided, and they arrived safely on the main island. As soon as they docked, Massine took off his clothes and swam to one of the smaller islands and back—a total distance of two hundred meters. The feat was clearly a sudden burst of rejoicing in his own capacity for survival as well as a reaffirmation of life when the end had seemed so near. This event also illustrates Massine's visceral rapport with the most basic aspects of nature. Though inclined to contemplation and analysis, he never relinquished a strong physical connection to his environment— a leitmotif from his childhood days at Zvenigorod-Moskovsky to his ageless form astride the landscape of Galli.[13]

During this period Massine wrote his memoirs, *My Life in Ballet*, published in 1968. *Massine on Choreography* followed in 1976. (When he died in 1979 he was working on a second volume of theory and practice, *Elaborations and Variants*.)

Massine with his students on the Isole dei Galli during the 1960s. The isles of Rotonda and Gigante are in the background.

Massine had begun seriously considering the idea of converting Galli into an international art center as early as 1963. He wanted musicians, choreographers, painters, and writers to be able to meet in the spirit of the Diaghilev tradition and create new works "away from the encroaching materialism of modern life."[14] He had two goals: to safeguard Diaghilev's ballet aesthetic, which he feared was being obliterated, and to reaffirm his own. For Massine, the survival of ballet as total theater became an engrossing crusade. A cultural center on Galli would be his final tribute to Diaghilev, the greatest any disciple could offer.

Surely this goal was in part a humble attempt to honor his artistic forebear. But was it also an acolyte's subtle reworking, and rewriting, of the past? It was true that Diaghilev's aesthetic sprang from a view of art and ballet that Massine himself continued to elaborate until the end of his life.[15] But now Massine's memories were filtering out all negative aspects of Diaghilev's character in favor of his finer qualities, which Massine idealized to almost cultlike dimensions. It was the tribute of the apostle through whom the master achieves his surest immortality. Anyone who knew Massine could also, if he simply looked deeply enough, know a piece of Diaghilev as well. Such veneration exalted Diaghilev at the same time it showed the world a shining path to him, and that path was Massine. Reverence and ultimate control of the revered one were deftly combined; the master was at last mastered.

Massine revived *Parade* in 1964 for Béjart's Ballet du XXE Siècle. It was the first time that he had revived the work since its final performance with Diaghilev's company. As he did so, he stressed over and over in the press the ballet's importance as a visual manifesto of Diaghilev's idea of the total theatrical work of art, of the balanced, equally important roles that decor, choreography, music, and literature play. In his memoirs Massine paid a posthumous homage to Diaghilev, and in later conversations and interviews he constantly relived their aesthetic relationship. At one point he told *Dance Magazine*: "I certainly regret having argued with him. A great genius he was. Now, the more distant he is the more I realize his principles and the way he conducted his artistic life are not to be deviated from." He added that Diaghilev "was intransigent. Uncompromising . . . he was like a comet—a star. Nothing like him will ever appear again. Meeting him changed my life and also changed the course of art in the West. Diaghilev was a perfectionist. Live life as it ought to be—not as it is, he would say."[16] It was Massine's concern for this legacy that prompted him to spend the last two decades of his life championing Diaghilev productions by Fokine and Nijinsky; he was personally responsible for revivals of *Petrouchka* and *L'Après-midi d'un faune.*[17]

ꙅꙅꙅꙅ

THE MASSINE FAMILY'S solidarity was beginning to deteriorate. Tatiana and Lorca ventured out to organize their own company, Les Ballets Europeéns—a natural step towards independence, but in this case accelerated by the choreographer's excessive demands. Massine's often tyrannical relationship with his family was due in part to the exigencies of his creative work. But even in the personal sphere he imposed upon himself and his environment, just as Diaghilev had, rigorous intellectual formulae by which he measured everything, from aesthetic issues to human relations. The resulting tensions were at times unbearable.

In 1963 Massine went to revive *Le Tricorne* in Cologne, where, in a café, he met Hannelore Holtwick, a Bayer Aspirin employee who offered to be his German interpreter and soon became his assistant and lover. Their child Peter was born in Switzerland in 1964, followed a year later by a second son, Theodor, who was born in Germany. Massine bought a house in Weseke, Germany, where he would stay with Holtwick and the children when he was not traveling to fulfill artistic commitments. In 1968 he and his wife were granted a divorce by a French court, yet he would not marry Holtwick until just before his death.

In addition to reviving his old ballets, Massine gave a great deal of his time to teaching. In 1968 he was invited to teach his theory of chore-ography at the Royal Ballet School in London, and in 1969 at Pittsburgh's Point Park College. By the 1970s his assignments would include several summer programs and workshops in Europe and the United States, where he also gave lecture-demonstrations and improvised choreogra-phy in front of an audience.

An important period of revivals began in 1969, when Massine staged *Le Tricorne* for the City Center Joffrey Ballet, the first time he had worked with an American company since 1954. The Massine association gave a serious boost to Robert Joffrey's prestige as a ballet director with a keen sense of historical consciousness. The company's thorough and faithful revivals of twentieth-century classics won acclaim in the 1970s and 1980s from a new generation of ballet critics who believed in letting the past speak for itself without making it accountable to the values and aesthetic principles of the present. Within the next few years Massine re-vived three more works for the Joffrey: *Le Beau Danube* (1972), *Parade* (1973), and *Pulcinella* (1974). *Parade* became a staple in the Joffrey reper-tory; indeed, today it remains the only American company where Mas-sine has been consistently represented. In the 1970s he would also stage major revivals for American Ballet Theatre, the Australian Ballet, the London Festival Ballet, the Royal Ballet, the Sadler's Wells, La Scala, and the Vienna State Opera Ballet.

The last major chapter in Massine's creative life opened in 1975, when he choreographed *Till Eulenspiegel* for his students at Point Park College. No offers to create new works from ballet companies were forthcoming, so he produced them in workshops, in which he could put into practice his concepts and theory of choreography. Unfortunately,

Till Eulenspiegel, with its slow rhythmic movements and choreographic asymmetry, was never performed outside of the rehearsal studio.

After reviving Nijinsky's *L'Après-midi d'un faune* with Romola Nijinsky for the Paris Opéra in 1976, Massine traveled to northern California to give a series of seminars at the invitation of Mary Otis Clark of the Rossmoor Ballet Guild. These seminars caused a stir in the Bay Area dance community, and Massine was invited back to the guild the following year.

In December 1976 he went to Palm Beach for the premiere of the newly organized ballet company Dancers, whose director, Dennis Wayne, hoped to commission a ballet from him. In Florida Massine met Ariane Csonka, an attractive young opera singer who managed two ballet studios in the area. Csonka fell under "the spell of his magical and mystical presence"[18] and soon became a supporter and collaborator who would accompany him in some of his travels. It is fascinating to note how the eighty-one-year-old Massine still exerted a seductive power over women, especially younger women. His enigmatic personality, larger-than-life allure, and almost Machiavellian sense of control never failed him until the very end of his life. Women gravitated to him until his death, and throughout his final years he continued to form intense relationships with them that provided him with emotional support, vitality, and renewed inspiration.

In the spring of 1977 Massine returned to the Bay Area to conduct a series of successful seminars and workshops in choreography. Again he was a hit, and a revival of *Le Beau Danube* for the San Francisco Conservatory of Ballet (now the Marin Civic Ballet) soon followed. Massine was beginning to find himself a force in the Bay Area ballet community, and to this end Fred and Elena Maroth became a constant source of support and friendship. Fred was a National Public Radio music producer, and Elena a onetime dancer from Cuba who now taught ballet. The Maroths became a sort of surrogate family for Massine during his sojourns in northern California, helping him to meet his professional commitments and serving as his assistants. He was also more than once a guest in their Oakland Hills home.

The summer of 1977 spent in Galli was productive. Massine invited Ariane Csonka and Susan Gieliotti-Ford, a dancer from the Palm Beach area, to join him on the island in June. Lorca and his wife joined them two weeks later. (Massine's personal guests stayed in the tower along with their host, while Lorca and his family were lodged in the main villa.)

As usual, life on Galli was disciplined, revolving around work and

Massine rehearsing in California during the 1970s

rest. After breakfast Ariane, Susan, and later Lorca (whom Massine, standing in a window, always summoned from the main villa with a megaphone) would join the choreographer in the tower's second-floor dance studio, where film and sound equipment stood ready to record each new choreographic session.[19] The first piece that Massine worked on, *The Inconstant Lover* (inspired by Shakespeare's poetry), was choreographed without music, although Massine later asked Csonka to improvise music to it in performance. *The Inconstant Lover* was a pas de deux staged on Ariane and Susan, and Csonka describes its creation as both a phenomenon and a revelation. "It was fascinating to see how he worked with both of us, even though we are both so different. To begin with, I am not a professional dancer and Susan is. . . . The movements he created for Susan and the mood that he gave to them absolutely depicted Susan's personality, while those he devised for me felt absolutely right. . . . The spirit of the characters reminded me of Ariadne and Zerbinetta in *Ariadne auf Naxos*.

"The choreography itself was slow, consisting of bodily interweaving. It was a pas de deux for two women who could have been lovers, friends, or any other kind of human relationship. We came together and parted, and yet Massine somehow showed through our gestures that upon parting we took along something of the other. She took with her some of my movements and I some of hers. It was so to the heart of life. Everything he did, even if it was abstract, was emotional, to the heart.

"Throughout the choreographic process he applied his theory of choreography to give us directions, since he could not actually show the movements. Yet he explained very little. The movements themselves would give the emotions, and he would only make a remark like, 'Surrender to it,' and in so doing he brought out my personality through his movements. He would give a movement that was so right for me that it was like finding my own center."[20]

Working with Lorca, Massine began to experiment with Bach's *Art of the Fugue*; Fred Maroth had recently given Massine a recording of it with a new orchestration by William Mallock. Massine also choreographed the Italian song "Se tu m'ami" on Lorca and Csonka, and Lorca found the wealth of movement that his father conceived astonishingly innovative.[21]

Csonka was touched by Lorca's compliance and patience with his father, who was never easy to work with or to please. In fact Lorca was spending most of his vacation time in the tower instead of with his family. Even his wife, a Béjart dancer who was pregnant at the time, joined some of the choreographic sessions.

But most rehearsal time was allocated to *Parisina,* a ballet based on Lord Byron's poem of the same name and set to Villa-Lobos's *Bachianas Brasileiras.* The piece had been commissioned in San Francisco by ballerina Natalia Makarova. The scenario revolved around Parisina's infidelity to her husband, Prince Ago of the house of Brunswick, with her son-in-law, Hugo. It was conceived by Massine and Csonka in three scenes: in the palace Ago discovers that Parisina has been unfaithful to him; in the garden the lovers meet and dance an ardent pas de deux; in the closing scene Parisina is executed. The sections of *Parisina* created in Galli were staged on Susan, and according to Csonka the choreography was beautiful and intensely emotional. "What was prominent in Massine's choreography was the image of this girl being caught in the agony of her guilt and remorse. . . . She danced out her passions as well as her memories of her love affair with her son-in-law and how he had loved her. At the end the guards came for her . . . Susan was standing in the middle of the studio and suddenly Massine had her listening to the guards coming and depicting her reaction when they finally came. He put all those feelings into physical motion. And then at the end, she went off with her arms behind her and head down as if they were dragging her off. Each minute detail was imbued with that emotion. It was very strong." [22]

In the autumn Massine began working with Makarova in San Francisco, but unfortunately their efforts came to nothing. It was unlikely that two such mercurial personalities could ever mesh. And Makarova simply could not accept the fact that *Parisina* had already been partially staged on someone else.

But being back in the Bay Area gave Massine the opportunity to resume work with the Marin Civic Ballet. He choreographed two new works for the company, *Venus and Adonis* and Mozart's *Bastien und Bastienne.*

During his final years Massine became an avid reader of poetry; *Venus and Adonis* was a pas de deux inspired by Shakespeare's poem of that name. Young Adonis, roving through the woods, comes upon Venus, who helplessly succumbs to his beauty. She bares herself to him in hopes of enticing him, but he turns from her, horrified. The choreography was in the simple and economical style of Massine's later oeuvre, stressing slow, sculptural movements rather than the staccato passages that had characterized his earlier work. He wanted very much to make a powerful connection with young, talented artists in the community, so he set the pas de deux to an electronic score commissioned from a young local composer. But Massine was still Massine, and he asserted his control by giving strict directives about length and measures for each section of the piece.[23] Unfortunately, as in the case of *Till Eulenspiegel, Venus and Adonis* was never performed outside the rehearsal room.

Late in life Massine took up yet another challenge: choreographing vocal compositions. Although Mozart's Mass in C Minor was one of the projects he longed to see realized, he knew that its scale was too vast for the resources of the Marin Civic Ballet. From Palm Beach, Csonka proposed the one-act opera *Bastien und Bastienne* instead and promptly brought its score to Massine in the Bay Area. They immediately began collaborating on the scenario.

Mozart's chamber opera centers on the shepherdess Bastienne and her lover Bastien; the only other character is the wise man/magician Colas, who ill advises the young lovers. (The three-character ballet also featured children playing a flock of sheep.) The ballet closely followed the opera's action, though it did manage to trim ten minutes from its forty-five-minute length.

Choreographing *Bastien und Bastienne* was made difficult by the working conditions. Massine had been invited by the Marin Civic Ballet to choreograph a full-length version of the Hans Christian Andersen story "The Red Shoes" (a work that, though he busied himself preparing for it, in the end never materialized). He was also peremptorily asked to donate to the company a second ballet, for which he was not to be paid. If this siphoning off of his energies weren't enough, when work on the Mozart piece got under way, the company's administrators had so poor an understanding of his requirements that they neglected to provide him with a rehearsal pianist. On top of that, it was *Nutcracker* season, so practically no rehearsal time was allocated to him.[24] It sometimes seemed that the company, rather than truly respecting Massine, only wanted the luster of his name. Massine, however, endured the annoyances with great dignity and was delighted with the artistic result. He hoped to recruit André Beaurepaire, with whom he had worked in Nervi, to design the ballet. Unfortunately, *Bastien und Bastienne* was never performed outside the studio. Yet according to eyewitnesses, especially the Maroths, the ballet was a first-rate addition to Massine's oeuvre.

Massine spent the Christmas holidays of 1977 with Hannelore and their children. In January 1978 he returned to the Bay Area, which he considered his working base. His life became more settled, due in great part to his devoted new personal assistant, twenty-five-year-old Mary Ann de

Vlieg. A native of Detroit, de Vlieg was studying linguistics at the University of California at Berkeley when she met Massine. She also held down a job as day supervisor of the Holiday Inn that Massine always stayed in when he visited the area.

One day, while he was staging *Le Beau Danube*, he approached de Vlieg with his easy, old-world grace. He kissed her hand, addressed her as "Madame," then extolled her diligence, efficiency, and discretion (he had taken particular notice of the fact that she rarely spoke with anyone). He promptly offered her a job. De Vlieg was knocked off her feet. Of course she had noticed this eccentric stranger, dressed in black and gray, of whom it was whispered around the hotel that he was Russian and a great man of ballet. His air of self-esteem and poised eminence suggested to her a recently fallen grand duke.

She began handling Massine's correspondence, accounts, and urgent business matters in the evenings.[25] Shortly she dropped out of college, quit her job, and, working as Massine's assistant from eight a.m. to midnight (with an afternoon break), became his most devoted and constant companion. In Diaghilev's manner, Massine provided for her room and board as well as all her personal travel expenses. But the salary he had promised her at the beginning of their association was never forthcoming (though when she needed money to buy her father a birthday gift, Massine delightedly handed it over at once). By now most of Massine's precious art collection had been sold, and de Vlieg soon realized that he was plagued with financial obligations that were quite beyond his means, including the caretakers' salaries on Galli, tuition for the children in Germany, taxes on the Swiss apartment, and heating bills for the house in Paris. Nevertheless, de Vlieg recalls, at difficult moments a royalty check for performances of his ballets in Vienna would miraculously arrive, or Massine would discover a forgotten Picasso drawing—stuck between the pages of an old book in his library—that could be sold. Thus was more than one financial crisis averted.[26]

The octogenarian Massine had conceded nothing to the coming of age, and de Vlieg quickly grew to appreciate his methodical, almost ritualistic physical regimen. He would rise early to do his Cecchetti barre, followed by a steam bath (a habit he had acquired at the Piešťany spa, which he still visited every three years), then rest in bed for forty-five minutes. Breakfast, the main meal of the day, varied according to the country he was in, though it always included freshly squeezed orange juice. As they rode in de Vlieg's car, he did not permit any conversation— he often wore a black eye mask—or radio playing, an act he considered disrespectful to the music as well as a distraction to the driver. In the afternoon he always took in healthy amounts of fresh air. De Vlieg would drive him into the hills, where to her amazement he would climb to the highest accessible spot. There he would sit with his eyes closed, in silence. (It seemed to her that he meditated.) He allowed conversation only if the matter was urgent or related directly to his work—a stricture, he claimed, that had also been insisted upon by Diaghilev. His days were usually occupied by near-compulsive work or study, along with the continual mapping out of new projects. He believed that as an artist he followed a path not chosen of his own free will but divinely ordained.

In 1978 Massine's schedule in the Bay Area was extremely hectic. He worked intensely with Fred Maroth to complete a television documentary on Diaghilev, and continued to conduct lecture-demonstrations. Igor Youskevitch and Walter Ducloux from the dance and music departments, respectively, of the University of Texas at Austin invited him to create a new work to inaugurate a new campus theater scheduled to open in December 1979. Massine chose to choreograph a version of Handel's *Messiah,* on which he began work with dancers from the Contra Mesa Ballet. De Vlieg later arranged for a group of modern dancers to work with him. These rehearsals were a great success, Massine felt, because the dancers seemed to grasp his style more readily than did ballet dancers, who he maintained were too stiff. Also that year, through the intercession of Fred Maroth, the Oakland Ballet commissioned from Massine a revival of *La Boutique fantasque* as well as a new work, which the choreographer decided would be a new version of *Le Soleil de nuit,* now titled *Snow Maiden.*

In the spring Tatiana Riabouchinska invited Massine to Los Angeles for the opening performances of the Southern California Ballet at UCLA, a company of which Riabouchinska is founder-director. The purpose of this invitation was to allow Massine to assess the young company and decide whether he wished to create a new work or revive an old one for it. The Massine-Riabouchinska reunion was poignant, and at the close of the master class he taught in her studio the pair performed the initial section of their mazurka from *Le Beau Danube* before the spellbound company and guests. The outcome of this trip to Los Angeles was to have been a 1979 revival of *Jeux d'enfants.* Miró was immediately contacted, declared himself thrilled by the prospect, and agreed to design a souvenir program for the occasion.[27]

After his usual summer in Galli, this time accompanied by Hannelore and the children, Massine revived *La Boutique fantasque* for the

Sadler's Wells touring company, then returned to the Bay Area to complete his work on *Snow Maiden,* which was scheduled for the following year.

Before leaving northern California in December 1978 Massine worked with a local pianist-composer, Bruce Nalezny, on an album for Terpsichore Records in Berkeley. Nalezny's original concept was to produce a ballet class record as a teaching aid, a proposal to which Massine objected, because he never had been interested in teaching basic ballet classes, only choreography.[28] Instead he selected five pieces to choreograph, which were notated according to Massine's own theory by a local dancer, Janet Karkowski, in the record's instruction booklet. Massine choreographed two additional pieces, a Tchaikovsky work for eight dancers and a solo dedicated to Nijinsky, which were not included in this album but were intended to appear on a second recording (which never came to pass).[29] These seven pieces were Massine's last choreographic works.

During the summer Massine had been taken seriously ill on Galli for a few days. Fearing the worst, he prepared a handwritten will. The episode took place during a storm, so it was difficult to get medical assistance to the island. After the crisis had passed, he never complained to de Vlieg about any pain or discomfort. He had a general physical examination and was declared in good health.

Massine returned to Germany to spend the Christmas holidays with Hannelore and the children. He planned to meet de Vlieg in New York afterwards. But de Vlieg remembers that at the airport, as he was departing for Germany, he somberly told her, "You'll never see me again."

In Germany Massine's condition—prostate cancer—worsened. In March de Vlieg received a telephone call in New York informing her that he was gravely ill. She immediately flew to Germany and went directly to the hospital in Borken. "You must hurry," the staff told her as she strode down the hallway. She found Massine alone in his room. He recognized her, tried to speak, but could not. She stayed with him awhile, but once she realized how critically ill he was she went into the hallway to telephone his daughter, Tatiana, in New York.

By the time she returned to the room Massine had died. It was March 15, 1979.[30]

EPILOGUE

AFTER DECADES OF NEGLECT of Massine's serious works (his *demi-caractère* and character ballets have always found a place in the international repertory), the last few years have seen a renewed interest in the symphonic ballets. This revival has stimulated both critics and balletomanes. Rudolf Nureyev took the first valiant step by commissioning a revival of *Les Présages* (1933) for the Paris Opéra. The work, though representative of the expressionistic aesthetics of its time, received high critical acclaim. Anna Kisselgoff wrote in the *New York Times* (March 9, 1989):

> In fact, the production is a complete triumph not only because it is exceedingly well danced by the Paris Opera Ballet, but also because the choreography has a dynamic invention that stands up on its own. . . .
>
> A revelation of the production is how strongly classical and formal the choreography looks. Massine's influence over Sir Frederick Ashton (his pupil) and even George Balanchine is evident. . . .
>
> The original criticism about the heaviness of the allegory—man battling his destiny—still holds true. In this production, however, the message falls by the wayside. One is left with the complexity of Massine's contrapuntal groups of dancers . . . and the sheer and striking classicism of most of the choreography. . . . The pas de deux in the second movement is actually a neoclassic duet of superb invention and fluidity. . . .
>
> We see the Ashton of the future in fleeting passages. His walking-on-air

trademark is visible in the duet, and the arm movements he used in Symphonic Variations are also present. To see the martial gestures in Les Présages *is to recall similar arm work in the Balanchine-Stravinsky Symphony in Three Movements. One can note a passing resemblance to certain lifts and images in other Balanchine ballets. . . . It is time to see* Les Présages *in a new light.*

And later, on May 7, 1989, Kisselgoff added:

Les Présages *suggests that a revisionist view of Massine is in order. In this revival, he emerges as a major neo-classical choreographer. For all the so-called Expressionist influences in the torso and gestures, the footwork is in the classical idiom, fluent and inventive. . . .*

Les Présages *shows us something else: a choreographer in firm command of the classical idiom and a complex interplay of dance structures. . . .*

Les Présages *also clarifies the relationship of Massine's work to Balanchine and Frederick Ashton, 20th century ballet's greatest neo-classicists. Ashton, Massine's pupil, acknowledged the older choreographer's influence. . . .*

The Joffrey Ballet subsequently revived *Les Présages,* in 1991.

Of paramount importance was the revival of *Choreartium* (1933)—Massine's first absolutely abstract ballet, a forerunner of abstraction, musical visualization, and neoclassicism. The staging by the Birmingham Royal Ballet in 1991 received rapturous reviews. Clement Crisp wrote in the *Financial Times* (October 28, 1991): "What Massine proposes in *Choreartium* is certainly a response to Brahmsian device in the immediate terms of thematic and formal structure, but it is one overlaid with an emotional—a Russian emotional—interpretation of mood. . . . The restoration of Choreartium to the repertory brings back to life a work that should retain an honoured place in any assessment of this century's ballet." The *Sunday Times* (November 3, 1991) declared that "it is time to reinstate Léonide Massine's full worth as a choreographer. . . . What first hits you about Choreartium is its epic scale." *The Times* (October 28, 1991) noted that "Massine created a complexity of detailed, distinct choreography, not just for the ten soloists, but for the entire ensemble. His patterns extend across the whole stage in contrast and variety, but are always possible for the eye to take in at once (this is surely something learned from his study of paintings)." And Jack Anderson wrote in the

New York Times (December 1, 1991): *"Choreartium* is a vast mural in motion that makes much recent choreography seem puny by comparison."

Ninette de Valois called Massine a "genius" and predicted that "[his] works will come back and [he] will be again a very prominent figure in our history." Now at last the reconsideration and re-evaluation of Massine's oeuvre are irreversibly on the ascent. He has been re-established as one of the century's most influential and innovative choreographers.

Notes

1. Moscow, July 1895–November 1913

1. Massine's school records, Central State Archives of Literature and the Arts, Moscow, fond. 659. Letter from Elizabeth Souritz to the author, April 21, 1991.
2. Mr. Miassine retired on September 1, 1911, and Mrs. Miassine retired on September 1, 1904.
3. Léonide Massine, *My Life in Ballet* (London: Macmillan, 1968), p. 13.
4. Ibid., p. 15.
5. Ibid., p. 13.
6. Ibid., pp. 12–13.
7. Ibid., p. 13.
8. Ibid., p. 20.
9. Ibid.
10. Ibid., p. 14.
11. Ibid., p. 17.
12. *Dance Magazine*, 51, no. 12 (December 1977), p. 68.
13. Ibid., pp. 20–21.
14. Miassine's school records, Central State Archives of Literature and the Arts, Moscow, fond. 682.
15. Undoubtedly a driving force in early-twentieth-century Russian ballet was Vladimir Telyakovsky, who was appointed director of the Moscow Imperial Theaters in 1897, and later was promoted to general director of the Imperial Theaters. Telyakovsky's greatest concern was to elevate the standards of artistic excellence at the Imperial Theaters. It is he who should be credited with hiring the bass Feodor Chaliapin for the Bolshoi in 1899, transferring Gorsky to the Bolshoi Ballet in 1900, appointing Vsevolod Meyerhold the Imperial Theaters' principal producer in 1907, helping to launch the career of Michel

Fokine, and supporting Stanislavsky's reforms to the extent of persuading him in 1915 to teach acting to the singers at the Bolshoi. See Natalia Roslavleva, *Era of the Russian Ballet* (London: Victor Gollancz, 1966).

16. A Russian cultural renaissance had blossomed during the nineteenth century, perhaps as an artistic revolt against the Europeanization of the Russias under Peter the Great in the late 1700s and early 1800s. This Russian renewal was responsible for the development of a strong Russian identity in the arts. The subsequent artistic fermentation reached its apogee in the early part of this century and continued until the 1930s, when art became a voice for ideological propaganda.

    Moscow had been Russia's capital from the end of the Mongol occupation in the fourteenth century until the beginning of the eighteenth, when Peter the Great designated St. Petersburg as his capital. Nevertheless, Moscow remained the economic center of the country, and with the help of industrialization the city in 1900 reached its peak rate of economic growth. Prosperity detonated a population explosion, from 1,038,000 in 1897 to 1,762,700 by 1914.

    The cultural renaissance in Moscow was shaped by two vital forces. First, there was the affluence provided by the eco-social phenomenon of the wealthy merchant class, which reached its heyday by the close of the nineteenth century. This group—bankers, manufacturers, industrialists, and railroad tycoons, most of whom came from peasant stock—spent their fortunes on art patronage as well as on industrial and scientific development, thus enriching Russia's cultural and intellectual life. They founded art and literary journals, libraries, and drama and opera companies. Their extensive private art collections, some of which were open to the public, provided sponsorship for Russian and European modernist artists, thus helping to create a market for modern art. Among the most notable members of this class were the Shchukins, the Morozovs, the Mamontovs, the Riabouchinskys, and the Tretyakovs, all of whom were champions of the Slavophile movement, whose philosophy was rooted in a revitalization of the national heritage.

    Another factor in the cultural renaissance was Moscow's nationalistic tradition, which so differed from the sophisticated cosmopolitanism of St. Petersburg, which was defined by European criteria. Moscow's search for artistic identity was opposed to St. Petersburg's occidentalism and sought to revitalize and reassert the Russian traditions venerated by the Slavophile movement. This search gave Moscow its pre-eminence as a center for experimentation and modernism.

    The Wanderers were a group of Slavophile artists formed in 1863 that rebelled against St. Petersburg's Academy of the Arts (founded in 1757), after which they settled in Moscow and enjoyed the support of the wealthy merchants. In 1870, with the assistance of Pavel Tretyakov, this group founded the Traveling Exhibition Society, whose primary objective was to bring in art from outside the country's two leading cities, and whose artistic credo was to free itself from Western influences so that a national art could be created that depicted Russian themes and the true realities of the Russian social landscape. Understandably, the Wanderers' hero was Leo Tolstoy.

Four years after the creation of the Traveling Exhibition Society, Savva and Elizaveta Mamontov, leading members of the Muscovite merchant class, gathered together a colony of artists at their estate at Abramtsevo, near Zagorsk. Abramtsevo became a center of Russian arts and crafts and came to include among its members Konstantin Korovin, Mikhail Vrubel, the Vasnetsov brothers, and Valentin Serov. It provided the site for the genesis of one of the most important theatrical manifestations of the time: out of the colony of artists gathered by Mamontov emerged his Private Opera Company, which opened in 1885 with the artistic objective of staging works by Russian composers and achieving a theater of synthesis. The productions, mounted in collaboration with the Abramtsevo artists, signaled the future importance of theatrical design.

The creation of the Private Opera Company heralded the development of Moscow as a theatrical center. In 1896, Mamontov invited the bass Feodor Chaliapin to join his company. Unhappy with the conditions at the Maryinsky Theater, Chaliapin gladly joined Mamontov's enterprise, where in three seasons he sang twenty roles. The singer's association with the Private Opera Company was vital for his artistic growth, and the mood of experimentation in the company encouraged him to focus on developing his approach to interpretation. According to historian Varvara Strakhova-Ermans, "The years Chaliapin spent at Mamontov's theater must be regarded as a period of extreme intellectual exertion and great fecundity. . . . This was the moment when his genius burst forth. . . . when Fedor Ivanovich became *Chaliapin*" (Quoted in Victor Borovsky, *Chaliapin: A Critical Biography* [New York: Alfred A. Knopf, 1988], p. 252). Stanislavsky, the great theatrical innovator, who had considered opening an acting workshop for opera singers, stated that "the only correct approach to opera is Chaliapin's approach, which proceeds not from the external reality of the character being portrayed, but from its inner reality, its psychological depth" (Borovsky, p. 9). See Beverly Whitney Kean, *All the Empty Palaces: The Merchant Patrons of Modern Art in Pre-Revolutionary Russia* (New York: Universal Books, 1983), and Serge Fauchereau, *Moscow, 1900–1930* (New York: Rizzoli, 1988).

17. The theater had always occupied a revered place in the hearts of the Russian intelligentsia; and even though since the early eighteenth century the Russian theater had been couched in Western European traditions, by the last two decades of the nineteenth century it had begun to find its own identity. Theater would eventually become one of the most artistically fertile areas of the Russian cultural renaissance, with Moscow emerging as the country's theatrical capital.

One of the most influential theatrical movements at the turn of the century was the Moscow Art Theater, founded in 1898 by Konstantin Stanislavsky (born Alexeyev to a merchant family) and Vladimir Nemirovich-Danchenko. The Art Theater introduced new concepts in acting and production that enlisted decor, costumes, props, lighting, music, and sound to create a cohesive dramatic whole that gave birth to a new realism and artistic truth on the stage. From its inception up until 1904, the Art Theater concentrated on realism and naturalism. Yet the emphasis on the outer truth of the theatrical experience led, paradoxically, to its discovery of the inner dimension; and thus from 1905 on the theater's creative direction moved toward psychological realism and the theater of mood. See Nicolai A. Gorchakov, *The Theater in Soviet Russia* (New York: Columbia University Press, 1957), and Marc Slonim, *Russian Theatre from the Empire to the Soviets* (Cleveland: World Publishing, 1961).

18. Elizabeth Souritz, *Soviet Choreographers in the 1920s* (Durham, N.C.: Duke University Press, 1990), p. 86.
19. Among Miassine's classmates, only Margarita Kandourova, a leading ballerina in the 1920s, became famous. Vera Svetinskaya, although only a coryphée, became known as the object of Gorsky's love letters and poetry.
20. Massine, *My Life*, p. 23.
21. Ibid., p. 24.
22. Ibid., p. 26.
23. Ibid., p. 27.
24. Souritz, *Soviet Choreographers*, p. 104.
25. Massine files, Central State Archives of Literature and the Arts, Moscow, fond. 682. On May 4, 1909, Leonid was moved to third class. On April 20, 1911—a year before his graduation—he was moved to fifth class with a special certificate of merit.
26. Letter from Elizabeth Souritz to the author, March 8, 1991.
27. Natalia Roslavleva, *Era of the Russian Ballet* (London: Victor Gollancz, 1966), p. 160.
28. Massine, *My Life*, p. 29.
29. Ibid. pp. 29–30.
30. Ibid., p. 30.
31. Ibid., p. 41.
32. Ibid., p. 32.
33. Ibid., p. 33.
34. Ibid., p. 34.
35. Ibid., p. 30–31.
36. In the certificate of christening in Massine's school records she appears as Alexandra Alexandrovna Minina—probably her maiden name.
37. Massine, *My Life*, pp. 38–39.
38. *Theatre*, no. 976, December 13, 1911.
39. *Theatre*, no. 979, December 16, 1911.
40. *Season News*, no. 2306, December 14, 1911.
41. Massine, *My Life*, p. 32.
42. Ibid., p. 37.

Anatoli Petrovich Bolchakov was born on November 5, 1870, in the village of Novaya Andronovka, near Moscow, and came from a family of peasants. In 1883 he applied for admission at the School of Painting, Sculpture, and Architecture in Moscow, and during his studies there he was so poor that he had to repeatedly petition for his tuition to be waived. (Central State Archives of Literature and the Arts, Moscow, fond. 680). Upon his graduation, probably in 1895, he taught drawing at several ordinary Moscow schools and opened his own art school in his private apartment. (Letters from Elizabeth Souritz to the author, April 21 and May 12, 1991.)

43. Massine, *My Life*, p. 38.
44. Letter from Massine to Anatoli Petrovich Bolchakov, October 9, 1914, State Central Theatrical Museum, Moscow, no. 181575.
45. Massine, *My Life*, p. 71.
46. Ibid., p. 38.
47. Ibid.
48. Letters from Massine to Bolchakov sending his regards to these friends, State Central Theatrical Museum, Moscow.
49. School records, Central State Archives of Literature and the Arts, Moscow, fond. 682.
50. Personal file of L. F. Massine, Central State Archives of Literature and the Arts, Moscow, fond. 659, reg. 3, unit 2532, p. 20.
51. Ibid., p. 21.
52. Massine, *My Life*, p. 35.
53. Souritz, *Soviet Choreographers*, p. 30.
54. Ibid., quoting the critic B. Asafiev, p. 93.
55. Ibid., p. 116.
56. Ibid., pp. 116–17.
57. Massine, *My Life*, p. 39.
58. Ibid., p. 40.
59. Gorchakov, *Theater in Soviet Russia*, p. 12.
60. Massine in conversations with the author, Rennes, France, 1978.

2. Moscow, December 1913–Paris, August 1914

1. Richard Buckle, *Diaghilev* (New York: Atheneum, 1979), p. 41. For a closer analysis of Diaghilev's relationship with Filosofov, see Vladimir Zlobin, *A Difficult Soul: Zinaida Gippius* (Berkeley: University of California Press, 1980).
2. Quoted in William Richardson, *Zolotoe Runo and Russian Modernism: 1905–1910* (Ann Arbor, Mich.: Ardis Publishers, 1986), p. 17.
3. Buckle, *Diaghilev*, p. 61.
4. Ibid., p. 91.
5. Alexandre Benois, *Reminiscences of the Russian Ballet* (London: Putnam, 1941), p. 238.
6. Buckle, *Diaghilev*, p. 102.
7. Ibid., pp. 158–280. See also Arnold Haskell, *Diaghileff* (New York: Simon and Schuster, 1935), pp. 184–255.
8. While in Moscow, Diaghilev also approached Gorsky about producing Nicolas Tcherepnine's *The Masque of the Red Death* for his Ballets Russes. Elizabeth Souritz, *Soviet Choreographers in the 1920s* (Durham, N.C.: Duke University Press, 1990), p. 163.

9. Buckle, *Diaghilev*, p. 269.

10. Ibid., p. 270.

11. Léonide Massine, *My Life in Ballet* (London: Macmillan, 1986), p. 42.

12. Ibid., p. 270.

13. Massine in conversations with the author, Rennes, France, 1978.

14. Massine, *My Life*, p. 43.

15. The date on which this trip took place cannot be determined. In Massine's records from the Imperial Theater School there are several one-day petitions to visit his family.

16. Massine, *My Life*, p. 45.

17. Ibid., p. 46.

18. Petition in Massine's personal school records at the Imperial Theater School, Central State Archives of Literature and the Arts, Moscow, fond. 659, reg. 3, unit 2532.

19. Hugo von Hofmannsthal and Richard Strauss, *Correspondence Between Richard Strauss and Hugo von Hofmannsthal* (London: Collins, 1961), p. 222.

20. Personal school records from the Imperial Theater School, Central State Archives of Literature and the Arts, Moscow, fond. 659, reg. 3, unit 2532.

21. Letter from Diaghilev to Massine, January 22, 1914, Massine's private collection. The contract was extended an additional year, to August 1, 1916.

22. Massine, *My Life*, p. 51.

23. Ibid., p. 48.

24. Lydia Sokolova, *Dancing for Diaghilev* (London: John Murray, 1960), pp. 60–61.

25. Massine, *My Life*, p. 51.

26. Ibid., p. 52.

27. Ibid.

28. Ibid., pp. 53–54.

29. Telegram from Bakst to Misia Edwards, Massine's private collection.

30. Massine, *My Life*, p. 54.

31. Ibid., p. 57.

32. Ibid.

33. Massine in conversations with the author, Galli, 1978.

34. The 1917 cubist ballet *Parade* (music by Satie; libretto by Cocteau; scenery, costumes, and curtain by Picasso; and choreography by Massine) was to be the result of this meeting.

35. Massine, *My Life*, p. 60.

36. *The Lady*, March 7, 1914.

37. *Sunday Times* (London), June 28, 1914.

38. Tamara Karsavina, *Theatre Street* (London: Dance Books, 1981), pp. 298–300.

39. The letters from Massine to Anatoli Petrovich Bolchakov were deposited at the State Central Theatrical Museum, Moscow, by Bolchakov's widow.

40. Letter from Massine to Bolchakov, June 13/1, 1914, State Central Theatrical Museum, Moscow, no. 181566.

3. Italy, August 1914–United States, April 1916

1. In his autobiography Massine sometimes tries to play down his relationship with Diaghilev by implying that on certain occasions he traveled or lived independently. This trip to Milan, which he says he made alone, is an example. In fact, up to the time their relationship began to crumble, it is unlikely that Massine was ever far from Diaghilev's sight for long; and when he was, Diaghilev almost certainly knew his precise whereabouts.
2. Léonide Massine, *My Life in Ballet* (London: Macmillan, 1968), p. 66.
3. Ibid.
4. Richard Buckle, *Diaghilev* (New York: Atheneum, 1979), p. 284.
5. Letter from Massine to Anatoli Petrovich Bolchakov, October 9, 1914, State Central Theatrical Museum, Moscow, no. 181575.
6. Massine, *My Life*, p. 66.
7. Ibid., pp. 67–69.
8. Ibid., p. 69.
9. Ibid.
10. Ibid., p. 70.
11. Ibid., p. 71.
12. Ibid., p. 69.
13. Ibid.
14. Massine in conversations with the author, Galli, 1978.
15. Massine interview with Fred Maroth, Oakland, California, 1978.
16. Massine, *My Life*, p. 70.
17. Buckle, *Diaghilev*, p. 286.
18. Massine, *My Life*, pp. 71–72. Original letter in State Central Theatrical Museum, Moscow.
19. Letter from Massine to Bolchakov, December 20, 1914, State Central Theatrical Museum, Moscow, no. 181574.
20. Letter from Massine to Bolchakov, December 22, 1914, State Central Theatrical Museum, Moscow, no. 181573.
21. Massine in conversations with the author, Galli, 1978.
22. Caroline Tisdall and Angelo Bozzolla, *Futurism* (New York: Oxford University Press, 1978), p. 103.
23. Lynn Garafola, *Diaghilev's Ballets Russes* (New York: Oxford University Press, 1989), p. 77.
24. *Stravinsky: Selected Correspondence,* ed. Robert Craft, vol. 2, letter dated November 25, 1914 (New York: Knopf, 1984), p. 16.
25. Letter from Massine to Bolchakov, January 19, 1915, State Central Theatrical Museum, Moscow, no. 181571.
26. Buckle, *Diaghilev*, p. 288.
27. *Stravinsky: Selected Correspondence,* vol. 2, p. 138.

28. Tisdall and Bozzola, *Futurism*, p. 117.

29. Tatiana Loguine, *Gontcharova et Larionov* (Paris: Klincksieck, 1971), p. 197.

30. Aline Isdebsky-Pritchard, *The Art of Mikhail Vrubel* (Ann Arbor, Mich.: UMI Research Press, 1982), passim.

31. Valentina Kachuba in conversations with the author, Madrid, 1987.

32. Ibid.

33. Buckle, *Diaghilev*, p. 291.

34. Ibid., p. 295.

35. Massine, *My Life*, p. 288.

36. Ibid.

37. Letter from Massine to Bolchakov, January 1916, State Central Theatrical Museum, Moscow, no. 181570.

38. Ibid.

39. Buckle, *Diaghilev*, p. 288.

40. *Stravinsky: Selected Correspondence*, ed. Robert Craft, vol. 1 (New York: Knopf, 1982), p. 138.

41. Gontcharova's remarks read:

> *Dès le début, Diaghilev ébaucha une chorégraphie en cinq épisodes de la vie du Christ: la Nativité et l'Adoration des Mages, l'entrée dans Jérusalem, la prière dans le Jardin de Gethsémané, le Portement de la Croix, Golgotha. Plus tard fut ajouté le Sermon sur la montagne et une version de l'Annonciation: le dernier épisode fut, symboliquement et chronologiquement, une introduction à tous les Mystères. Les projets de Diaghilev étaient très vastes.*
>
> *Le Sermon sur la montagne était figuré exclusivement par le mouvement, la plastique et le développement des situations dramatiques. Parfois l'action était précédée par la musique et le choeur. D'autres fois, l'action était accompagnée par la musique et le chant à l'unisson, comme cela faisait dan l'ancienne Russie. La transportation du vieux motif musical fut en partie réalisée par le maître de chapelle de la Cathédrale orthodoxe de Genève, Kibaltchitch, qui était le fils du célèbre révolutionnaire russe. Suivant les exigences de l'action, soit le choeur se déployait au milieu de la scène, soit il en partait, soit encore il se tenait "en escalier" sur les côtés des premières coulisses. Sur scène apparaissaient les personnages principaux. . . .*
>
> *L'entrée dans Jérusalem se déroulait sur l'avant-scène avec pour fond le rideau baissé, réalisé sur le modèle des châssis qui entourent les icônes. Les quatre évangélistes portaient une reproduction d'âne stylisé, aux pattes projetées en avant et en arrière. Sur le dos de l'animal était placée une sculpture qui représentait l'entrée du Christ dans Jérusalem. Les apôtres marchaient sur les toits de la ville, figurés au niveau de la scène. Le sol devait avoir une certaine résonance, le rythme de la danse et le bruit des pas devaient être perçus distinctement par les spectateurs dans la salle. C'est porquoi on installa, à vint-cinq centimètres du sol, un faux-plancher fabriqué dans un bois "sonore," une espèce de chêne à la texture sèche. Après le passage de la procession, le rideau se levait et l'épisode suivant se déroulait sur la scène.*
>
> *Les Nouvelles Russes*, 1953, no. 427, p. 6.

42. Massine, *My Life*, p. 74.

43. Ibid.

44. Ibid.

45. Serge Grigoriev, *The Diaghilev Ballet, 1909–1929*, trans. and ed. by Vera Bowen (London: Constable, 1953; rpnt. Penguin Books, 1960), p. 117.
46. Kachuba in conversations with the author.
47. Lydia Sokolova, *Dancing with Diaghilev* (London: John Murray, 1960), p. 71.
48. Kachuba in conversations with the author.
49. Massine, *My Life*, p. 76.
50. Massine in conversations with the author, Galli, 1978.
51. Kachuba in conversations with the author.
52. Arthur Gold and Robert Fizdale, *Misia* (New York: Knopf, 1980), p. 173.
53. *Journal de Genève*, December 22, 1915.
54. Massine, *My Life*, p. 77.
55. Ibid.
56. Ibid.
57. Ibid.
58. *The New Republic*, January 15, 1916.
59. Massine, *My Life*, p. 80.
60. Ibid.
61. *New York Tribune*, January 18, 1916.
62. *New York Sun*, January 26, 1916.
63. *New York Times*, January 26, 1916.
64. Ibid.
65. Massine, *My Life*, p. 82.
66. Ibid., p. 81.
67. Ibid., p. 84.
68. Ibid.
69. Ibid.
70. Letter from Massine to Bolchakov, January 1916, State Central Theatrical Museum, Moscow, no. 181570.
71. Sokolova, *Dancing*, p. 75.
72. Ibid.
73. *Musical Courier*, April 1916.
74. Milo Keynes, *Lydia Lopokova* (New York: St. Martin's Press, 1982), p. 211.
75. Massine, *My Life*, p. 97.

4. Spain, May–September 1916

1. Richard Buckle, *Diaghilev* (New York: Atheneum, 1979), p. 311.
2. Léonide Massine, *My Life in Ballet* (London: Macmillan, 1968), p. 88.
3. Letter from Massine to Anatoli Petrovich Bolchakov, June 5, 1916, State Central Theatrical Museum, Moscow, no. 181580.
4. *ABC* (Madrid), May 28, 1916.
5. *ABC* (Madrid), May 31, 1916.
6. *ABC* (Madrid), May 29, 1916.

7. Letter from Manuel de Falla to María Martínez Sierra, June 18, 1916, Archivo Manuel de Falla, Granada.

8. Igor Stravinsky, *Chronicle of My Life* (London: Victor Gollancz, 1936), p. 47.

9. Letter from Massine to Bolchakov, June 13, 1916, State Central Theatrical Museum, Moscow, no. 181519.

10. María Martínez Sierra, *Gregorio y yo* (Mexico, D.F.: Biografías Gandesa, 1953), p. 144.

11. Falla, in a letter to the dancer Nirva del Río dated June 20, 1929, states: "It has always been a definite criterion of mine not to change the character or destiny of my works. The *Noches* were composed as a symphonic piece. . . . I had already received several propositions (especially from Diaghilev's Ballets Russes, even before the premiere of *Tricorne*)." Archivo Manuel de Falla.

12. Jaime Pahissa, *Cuando el maestro Falla fue al pueblo de Goya,* Archivo Manuel de Falla.

13. Letter from Falla to María Martínez Sierra, June 18, 1916, Archivo Manuel de Falla.

14. Pahissa, *Cuando el maestro Falla.*

15. Letter from de Falla to María Martínez Sierra, June 18, 1916, Archivo Manuel de Falla.

16. Ibid.

17. Diaghilev offered Falla 5,000 francs for a five-year exclusivity for each work and a 100-franc royalty per performance for a minimum of ten performances a year. Falla proposed instead 6,000 francs for a three-year exclusivity for each work, a 125-franc royalty per performance and a minimum of fifteen performances a year, and his right to retain the exclusivity of these works for Spain. Diaghilev's counteroffer was of 5,000 francs for a three-year exclusivity and a 100-franc royalty per performance for a minimum of ten performances a year. Falla was to retain the exclusivity for concert performances in Spain. Archivo Manuel de Falla.

18. Ibid.

19. Letter from Massine to Bolchakov, June 5, 1916, State Central Theatrical Museum, Moscow, no. 181580.

20. Massine, *My Life,* p. 89.

21. Doctor's certificate, dated June 4/17, 1916, presented at the Russian embassy in Madrid, private collection.

22. Letter from Massine to Stravinsky, undated, quoted in *Stravinsky: Selected Correspondence,* ed. Robert Craft, vol. 2 (New York: Knopf, 1984), p. 160.

23. Massine, *My Life,* p. 144.

24. Letter from Massine to Bolchakov, June 25, 1916, State Central Theatrical Museum, Moscow, no. 181578.

25. Letter from Falla to Stravinsky, July 7, 1916, quoted in *Stravinsky,* vol. 2, p. 160.

26. Ibid.

27. The *modernismo* movement was the Catalonian expression of European modernism.

28. Massine, *My Life,* p. 89.

29. Ibid.

30. Lydia Sokolova, *Dancing for Diaghilev* (London: John Murray, 1960), p. 83.
31. Arthur Rubinstein, *My Young Years* (New York: Knopf, 1973), p. 469.
32. Letter from Gerald Tyrwhitt to Stravinsky, August 16, 1916, quoted in *Stravinsky*, vol. 2, p. 136. Tyrwhitt informs Stravinsky that Mme Khvoshchinsky has fallen ill in San Sebastián, where she has been for a month.
33. Zinaida Hippius and her husband, Dmitri Merezhkovsky, were pioneers of symbolism in Russia at the turn of the century. They were key figures in the St. Petersburg literary life and collaborated with the *World of Art* circle. One of the most influential poets of the Russian Silver Age, Hippius was instrumental in the Russian religious revival within the turn-of-the-century intelligentsia.
34. Both Massine and Sokolova give August 22 as the date of the premiere of *Las meninas*. But the first gala took place on August 21, and no new works were presented that evening. Ansermet in a letter to Falla dated August 22 mentions that the first gala had taken place the night before and that the program consisted of *Les Sylphides, Sadko, Prince Igor,* and *Schéhérazade.* He adds that *Las meninas* is being rehearsed and that Diaghilev wants to hear nothing except about *Las meninas* and *Kikimora,* which obviously were to be premiered at the second gala on August 25.
35. Cited in Fernando García-Pérez, "A la busqueda de Mrs. Keynes," *Papeles de Economía Española* (Madrid, 1983), pp. 341–71.
36. Alfredo Salazar, "Algo más sobre los Bailes Rusos," *Revista Musical Hispano-Americana,* August 1916.
37. Massine, *My Life,* p. 111.
38. Massine in conversations with Fred Maroth, 1978.
39. Draft of *Tricorne* contract, Archivo Manuel de Falla.
40. During the Ballets Russes' stay in San Sebastián, Falla wrote several times to Ansermet asking him to persuade Diaghilev to drop his initial idea to use the *Noches* for a ballet. Letters from Ansermet to Falla, August 22, September 2, and undated, Archivo Manuel de Falla.

5. Rome, September 1916–Paris, May 1917

1. *Stravinsky: Selected Correspondence,* ed. Robert Craft, vol. 2 (New York: Knopf, 1984), p. 489.
2. Romola Nijinsky, *Nijinsky* (New York: Simon and Schuster, 1980), p. 374.
3. Léonide Massine, *My Life in Ballet* (London: Macmillan, 1968), p. 107.
4. Massine in conversations with the author, Galli, 1978.
5. In his memoirs Massine claims that he bought the books, but I share Richard Buckle's opinion, in his biography *Diaghilev* (New York: Atheneum, 1979), that it was the impresario who did (p. 319).
6. Massine, *My Life,* pp. 96–97.
7. Ibid., p. 97.
8. Ibid.

9. Ibid., p. 98.
10. Ibid., p. 95.
11. Lydia Sokolova, *Dancing for Diaghilev* (London: John Murray, 1960), p. 98.
12. Milo Keynes, *Lydia Lopokova* (New York: St. Martin's Press, 1982), p. 210.
13. Lynn Garafola, *Diaghilev's Ballets Russes* (New York: Oxford University Press, 1989), p. 86.
14. Caroline Tisdall and Angelo Bozzolla, *Futurism* (New York: Oxford University Press, 1978), pp. 143–45.
15. Ibid., p. 145.
16. By 1916 Massine already had the visionary idea of documenting ballet on film, for it was about this time in Rome that he bought his first camera, to shoot rehearsals and performances of his ballets. However, in a letter to Anatoli Petrovich Bolchakov the choreographer wrote: "I take great interest in cinematography. I tried to shoot movies, but so far did not succeed. I hope the cinema will not replace choreographic notation." (July 4, 1917, State Central Theatrical Museum, Moscow, no. 181569.) The surviving films are now part of the Dance Collection of the New York Public Library.
17. *Stravinsky,* vol. 2, p. 34.
18. Buckle, *Diaghilev,* p. 346.
19. *Stravinsky,* vol. 2, pp. 29–30.
20. Ibid.
21. Ibid., p. 23.
22. Serge Lifar, *Serge Diaghilev* (New York: G. P. Putnam's Sons, 1940), p. 208.
23. *Stravinsky,* vol. 2, p. 30.
24. Ibid.
25. Massine, *My Life,* p. 98.
26. Ibid., p. 100.
27. Ibid., pp. 99–100.
28. Prince Peter Lieven, *The Birth of the Ballets-Russes* (Boston: Houghton Mifflin, 1936), p. 170.
29. Quoted in Francis Steegmuller, *Cocteau* (Boston: Little, Brown, 1970), pp. 75–76.
30. Ibid., p. 82.
31. Ibid., p. 167.
32. Ibid.
33. Steegmuller, *Cocteau,* p. 165.
34. Douglas Cooper, *Picasso Theatre* (London: Weidenfeld, 1968), p. 21.
35. Massine in conversations with the author, Galli, 1978.
36. Massine, *My Life,* pp. 106–107.
37. Massine in conversations with Fred Maroth, Oakland, Calif., 1977.
38. Ibid.
39. Massine in conversations with the author.
40. Letter from Cocteau to Misia Sert, undated, cited in Vicente García-Márquez's *España y los Ballets Rusos,* catalogue to exhibition in Granada, 1989, p. 25.
41. The original letter read:

    Mon cher Massine:

    Une collaboration est faite de surprises.

J'ai surpris Satie et Picasso avec mon thème, ils me surprennent avec la manière dont ils le traitent.

Reste un vide

Exprès

C'est le votre—c'est à vous de la remplir, de nous "surprendre" et ils ne restera plus à surprendre que le public.

Ne prenez pas ce vide pour du vague, mais pour un preuve de la bonne architecture de Parade *et de notre confiance en vous.*

Letter from Cocteau to Massine, undated, private collection.

42. In his memoirs Massine mistakenly dates the trip to Naples with Cocteau after the Ballets Russes' performance at the Teatro Costanzi in Rome, which took place in April. Cocteau was by then in Paris.

43. Massine, *My Life*, p. 108.

44. Ibid.

45. Ibid.

46. Buckle, *Diaghilev*, p. 325.

47. "... *un'organismo puramente musicale che si svolge con lo stesso andare di un fuoco d'artificio anche nell'ordine visuale.*" From the original program for the April 12 gala, private collection.

48. The original French reads:

Voici une Bonne fin que J'ai trouvée en sleeping. Elle arrange Serge et elle souligne Parade: *Pendant la final où les managers se detraquent les acrobates, la petite fille américaine et le chinois peuvent apparaître craintivement, assister avec épouvant à la chute des managers et se mettre à leur tour à indiquer de toutes leurs forces l'"ingresso" ils comprennent que les managers y renoncent. C'est une manière honnête de les ramener en scène et d'aider à faire comprendre qu'ils sont la* Parade *et non le spectacle intérieur.*

49. Massine, *My Life*, pp. 108–9.

50. Ibid., p. 109.

51. Nesta Macdonald, *Diaghilev Observed* (New York: Dance Horizons, 1975), p. 239. Also Marianne Martin, *Futurist Art and Theory, 1909–1915* (New York: Oxford University Press, 1968), p. 103.

52. Massine in conversations with the author, Galli, 1978.

53. Ibid.

54. Steegmuller, *Cocteau*, pp. 513–14.

55. Quoted in Lifar, *Serge Diaghilev*, pp. 217–18.

56. Ibid.

57. Ibid.

58. Cited in Garafola, *Diaghilev's Ballets Russes*, p. 87.

59. Francis Poulenc, *Moi et mes amis* (Paris: La Palatine, 1963), p. 88.

60. Steegmuller, *Cocteau*, p. 186.

61. Ibid., pp. 187–88.

62. Ibid., p. 190.

63. Ibid.

64. Ibid., p. 188.

65. The original French reads:

Vous avez assumé auprès de Diaghilev le rôle le plus important vis à vis de l'art scenique d'aujourd'hui en générale.

Mais ce qui nous interesse le plus c'est cette danse sur laquelle vous dessinez ave une grâce étrangement forte.

Cette force, cette simplicité dirai-je même sont les qualités qui vous distinguent. . . .

La chorégraphie et la musique sont par excellence des arts sur-réalistes puisque la réalité qu'ils expriment dépasse toujours la nature.

Voilà la raison même de l'importance de votre art et de votre propre importance artistique.

Vous m'avez apparu si appliqué à pénétrer les arcanes de l'imprévu chorégraphique que je n'ai aucune crainte sur l'avenir de cet art moderne.

Pour ce qui touche Parade *et peut-être les ballets en générale je crois que les genoux et les coudes n'ont pas obtenu tous les égards qu'ils méritent. . . .*

Vous été sans doute le premier qui ayez donné occasion d'employer ce mot à propos de danse.

Letter from Apollinaire to Massine, Paris, May 21, 1917, Archives de la Fondation Erik Satie, Paris.

6. Spain, June 1917–July 1918

1. Nijinsky previously had danced in Spain in 1914 in Madrid, at the wedding reception of Kermit Roosevelt.
2. Letter from Falla to María Martínez Sierra, June 4 and June 8, 1917, Archivo Manuel de Falla, Granada.
3. See C. E. Gauss, *The Aesthetic Theory of French Artists* (Baltimore, 1966), pp. 24–25. Chevreul concentrated on experiments in the physics of light and color.
4. Letter from Falla to María Martínez Sierra, June 8, 1917, Archivo Manuel de Falla.
5. Ibid.
6. Léonide Massine, *My Life in Ballet* (London: Macmillan, 1968), p. 115.
7. Letter from Falla to María Martínez Sierra, June 12, 1917, Archivo Manuel de Falla.
8. Letter from María Martínez Sierra to Falla, June 22, 1917, Archivo Manuel de Falla.
9. Massine, *My Life*, p. 115.
10. Douglas Cooper, *Picasso Theatre* (London: Weidenfeld, 1968), p. 37.
11. Carlos Bosch, *Mneme* (Madrid: Espasa-Calpe, 1942), p. 155.
12. Massine, *My Life*, p. 113.
13. Ibid.
14. Massine's autobiography is not accurate in its chronology of events. It was during the 1916 trip that he met Felix in Seville; he re-encountered him in Madrid in 1917, the year Felix joined the company.

15. Lydia Sokolova, *Dancing for Diaghilev* (London: John Murray, 1960), p. 113.
16. Massine, *My Life*, p. 114.
17. In his diary for 1918, Nijinsky expresses his feelings of resentment towards Diaghilev, as a betrayed lover.
18. Richard Buckle, *Nijinsky* (New York: Avon, 1971), p. 115.
19. Letter from Massine to Anatoli Petrovich Bolchakov, July 4 1917, State Central Theatrical Museum, Moscow, no. 181569.
20. Massine, *My Life*, p. 115.
21. Ibid., p. 117.
22. Ibid., p. 118.
23. Ibid., p. 119.
24. Ibid., p. 116.
25. Ibid., p. 117.
26. Ibid., p. 118.
27. Ibid.
28. For a more detailed study of the differences between the pantomime and the ballet, see Andrew Budwig, "The Evolution of Manuel de Falla's 'The Three-Cornered Hat,' 1916–1920," *Musicological Research* 5 (1984), pp. 191–212.
29. Massine in conversations with the author, Galli, 1978.
30. Manuel de Falla, *Escritos* (Madrid, 1947), p. 77.
31. Diaghilev-Falla correspondence from July 1916 to February 1917, Archivo Manuel de Falla.
32. Archivo Manuel de Falla.
33. Massine, *My Life*, p. 119.
34. Ibid., p. 121.
35. Jaime Pahissa, *Cuando el maestro Falla fue al pueblo de Goya*, Archivo Manuel de Falla.
36. Massine, *My Life*, p. 122.
37. Massine in conversations with Fred Maroth, Oakland, Calif., 1978.
38. Alfredo Morán, *Joaquín Turina: A través de sus escritos*, vol. 1 (Madrid, 1981), pp. 227–28.
39. Letter from Diaghilev to Massine, undated (Wednesday), Madrid, Palace Hotel, private collection.
40. Ibid.
41. Bernard Dorival, *Robert Delaunay* (Paris: Jacques Dermase Editions, 1975).
42. Letter from Sonia Delaunay to Massine, January 18, 1928, private collection.
43. Letter from Robert Delaunay to Massine, 1918, quoted in Dorival, *Robert Delaunay.*
44. Letter from Sonia Delaunay to Massine, January 18, 1928, private collection.

7. *Paris, August 1918–London, August 1919*

1. Léonide Massine, *My Life in Ballet* (London: Macmillan, 1968), p. 127.
2. Ibid.

3. Jean Hugo, *Le Regard de la mémoire* (Paris: Actes Sud, 1983), p. 137.

4. Massine, *My Life*, p. 128.

5. Ibid., p. 129.

6. Serge Grigoriev, *The Diaghilev Ballet, 1909–1929*, trans. and ed. by Vera Bowen (London: Constable, 1953; rpnt. Penguin Books, 1960), p. 150.

7. *The Observer*, September 11, 1918.

8. Cyril Beaumont, *The Diaghilev Ballet in London* (London: Adam and Charles Black, 1951), p. 107.

9. Ibid., p. 108.

10. Ibid.

11. Cited in John Pearson, *The Sitwells: A Family Biography* (New York: Harcourt Brace Jovanovich, 1978), p. 123.

12. Richard Buckle, *Diaghilev* (New York: Atheneum, 1979), pp. 349–50.

13. *Sunday Times* (London), November 24, 1918.

14. Roger Fry, *Letters of Roger Fry*, ed. by Denys Sutton (London: Chatto & Windus, 1972), p. 440.

15. Grigoriev, *Diaghilev Ballet*, p. 150.

16. *The Times* (London), December 24, 1918.

17. Beaumont, *Diaghilev Ballet*, pp. 117–18.

18. Letters in private collection.

19. Massine, *My Life*, p. 132.

20. Ibid.

21. Ibid., p. 133.

22. Ibid.

23. Massine in conversations with the author, Galli, 1978.

24. Clive Bell, "The New Ballet," *The New Republic*, July 30, 1919, pp. 414–16.

25. Lydia Sokolova, *Dancing for Diaghilev* (London: John Murray, 1960), p. 138.

26. Massine, *My Life*, p. 137.

27. Ballets Russes souvenir program, London, 1918.

28. Alexandra Danilova, *Choura* (New York: Knopf, 1986), p. 141.

29. Massine in conversations with the author.

30. Cited in *Diaghilev, Les Ballets Russes*, exhibition catalog (Paris: Bibliothèque Nationale, 1979).

31. Beaumont, *Diaghilev Ballet*, p. 134.

32. Ibid.

33. *Vogue* (London), August 1, 1919.

34. Roy Harrod, *The Life of John Maynard Keynes* (London: Macmillan, 1951), p. 334.

35. Massine in conversations with Fred Maroth, Oakland, Calif., 1977.

36. According to Nesta Macdonald, some of the characters in the front of the curtain can be identified, from left to right, as: Picasso (the man in the cape), Olga Khokhlova (the woman with the mantilla next to him), Stanislas Idzikowski (the little boy), Massine (the young man in the bull ring), and Diaghilev (disguised as a woman in blue sitting down). *The Observer*, November 2, 1986.

37. Letter from Diaghilev to Falla, London, May 24, 1919, Archivo Manuel de Falla, Granada.

38. Letter from Falla to Diaghilev, May 24, 1919, Archivo Manuel de Falla.
39. Sokolova, *Dancing*, p. 135.
40. Ibid.
41. This is probably why the tarantella employed a variety of Spanish folk steps.
42. Sokolova, *Dancing*, p. 134.
43. Tamara Karsavina, *Theatre Street* (London: Dance Books, 1981), p. 298.
44. Ibid., p. 300.
45. Sokolova, *Dancing*, pp. 136–37.
46. Massine, *My Life*, p. 143.
47. Quoted in Nesta Macdonald, *Diaghilev Observed* (New York: Dance Horizons, 1975), p. 230.
48. Copy of a letter from Falla to the director of the Teatro Colón, Buenos Aires, in regard to a revival of *Le Tricorne*, Manuel de Falla Archives, Granada.
49. Macdonald, *Diaghilev*, p. 231.
50. Beaumont, *Diaghilev Ballet*, p. 144.
51. Sokolova, *Dancing*, p. 142.
52. Ibid.
53. *Sunday Times* (London), July 27, 1919.
54. W. A. Propert, *The Russian Ballet in Western Europe, 1909–1920* (London: John Lane, 1921), p. 52.

The French reception of *Le Tricorne* was more controversial. Nevertheless, following its French premiere at the Paris Opéra on January 23, 1920, it was well received by the daily press; *Le Figaro* (January 24, 1920) reported long ovations after each entrée. But those French intellectual critics who had championed the prewar Ballets Russes (Henri Ghéon, Jacques Rivière, André Suarez, Fernand Gregh) did not subscribe so quickly to Diaghilev's abandonment of his earlier Russian aesthetic in favor of modernism. Massine the performer was much admired; for Rivière, his *farruca* was almost a "hallucination" ("Les Ballets Russes à l'Opéra," *La Nouvelle Revue Française* 78 [1920]: 463). Unfortunately, no other dancer has been able, as Massine was, to give this character its dramatic and essentially archetypal symbolic quality.

When the ballet was presented in Spain the following year, the issue became modernism versus traditionalism, internationalism versus nationalism. While intellectuals like Adolfo Salazar (*El Imparcial*, April 6, 1921), the dean of Spanish critics, championed *Le Tricorne*, the conservative Spanish press charged the ballet with modernist snobbery and with inaccuracy in its combination of styles of various regions, as well as contending that it departed from Alarcón's original and that even Falla's and Picasso's own work lacked authenticity. Here again, some of the critical objections to modernism were brought to bear.

55. Marilyn McCully, paper given at the symposium "España y Los Ballets Russes," Granada, 1989.
56. Massine, *My Life*, p. 141.
57. Ibid.
58. Ibid., pp. 141–42.
59. Beaumont, *Diaghilev Ballet*, p. 145.
60. Massine in conversations with the author.

61. Massine, *My Life,* p. 142.
62. Bell, "The New Ballet," loc. cit.
63. Ibid.
64. Ibid.
65. Ibid.
66. T. S. Eliot, "Dramatis Personae," *Criterion,* April 1923, pp. 303–06.

8. *London, August 1919–Rome, February 1921*

1. Léonide Massine, *My Life in Ballet* (London: Macmillan, 1968), p. 144.
2. Ibid.
3. Ibid.
4. Massine in conversations with the author, Galli, 1978.
5. Vera Stravinsky and Robert Craft, *Stravinsky in Pictures and Documents* (London: Hutchinson, 1979), pp. 183–84.
6. Ibid.
7. Igor Stravinsky and Robert Craft, *Expositions and Developments* (New York: Doubleday, 1962), pp. 126–27.
8. *Stravinsky: Selected Correspondence,* ed. Robert Craft, vol. 1 (New York: Knopf, 1982), p. 134. However, according to Massine the three met in Paris in 1918.
9. V. Stravinsky and Craft, *Stravinsky,* pp. 177–81.
10. Igor Stravinsky, *Chronicle of My Life* (London: Victor Gollancz, 1936), p. 37.
11. "Conversations with Henri Matisse," unpublished manuscript of interviews conducted by Pierre Courthion, 1941 (trans. by V. G.-M.), Special Collections, Getty Center for the History of Art and the Humanities, Los Angeles.
12. Ibid.
13. Ibid.
14. Ibid.
15. Ibid.
16. Ibid.
17. Ibid.
18. Ibid.
19. Massine, *My Life,* p. 147.
20. "Conversations with Matisse."
21. *Comoedia,* February 4, 1920.
22. Lydia Sokolova, *Dancing for Diaghilev* (London: John Murray, 1960), p. 147.
23. Nancy van Norman Baer, *The Art of Enchantment: Diaghilev's Ballets Russes, 1909–1929,* exhibition catalog, Fine Arts Museum of San Francisco, 1989, p. 75. Quote within extract is from Walter A. Propert, *Russian Ballet in Western Europe, 1909–1920* (London, 1921), p. 60.
24. *The Times* (London), July 17, 1920.
25. *Sunday Times* (London), July 18, 1920.

26. *Daily Herald* (London), July 17, 1920.
27. Douglas Cooper, *Picasso Theatre* (New York: H. N. Abrams, 1968), p. 46.
28. Igor Stravinsky, *Conversations with Igor Stravinsky* (New York: Doubleday, 1959).
29. Cyril W. Beaumont, *The Diaghilev Ballet in London* (London: Adams and Charles Black, 1951), p. 159.
30. Stravinsky, *Chronicle* (London: Victor Gollancz, 1936), p. 42.
31. Massine, *My Life*, pp. 148–49.
32. Serge Grigoriev, *The Diaghilev Ballet, 1909–1929* (London: Penguin Books, 1960), pp. 161–62.
33. Massine interview with Maroth, Maroth Collection.
34. Massine, *My Life*, p. 149.
35. André Levinson, "Stravinsky and the Dance," *Theatre Arts Monthly* 8 (November 1924), pp. 741–54.
36. *Daily Mail* (London), June 11, 1920.
37. *The Observer* (London), June 13, 1920.
38. Beaumont, *Diaghilev Ballet*, p. 160.
39. Ibid.
40. *Athenaeum*, June 18, 1920.
41. Stravinsky, *Chronicle*, p. 39.
42. *Sunday Times* (London), June 27, 1920.
43. *Athenaeum*, July 2, 1920.
44. Later a pas de quatre was added with choreography by Bronislava Nijinska.
45. Arnold Haskell, "The Younger Russian Dancers," *Dancing Times,* London, May 1928, pp. 135–37.
46. Ibid.
47. Sokolova, *Dancing*, p. 159.
48. Ibid., p. 160.
49. Ibid., p. 161.
50. *The Observer*, July 3, 1921.
51. Massine interview with Fred Maroth, Maroth Collection.
52. Ibid.
53. *Comoedia*, December 11, 1920.
54. Massine, *My Life*, p. 152.
55. Sokolova, *Dancing*, p. 162.
56. Ibid., pp. 160, 166.
57. Grigoriev, *Diaghilev Ballet*, p. 167.
58. *Comoedia*, December 11, 1920; *The Observer*, July 3, 1921.
59. Emile Vuillermoz, "La nouvelle version chorégraphique du Sacre du printemps, au Théâtre des Champs-Elysées," *La Revue Musicale*, February 1, 1921.
60. Levinson, "Stravinsky and the Dance," pp. 741–54.
61. Jean Bernier, "La Chorégraphie du Sacre du printemps," *Comoedia Illustré*, January 1921, p. 171.
62. Quoted in Arnold Haskell, *Balletomania Then and Now* (New York: Knopf, 1977), p. 104.

63. *Morning Post* (London), June 28, 1921.
64. *The Times* (London), June 28, 1921.
65. *Ballet Review* 6, no. 3 (1977–78), p. 59.
66. *The Times* (London), July 23, 1929.
67. Sokolova, *Dancing*, p. 163.
68. Ibid., pp. 163–64, 167.
69. Ibid., pp. 167–68.
70. Grigoriev, *Diaghilev Ballet*, p. 168.
71. Ibid.
72. Richard Buckle, *Diaghilev* (New York: Atheneum, 1979), p. 370.
73. Ibid., p. 371.
74. Ibid.
75. Grigoriev, *Diaghilev Ballet*, p. 169.
76. Ibid., p. 170.
77. Ibid.
78. Ibid.
79. Sokolova, *Dancing*, p. 171.
80. Arnold Haskell, *Diaghileff: His Artistic and Private Life* (New York: Simon and Schuster, 1935), p. 289.
81. Buckle, *Diaghilev*, p. 371.
82. Haskell, *Diaghileff*, p. 272.
83. Serge Lifar, *Serge Diaghilev: His Life, His Work, His Legend* (New York: G. P. Putnam's Sons, 1940), p. 208.

9. Rome, February 1921–Paris, September 1928

1. Léonide Massine, *My Life in Ballet* (London: Macmillan, 1968), p. 154.
2. Letter from Massine to Anatoli Petrovich Bolchakov, Barcelona, July 4, 1917, State Central Theatrical Museum, Moscow, no. 181569.
3. Massine, *My Life*, p. 154.
4. Copy of telegram from Massine to Mikhail Semenov, Avenida Palace Hotel, Lisbon, December 24, 1917, private collection.
5. Serge Lifar, *Serge Diaghilev: His Life, His Work, His Legend* (New York: G. P. Putnam's Sons, 1940), p. 208.
6. Correspondence between Massine and Jan Kawetzky, February and March 1921, private collection.
7. Contract between Massine and Raoul Gunsbourg, May 24, 1921, private collection.
8. Massine, *My Life*, p. 156.
9. Letter from Massine to Picasso, São Paulo, August 19, 1921, Musée Picasso, Paris.
10. Handwritten draft of a letter from Massine to Picasso, undated, private collection.

11. Cable from Massine to Picasso, Buenos Aires, November 18, 1921, Musée Picasso, Paris.

12. Draft of letter on the Parque Hotel letterhead, Montevideo, undated, private collection.

13. Copies of cables from Massine to Gunsbourg, undated, private collection.

14. Contract with Walter Wanger dated March 25, 1922, private collection.

15. *The Times* (London), April 4, 1922.

16. Ninette de Valois in conversations with the author, London, 1987.

17. T. S. Eliot, *The Letters of T. S. Eliot,* ed. Valerie Eliot, vol. 1 (London: Faber and Faber, 1988), p. 253.

18. Ibid., p. 530.

19. Massine, *My Life,* p. 134.

20. Correspondence between Ottoline Morrell and Massine, private collection.

21. Postcard from Morrell to Massine, October 16, 1922, private collection.

22. Postcard from Morrell to Massine, private collection.

23. Letter from Morrell to Massine, April 23, 1922, private collection.

24. Lydia Sokolova, *Dancing for Diaghilev* (London: John Murray, 1960), p. 198.

25. Tallulah Bankhead, *Tallulah: My Autobiography* (New York: Harper and Brothers, 1952), p. 13.

26. Entrance forms dated October 1, 1924, private collection.

27. Bernard Faÿ, *Les Précieux* (Paris: Librairie Académique, 1966), p. 69.

28. Francis Steegmuller, *Cocteau* (Boston: Little, Brown, 1970), p. 327.

29. Ibid., p. 328.

30. Milo Keynes, *Lydia Lopokova* (New York: St. Martin's Press, 1982), p. 98.

31. Richard Buckle, *Diaghilev* (New York: Atheneum, 1979), p. 426.

32. Polly Hill and Richard Keynes, *Lydia and Maynard: The Letters of L.L. and J.M.K.* (New York: Charles Scribner's Sons, 1989), p. 169.

33. Ibid., p. 174.

34. Ibid., p. 194.

35. Ibid., p. 197.

36. Ibid., p. 207.

37. Ibid., p. 219.

38. Ibid.

39. Massine in conversations with the author, Galli, 1978.

40. Ornella Volta, "Parade et Mercure," unpublished paper given at the conference "España y los Ballets Rusos," Granada, 1989. (According to Douglas Cooper, the whole conception of the ballet's mise-en-scène was essentially Picasso's. This probably explains why Massine in his autobiography does not discuss *Mercure.* It is evident that by 1924 the choreographer was moving away from this modernist trend.)

41. Volta, ibid.

42. Gertrude Stein, *Picasso* (London: Scribner's Sons, 1939), p. 54.

43. Volta, "Parade et Mercure."

44. Volta in conversations with the author, Paris, 1989. Jean Hugo, in his memoirs, *Avant d'oublier* (Paris: Fayard, 1976), p. 177, recalls a conversation in which Picasso claimed that the gloves were not his idea but that he liked it.

45. Cited in Lincoln Kirstein, *Ballet: Bias and Belief* (New York: Dance Horizons, 1983), p. 16.

46. *Paris-Journal*, May 30, 1924.

47. Madeleine Milhaud in conversations with the author, Paris, 1987.

48. "Chronique dramatique: Les Soirées de Paris," *Les Nouvelles Littéraires*, May 24, 1924.

49. Quoted by Anne Bertrand in *Les Soirées de Paris du Comte Etienne de Beaumont*, unpublished dissertation, Université de Paris X, Nanterre, p. 212.

50. Hill and Keynes, *Lydia and Maynard*, p. 196.

51. Ibid., p. 194.

52. Ibid.

53. Quoted in Bertrand, *Les Soirées*, p. 210.

54. Darius Milhaud, *Ma Vie heureuse* (Paris: Belfond, 1973), p. 131.

55. Bertrand, *Les Soirées*, p. 212.

56. Arnold Haskell, *Balletomania Then and Now* (New York: Knopf, 1977), p. 94.

57. Hill and Keynes, *Lydia and Maynard*, p. 180.

58. Jean Hugo, *Le Regard de la mémoire* (Paris: Actes Sud, 1983), p. 232.

59. Boris Kochno in conversations with the author, Paris, 1983–89.

60. Hill and Keynes, *Lydia and Maynard*, p. 200.

61. Massine in conversations with the author. Massine could not conceal his satisfaction that *Le Beau Danube*, which Diaghilev had called "pure trash" in 1924, became in the 1930s and well into the 1950s one of the most popular works in the international ballet repertory.

62. Massine, *My Life*, p. 142.

63. Quoted in Bertrand, *Les Soirées*, p. 229.

64. Hill and Keynes, *Lydia and Maynard*, p. 140.

65. Massine, *My Life*, p. 162.

66. Hill and Keynes, *Lydia and Maynard*, p. 145.

67. Massine in conversations with the author and with Fred Maroth.

68. Massine, *My Life*, p. 162.

69. Handwritten copy of telegram, undated, private collection.

70. Lynn Garafola, *Diaghilev's Ballets Russes* (New York: Oxford University Press, 1989), p. 266.

71. Massine, *My Life*, p. 161.

72. Ibid., p. 163.

73. Ibid., pp. 162, 163.

74. Kochno in conversations with the author, Paris, 1989.

75. Sokolova, *Dancing*, pp. 229–30.

76. Vernon Duke, *Passport to Paris* (Boston: Little, Brown, 1955), p. 135.

77. Ibid., p. 137.

78. Ibid.

79. Ibid., p. 135.

80. Kochno in conversations with the author, Paris, 1989.

81. Ibid.

82. *Morning Post*, November 13, 1925.

83. *The Times*, November 13, 1925.

84. Massine, *My Life*, p. 166.
85. Cyril W. Beaumont, *Diaghilev's Ballet in London* (London: Adam and Charles Black, 1951), p. 248.
86. Quoted in Garafola, *Diaghilev's Ballets Russes*, p. 136.
87. Nesta Macdonald, *Diaghilev Observed* (New York: Dance Horizons, 1975), p. 312.
88. *The Times* (London), June 30, 1925.
89. *Morning Post*, May 20, 1925.
90. Massine, *My Life*, p. 166.
91. Letter from Charles B. Cochran to Massine, May 19, 1925, private collection.
92. Quoted in *Dancing Times*, August 1925, p. 1139.
93. Letter from Cochran to Massine, May 19, 1925.
94. Note to Massine attributed to Coward, private collection.
95. Massine, *My Life*, p. 168.
96. Ibid.
97. Garafola, *Diaghilev's Ballets Russes*, p. 235.
98. Letter from Massine to Edith de Beaumont, January 23, 1926, Archives de la Fondation Erik Satie; correspondence between E. de Beaumont and Diaghilev from January 28, 1926, through April 29, 1926, Fonds Kochno, Bibliothèque de l'Opéra, Paris.
99. Kochno in conversations with the author, Paris, 1989.
100. Ibid.
101. Elizabeth Souritz, "Soviet Ballet of the 1920's and the Influence of Constructivism," *Soviet Union* 7, pts. 1–2 (1980), p. 122.
102. Letter from Marcel Ballot of the Société des Auteurs et Compositeurs Dramatiques, stating that Massine was to receive a percentage as co-author with Prokofiev and Yakoulov, private collection.
103. Kochno in conversations with the author, Paris, 1989.
104. *The Times* (London), July 5, 1927.
105. *Daily Express*, July 7, 1927.
106. Beaumont, *Diaghilev Ballet*, p. 279.
107. Ibid.
108. Massine, *My Life*, p. 174.
109. Eugenia Delarova in conversations with the author, New York, 1981–90.
110. Massine papers, private collection.
111. Letter from Sonia Delaunay to Massine, January 18, 1928, private collection.
112. Ibid.
113. Private collection.
114. Parker Tyler, *The Divine Comedy of Pavel Tchelitchew* (New York: Fleet Publishing Corporation, 1967), p. 328.
115. Ibid.
116. Kochno in conversations with the author, Paris, 1983–89.
117. Nicholas Nabokov, *Bagazh* (New York: Atheneum, 1975), p. 152.
118. Arnold Haskell, *Diaghileff* (New York: Simon and Schuster, 1935), p. 135.
119. Cecil Beaton, *Dance Index* 5, no. 8, August 1946, pp. 194–95.
120. Massine, *My Life*, p. 173.
121. Felia Doubrovska in conversations with the author, New York City, 1981.

122. *Dancing Times*, no. 215, August 1928, p. 491.
123. Beaumont, *Diaghilev Ballet*, p. 287.
124. Ibid., pp. 287–88.
125. A. V. Coton, *A Prejudice for Ballet* (London: Methuen and Co., 1938), p. 90.
126. Garafola, *Diaghilev's Ballets Russes*, p. 142.
127. Massine, *My Life*, pp. 176–77.
128. Nabokov, *Bagazh*, p. 153.
129. Delarova in conversations with the author.

10. New York, December 1928–London, June 1936

1. Letter from Massine to Charles B. Cochran, April 25, 1928, private collection.
2. Ibid.
3. Léonide Massine, *My Life in Ballet* (London: Macmillan, 1968), p. 174.
4. Ibid., p. 175.
5. Ibid., p. 176.
6. Ibid., p. 177.
7. Anne Bertrand, *Les Soirées de Paris du Comte Etienne de Beaumont*, unpublished dissertation, Université de Paris X, Nanterre, p. 358.
8. Vicente García-Márquez, *The Ballets Russes* (New York: Knopf, 1990), pp. 3–4.
9. Copies of cables, private collection.
10. García-Márquez, *Ballets Russes*, p. 4.
11. Oliver Daniel, "Rite of Spring, First Staging in America: Stokowski-Massine-Graham." *Ballet Review* 10, no. 2 (Summer 1982), pp. 67–71.
12. These stories have been handed down mainly by Claire Reis and Dick Hammond, who were closely involved in the production.
13. Transcript of the Dance Critics Association panel on Léonide Massine's *Le Sacre du printemps*, New York City, November 7, 1987.
14. Ibid.
15. Ibid.
16. Ibid.
17. Massine, *My Life*, pp. 178–79.
18. Daniel, "Rite of Spring," p. 70.
19. Transcript of Dance Critics Association panel.
20. Ibid.
21. *New York Herald Tribune*, April 20, 1930.
22. *New York Times*, April 27, 1930.
23. Cable from Walter Nouvel to Massine, April 1, 1931, private collection.
24. Huguette Laurenti, *Paul Valéry et le théâtre* (Paris: Gallimard, 1973), p. 430.
25. *Revue de France*, August 1931.
26. *Les Nouvelles Littéraires*, July 18, 1931.
27. *Temps*, July 1, 1931.

28. André Levinson, *Les Visages de la danse* (Paris: Editions Bernard Grasset, 1933), p. 111.
29. Ibid., pp. 111–12.
30. *L'Excelsior,* June 29, 1931.
31. *Candide,* July 2, 1931.
32. Confirmation of Massine's engagement with British and Dominions Film Corporation, July 28, 1931, private collection.
33. Igor Markevitch, *Être et avoir été* (Paris: Gallimard, 1980), pp. 210–11.
34. Massine, *My Life,* pp. 180–81.
35. Markevitch, *Être et avoir été,* p. 212.
36. Massine, *My Life,* p. 181.
37. *Dancing Times* 258 (March 1932).
38. Letter from Cochran to Massine, September 19, 1931, private collection.
39. Massine, *My Life,* p. 182.
40. Ibid.
41. Delarova in conversations with the author, New York City, 1981–90.
42. Massine, *My Life,* p. 185.
43. Philip Ziegler, *Diana Cooper* (London: Hamish Hamilton, 1981), pp. 147–49.
44. *The Times* (London), April 11, 1932.
45. Ibid.
46. Diana Cooper, *The Light of Common Day* (London: Rupert Hart-Davis, 1959), p. 112.
47. Cable from Max Reinhardt to Massine, May 15, 1932, private collection.
48. Cf. my discussion of *Jeux d'enfants* in *Ballets Russes,* pp. 28–37.
49. Ibid., p. 31.
50. A. V. Coton, *A Prejudice for Ballet* (London: Methuen & Co., 1938), p. 213.
51. Toumanova in conversations with the author.
52. Riabouchinska in conversations with the author.
53. *Sunday Times* (London), July 11, 1933.
54. Copy of letter to Rothafel and Jay Kaufman, July 11, 1932, private collection.
55. Arnold Haskell, *Balletomania Then and Now* (New York: Knopf, 1977), p. 94.
56. Verchinina in conversations with the author, Rio de Janeiro, March 18, 1990.
57. Pierre Michaut, *Le Ballet contemporain* (Paris: Pion, 1950), p. 93.
58. Verchinina in conversations with the author.
59. Ibid.
60. Massine, *My Life,* p. 187.
61. Ibid.
62. Riabouchinska in conversations with the author, July 1980, May 1983, and August 1985.
63. Levinson, *Visages de la danse,* p. 83.
64. Lifar was quite outspoken against Massine's symphonic ballets. In 1936 he wrote: "One could discuss his method of transposing an orchestral score onto a dance-canvas. At the present, Massine never idealizes material images; he submits entirely to the power of the sentiments aroused in him by those musical symphonies whose choreographic translator he wants to be." Undated clipping, Bibliothèque de l'Opéra, Paris.

65. Michaut, *Ballet contemporain*, p. 94.
66. *Sunday Times* (London), July 9, 1933.
67. Coton, *Prejudice for Ballet*, p. 65.
68. Ibid., p. 68.
69. Riabouchinska in conversations with the author.
70. Baronova in conversations with the author.
71. Ibid.
72. Massine, *My Life*, pp. 190–91.
73. *New York Times*, January 3, 1934.
74. *L'Excelsior*, June 16, 1933.
75. Levinson, *Visages de la danse*, p. 89.
76. Haskell, *Balletomania*, p. 172.
77. Toumanova in conversations with the author.
78. *Sunday Times* (London), July 16, 1933.
79. Coton, *Prejudice for Ballet*, p. 207.
80. Haskell, *Balletomania*, p. 167.
81. Coton, *Prejudice for Ballet*, p. 212.
82. Ibid., p. 214.
83. Agnes de Mille, *Dance to the Piper* (Boston: Little, Brown, 1952), p. 152.
84. Haskell, *Balletomania*, p. 92.
85. Ibid., p. 101.
86. Massine, *My Life*, p. 191.
87. Ibid.
88. Ibid., pp. 191–92.
89. Verchinina in conversations with the author.
90. Ibid.
91. Cf. my discussion of *Choreartium* in García-Márquez, *The Ballets Russes*, p. 92.
92. Coton, *Prejudice for Ballet*, p. 88.
93. *Sunday Times* (London), October 29, 1933.
94. Ibid., July 5, 1936.
95. Haskell, *Balletomania*, p. 174.
96. Ibid.
97. Coton, *Prejudice for Ballet*, p. 89.
98. Ibid., p. 5.
99. Ibid., p. 126.
100. Delarova in conversations with the author.
101. Official visa granted by the Spanish consulate in Nice, April 30, 1935, private collection.
102. Vera Zorina, *Zorina* (New York: Farrar, Straus & Giroux, 1986), p. 106.
103. Ibid., pp. 106–07.
104. Ibid., p. 110.
105. Ibid., pp. 111–12.
106. Letter from Voltaire A. Gicca (Mexican and Brazilian attorney) to George Boochever, January 17, 1936, private collection.
107. Letter from George Boochever to Massine, January 17, 1936, private collection.
108. Ibid.

109. Zorina, *Zorina*, pp. 111–12.
110. Ibid.
111. Ibid., p. 118.

11. London, June 1936–Paris, June 1939

1. Letter from J. D. Langton and Passmore to Colonel de Basil, July 12, 1934, private collection.
2. Letter from J. D. Langton and Passmore to the managing director, Covent Garden Opera House, July 17, 1934, private collection.
3. Agreement between Colonel de Basil and Massine, August 10, 1934, Mme de Basil Collection, Paris.
4. Alexandra Danilova, *Choura* (New York: Knopf, 1986), p. 118.
5. Draft of letter from Massine to de Basil and letter from de Basil to Massine, March 27, 1936, private collection.
6. Correspondence between Massine and Blum and Stoll throughout March 1936, private collection.
7. Copies of cables to Lifar, Woizikowski, and Balanchine, May 3, 1936, private collection.
8. Tamara Tchinarova in conversations with the author, 1982.
9. Grace Robert, *The Borzoi Book of Ballets* (New York: Knopf, 1946), p. 346.
10. *Daily Telegraph*, July 24, 1935.
11. Toumanova in conversations with the author, Beverly Hills, 1985.
12. Letter from Ernest Ansermet to Massine, January 15, 1933, Mme de Basil Collection, Paris.
13. Letter from Etienne de Beaumont to Massine, August 9, 1935, private collection.
14. Vera Newman, *Ernest Newman: A Memoir by His Wife* (New York: Knopf, 1964), p. 155.
15. Cf. my discussion of *Symphonie fantastique* in *Ballets Russes*, pp. 158–68.
16. *Sunday Times* (London), August 2, 1936.
17. Léonide Massine, *My Life in Ballet* (London: Macmillan, 1968), pp. 201–02.
18. *Sunday Times* (London), July 5, 1936; July 12, 1936; July 19, 1936; July 26, 1936.
19. A. V. Coton, *A Prejudice for Ballet* (London: Methuen and Co., 1938), p. 127.
20. *Sunday Times* (London), August 2, 1936.
21. *The Times* (London), July 25, 1936.
22. Coton, *Prejudice for Ballet*, p. 140.
23. *Sunday Referee*, August 2, 1936.
24. *Sunday Times* (London), August 2, 1936.
25. Letter from W. J. Turner to Massine, July 25, 1936, private collection.
26. *New York Sun*, October 30, 1936.
27. Edwin Denby, *Dance Writings* (New York: Knopf, 1986), pp. 39–40.
28. Ibid.

29. Letter from Etienne de Beaumont to Massine, June 26, 1936, private collection.
30. Copy of a letter from Massine to Zoltán Kodály, December 14, 1926, enclosed with a draft of a contract, private collection.
31. Letter from Massine to Serge Denham, January 2, 1937; letter from Denham to Massine, October 1, 1937; Denham Papers, Dance Collection, New York Public Library.
32. Letter from Massine to Sol Hurok, April 13, 1937, Denham Papers.
33. *New York Times*, November 20, 1937.
34. *Dancing Times* 322 (July 1937), p. 413.
35. Copy of a letter from Massine to Beaumont, March 3, 1937, private collection.
36. Frederic Franklin in conversations with the author, New York, 1986.
37. *Sunday Times* (London), July 17, 1938.
38. *Dancing Times*, August 1938.
39. Cyril Beaumont, *Supplement to Complete Book of Ballets* (London: Putnam, 1952), pp. 47–48.
40. *New York Times*, October 13, 1938.
41. *New York Times*, April 24, 1938.
42. Sol Hurok, *Impresario* (New York: Random House, 1946), p. 204.
43. *Sunday Times* (London), July 26, 1936.
44. Massine, *My Life*, p. 206.
45. Massine in conversation with the author, Galli, 1978.
46. Jack Anderson, *The One and Only: The Ballet Russe de Monte Carlo* (New York: Dance Horizons, 1981), p. 69.
47. *Daily Telegraph*, July 13, 1938.
48. *Sunday Times* (London), July 24, 1938.
49. Ibid.
50. Anderson, *The One and Only*, p. 19.
51. Denby, *Dance Writings*, pp. 52–53.
52. *Excelsior*, June 3, 1939.
53. *Le Temps*, June 17, 1939.
54. *Le Jour*, June 3, 1939.
55. Massine, *My Life*, p. 207.
56. François Mauriac, foreword, Ballet Russe de Monte Carlo souvenir program, n.d.
57. Letters from Massine to Paul Hindemith, August 8 and August 29, 1937, Dunham Papers, Dance Collection, New York Public Library.
58. Massine, *My Life*, p. 209.
59. Ibid.
60. Danilova, *Choura*, p. 140.
61. Letter from Hindemith to Massine, August 1938, private collection.
62. *Bystander*, August 10, 1938.
63. *Daily Telegraph*, July 22, 1938.
64. Robert, *Borzoi Book of Ballets*, p. 266.
65. Denby, *Dance Writings*, pp. 53–54.
66. Ibid., p. 66.
67. *New York Times*, October 23, 1938.

68. Solomon Hurok, *S. Hurok Presents . . . The World of Ballet* (London: Robert Hale, 1955), p. 129.
69. George Amberg, *Ballet in America* (New York: Mentor, 1955), p. 53.
70. *Le Temps*, June 24, 1939.
71. *Le Jour*, June 4, 1939.
72. *Ce Soir*, June 6, 1939.
73. *Le Jour*, June 4, 1939.
74. Danilova in conversations with the author, New York, 1986.
75. Frederic Franklin in conversations with the author.
76. Massine, *My Life*, p. 211.
77. Denby, *Dance Writings*, pp. 59–60.
78. Massine, *My Life*, p. 211, and in conversations with the author, Rennes, 1978.
79. "Conversations with Henri Matisse," unpublished manuscript of interviews conducted by Pierre Courthion, 1941 (trans. by V. G-M), Special Collections, The Getty Center for the History of Art and the Humanities, Los Angeles.
80. Letter from Matisse to Massine, May 18, 1938, private collection.
81. Letter from Matisse to Massine, undated, private collection.
82. Danilova in conversations with the author.
83. *L'Opinion*, July 1, 1939.
84. Ibid.
85. Anderson, *The One and Only*, p. 34.
86. Danilova, *Choura*, p. 140.
87. Robert, *Borzoi Book of Ballets*, pp. 257–58.
88. *L'Opinion*, July 1, 1939.
89. Denby, *Dance Writings*, p. 60.
90. *New York Times*, November 5, 1939.
91. Robert, *Borzoi Book of Ballets*, p. 258.
92. Robert Lawrence, *The Victor Book of Ballets and Ballet Music* (New York: Simon and Schuster, 1950), p. 374.
93. *Theatre Arts*, July 1940, p. 26.
94. *L'Opinion*, July 1, 1939.

12. Paris, June 1939–New York, August 1946

1. Delarova in conversations with the author, New York, 1981–1990.
2. Ballet libretto handwritten by Salvador Dalí, signed and dated Monte Carlo, April 20, 1938, private collection. (According to a letter from Stravinsky to Massine, the composer was eager to collaborate with the choreographer on a Dalí ballet. Obviously, the collaboration did not materialize. Letter from Stravinsky to Massine, March 27, 1938, private collection.)
3. Ibid., specifications in ballet libretto by Dalí.
4. This contract was rectified on July 6, 1938. Letter from Dalí to Massine, October 23, 1938, private collection.

5. Robert Descharnes, *Salvador Dalí* (New York: H. N. Abrams, 1985).

6. Gerald Goode, *The Book of Ballets* (New York: Crown, 1939), p. 19.

7. Léonide Massine, *My Life in Ballet* (London: Macmillan, 1968), p. 215.

8. Ibid.

9. Alexandra Danilova, *Choura* (New York: Knopf, 1986), p. 142.

10. Jack Anderson, *The One and Only: The Ballet Russe de Monte Carlo* (New York: Dance Horizons, 1981), p. 37.

11. *New York Times,* November 19, 1939.

12. Robert Lawrence, *The Victor Book of Ballets and Ballet Music* (New York: Simon & Schuster, 1950), p. 46.

13. *San Francisco Chronicle,* February 3, 1940.

14. George Amberg, *Ballet in America* (New York: Mentor, 1949), p. 53.

15. *Dance,* November 1940, p. 9.

16. Ibid.

17. Letter from Massine to Denham, June 7, 1940, Denham Papers, Dance Collection, New York Public Library.

18. Letter from Massine to Denham, June 16, 1940, Denham Papers.

19. Letter from Massine to Denham, August 24, 1940, Denham Papers.

20. Ibid.

21. Letter from Massine to Denham, September 7, 1940, Denham Papers.

22. Letter from Massine to Denham, August 16, 1940, Denham Papers.

23. Ibid.

24. *Dance,* November 1940.

25. Edwin Denby, *Dance Writings* (New York: Knopf, 1986), p. 66.

26. *New York Times,* October 30, 1940.

27. *New York Sun,* October 19, 1940.

28. Letter from Massine to Etienne de Beaumont, June 4, 1936, private collection.

29. *Dance,* November 1940, p. 9.

30. Letter from Denham to Jacques Rubinstein, December 19, 1939, cited in Anderson, *The One and Only.*

31. Massine, *My Life,* p. 216.

32. Massine in conversations with the author, Galli, 1978.

33. Massine, *My Life,* p. 218.

34. Ibid., pp. 218–19.

35. Ibid., p. 219.

36. Lawrence, *Victor Book of Ballets,* p. 255.

37. Denby, *Dance Writings,* p. 80.

38. *New York Herald Tribune,* October 19, 1941.

39. Massine, *My Life,* p. 220.

40. Amberg, *Ballet in America,* p. 50.

41. *Dance,* January 1941.

42. *New York Herald Tribune,* April 19, 1942.

43. Letter from Serge Denham to Julius Fleischmann, April 15, 1942, Denham Papers.

44. Letter from Denham to Massine, August 26, 1937, Denham Papers.

45. Letter from Massine to Denham, August 13, 1938, Denham Papers.

46. Anderson, *The One and Only,* p. 46.
47. *Dance,* November 1940, p. 9.
48. Letter from Denham to Fleischmann, July 5, 1939, Denham Papers. .
49. *Dance,* November 1940, p. 9.
50. Anderson, *The One and Only,* p. 50.
51. Ibid.
52. The list reads as follows:
    1. *Dulle Griet* ("Mad Meg") (based upon paintings by Pieter Brueghel the Elder, scenery and costumes by Dalí);
    2. *Audubon* (character ballet by Glenway Wescott, music by David Diamond, scenery and costumes by [?] Platt);
    3. *Don Pasquale* (classical ballet, music by Donizetti, scenery and costumes by Giorgio de Chirico);
    4. *Brazilian Ballet* (music by Heitor Villa-Lobos, scenery and costumes by Cándido Portinari);
    5. *Lieutenant Kije* (music by Serge Prokofiev, scenery and costumes by Sergei Soudeikine);
    6. *Johnny Goes to Town* (American ballet, music to be composed by Roy Harris, libretto by Archibald MacLeish, scenery and costumes by [?] Saalburg or Aron Borhod);
    7. *Mayan Ballet* (music to be composed by Carlos Chávez, scenery and costumes by Diego Rivera);
    8. *Sacrifice* (Spanish ballet by Dalí, music by Bach or Handel to be arranged, scenery and costumes by Dalí);
    9. *English Ballet* (based on work of Gilbert and Sullivan, scenery and costumes by Oliver Smith and Alvin Colt);
    10. *The Gypsies* (by Pushkin, music by Tchaikovsky, scenery and costumes by [?] Anisfeld);
    11. *The Golden Age* (suite of dances by Dmitri Shostakovich, scenery and costumes by Alexander Calder);
    12. *Golden Wife* (based upon Finnish legend, music by Sibelius (En Saga), scenery and costumes by Pavel Tchelitchev);
    13. *Le Mariage Forcé* (by Molière, music by Mozart to be arranged, scenery and costumes by [?] De Molas);
    14. *Elegie* (classical ballet, music by Chopin to be arranged, scenery and costumes by Lydia Doboujinsky);
    15. *Hungarian Rhapsody* (music by Liszt);
    16. *Astuzie Femminili* (revival);
    17. *Soleil de nuit* (revival);
    18. *Pulcinella* (revival);
    19. *Le Sacre du printemps* (revival); and
    20. *Le Roi valet* (story by Derain, music to be composed by Jean Françaix, scenery by Tchelitchev (if André Derain was not available).
53. Letter from Massine to Manuel de Falla, November 27, 1941, Archivo Manuel de Falla, Granada.

54. Letter from Denham to Fleischmann, January 23, 1942, Denham Papers.
55. Letter from Denham to Fleischmann, April 15, 1942, Denham Papers.
56. *Time,* April 20, 1936.
57. Hurok, *The World of Ballet,* p. 130.
58. Ibid.
59. Ibid., p. 132.
60. Letter from Denham to Fleischmann, May 5, 1942, Denham Papers.
61. Massine, *My Life,* p. 221.
62. Ibid., p. 222.
63. Ibid., p. 223.
64. Franz Meyer, *Marc Chagall: Life and Work* (London: Thomas Hudson, 1964), p. 438.
65. Ibid.
66. Ibid.
67. Jean-Paul Crespell, *The Love, the Dreams, the Life of Marc Chagall* (New York: Coward-McCann, 1970), p. 231.
68. Massine, *My Life,* p. 225.
69. Peter Anastos, "A Conversation with George Skibine," *Ballet Review* 10, no. 1 (Spring 1982), p. 75.
70. Leland Windreich, "Massine's *Aleko,*" *Dance Chronicle* 8 (1985), p. 160.
71. Meyer, *Chagall,* p. 438.
72. Jacques Lassaigne, *Marc Chagall: Drawings and Watercolors for the Ballet* (New York: Tudor, 1959), pp. 14–15.
73. Meyer, *Chagall,* p. 438.
74. Windreich, "Massine's *Aleko,*" p. 170.
75. Grace Robert, *The Borzoi Book of Ballets* (New York: Knopf, 1946), p. 26.
76. Ibid.
77. Alonso in conversations with the author, Rome, 1988.
78. Charles Payne, *American Ballet Theatre* (New York: Knopf, 1979), p. 335.
79. Marcia Siegel, *The Shape of Change* (Boston: Houghton Mifflin, 1979), p. 100.
80. *Novedades,* September 9, 1942.
81. *New York Herald Tribune,* October 25, 1942.
82. Denby, *Dance Writings,* p. 98.
83. Ibid., p. 99.
84. Ibid., p. 118.
85. *San Francisco Chronicle,* July 3, 1943.
86. Robert, *Borzoi Book,* p. 25.
87. Payne, *American Ballet Theatre,* p. 77.
88. Massine, *My Life,* pp. 215–16.
89. Ibid., p. 220.
90. Ibid., p. 226.
91. Ibid., p. 227.
92. Ibid., p. 226.
93. Souvenir program, Ballet Theatre, October 10, 1943.
94. T. S. Eliot, "Tradition and the Individual Talent," in *Selected Essays* (New York: Harcourt, Brace & World, 1964), p. 7.

95. Denby, *Dance Writings*, pp. 148–49.
96. Ibid., p. 154.
97. Ibid., p. 275.
98. Ibid., pp. 275–76.
99. Robert, *Borzoi Book of Ballet*, p. 37.
100. Amberg, *Ballet in America*, p. 167.
101. Ibid., p. 53.
102. Massine, *My Life*, pp. 227–28.
103. Ibid.
104. Denby, *Dance Writings*, p. 113.
105. Ibid., pp. 118–19.
106. *Dance*, July 1941, p. 7.
107. *Dance*, November 1940, p. 9.
108. Amberg, *Ballet in America*, p. 47.
109. Marcia Siegel, *At the Vanishing Point* (New York: Saturday Review Press, 1972), p. 109.
110. Agnes de Mille, *Dance to the Piper* (Boston: Little, Brown, 1952), p. 220.
111. Amberg, *Ballet in America*, p. 42.
112. Lincoln Kirstein, *Ballet: Bias and Belief* (New York: Dance Horizons, 1983), p. 168.
113. Anderson, *The One and Only*, p. 71.
114. Lincoln Kirstein, *P.M.*, December 1, 1940.
115. Kirstein, *Ballet: Bias and Belief*, p. 245.
116. Amberg, *Ballet in America*, p. 45.
117. Eugene Loring in conversations with the author, Irvine, California, 1980.
118. Denby, *Dance Writings*, p. 52.
119. Amberg, *Ballet in America*, p. 54.
120. *Dance*, February 1940, p. 31.

13. *London, September 1946–Edinburgh, September 1960*

1. Brahms was the editor of *Footnotes to Ballet* (London, 1936) and the author of *Robert Helpmann, Choreographer*.
2. Richard Buckle, *The Adventures of a Ballet Critic* (London: Cresset Press, 1953), p. 90.
3. Ninette de Valois in conversations with the author, London, 1987.
4. Ibid.
5. Ibid.
6. Alexander Bland, *The Royal Ballet* (New York: Doubleday, 1981), p. 90.
7. Ibid.
8. Ibid.
9. Léonide Massine, *My Life in Ballet* (London: Macmillan, 1968), p. 230.
10. Alexander Grant in conversations with the author, London, 1987.

11. Margot Fonteyn, *Autobiography* (New York: Warner Books, 1967), p. 97.
12. Ibid.
13. Moira Shearer in conversations with the author, Wiltshire, England, 1987.
14. *Dance Magazine* 22, no. 4 (April 1948), p. 29.
15. De Valois in conversations with the author.
16. Grant in conversations with the author.
17. *Ballet Review* 6, no. 3 (1977–78), p. 72.
18. Michael Powell in conversations with the author, Avening, England, 1987.
19. Michael Powell, *A Life in Movies* (New York: Knopf, 1987), p. 627.
20. Powell in conversations with the author.
21. Cited in Monk Gibbon, *The Red Shoes Ballet* (London: Saturn Press, 1948), p. 51.
22. Powell, *A Life,* p. 642.
23. Ibid.
24. Ibid.
25. Ibid.
26. Powell in conversations with the author.
27. Gibbon, *Red Shoes,* p. 68.
28. Ibid., p. 30.
29. Shearer in conversations with the author.
30. Powell in conversations with the author.
31. Gibbon, *Red Shoes,* pp. 77–78.
32. Powell in conversations with the author.
33. Massine, *My Life,* p. 233.
34. Gibbon, *Red Shoes,* p. 17.
35. Ibid., p. 58.
36. Shearer in conversations with the author.
37. Gibbon, *Red Shoes,* p. 14.
38. Ibid., pp. 67–68.
39. Powell in conversations with the author.
40. Ibid.
41. Massine, *My Life,* p. 237.
42. Shearer in conversations with the author.
43. Ibid.
44. Ian Christie, *Powell, Pressburger and Others* (London: British Film Institute, 1978), p. 37.
45. Powell, *A Life,* p. 654.
46. Ibid., p. 653.
47. Shearer in conversations with the author.
48. De Valois in conversations with the author.
49. Grant in conversations with the author.
50. Shearer in conversations with the author.
51. Grant in conversations with the author.
52. *Dance Magazine* 22, no. 4 (April 1948), p. 28.
53. *Dancing Times* 448 (January 1948), pp. 180–81.
54. *Dance Magazine* 22, no. 4 (April 1948), pp. 28–29.
55. For de Cuevas, Massine danced in *Le Tricorne* with Toumanova and Lichine

and in *Le Beau Danube* and *Les Femmes de bonne humeur* with Riabouchinska and Lichine.

56. Massine, *My Life*, p. 231.
57. Ibid., p. 232.
58. Grant in conversations with the author.
59. Shearer in conversations with the author.
60. Ibid.
61. *Dancing Times* 455 (August 1948), p. 578.
62. Lorca Massine in conversations with the author, Rome, 1987.
63. Tatiana Massine in conversations with the author, New York, 1990.
64. *The Simon and Schuster Book of Ballet* (New York: Simon and Schuster, 1979), p. 254.
65. Tamara Toumanova in conversations with the author, Beverly Hills, 1990.
66. Irene Skorik in conversations with the author, Paris, 1989.
67. Massine, *My Life*, p. 237.
68. Powell in conversations with the author.
69. Ibid.
70. Shearer in conversations with the author.
71. Powell in conversations with the author.
72. Monk Gibbon, *The Tales of Hoffmann: A Study of the Film* (London: Saturn Press, 1951), p. 58.
73. Ibid., p. 57.
74. Ibid., pp. 57–58.
75. Powell in conversations with the author.
76. Gibbon, *Tales of Hoffmann*, pp. 58–59.
77. Ibid., p. 60.
78. Christie, *Powell, Pressburger*, p. 41.
79. Fernau Hall, *Anatomy of Ballet* (London: Andrew Melrose, 1953), p. 197.
80. Christie, *Powell, Pressburger*, p. 62.
81. Grant in conversations with the author.
82. Pigeon Crowle, *Beryl Grey* (London: Faber and Faber, 1952), pp. 69–70.
83. David Gillard, *Beryl Grey: A Biography* (London: W. H. Allen, 1977), p. 81.
84. *Dance and Dancers* 3, no. 2 (February 1952), p. 14.
85. *Dancing Times* 496 (January 1952), p. 202.
86. *Dance and Dancers* 3, no. 2 (February 1952), pp. 13–14.
87. *Ballet Annual*, no. 7 (1953), p. 17.
88. Hall, *Anatomy of Ballet*, pp. 134–35.
89. *Dancing Times* 496 (January 1952), p. 204.
90. De Valois in conversations with the author.
91. Grant in conversations with the author.
92. Bland, *Royal Ballet*, p. 104.
93. Massine, *My Life*, p. 239.
94. Ibid.
95. Ibid., p. 241.
96. *Simon and Schuster Book of Ballet*, p. 260.
97. Ibid.

98. Massine, *My Life*, p. 241.
99. Arnold Haskell, *Balletomania Then and Now* (New York: Knopf, 1977), p. 105.
100. *New York Herald Tribune*, April 9, 1962.
101. *New York Times*, April 9, 1962.
102. *Arts*, June 5, 1953.
103. Ettore Giannini in conversations with the author, Rome, 1987.
104. Ibid.
105. Ibid.
106. Ibid.
107. Ibid.
108. *Le Figaro*, Paris, April 6, 1954.
109. *Ballet Today*, November 1954, p. 9.
110. Gian Piero Brunetta, *Storia del cinema italiano* (Rome: Editori Riuniti, 1980), p. 246.
111. Massine, *My Life*, p. 245.
112. *Le Monde*, July 16, 1954.
113. Correspondence between Serge Denham and Massine, Denham Papers, Dance Collection, New York Public Library.
114. Letter from Massine to Denham, October 1, 1953, Denham Papers.
115. Letter from Denham to Massine, June 23, 1954, Denham Papers.
116. Letter from Massine to Columbia Concerts, February 5, 1954, Denham Papers.
117. Frederic Franklin in conversations with the author, New York, 1986.
118. Jack Anderson, *The One and Only: The Ballet Russe de Monte Carlo* (New York: Dance Horizons, 1981), p. 59.
119. *Dance Magazine* 28, no. 12 (December 1954), p. 57.
120. *Dance News* 25, no. 3 (November 1954), p. 7.
121. *Ballet Annual*, no. 10, p. 118.
122. Ibid.
123. Anderson, *The One and Only*, p. 71.
124. Letter from Denham to Massine, November 23, 1954, Denham Papers.
125. *Lyra* (Buenos Aires), August 1955.
126. Dora Kriner, *Ensayos sobre ballet* (Buenos Aires: Ricordi Americana, 1964), p. 106.
127. *Lyra*, August 1955.
128. Ricardo Naymanovich in conversations with the author, Buenos Aires, 1990.
129. Massine, *My Life*, p. 248.
130. Gaia Servadio, *Luchino Visconti* (New York: Franklin Watts, 1983), p. 127.
131. Ibid., p. 141.
132. Jean Babilée in conversations with the author, Paris, 1987.
133. Ibid.
134. Ibid.
135. Ibid.
136. Ibid.
137. Ibid.
138. Ibid.

139. Letter from Lila de Nobili to the author, November 1987.
140. Ibid.
141. *Simon and Schuster Book of Ballet,* p. 264.
142. Massine, *My Life,* p. 256.
143. *Saturday Review* 42, no. 20 (May 16, 1959), p. 83.
144. Vasili Sulich in conversations with the author, Los Angeles, 1990.
145. *Ballet Annual,* no. 15 (1961), p. 698.
146. André Beaurepaire in conversations with the author, Paris, 1987.
147. Vladimir Augenblick in conversations with the author, Paris, 1987.
148. Sulich in conversations with the author.
149. Lorca Massine in conversations with the author.
150. Irène Lidova in conversations with the author, Paris, 1987, 1989.
151. Beaurepaire in conversations with the author.
152. Massine, *My Life,* p. 266.
153. Lidova in conversations with the author.
154. Sulich in conversations with the author.
155. *Le Figaro,* July 16, 1960.
156. *Dance and Dancers* 11, no. 11 (November 1960), p. 23.
157. *Simon and Schuster Book of Ballet,* pp. 269–70.
158. Massine, *My Life,* pp. 261–62.
159. Ibid., p. 260.
160. Beaurepaire in conversations with the author.
161. Lidova in conversations with the author.
162. *Dance and Dancers* 11, no. 11 (November 1960), p. 23.

14. *Moscow, June 1961–Borken, West Germany, March 1979*

1. Tatiana Massine in conversations with the author, New York, 1987.
2. Massine, *My Life in Ballet* (London: Macmillan, 1968), p. 268.
3. Ibid., pp. 267–68.
4. Ibid., p. 269.
5. Ibid., p. 270.
6. Tatiana Massine in conversations with the author.
7. Massine, *My Life,* p. 271.
8. Tatiana Massine Weinbaum in conversations with the author, New York, 1987.
9. Massine had first suggested to La Scala that the organization would do well to invite Nijinska to stage *Les Noces.* When Nijinska declined, however, Massine sought her permission to choreograph his own version. Draft of telegram from Massine to Nijinska at the Hotel Rembrandt, London, undated, private collection.
10. Letter from Massine to Anatoli Petrovich Bolchakov, Barcelona, July 4, 1917, State Central Theatrical Museum, Moscow, no. 181569.
11. *Dance Magazine* 51, no. 12 (December 1977), p. 70.

12. Massine, *My Life,* p. 276.
13. Vlademir Augenblick in conversations with the author, Paris, 1987.
14. Massine, *My Life,* p. 277.
15. Massine in conversations with the author, Galli, 1978.
16. *Dance Magazine,* December 1977.
17. Even during his years with de Basil's and Denham's companies Massine had supervised revivals of *L'Après-midi d'un faune.* In 1958 he revived *Petrouchka* for the first time, for the Vienna State Opera Ballet. In the ensuing years he became a vocal champion of both of these works. The enshrinement of his past continued to the end of his life. He included *Schéhérazade* in the repertory of the 1960 Nervi Festival, and just before his death he offered to revive *Petrouchka* for the Oakland Ballet.
18. Ariane Csonka in conversations with the author, Palm Beach, Fla., 1988.
19. Lorca Massine in conversations with the author, Rome, 1987.
20. Csonka in conversations with the author.
21. Lorca Massine in conversations with the author.
22. Csonka in conversations with the author.
23. Fred Maroth in conversations with the author, Oakland, Calif., 1987.
24. Ibid.
25. Mary Ann de Vlieg in conversations with the author, London, 1987.
26. Ibid.
27. Letter from Joan Miró to Tatiana Riabouchinska, Los Angeles, March 24, 1978, Riabouchinska collection.
28. Bruce Nalezny in conversations with the author, Oakland, Calif., 1987.
29. Ibid.
30. Mary Ann de Vlieg in telephone conversation with the author, September 1992.

Bibliography

Acton, Harold. *Memoirs of an Aesthete*. London: Methuen, 1948.

Amberg, George. *Ballet in America*. New York: Mentor, 1955.

Anderson, Jack. *The One and Only: The Ballet Russe de Monte Carlo*. New York: Dance Horizons, 1981.

Apollinaire, Guillaume. *Apollinaire on Art: Essays and Reviews, 1902–1918*. Edited by LeRoy C. Breunig. New York: Da Capo Press, 1988.

Auric, Georges. *Quand j'étais là . . .* Paris: Bernard Grasset, 1979.

Axson, Richard H. *"Parade": Cubism as Theatre*. New York: Garland, 1979.

Baer, Nancy van Norman. *The Art of Enchantment: Diaghilev's Ballets Russes, 1909–1929*. San Francisco: Fine Arts Museum, 1989.

Bankhead, Tallulah. *Tallulah: My Autobiography*. New York: Harper and Brothers, 1952.

Barnes, Albert C., and Violette de Mazia. *The Art of Henri Matisse*. Merion, Pa.: Barnes Foundation Press, 1963.

Beaton, Cecil. *Diaries, 1922–1929: The Wandering Years*. London: Weidenfeld and Nicolson, 1961.

———. *Ballet*. Garden City, N.Y.: Doubleday, 1951.

Beaumont, Cyril. *The Diaghilev Ballet in London*. London: Adams and Charles Black, 1951.

———. *Supplement to Complete Book of Ballets*. London: Putnam, 1952.

Benois, Alexandre. *Reminiscences of the Russian Ballet*. London: Putnam, 1941.

Berg, Shelley C. *"Le Sacre du printemps": Seven Productions from Nijinsky to Martha Graham*. Ann Arbor, Mich.: UMI Research Press, 1988.

Bland, Alexander. *The Royal Ballet*. New York: Doubleday, 1981.

Borovsky, Victor. *Chaliapin: A Critical Biography*. New York: Knopf, 1988.

Bosch, Carlos. *Mneme*. Madrid: Espasa-Calpe, 1942.

Bowlt, John E. *The Silver Age: Russian Art of the Early Twentieth Century and the "World of Art" Group*. Newtonville, Mass.: Oriental Research Partners, 1979.

Braunsweg, Julian. *Ballets Scandals*. London: George Allen and Unwin, 1977.

Brodovitch, Alexey. *Ballet*. Text by Edwin Denby. New York: J. J. Augustin, 1945.

Brunetta, Gian Piero. *Storia del cinema italiano*. Rome: Editori Riuniti, 1980.

Buckle, Richard. *The Adventures of a Ballet Critic*. London: Cresset Press, 1953.

―――. *Diaghilev*. New York: Atheneum, 1979.

―――. *Nijinsky*. New York: Avon Books, 1971.

Cabanne, Pierre. *Le Siècle de Picasso: 1887–1937*. Paris: Editions Denoël, 1975.

Carrieri, Raffaele. *Futurismo*. Milan: Edizione del Milione, 1963.

Castillo, Alberto del. *José María Sert: Su vida y su obra*. Barcelona: Librería Editorial Argos, 1947.

Chase, Gilbert, and Andrew Budwig. *Manuel de Falla: A Bibliography and Research Guide*. New York: Garland, 1986.

Christie, Ian. *Powell, Pressburger and Others*. London: British Film Institute, 1978.

Chujoy, Anatole. *Ballet*. New York: Robert Speller, 1936.

Clarke, Mary. *The Sadler's Wells Ballet*. London: Adam and Charles Black, 1955.

Cochran, Charles B. *I Had Almost Forgotten*. London: Hutchinson, 1932.

Cooper, Diana. *The Light of Common Day*. London: Rupert Hart-Davis, 1959.

Cooper, Douglas. *Picasso Theatre*. London: Weidenfeld, 1968.

Coton, A. V. *A Prejudice for Ballet*. London: Methuen, 1938.

Crespell, Jean-Paul. *The Dove, the Dreams: The Life of Marc Chagall*. New York: Coward-McCann, 1970.

Crowle, Pigeon. *Beryl Grey*. London: Faber and Faber, 1952.

Danilova, Alexandra. *Choura*. New York: Knopf, 1986.

Deaken, Irving. *Ballet Profile*. New York: Dodge, 1936.

Delaunay, Sonia. *Nous irons jusqu'au soleil*. Paris: R. Lafont, 1978.

Demarques, Suzanne. *Manuel de Falla*. Paris: Flammarion, 1963.

Denby, Edwin. *Dance Writings*. New York: Knopf, 1986.

Desanti, Dominique. *Sonia Delaunay: Magique magicienne*. Paris: Editions Ramsay, 1988.

Descharnes, Robert. *Salvador Dalí*. New York: Harry N. Abrams, 1985.

de Valois, Ninette. *Come Dance with Me: A Memoir*. London: Dance Books, 1973.

―――. *Invitation to the Ballet*. London: John Lane, 1937.

Dorati, Antal. *Notes of Seven Decades*. London: Hodder and Stoughton, 1979.

Dorival, Bernard. *Robert Delaunay*. Paris: Jacques Darmasse Editions, 1975.

Duke, Vernon. *Passport to Paris*. Boston: Little, Brown, 1955.

Eliot, T. S. *The Letters of T. S. Eliot*. Edited by Valerie Eliot. Vol. 1. London: Faber and Faber, 1988.

———. *Selected Essays*. New York: Harcourt, Brace & World, 1964.

Falla, Manuel de. *Escritos*. Madrid, 1947.

Fauchereau, Serge, ed. *Moscow, 1900–1930*. New York: Rizzoli, 1988.

Faÿ, Bernard. *Les Précieux*. Paris: Librairie Académique, 1966.

Ferreira, Paulo. *Correspondance de quatre artistes portugais avec Robert et Sonia Delaunay*. Paris: Presses Universitaires de France, 1972.

Fokine, Michel. *Memoirs of a Ballet Master*. Boston: Little, Brown, 1961.

Fonteyn, Margot. *Autobiography*. New York: Warner Books, 1976.

Fry, Roger. *Letters of Roger Fry*. Edited by Denis Sutton. London: Chatto and Windus, 1972.

Gambillo, Maria Drudi, and Teresa Fiori, eds. *Archivi del futurismo*. 2 vols. Rome: Lucia Editore, 1958.

Garafola, Lynn. *Diaghilev's Ballets Russes*. New York: Oxford University Press, 1989.

García-Márquez, Vicente. *The Ballets Russes*. New York: Knopf, 1990.

Gauss, C. E. *The Aesthetic Theory of French Artists*. Baltimore, 1966.

Gibbon, Monk. *The Red Shoes Ballet*. London: Saturn Press, 1948.

Gillard, David. *Beryl Grey: A Biography*. London: W. H. Allen, 1977.

Gold, Arthur, and Robert Fizdale. *Misia: The Life of Misia Sert*. New York: Knopf, 1980.

Goode, Gerald. *The Book of Ballets*. New York: Crown, 1939.

Gorchakov, Nikolai A. *The Theater in Soviet Russia*. New York: Columbia University Press, 1957.

Grigoriev, Serge. *The Diaghilev Ballet*. London: Penguin Books, 1960.

Hall, Fernau. *An Anatomy of Ballet*. London: Andrew Welrose, 1953.

Harrod, Roy. *The Life of John Maynard Keynes*. London: Macmillan, 1951.

Haskell, Arnold. *Balletomania Then and Now*. New York: Knopf, 1977.

———. *Diaghilev*. New York: Simon and Schuster, 1935.

Hill, Polly, and Richard Keynes, eds. *Lydia and Maynard: The Letters of Lydia Lopokova and John Maynard Keynes*. New York: Charles Scribner's Sons, 1989.

Hippius, Zinaida. *Selected Works*. Edited and translated by Temira Pachmuss. Urbana: University of Illinois Press, 1972.

Hugo, Jean. *Le Regard de la mémoire*. Paris: Actes Sud, 1983.

Hurard-Viltard, Eveline. *Le Groupe des Six*. Paris: Méridiens Klincksieck, 1987.

Hurok, Solomon. *S. Hurok Presents . . . The World of Ballet*. London: Robert Hale, 1955.

Isdebsky-Pritchard, Aline. *The Art of Mikhail Vrubel*. Ann Arbor, Mich.: UMI Research Press, 1982.

Karsavina, Tamara. *Theatre Street*. London: Dance Books, 1981.

Kean, Beverly Whitney. *All the Empty Palaces*. New York: Universe Books, 1983.

Keynes, Milo. *Lydia Lopokova*. New York: St. Martin's Press, 1982.

Kirstein, Lincoln. *Ballet: Bias and Belief*. New York: Dance Horizons, 1983.

Kochno, Boris. *Diaghilev and the Ballets Russes*. New York: Harper & Row, 1970.

Kriner, Dora. *Ensayos sobre ballet*. Buenos Aires: Ricordi Americana, 1964.

Kupferman, Fred. *Mata Hari*. Brussels: Editions Complexe, 1982.

Lassaigne, Jacques. *Marc Chagall: Drawings and Watercolors for the Ballet*. New York: Tudor, 1959.

Laurenti, Huguette. *Paul Valéry et le théâtre*. Paris: Gallimard, 1973.

Lawrence, Robert. *The Victor Book of Ballets and Ballet Music*. New York: Simon and Schuster, 1950.

Levinson, André. *Ballet Old and New*. New York: Dance Horizons, 1982.

———. *Les Visages de la danse*. Paris: Editions Bernard Grasset, 1933.

Lifar, Serge. *Serge Diaghilev: His Life, His Work, His Legend*. New York: G. P. Putnam's Sons, 1940.

Litvinoff, Valentina. *The Use of Stanislavsky Within Modern Dance*. New York: American Dance Guild, 1972.

Loguine, Tatiana, ed. *Gontcharova et Larionov*. Paris: Klincksieck, 1971.

Macdonald, Nesta. *Diaghilev Observed*. New York: Dance Horizons, 1975.

Magarshack, David. *Stanislavsky: A Life*. London: Macgibbon & Kee, 1950.

Marcadé, Valentine. *Le Renouveau de l'art pictural russe*. Lausanne, 1971.

Markevitch, Igor. *Etre et avoir été*. Paris: Gallimard, 1980.

Martin, Marianne W. *Futurist Art and Theory*. Oxford: Clarendon Press, 1968.

Martínez Sierra, María. *Gregorio y yo*. Mexico City: Biografías Gandesa, 1953.

Massine, Léonide. *My Life in Ballet*. London: Macmillan, 1968.

Masson, André. *Peindre et une gaguere, le plaisir de peindre*. Paris, undated.

Meyer, Franz. *Marc Chagall: Life and Work*. London: Thomas Hudson, 1964.

Michaut, Pierre. *Le Ballet contemporain*. Paris: Librairie Plon, 1950.

Milhaud, Darius. *Ma Vie heureuse*. Paris: Belfond, 1973.

Morán, Alfredo. *Joaquín Turina a través de sus escritos*. Vols. 1 and 2. Madrid, 1981.

Morrell, Lady Ottoline. *Ottoline*. Edited by Robert Gathorne-Hardy. London: Faber, 1963.

Muñoz, Matilde. *Historia del Teatro Real*. Madrid: Editorial Tesoro, 1946.

Nabokov, Nicholas. *Bagazh*. New York: Atheneum, 1975.

Naifeh, Steven, and Gregory White Smith. *Jackson Pollock: An American Saga*. New York: Clarkson N. Potter, 1989.

Newman, Vera. *Ernest Newman: A Memoir by His Wife*. New York: Knopf, 1964.

Nijinsky, Romola. *Nijinsky*. New York: Simon and Schuster, 1980.

Obolensky, Serge. *One Man of His Time*. New York: McDowell, Obolensky, 1958.

Orozco, Manuel. *Manuel de Falla*. Barcelona: Ediciones Destino, 1985.

Payne, Charles. *American Ballet Theatre*. New York: Knopf, 1979.

Pearson, John. *The Sitwells: A Family Biography*. New York: Harcourt Brace Jovanovich, 1978.

Penrose, Roland. *Picasso: His Life and Work*. London: Victor Gollancz, 1958.

Powell, Michael. *A Life in Movies*. New York: Knopf, 1987.

Propert, W. A. *The Russian Ballet, 1921–1929*. London: Bodley Head, 1931.

———. *The Russian Ballet in Western Europe, 1909–1920*. London: Bodley Head, 1921.

Richardson, William. *Zolotoe Runo and Russian Modernism: 1905–1910*. Ann Arbor, Mich.: Ardis Publishers, 1986.

Robert, Grace. *The Borzoi Book of Ballets*. New York: Knopf, 1946.

Roslavleva, Natalia. *Era of the Russian Ballet*. London: Victor Gollancz, 1966.

———. "Stanislavsky and the Ballet." *Dance Perspectives,* no. 23 (1965).

Rubin, William, and Carolyn Lancher. *André Masson*. New York: Museum of Modern Art. 1976.

Rubinstein, Arthur. *My Young Years*. New York: Knopf, 1973.

Rusiñol, Santiago. *Obres completes*. Barcelona: Editorial Selecta, 1956.

Servadio, Gaia. *Luchino Visconti*. New York: Franklin Watts, 1983.

Siegel, Marcia B. *At the Vanishing Point*. New York: Saturday Review Press, 1972.

———. *The Shapes of Change*. Berkeley: University of California Press, 1985.

The Simon and Schuster Book of Ballet. New York: Simon and Schuster, 1979.

Sitwell, Osbert. *Laughter in the Next Room*. London: Macmillan, 1949.

———. *Great Morning*. London: Macmillan, 1948.

Slonim, Marc. *Russian Theater, from the Empire to the Soviets*. Cleveland: World, 1961.

Smakov, Gennady. *The Great Russian Dancers*. New York: Knopf, 1984.

Soby, James Thrall. *Joan Miró*. New York: Museum of Modern Art, 1959.

Sokolova, Lydia. *Dancing for Diaghilev*. London: John Murray, 1960.

Sopeña, Federico. *Vida y obra de Falla*. Madrid: Turner Música, 1988.

Souritz, Elizabeth. *Soviet Choreographers in the 1920's*. Durham, N.C.: Duke University Press, 1990.

Stanislavsky, Constantin. *My Life in Art*. Boston: Little, Brown, 1924.

Steegmuller, Francis. *Cocteau*. Boston: Little, Brown, 1970.

Stein, Gertrude. *Picasso.* London: Charles Scribner's Sons, 1939.

Stokes, Adrian. *Russian Ballets.* London: Faber and Faber, 1946.

———. *To-night the Ballet.* London, 1935.

Strauss, Richard, and Hugo von Hofmannsthal. *Correspondence Between Richard Strauss and Hugo von Hofmannsthal.* London: Collins, 1961.

Stravinsky, Igor. *Conversations with Igor Stravinsky.* New York: Doubleday, 1959.

———. *Chronicle of My Life.* London: Victor Gollancz, 1936.

———. *Stravinsky: Selected Correspondence.* 3 vols. Edited by Robert Craft. New York: Knopf, 1984.

——— and Robert Craft. *Expositions and Developments.* London: Hutchinson, 1979.

Thomson, Virgil. *Virgil Thomson.* New York: Knopf, 1966.

Tisdall, Caroline, and Angelo Bozzolla. *Futurism.* New York: Oxford University Press, 1989.

Tyler, Parker. *The Divine Comedy of Pavel Tchelitchew.* New York: Fleet, 1967.

Vaughan, David. *Frederick Ashton and His Ballets.* New York: Knopf, 1977.

White, Eric Walter. *Stravinsky: The Composer and His Works.* Berkeley: University of California Press, 1984.

Ziegler, Philip. *Diana Cooper.* London: Hamish Hamilton, 1981.

Zlobin, Vladimir. *A Difficult Soul: Zinaida Gippius.* Berkeley: University of California Press, 1980.

Zorina, Vera. *Zorina.* New York: Farrar, Straus & Giroux, 1986.

Index

Permissions Acknowledgments

Grateful acknowledgment is made to the following for permission to reprint previously published material:

A & C Black (Publishers) Limited: Excerpts from *The Diaghilev Ballet* by Cyril Beaumont (Huntingdon, England: A & C Black [Publishers] Limited, 1951). Reprinted by permission of A & C Black (Publishers) Limited.

Richard Buckle: Excerpts from *Dancing for Diaghilev* by Lydia Sokolova, edited by Richard Buckle (San Francisco: Mercury House, 1989), copyright © 1960 by Richard Buckle. Reprinted by permission of Richard Buckle.

Robert Craft: Excerpts from *Stravinsky: Selected Correspondence,* vol. 2, edited by Robert Craft (New York: Alfred A. Knopf, Inc., 1984). Reprinted by permission of Robert Craft.

Dance Horizons: Excerpts from *The One and Only: The Ballet Russe de Monte Carlo* by Jack Anderson, copyright © 1981 by Jack Anderson. Reprinted by permission of Dance Horizons.

Farrar, Straus & Giroux, Inc.: Excerpt from *Zorina* by Vera Zorina, copyright © 1986 by Brigitta Lieberson. Reprinted by permission of Farrar, Straus & Giroux, Inc.

David R. Godine, Publisher, Inc., and Constable & Co. Ltd.: Excerpts from *Cocteau* by Francis Steegmuller, copyright © 1970 by Francis Steegmuller. Rights in the United Kingdom administered by Constable & Co. Ltd., London. Reprinted by permission of David R. Godine, Publisher, Inc.

William Heinemann Ltd.: Excerpts from *A Life in Movies* by Michael Powell (London: William Heinemann Ltd., 1987). Reprinted by permission of William Heinemann Ltd.

Alfred A. Knopf, Inc., and Robert Cornfield Literary Agency: Excerpts from *Dance Writings* by Edwin Denby, copyright © 1986 by Yvonne and Rudolph Burckhardt. Reprinted by permission of Alfred A. Knopf, Inc., and Robert Cornfield Literary Agency.

Alfred A. Knopf, Inc., and Weidenfeld and Nicolson: Excerpts from *Balletomania Then and Now* by Arnold Haskell, copyright © 1934, 1977 by Arnold Haskell, copyright renewed 1962 by Arnold Haskell. Rights outside the United States administered by Weidenfeld and Nicolson, London. Reprinted by permission of Alfred A. Knopf, Inc., and Weidenfeld and Nicolson.

Arnoldo Mondadori Editore S.p.A.: Excerpts from *The Simon and Schuster Book of the Ballet,* copyright © 1979 by Arnoldo Mondadori Editore S.p.A., Milano. Reprinted by permission of Arnoldo Mondadori Editore S.p.A.

Charles Scribner's Sons and Andre Deutsch Ltd.: Excerpts from *Lydia and Maynard: The Letters of John Maynard Keynes and Lydia Lopokova,* edited by Polly Hill and Richard Keynes. The letters of John Maynard Keynes and Lydia Lopokova copyright © 1989 by King's College, Cambridge; introduction, editorial work, notes, and all other matter copyright © 1989 by Polly Hill and Richard Keynes. Rights outside the United States administered by Andre Deutsch Ltd., London. Reprinted by permission of Charles Scribner's Sons and Andre Deutsch Ltd.

Tatiana Massine Weinbaum and Lorca Massine: Excerpts from *My Life in Ballet* by Léonide Massine (London: Macmillan, 1968). Reprinted by permission of Tatiana Massine Weinbaum and Lorca Massine.

Photographic Sources

Central State Archives of Literature and the Arts, Moscow: 3, 11, 14 (both), 15, 19 (both), 22

The Hulton-Deutsch Collection: ii, 137, 167, 193, 197 (both), 257 (all), 311, 331

 40: Photographs by Durnkoof, Berlin, 1914, private collection
106: Fundación Archivo Manuel de Falla, Granada
141: Photograph by Foulsham & Banfield Ltd, private collection
207: Photograph by Maurice Seymour, private collection
218: Photograph by Pearl Freeman, private collection
231: Photograph by Hoyningen-Huene, private collection
243: Photograph by Anthony, private collection
245: Photograph by Iris, private collection
264: Photographs by Maurice Seymour, private collection
277: Photograph by Max Erlanger de Rosen, private collection
314: Photograph by Baron, private collection
333: Photograph by Robert Cann, private collection

All other photographs are from private collections.

A NOTE ABOUT THE AUTHOR

Vicente García-Márquez, the author of The Ballets Russes:
Colonel de Basil's Ballets Russes de Monte Carlo,
1932–1952, *was director of the 1992 Tribute to Diaghilev in
Granada. He consulted with the Paris Opéra Ballet and other
companies when they mounted Massine revivals.*
Mr. García-Márquez died in 1993.

A NOTE ON THE TYPE

*This book was set in a PostScript version of Dante,
a typeface designed by Giovanni Mardersteig. Conceived
as a private type for the Officina Bodoni at Verona, Italy,
Dante was originally cut only for hand composition by Charles
Malin, the famous Parisian punchcutter, between 1946 and 1952.
Its first use was in an edition of Boccaccio's* Trattatello in laude di
Dante *that appeared in 1954. The Monotype Corporation's version of
Dante followed in 1957. Although modeled on the Aldine type used
for Pietro Cardinal Bembo's* De Aetna *in 1945, Dante is a
thoroughly modern interpretation of that venerable face.*

Composed by Dix!, Syracuse, New York

*Printed and bound by Quebecor Printing Martinsburg,
Martinsburg, West Virginia*

Designed by Iris Weinstein